I0474116

Nervous
Systems

EDITED BY JOHANNA GOSSE AND TIMOTHY STOTT
FOREWORD BY JUDITH RODENBECK

Nervous Systems

Art, Systems, and Politics since the 1960s

Duke University Press
Durham and London
2022

© 2022 Duke University Press
All rights reserved
Designed by Courtney Leigh Richardson
Typeset in Minion Pro and Helvetica LT Std
by Westchester Publishing Services

Library of Congress Cataloging-in-Publication Data
Names: Gosse, Johanna, [date] editor. | Stott, Tim, [date] editor. |
Rodenbeck, Judith F. [date], writer of foreword.
Title: Nervous systems : art, systems, and politics since the 1960s /
edited by Johanna Gosse and Timothy Stott ; foreword by Judith
Rodenbeck.
Description: Durham : Duke University Press, 2021. | Includes
bibliographical references and index.
Identifiers: LCCN 2021014276 (print)
LCCN 2021014277 (ebook)
ISBN 9781478013822 (hardcover)
ISBN 9781478014768 (paperback)
ISBN 9781478022053 (ebook)
Subjects: LCSH: Art—Philosophy. | Aesthetics. | Art, Modern—
20th century. | Art, Modern—20th century—Social aspects. | Art,
Modern—20th century—Political aspects. | Art criticism. | BISAC:
ART / History / Contemporary (1945–) | ART / Criticism & Theory
Classification: LCC N66.N478 2021 (print) | LCC N66 (ebook) |
DDC 700.1—dc23
LC record available at https://lccn.loc.gov/2021014276
LC ebook record available at https://lccn.loc.gov/2021014277

Cover art: Charles Gaines, *Faces: Men and Women Set #4,*
"*Stephen W. Walls,*" 1978. Photograph, ink on paper, three sheets.
Each sheet: 61 × 50.8 × 3.8 cm / 24 × 20 × 1 1/2 in. © Charles
Gaines. Courtesy the artist and Hauser and Wirth.

Contents

Foreword [vii]
JUDITH RODENBECK

Acknowledgments [ix]

After the Breakdown: Sixty Years of Systems Art [1]
JOHANNA GOSSE AND TIMOTHY STOTT

Section I: Systems Aesthetics to Systems Politics

1. Jack Burnham Redux: Reappraising Systems Aesthetics [31]
LUKE SKREBOWSKI

2. The Artist as "Weatherman":
Hans Haacke's Critical Meteorology [55]
JOHN TYSON

3. Desalineación: Open Systems
as Social Transformation in Tucumán Arde [78]
CHRISTINE FILIPPONE

Section II: Nervous Interfaces

4. The Irresolutions of Charles Gaines [103]
KRIS COHEN

5. Light and Space as Institutional Critique [125]
DAWNA SCHULD

6. One among Many: Experiencing Complexity
in Participatory Art Systems [148]
CRISTINA ALBU

Section III: The Contemporary Art World Described as a System

7. Abstraction, Dispersion, Deflation, and Noise:
Liam Gillick's Disappointing Systems [173]
FRANCIS HALSALL

8. Aesthetic Action as Planetary Praxis: Mel Chin's *The Arctic Is . . .* [192]
AMANDA BOETZKES

9. Mapping, *SEA STATE*, and State Violence on
the Shores of Singapore [213]
BRIANNE COHEN

10. Toward Infrastructure Art: Containerization,
Black Box Logistics, and New Distribution Complexes [235]
JAIMEY HAMILTON FARIS

Selected Bibliography [261]
Contributors [277]
Index [281]

Foreword

Scratch the surface of postwar Western cultural production and you'll find, just a few layers down, systems thinking. Those aspects of *techne* that are embodied in the technocratic projects or communications devices that make up the most obvious referents have dominated discussion, but a newly invigorated discourse has returned attention to the complex phenomenologies of flow and feedback, of social dynamics recrafted, of emergent ecologies—of *poiesis*—that make up cultural complexity.

Doing history—that surface-scratching—more often than not has rested precisely there, at the surface as a technical exercise, its process held in check by intellectual filiation and ideological prescription, atavistic loyalties and ambitions, carefully bounded and bracketed discursive territories. But thinking about art in terms of systems requires we think of art as not just a formal, reflective, or ideological object—not simply as an object (or "object") emerging from an air-locked internal discourse or a tidy confirmation of some truism about its cultural moment or the fulfillment in allegorical form of a carefully crafted role in some grand totalizing theory. For it is never "simply" any one of those things.

For the historian of culture, stepping away from the prescriptions of grand narrative can mean going with the gut or the hunch, allowing open-ended exploration in the blind field rather than settling for closed sets generating confirmatory hypotheses: dwelling in the negative. In the past decade, a network of historians, artists, and cultural critics has gradually coalesced, with remarkable creative and collective energy, through a series of dialogues, exchanges, panels, and mutual discoveries. What is emerging is a new history of recent art that is radically transdisciplinary yet materially precise. This volume, *Nervous Systems*, presents a vital set of living core samples.

The systems approaches demonstrated here ask us to think in terms of flows and nodes, of dynamically linked discourses, materialities, persons, and locales, to grapple with and dwell in process—and to understand process itself as fully embedded in its environment. A systems approach demonstrates that the feedback loops of individual works and projects are part of much larger historical and social dynamics—integral to the ecologies, if you will, of *culture* as a verb.

Judith Rodenbeck
Associate Professor of Media and Cultural Studies
University of California, Riverside

Acknowledgments

The editors would like to thank our brilliant and committed team of contributors and give special acknowledgment to Christine Filippone and Francis Halsall, whose work and thought provided the initial impetus to this project. We want to thank Judith Rodenbeck for her support and encouragement along the way, and Lucy Lippard for permission to reprint a manuscript page from *Six Years*. We want to express our gratitude to Elizabeth Ault, our skillful and steadfast editor, and to editorial associate Ben Kossak and the rest of the editorial team at Duke University Press for their excellent work in shepherding this book to publication. We are especially grateful to the anonymous external reviewers for their generous and perceptive feedback. In addition, Johanna would like to thank James Coupe, Erica Levin, and Kevin Hamilton for their intellectual support and kinship, and Tim would like to thank May Ann Bolger and Glenn Loughran for conversations about this collection.

Sixty Years of Systems Art

JOHANNA GOSSE AND TIMOTHY STOTT

The murder of Martin Luther King pressed into focus something that I had known for a long time but never realized so bitterly and and [sic] helplessly—namely, what we are doing: the production and the talk about sculpture has nothing to do with the urgent problems of our society. Whoever believes that art can make life more human is utterly naïve. Mondrian was one of those naïve saints. . . . Nothing, but absolutely nothing, is changed by whatever type of painting, or sculpture, or happening you produce. All the shows of Angry Arts will not prevent a single Napalm bomb from being dropped. We must face the fact that art is unsuited as a political tool. —Hans Haacke, reproduced in Lucy Lippard, manuscript for *Six Years*

In an original typewritten draft of her book *Six Years: The Dematerialization of the Art Object from 1966–1972*, Lucy Lippard includes a transcribed passage from a letter written by the artist Hans Haacke to the artist, critic, and theorist Jack Burnham (figure I.1). Dated April 10, 1968, and sandwiched between two unannotated citations in the book's "1968" section, the letter conveys Haacke's pessimism and despair in the wake of King's assassination less than a week earlier, on April 4. The targets of Haacke's frustration are many. He dismisses the previous generation of modernists like Piet Mondrian as naïve utopians but is equally disappointed with contemporary activist efforts

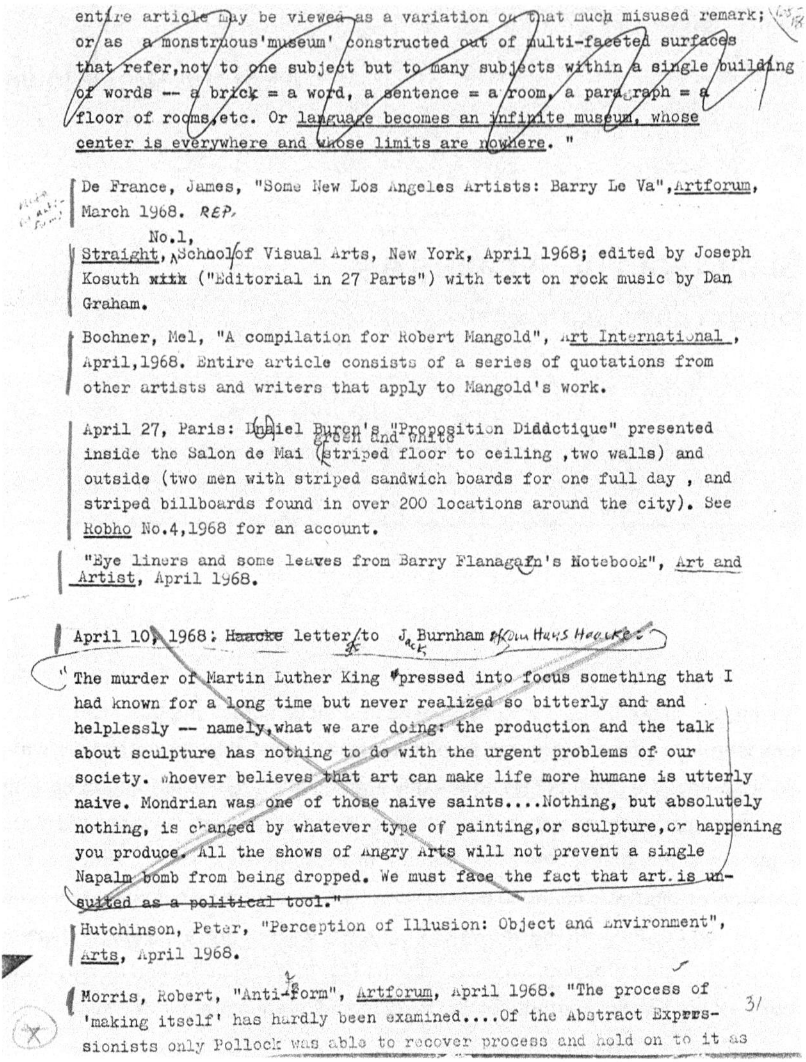

entire article may be viewed as a variation on that much misused remark;
or as a monstrous 'museum' constructed out of multi-faceted surfaces
that refer, not to one subject but to many subjects within a single building
of words -- a brick = a word, a sentence = a room, a paragraph = a
floor of rooms, etc. Or language becomes an infinite museum, whose
center is everywhere and whose limits are nowhere. "

De France, James, "Some New Los Angeles Artists: Barry Le Va", Artforum,
March 1968. REP.

    No.1,
Straight, School of Visual Arts, New York, April 1968; edited by Joseph
Kosuth ("Editorial in 27 Parts") with text on rock music by Dan
Graham.

Bochner, Mel, "A compilation for Robert Mangold", Art International,
April, 1968. Entire article consists of a series of quotations from
other artists and writers that apply to Mangold's work.

April 27, Paris: Daniel Buren's "Proposition Didactique" presented
inside the Salon de Mai (striped floor to ceiling, two walls) and
outside (two men with striped sandwich boards for one full day, and
striped billboards found in over 200 locations around the city). See
Robho No.4, 1968 for an account.

"Eye liners and some leaves from Barry Flanagan's Notebook", Art and
Artist, April 1968.

April 10, 1968: Haacke letter to J. Burnham from Hans Haacke

"The murder of Martin Luther King pressed into focus something that I
had known for a long time but never realized so bitterly and and
helplessly -- namely, what we are doing: the production and the talk
about sculpture has nothing to do with the urgent problems of our
society. Whoever believes that art can make life more humane is utterly
naive. Mondrian was one of those naive saints....Nothing, but absolutely
nothing, is changed by whatever type of painting, or sculpture, or happening
you produce. All the shows of Angry Arts will not prevent a single
Napalm bomb from being dropped. We must face the fact that art is unsuited as a political tool."

Hutchinson, Peter, "Perception of Illusion: Object and Environment",
Arts, April 1968.

Morris, Robert, "Anti-form", Artforum, April 1968. "The process of
'making itself' has hardly been examined....Of the Abstract Expres-
sionists only Pollock was able to recover process and hold on to it as

FIGURE I.1. Lucy R. Lippard, manuscript page 68-18 from *Six Years: The Dematerialization of the Art Object from 1966–1972*, c. 1972. Lucy R. Lippard papers, 1930s–2007, Archives of American Art, Smithsonian Institution.

like the Angry Arts week, a festival of antiwar performances and exhibitions staged in early 1967. To Haacke, both approaches exemplify art's inadequacy in the face of "the urgent problems of our society," from the imperialist war in Vietnam to racism, political assassinations, and violent unrest at home.[1]

Haacke's bitter indictment of art's political impotence is a provocative artifact of its historical moment. Yet, in her typescript, Lippard crossed out this entire passage with green marker. Ultimately, the passage was not included in the published version of *Six Years*, which Lippard described as "a cross-reference book of information" on "vaguely designated areas" of contemporary art, including "minimal, anti-form, systems, earth, or process art, occurring now in the Americas, Europe, England, Australia, and Asia (with occasional political overtones)."[2] This omitted excerpt then featured in a 1975 essay by Burnham, "Steps in the Formulation of Real-Time Political Art," to illuminate Haacke's role in cofounding the Art Workers' Coalition in 1969 and his subsequent turn to institutional critique, which extended his interest in social systems and generated some of the most confrontationally political moments in postwar art history.[3] The recurrence of this passage in both the literature on Haacke and within Lippard's canonical examination of post-1960s art prompts a reconsideration of the role that politics—and more specifically, political frustration—played in debates around the intersection of art and systems, a major theme in *Six Years* and in Haacke and Burnham's intellectual exchanges during this same period.

A few months after he received Haacke's letter, Burnham published an essay in the September 1968 issue of *Artforum* in which he declared: "A 'systems esthetic' will become the dominant approach to a maze of socio-technical conditions rooted only in the present."[4] To most readers, this invocation of "the present" would not have been interpreted as an abstract phenomenological condition, akin to the "presentness" famously described by Michael Fried in "Art and Objecthood," the landmark critique of minimalism published in *Artforum* the previous year. Rather, to speak of "the present" as a "maze of conditions" in the fall of 1968 would immediately gesture toward the heightened sense of urgency, tension, and uncertainty that attended the fraught sociopolitical atmosphere of the moment. The year 1968 was a political watershed punctuated by protests, sit-ins, uprisings, riots, high-profile assassinations, government surveillance, and violent repression, events animated in no small part by the escalating US war in Vietnam, which signaled a breaking point in the Cold War era's so-called culture of consensus. To many, 1968 also signified the beginning of the end of the 1960s, at once the climactic culmination and unsatisfying conclusion to a decade marked by dramatic cultural and political upheaval.

Just as Burnham's invocation of "the present" requires historical contextualization, so, too, does his use of the term "systems." In 1968, this was less likely to prompt considerations of aesthetics than to conjure the ominous figure of "the system," a popular euphemism for the "establishment" and its representative institutions, such as government, organized religion, the military-industrial complex, the mass media, corporate America, and mainstream Cold War ideology more broadly. As an umbrella category, "the system" offers a shorthand for mutually reinforcing structures of domination, including capitalism, heteropatriarchy, racism, militarism, surveillance, and imperialism. While "the system" is often personified by "the man," or, per bestselling corporate journalist William H. Whyte, the "organization man,"[5] it is also feminized insofar as it functions as a metonymic reference to coercive, intrusive, emasculating bureaucracies and social obligations that infringe on individual (and thus artistic) freedom—hence, the "nanny state," or, in the lyrical imaginary of a leading voice of the 1960s counterculture, Bob Dylan, "Maggie's Farm" (1965). Whether one props up, defends, supports, resists, critiques, drops out of, or smashes "the system," it is impossible, today as much as in 1968, to ignore or avoid its reach.

Importantly, rather than the hegemonic thrust of "the system," Burnham uses the plural, "systems," which suggests the distribution and dispersal of power across multiple arenas rather than its consolidation and coordination into a single monolithic body. As the art historian Pamela M. Lee notes, framing social issues in terms of "systems" allowed 1960s artists (and members of the counterculture more broadly) to generate "a more ecological perspective on the world at large: the sense of interdependence or mutual causation organizing operations of both the social and biological."[6] Furthermore, by observing the ways in which various systems connect and overlap, artists who engage in systems thinking reveal "how one system exists by dint of the other it critiques or excludes, in an ongoing process of mutual differentiation."[7] Similarly, James Nisbet shows how the spread of systems thinking among artists in the 1960s and 1970s transformed their art from "artificially confined environments and simplified allegories of the planet" to art that engaged the complexities and entanglements of "global ecologies of information and power."[8] This ecological perspective provided artists and the counterculture more broadly with an opportunity to observe, analyze and then transform systems. For example, during the well-publicized 1968 protests over the curriculum at Hornsey College of Art and Guildford School of Art in London, demands to "smash the system" functioned as calls for institutional reform. Hornsey students proposed to replace the closed, "linear system" of education with a "network system," based on open and nonspecialized pedagogy.[9] These key distinctions—between open and closed, linear and networked systems—help clarify the stakes behind Burnham's prescription, which called on artists to turn toward the real world rather than distance themselves from it. A direct disavowal of modernist autonomy's demand for distance and separation, Burnham's systems aesthetics demanded that artists adopt the logic of, and even directly infiltrate, existing systems to transform them from within. In this, Burnham participated in the emergence of a late 1960s "systems counterculture," one which Bruce Clarke has described as an interdisciplinary contingent that sought to "detoxify the notion of 'system' of its military, industrial, and corporate connotations of command and control and to redeploy it in the pursuit of holistic ideals and ecological values."[10]

The second-order cybernetics of anthropologists Gregory Bateson and Margaret Mead, and of physicist Heinz von Foerster, offered an integrative model of planetary ecology along with an epistemology of consciousness that was ripe for psychiatric and, at times, hallucinogenic experimentation. The experimental and speculative potential of cybernetics evolved into numerous "weird" interpretations of open, nonlinear, and observer-dependent systems. Weird systems became a central feature of the counterculture and various subcultures—folk, outsider, mystical, spiritualist, underground, new age, and cult. Neurophysiologist John Lilly, for example, expanded cybernetic theories of communication to nonhuman minds such as dolphins in his *The Mind of the Dolphin* (1967), then to cosmic beings in *The Scientist: A Novel Autobiography* (1978).[11] From the 1950s on, Stafford Beer was the first to apply cybernetics to the study of firms, production lines, and management structures, and by 1972, he had introduced a cybernetic model of organization called the viable system model.[12] Alongside his more straitlaced management cybernetics, however, Beer also developed an animist understanding of nature and an interest in tantrism, which led him in 1974 to retire to a frugal life in a remote stone cottage near Lampeter in Wales. Beer's evolution connects cybernetics to the many other weird systems aesthetics, imaginary taxonomies, and personal cosmologies that were invented by reclusive outsider artists, underground iconoclasts, and schools-of-one, from Henry Darger's Vivian Girls, James Hampton's assemblages, and Simon Rodia's *Watts Towers* to the queer systems of Jack Smith's loft performances and Ray Johnson's mail art network, the New York Correspondence School. In turn, systems aesthetics allows us to better understand practices that are often reductively understood in terms of individual eccentricity; for instance, as Gloria Sutton has suggested, Yayoi Kusama's patterned, mirrored, immersive interiors make sense not as the result of some personal pathology but as explorations of the new understanding of cognition and networked intelligence provided by cybernetics.[13]

Thus, the migration of systems scientists into nonacademic, subcultural, mystical, or just weird applications of systems, and the systems thinking demonstrated by art-world outliers and outsiders, mutually demonstrate the heuristic utility of "nervous systems" as an interdisciplinary interpretive category. Yet, divorced from broader cultural and historical contexts and situated strictly within the disciplines of art history and criticism, the sociopolitical valence of systems aesthetics, as well as its weirder dimensions, tends to get lost in translation. More reductively, artistic engagement with systems is often reduced to a passing technophilic fascination with cybernetic feedback and computing, which sparked a temporary fashion for "art and technology" collaboration and residencies across powerful industries, from public broadcasting to research universities to major corporations like Bell Labs and RAND. As a result, systems aesthetics is often associated with an uncritical stance toward the Cold War corporate military-industrial complex rather than with artistic efforts to undermine it. We argue that such depoliticized interpretations run afoul of Burnham's use of the compound adjective "sociotechnical" in his original formulation, by disproportionally privileging technical research to the detriment of the "social." Furthermore, we contend that this technocratic bias has obscured the diverse range of artistic practices that has utilized systems thinking to critique and transform the perceived political impotence of art in the wake of widespread social tension and uncertainty post-1968. Such practices are the focus of this volume.

The aim of this collection is to reassess the theorization and implementation of systems aesthetics by artists and critics since the 1960s and to demonstrate the continuing relevance of systems aesthetics within contemporary art. Our title, *Nervous Systems*, builds on the integrative spirit of early cybernetics and systems thinking, especially its attempts to forge an analytical and explanatory framework applicable across organic and nonorganic systems. It also expands on the transformed understanding of objects, bodies, and structures brought about by postwar information theory, systems theory, and cybernetics. No longer isolated, objects, bodies, and structures became communicative and mutable systems in networked complexes with other systems. This transformed art, design, and architecture into extended nervous systems. For example, already in 1957 the architect and industrial designer

George Nelson observed how "building is becoming less of a traditional art and more an integrated, sheltered network of 'nervous systems' for communication."[14] The "nervous systems" studied in this collection, however, expand beyond the informational to the affective, economic, and atmospheric, revealing, for example, the political valence of weather in the work of Haacke, the organization of affect in participatory art installations, and the mapping of global logistics infrastructures. Referring to these systems as "nervous" points to their informational character but also the cultural anxieties and social tensions that fueled these projects, as well as their implicit response to what Luke Skrebowski—following Mel Ramsden of the British conceptual art group Art & Language—frames as modernism's "nervous breakdown." This breakdown, Skrebowski argues, is exemplified by Haacke's dispirited diagnosis of art's predicament in 1968 and his dismissal of modernist utopianism.[15] Framed less as a breakdown than a turn outward toward systems, this nervousness, we argue, forms a line of continuity, not just between modern and contemporary art, but from the Cold War winter to the scorched Anthropocene summer.[16] Systems aesthetics, then as now, enables artists to respond to these political, cultural, and environmental anxieties, offering an integrative, intermedial, cross-disciplinary methodology that retools art for sociopolitical purposes.

To date, much of the art historical discourse on systems aesthetics traces how early computer art, telematics, and art and technology experimentation anticipated the emergence of contemporary digital and new media art. For instance, art historian Edward Shanken aims to "suture the wound" of art history's persistent omission of "science, technology, and new media from mainstream contemporary art discourses."[17] Shanken's intervention, and especially his recovery of Burnham's criticism from art historical obscurity, was an indispensable contribution that added key dimensions to the story of systems aesthetics and its legacy in the contemporary.[18] And yet, the recuperative tenor of this and parallel efforts often run the risk of reinscribing traditional medium-specific separations between new media, telematics, conceptual art, video, performance, and so forth, distinctions that the artists and artworks in question deliberately sought to destabilize. In this regard, the "wounded" relation between so-called mainstream contemporary art and new media art persist, we contend, due to the historical emphasis on technology that characterizes discourses on the latter.

The art historian Judith Rodenbeck clarifies the stakes for recovering and expanding the art historical scope of systems aesthetics beyond artworks that utilize advanced technologies:

Contemporary recuperation of systems theory and cybernetics has provided rich ground for the analysis of some of the most vital art and criticism of the 1960s. But this renewed interest has generally been arrived at recursively, that is, through thinking about systems-dependent technological means such as television, computers, and the networks that sustain them, and doing so from a position structured by ubiquitous computing. If much of this new digital-era scholarship privileges concept and machine, it just as often sidesteps the messier realms of feeling, sensation, and meat-space.[19]

Rodenbeck's insight into the neglected, "messier" dimensions of systems aesthetics is a common thread in the essays gathered in this collection, which highlight the eclectic, pluralistic, and idiosyncratic dimensions of artistic engagement with systems. Belonging not so much to institutions or an established movement than to outliers and radicals, we argue that this critical paradigm was and is buttressed by experimental, amateur appropriations, (mis)applications of advanced technologies and, at times, productive (mis)readings of systems theory rather than expert applications of the latest technoscientific research. In this sense, the project of this collection is less historiographical or teleological than genealogical, in the spirit of Michel Foucault's influential formulation, by demonstrating how artists have adopted and elaborated systems aesthetics "in piecemeal fashion from alien forms," as they sought to match their political concerns with the productive, distributive, and communicational systems available to them at the time.[20]

Nervous Systems historically expands systems aesthetics beyond the politically charged moment of the late 1960s to bridge two generations of art and systems thinking—the postwar and the contemporary. In doing so, it unravels some of the more reductive, technodeterminist connotations of this discourse. Building on a growing body of criticism and scholarship that places systems-based thinking and methodologies at the center of art historical and theoretical inquiry, the essays collected here propose an alternative genealogy by raising questions related to race, gender, class, sexuality, labor, embodiment, affect, subjectivity, ecology, extraction, and colonialism (all prominent concerns within the scholarship of contemporary art) and by linking them to discussions of systems.[21] Yet, rather than subsume social and political concerns under the master discourse of "systems aesthetics," the essays contained here consider how the sociopolitical was always already present, if latent or obliquely articulated, in systems art of the late 1960s and in subsequent systems-based approaches in contemporary art. Moving beyond the idea of systems art as a coherent, periodized movement, our contributors show how the intersection of artistic practice and systems thinking forged an evolving research methodology that prioritizes process over product, relations over autonomy, and which, in the words of Mitchell Whitelaw, signals a "turn outward" to the world.[22] More recent articulations of systems aesthetics by contemporary artists continue this turn outward, by building on and adapting the social and political commitments of an earlier generation of systems artists.

Here, we must add a proviso to our own "turn outward" in expanding a systems art genealogy, which is far from complete but is instead offered as a first step. In our attempt to disentangle systems art from the technophilic biases of most of its chroniclers to date, we have neglected some of its weirder and minoritarian practitioners, as noted above. We and our contributors also face an archive, extant discourse, and set of primary literatures that remain predominantly white and male, especially for the first generation of systems artists. As such, the turn outward remains a work in progress. For instance, if we turn our attention to Afrofuturism, a field of practice committed to multiple forms of spatiotemporal, perceptual, and archival expansion, we find an exemplar in Black Audio Film Collective's 1995 film essay *The Last Angel of History*. The director John Akomfrah and scriptwriter Edward George took inspiration from John Corbett's 1993 essay "Brothers from Another Planet," which unearths the origins of Afrofuturism in Sun Ra and the Arkestra, Lee "Scratch" Perry's studio the Black Ark, and George Clinton's music collective Parliament-Funkadelic. "Each (group) is working with a shared set of mythological images and icons such as space iconography, the idea of extraterrestriality and the idea of space exploration," writes Corbett.[23] Building from Corbett's account, Kodwo Eshun notes how, from 1997 through to 2003, he and other members of the Cybernetic Culture Research Unit in Warwick University's Philosophy Department sought to radicalize Donna Haraway's "Cyborg Manifesto" in order to wrestle alternative technofutures from the "corporate utopias that make the future safe for industry," including cyberculture, science fiction, and other capitalist media.[24]

Afrofuturist formations involve writers, artists, filmmakers, and musicians of the African diaspora who have appropriated and transformed those same cybercultures—reworking their gendered imaginaries, colonial logics, technological fetishes, and speculative fictions—that were central to many of the systems artists gathered in this collection. Insofar as Afrofuturism is a critical discourse that remaps the relationships between art and other systems—colonial, musical, economic, planetary—and seeks to uncouple futures from the technologies of prediction and control, any expanded conceptualization of systems aesthetics must account for it. Like many of the systems artists discussed in this collection, Afrofuturism too opens the discourse of modern science to speculative fiction that is feminist, queer, decolonial, and antiracist.[25] If, at first glance, artists like Sun Ra and Akomfrah might seem remote from Burnham and Haacke, one of the purposes of this collection is not to reassert the centrality of the latter but, rather, to insist on the inclusion and legibility of the former within a more capacious and politically attuned reconceptualization of systems aesthetics in contemporary art. We insist that expanding this genealogy is not merely a symbolic show of inclusivity. It yields hermeneutic value, for example, by illuminating the connections between the Afrofuturism of *The Last Angel of History* and the posthumanism of Akomfrah's more recent moving-image work *Vertigo Sea* (2015). Fusing the sublime aesthetics of nature documentary with the ethnographic gaze of found and archival footage, this multichannel installation renders visible the complex historical interconnections between the transatlantic slave trade, European imperialism, migration and refugees, the whaling industry and the ecology of oceans, and the history of cinema itself, analyzing them not as independent or isolated histories and phenomena but as co-constitutive, mutually entwined, and intrinsically social *systems*.[26]

Systems Genealogies

As we attempt to show here, an expanded genealogy of systems aesthetics requires, first and foremost, that the concept be uncoupled from Burnham, who was by no means the first or the only thinker of his day to adopt systems as a critical lens on cultural production. Two years prior to Burnham's *Artforum* essay, in the fall of 1966, the British critic and curator Lawrence Alloway curated *Systemic Painting* at the Solomon R. Guggenheim Museum in New York. The exhibition reframed the work of the painters Jo Baer, Frank Stella, Kenneth Noland, and Agnes Martin, among others, as *systemic*, thus displacing the label of "post-painterly abstraction" that had been applied by Clement Greenberg.[27] Most importantly for Alloway, the concept of systemic painting suggested that artworks operating as systems could develop from "human proposals" rather than from absolute, fundamental aesthetic principles. Systemic order, Alloway insisted, could be "as human as a splash of paint."[28]

Such was the popularity of systems thinking in the visual arts at the time that in a review of *Systemic Painting* Dore Ashton criticized Alloway's use of "systemic," which to her was no more than a marketing buzzword, a "brand name" to grab the attention of the museum-going public.[29] Undeterred, Alloway extended his systems thinking in an essay titled "Network: The Art World Described as a System," published in the September 1972 issue of *Artforum*, four years after Burnham's "Systems Esthetics" appeared. Alloway's essay drew from systems theory and cybernetics to describe how the social organization of the art world had changed due to rapidly expanding information technologies and distribution networks. His diagnosis of the postwar art world as a networked and multimodal but closed system anticipated the ways that the contemporary art world has adapted to meet the demands of global digital capitalism. Thus, whereas Burnham's call for artists to respond to "socio-technical conditions rooted only in the present" provides a foundation for this collection's inquiry, Alloway's analysis shows how the contemporary art world operates as a system among systems. Hence, our third section, "The Contemporary Art World Described as a System," which riffs on the title of Alloway's 1972 essay. In addition to performing genealogical work, the chapters contained in this final section (by Halsall, Boetzkes, Cohen, and Hamilton Faris) collectively identify a systems turn within post-1990s global contemporary art, as it grapples with increasingly networked conditions of artistic production under globalization.

Yet, more than two decades before Alloway and Burnham adopted the rhetoric and logic of systems to analyze the art of their moment, cyberneticians and systems theorists were developing a general theory that would be applicable across the sciences and the humanities. In March 1946, the Josiah Macy Jr. Foundation began a series of conferences to bring mathematicians and engineers into discussion with anthropologists and psychologists. The subject of the first meeting was circular causal systems, followed by a second and third later in the year on "Teleological Mechanisms in Society" and "Feedback Mechanisms and Circular Causal Systems in Biology and Society," respectively. These Macy conferences were largely responsible for the consolidation of cybernetics as a discipline and for its expansion to sociology and anthropology. In subsequent decades, cybernetics would extend from literature to architecture to art and design education.[30] Before describing in more detail their significance within art history, let us pause and provide some background on the development of these discourses.

Cybernetics is a science of organization for organic and inorganic systems that rose to prominence in the immediate postwar years. Norbert Wiener coined the term in his 1948 book *Cybernetics: Or Control in the Animal and Machine*: "We have decided to call the entire field of control and communication theory, whether in the machine or in the animal, by the name Cybernetics, which we form from the Greek κυβερνήτης or steersman."[31] Wiener's work from the 1940s and 1950s, alongside that of his contemporaries in cognate fields like information theory, falls under the heading of first-order cybernetics, with second-order cybernetics emerging later in the 1960s.[32] For first-order cybernetics, a system is linear and predictable, and it must be observed passively and objectively in order to be controlled or "steered." By contrast, second-order cybernetics understands that systems, far from being predictable, develop through nonlinear, recursive interactions between elements, which includes the observers of those systems. In sum, second-order cybernetics "stresses the recursive complexities of observation, mediation, and communication with regard to nonlinear and emergent systems."[33] A minor change in a system can thus have major consequences, and the future behavior of a system can be probable but not entirely predictable.

A further key development in systems thinking was the concept of "open systems," initially outlined by the Austrian biologist Ludwig von Bertalanffy. A decade prior to Wiener's theorization of cybernetics, von Bertalanffy theorized the "openness" of systems in terms of interdependence with the environment.[34] Before von Bertalanffy, systems theorists understood systems as closed, insofar as they reacted to changes in their environment but did not interact with them.[35] Von Bertalanffy demonstrated that the second law of thermodynamics, according to which all closed systems tend toward maximum entropy, did not adequately describe biological systems, which maintain their order and delay entropy by remaining open to their respective environments. In departing from the classical conception of systems as whole entities that preserve a closed organization, von Bertalanffy moved toward our current understanding of systems as complex, emergent, and in a state of what he calls "dynamic equilibrium" (*Fließgleichgewicht*), in which a system, open to its environment, continually changes its components in order to maintain its organization. In this view, only a general systems theory can account for this organizational model of complexity and change.[36] Von Bertalanffy's general systems theory provided a "general science of 'wholeness'" that studied isomorphisms across systems in order to integrate the otherwise disparate fields of biology, robotics, information theory, sociology, economics, and psychology.[37] This "new worldview of considerable impact" analyzed the world through wholes and interactions rather than discrete parts, and it provided tools for analyzing systems that are open, complex, dynamic, and unpredictable, and therefore difficult to manage and govern.[38]

Both cybernetics and general systems theory were influential on postwar artists who aimed to destabilize the ontology of the work of art, defined not as a discrete object but as an integrated and dynamic complex of elements—semiotic, visual, graphic, discursive, mechanical, or affective—and acting in relation to other artworks and to its environment. Disseminated through reading groups, lecture programs, and art and design schools from the late 1950s on, a generation of emerging artists believed that open, complex systems could offer a corrective to a technocratic and automated postwar society that was largely controlled by what Peter Galison has called the "Manichean sciences" of operations research, game theory, and military-industrial applications of cybernetics.[39] In the late 1960s, cyberneticians began to argue that art uniquely offered holistic knowledge of systems. In 1967, Gregory Bateson argued that artists, by modeling and observing open systems, could redirect a purposive but limited analysis of the world toward a more holistic, "wiser" view of the "circuits of contingency" on which life depends.[40] Three years later, the architect Sim Van der Ryn, founder of the Farallones Institute, wrote that "the purpose of life is to attain the state of full participation again—the state of the whole. Man has lost the totality of being because culture destroys it. We have made art the system that recombines fragments because our lives are not art."[41] In a similar vein, the architect Christopher Alexander described systems in 1967 as "not a special kind of thing, but a special way of looking at a thing," a holistic model for thinking about relationships and codependencies between things.[42] In 1969, psychologist Michael Apter declared cybernetics to be "a development in science which holds out the promise of taking art seriously" and which carried the potential to blur "the traditional distinctions between the work of art and the system which creates the work of art, and between the work of art and the system which observes the work of art."[43]

Along with Lippard, Haacke, Burnham, and Alloway, numerous other artists and critics contributed to this critical mass of discourse on the relationship between art and systems from the late 1960s onward. For them, systems offered a modus operandi distinct from the prevailing discourses of postformalism, dematerialization, and postmodernism that were also highlighted in *Six Years*. For instance, Haacke wrote of the importance of thinking "in terms of systems" in an untitled statement for the catalog to the 1970 exhibition *Conceptual Art and Conceptual Aspects* at the New York Cultural Center, which reveals the strong influence of von Bertalanffy's general systems theory on his thought: "The working premise is to think in terms of systems; the production of systems, the interference with and the exposure of existing systems. Such an approach is concerned with the operational structure of organization, in which the transfer of information, energy and/or material occurs. Systems can be physical, biological or social; they can be man-made, naturally existing, or a combination of any of the above."[44]

For his part, Burnham declared in his landmark 1968 essay: "We are now in transition from an *object-oriented* to a *systems-oriented culture*. Here change emanates, not from *things*, but from *the way things are done*."[45] In his book from that same year, *Beyond Modern Sculpture*, Burnham elaborated on this insight by arguing that artists had abandoned the "cultural obsession with the art object" in favor of a "systems consciousness," in turn signaling the decline of medium-specific paradigms for artistic production and critical evaluation that had dominated art discourse for centuries.[46] This "refocusing of aesthetic awareness . . . onto matter-energy information exchanges and away from the invention of solid artifacts," Burnham argues, prompted artists to look beyond the "skin of objects" to their systemic interactions and relations.[47] What is more, Burnham wrote, this "systems consciousness" transformed the status and ontology of the artist, who now considered "goals, boundary, structure, input, output, and related activity inside and outside the system," and who was, knowingly or not, a function of the "metaprograms" of the art world, itself framed, as Alloway later would, as a system.[48] In this sense, systems theory and cybernetics enabled artists to find analogies and isomorphisms between domains of social life, institutions, economies, and infrastructures that had previously been considered separate and distinct, freeing them to work not only with objects but to intervene directly into what the Brazilian conceptual artist Cildo Meireles called "the body of society."[49]

Art and systems thinking also converged in Great Britain during the late 1950s and 1960s, principally through the field of cybernetics. For example, the Independent Group's interest in information, telecommunications, and mass media led them to integrate various types of systems thinking. In 1955, for the cybernetician E. W. Meyer's address to the Independent Group (IG) at the Institute of Contemporary Arts, "Probability and Information Theory and Their Application to the Visual Arts," the artist John McHale made a first foray into information design. McHale recalled that having found an expert on cybernetics, his ideas would have to be explained to the IG through several diagrams on coding, information, and probability.[50] The previous year, McHale had already begun to make collages based on information processing, such as *Transistor* (1954), which reworked Claude Shannon's famous diagram from his "Mathematical Theory of Communication," published in 1948. Jacquelynn Baas describes *Transistor* as a "visual equivalent for the processing of information."[51] These works show McHale's interest in how data is processed, ordered, and reconfigured through both electronic and organic systems.

A decade later, cybernetics would provide an account of art that privileged participation and testability over expression or affect.[52] In a two-part essay published in 1966 and 1967, the artist Roy Ascott noted that the interdisciplinary and integrative character of cybernetics allowed a "cybernetic vision in art" to extend beyond a mere set of technical procedures or devices to become a "fundamental attitude toward events and human relationships."[53] For Ascott, modern artists constructed "a field of behavior" into which spectators were drawn as participants.[54] Ascott's student Stephen Willats, who by the late 1960s had developed a quasi-ethnographic and collaborative art practice based on cybernetic principles, exemplifies this best. To capture the "reality" of life in inner-city social housing schemes and to challenge the bureaucratic planning and architecture that rendered residents inert, dependent, and incapable of critical consciousness, Willats developed models of nested, adaptive systems to celebrate the "richness and complexity" of residents' lives. Willats understood that any work of art (or sign or image) produced collaboratively by him and the residents was entangled within complex systems of communication, observation, self-organization, and control.

In the summer and fall of 1968, the ICA showed *Cybernetic Serendipity*, a seminal exhibition of computers, painting machines, and other interactive devices curated by Jasia Reichardt. In her 1971 book *The Computer in Art*, Reichardt noted that the concept of cybernetic feedback "has entered the world of happenings as well as various environmental constructions, where audience participation and reaction can alter the appearance and even the content of the work in due course." Reichardt further noted that artists had begun to produce works that had "no significant aesthetic value" but were "do-it-yourself platform[s] [with an] important sociological implication," because they organized a field of complex social behavior.[55]

So far, this genealogy of systems aesthetics has privileged a familiar cast of Anglo-American figures, from Lippard to Ascott to Reichardt. However, artists from a wide range of national and political contexts have adopted systems thinking to organize public participation in dynamic environments. As contributor Christine Filippone has convincingly argued, feminist artists of the 1960s and 1970s such as Martha Rosler, Carolee Schneemann, and Agnes Denes were early adopters and adapters of theories of open systems as a means of critiquing patriarchal Cold War cultural values.[56] Filippone's chapter in the current collection argues that prominent Argentinian performance collective Grupo de artistas de vanguardia de Rosario (also known as the Rosario Group) used open systems as a "model for process-oriented, multisensory, collaborative works that not only engaged but infiltrated social and political contexts in the midst of dictatorship." Here, systems art was a "political-cultural action" aimed at radically dissolving "into the social." Argentina was in fact a central hub for postwar artists engaged in systems thinking, as evidenced by Centro de arte y comunicación, a group founded by Jorge Glusberg in 1968 in Buenos Aires, which used cybernetics to model and critique political oppression, most evident in the 1971 exhibition *Arte de sistemas* and in the "metabiotic" labyrinths of Luis Benedit.[57]

Two other key examples—the Russian arts group Dvizhenie and the Italian art movement Arte programmata—similarly reimagined the environment of art as a social space organized around interaction and exchange.[58] In 1967, Dvizhenie proposed the large-scale interactive and immersive *Cybertheatre*, a cybernetic environment that participants and programmed "cyber creatures" could modulate using light, movements, smoke, and gas. Lev Nusberg, the unofficial leader of Dvizhenie, described *Cybertheatre* as "one model of our man made world and the relationship between man and machine."[59] Arguing that Dvizhenie was the first Russian artist collective to adopt cybernetics, the art historian Margareta Tillberg details the group's plans for an *Artificial Bio Kinetic Environment* (1968), which, though strictly theoretical, imagined a fantasy future city attached to an artificial environment.[60] The artists envisaged participants' interactions with their surroundings as guiding the "management" of the city, by modifying the "plot of the game" in a continuous feedback loop.[61]

During the 1960s, Arte programmata explained its environments—composed of carefully chosen lights, colors, and simple wires—as organizational experiments. Organization, the group claimed, was "the necessary condition for all constructive engagement"[62] and went hand in hand with the new idea of the artist as "programmer" or systems planner, as described by member Bruno Munari: "In the works of programmed art, the fundamental elements . . . are in a free state or are arranged objectively in geometrically ordered systems so as to create the greatest number of combinations, often unpredictable in their mutations but all programmed in accordance with the system planned by the artist."[63]

The art historian Lindsay Caplan observes that Arte programmata did not consider its work hierarchical but rather as a flattened and reciprocal interaction between artists and participants.[64] Yet, by transforming artists into programmers, and therefore managers, of a field of social behaviors and relations, Arte programmata's practice inevitably reproduced certain operational and reputational hierarchies.[65]

In the examples above, systems aesthetics enabled artists to engage spectators in "a field of behavior" and recast them as participants. In this sense, systems thinking is a rarely acknowledged antecedent to the concept of "relational aesthetics" and the broader "social turn" in contemporary art noted since the early 1990s. Coined by French curator Nicolas Bourriaud in 1995, the term *relational aesthetics* describes a set of artistic practices that adopt a direct, one-to-one relation to social conditions, composing and authoring the work of art with and through these relations rather than depicting them representationally or metaphorically. Bourriaud writes, "The possibility of a *relational* art (an art that takes as its theoretical horizon the sphere of human interactions and its social context, rather than the assertion of an autonomous and *private* symbolic space) is testimony to the radical upheaval in aesthetic, cultural and political objectives brought about by modern art."[66] For Bourriaud, these practices are political because they occupy a "territory" that brings social conditions and relations to the fore: "Art, by modeling social functions through the amplification of those tensions and contradictions that hallmark the world of art, has been consigned to the sphere of politics."[67] Though he does not deploy the rhetoric of systems, we maintain that the arguments and concepts put forth in *Relational Aesthetics* correspond closely to earlier theorizations of art as system, particularly by Burnham, Alloway, and Ascott. Without citing systems aesthetics, Bourriaud nevertheless reiterated its central terms and approach and, most importantly, diagnosed its ongoing elaboration within contemporary art.[68]

Bourriaud's formulation has prompted much debate among art historians and critics in the intervening decades, most notably in Claire Bishop's 2004 article "Antagonism and Relational Aesthetics," which charges that relational aesthetics valorizes socially engaged art without offering any evaluative criteria, aesthetic or political, with which to assess the significance and experiential texture of this engagement.[69] Bishop warns that social engagement, pursued for its own sake and drained of conflict and friction, actually performs an affirmative function vis-à-vis existing structures of power rather than a democratic intervention or disruption. To substantiate this critique, Bishop targets many of Bourriaud's exemplars of relational aesthetics, pointing out that their work lacks political antagonism. As compelling as Bishop's polemic is, her critique aims more at Bourriaud's misapplication of "relational aesthetics" to a set of art practices that do not fulfill the concept's political promise, rather than at the logic of the conceptual formulation itself.

We propose our expanded genealogy of systems aesthetics as a response to this critical impasse. Rather than debate the political merits of works of contemporary art or the category of "relational aesthetics," this book helps to historicize Bourriaud's concept by demonstrating that his was not an entirely new paradigm but, in fact, a contemporary recuperation of the post-1960s discourse of art and systems.[70]

In the decades immediately preceding Bourriaud's coining of this signature concept, a more urgent contemporary elaboration of systems aesthetics emerged, one that responds directly to environmental and ecological crises. Here, systems thinking allows artists to include nonhuman agents, to join human history with geologic history, or "deep time," to combine human and natural ecologies, and to think across spatial and temporal scales, from a planetary "shared sense of catastrophe" to more local historical and cultural contingencies.[71] This integrated, *eco*-systems aesthetics, so to speak, is exemplified by Agnes Denes, who participated in the first wave of feminist artists invested in open systems, as identified by Filippone.[72] Through systemic diagrams, maps, drawings, and charts, Denes sought to create a language of perception that facilitated the flow of information among discrete systems and disciplines, eliminating their boundaries in favor of association and analogy. As Denes states, "Art is a specialization that need not feed upon itself. It is capable of imbibing key elements from other systems and unifying them into a unique, coherent vision."[73] For Denes, information design performs an epistemological function, enabling the artist to identify patterns normally hidden by "superfluous or erroneous information," to synthesize intellect and intuition, and to unify systems of knowledge into a "unique, coherent vision." As described by Giampaolo Bianconi, Denes's contributions to the 1970 exhibition at the Jewish Museum curated by Burnham, *Software: Information Technology; Its New Meaning for Art*, demonstrated her attempt to "map her artistic system of philosophical inquiry onto computer programs and exploit computation interactivity."[74] The two 1970 works included in that show, *Matrix of Knowledge* and *Trigonal Ballet*, thus functioned as "computational analogue(s) for the 'Philosophical Drawings' she was simultaneously creating."[75] Nevertheless, Denes's primary interests in these works were conceptual, linguistic, affective, ecological, and corporeal, not technical. Computing offered a language and a tool for developing her ecosystemic approach, not an end.

More recently, contemporary ecoartists have revived the concerns Denes initially explored in the 1970s. The art historian T. J. Demos compares contemporary artists who adopt a "systems ecology" approach to the "restorationist eco-aesthetics" of much first-generation environmental art, such as that surveyed in the exhibition *Fragile Ecologies*, curated by Barbara Matilsky at the Queens Museum of Art in 1992.[76] A systems-ecological art, by contrast, expands the definition of ecology to include not strictly environmental but also social, technological, and economic systems. Demos illustrates this approach through a discussion of Ursula Biemann's five-channel video installation *Egyptian Chemistry* (2012), which examines the Nile River as a "hybrid interactive system that has always been at once organic, technological, and social" instrumentalized for human benefit.[77] Biemann maps out a network of "water politics, hydraulic energy systems, the damming of the Nile, fish ecologies, nitrate industries, social revolution," in which "agency is distributed beyond humans to systems, infrastructure, ecologies, and so on; and these things and systems exist beyond anthropocentric epistemologies or determinations."[78]

In light of contemporary artists' interests in systems ecology, a more expansive genealogy of systems aesthetics enables art history to contribute more fully to the emerging field of environmental humanities, an early twenty-first-century response to the rise of ecologically minded cultural production and a renewed emphasis on connecting the humanities to biological, earth, and environmental sciences. A direct demonstration of the "turn outward" prescribed by Whitelaw, the environmental humanities emerged in response to the STEM fields' and social sciences' dominance over environmental scholarship. While these remain the principal disciplines for researching natural environments, it has become strikingly evident that fighting the combined specters of climate change, mass migration, biodiversity loss, pollution, fossil-fuel dependency, and other features of the environmental crisis will demand an analysis of cultural and aesthetic factors, a role that suits systems aesthetics perfectly.

Just as artists continue to adapt varieties of systems thinking to model, organize, and represent their projects, art historians have worked to recover systems thinking as a central theoretical discourse. Foremost among them is Pamela M. Lee, whose seminal book *Chronophobia: On Time in the Art of the 1960s* (2004) examines the role of seriality, duration, and process during this pivotal decade.[79] Lee's 2012 book, *Forgetting the Art World*, revisits systems theory to think through the increasingly complex set of infrastructures, economies, institutions, media, and distribution methods that constitute what she terms "the *work* of art's world."[80] Returning to Alloway's description of the postwar art world as a network, Lee challenges his characterization of this network as a closed system: "The purported integrity of this system enabled the work of art to function as a coherent and autonomous thing within that 'negotiated environment'—transparent to those who inhabited that system's still well-policed borders. Alloway's theorization of the art world, in other words, continues to authorize the language and secret handshakes that grant membership into a closed society."[81] Here, Lee asks whether the contemporary art world qualifies as an open (if nonetheless exploitative and hierarchical) system, in keeping with the rapidly shifting imperatives of neoliberal financialization and digital capitalism. If so, Lee wonders, is it still possible to distinguish the "negotiated environment" of the art world from the broader environment, or do "the theories and protocols that were once the exclusive purview of the art world take on the status of a new cultural and mental labor"?[82] Lee's questions provide a critical point of departure for our present collection. Analyzing a set of alternative convergences of art and systems thinking from the 1960s to the present day, our contributors reveal the broader and often unexpected influence of systems thinking on the social aspirations and political investments that have motivated artists to explore questions of infrastructure, affect, social relations, and environment. These case studies also enact a more capacious and politicized approach to systems aesthetics by transgressing disciplinary, medium-specific, historical, and geographic boundaries in order to question the status of art as just one system among many.

Chapter Summaries

The first section, "Systems Aesthetics to Systems Politics," consists of case studies on art, politics, and systems in the late 1960s and early 1970s, opening with Luke Skrebowski's insightful and overdue reassessment of the political underpinnings of Burnham's systems aesthetics, focusing on his indebtedness to the writings of the Marxist critical theorist Herbert Marcuse, an intellectual touchstone for the 1960s counterculture. John Tyson investigates what he calls Haacke's "systems politics," specifically in relation to the artist's interests in weather and the environment and his role as "critical meteorologist." Lastly, Christine Filippone provides an in-depth examination of the Rosario Group's adoption of "open systems" thinking to disrupt informational circuits and to critique the Argentine dictatorship's propaganda mechanisms during the late 1960s.

The second section, "Nervous Interfaces," examines art systems that encompass bodies, experience, interfaces, and environments in complex and often tense arrangements. Kris Cohen analyzes how African American artist Charles Gaines uses systems as a framework for his inquiry into subjectivity, labor, and racial blackness. Dawna Schuld examines a specific installation by California light and space artists Robert Irwin, Doug Wheeler, and Larry Bell and analyzes their phenomenological analysis of audience experience in terms of the emerging discourse of institutional critique. Cristina Albu investigates the role of sensory experience and visualization in participatory art projects by Gina Czarnecki, Mariko Mori, and Tomás Saraceno, which similarly emphasize complex phenomenological systems. Together, these essays think through the ways systems organize and reproduce experience—of users, participants, players, performers, and subjects.

The third and final section, "The Contemporary Art World Described as a System," references the title of Alloway's 1972 essay and updates his diagnosis of the art world for the contemporary moment. Francis Halsall considers how the work of the artist Liam Gillick, long associated with the concept of "relational aesthetics," deploys an aesthetics of disappointment to generate a mirror image of the contemporary art world as a system. Amanda Boetzkes discusses the recent work of the conceptual artist Mel Chin, focusing on *The Arctic Is . . .* (2015), in which the artist photographed two Inuit hunters wearing sealskin coats and carrying harpoons on the streets of Paris on the occasion of the 2015 Paris Climate Change Conference. Boetzkes argues that Chin's practice exemplifies new modes of contemporary artistic practice that accept ecological entanglements as political and economic realities that are aesthetically actionable. Brianne Cohen analyzes Singaporean artist Charles Lim's SEA STATE (2005–present), a ten-part multimedia project that maps the infrastructural and extractive changes occurring along the country's expanding shoreline. Cohen shows how Lim's "ecosystemic" approach seeks to counter the deleterious policies and practices that occur within this extractive zone. In conclusion, Jaimey Hamilton Faris examines "containerization" and how its invisible networks of global distribution are integral to the contemporary art market. Together, the contributions to this section reflexively examine the contemporary art world itself as an increasingly networked system.

Nervous Systems gathers these contributions at a moment when algorithmic governance and infrastructural inertia clash with the demands of multiscalar ecological thinking, and when the art world's operational closure (as one system among many) tends to disappoint art's claims to political efficacy. In light of these conditions, our contributors elucidate the diversity and theoretical generativity of systems aesthetics in the present. Far from an isolated art historical moment, passing technoutopian fad, or exercise in formal innovation, systems aesthetics constitutes, then as now, a political commitment to "turn outward" and again, quoting Denes, to develop a "unique, coherent vision" as urgent at the end of the 1960s as it is today.

NOTES

1   As just one system among many, the art world was not insulated from this pervasive atmosphere of violent unrest. In June 1968, Valerie Solanas infamously shot Andy Warhol at his New York Factory, just days before presidential hopeful Senator Robert F. Kennedy would be gunned down in Los Angeles.

2   Lucy R. Lippard, *Six Years: The Dematerialization of the Art Object from 1966 to 1972* (New York: Praeger, 1973), cover image and frontispiece. Since Lippard has never shied from discussions of politics, her parenthetical aside about "occasional political overtones" should be read as tongue-in-cheek.

3   Toward the end of 1968, large cross sections of the New York art world organized meetings and direct actions to protest the policies of major institutions like the Museum of Modern Art. These activities led to the founding of organizations like the Art Workers' Coalition (AWC) and the Women Artists in Revolution (WAR), which called for these powerful entities to enact reforms on issues like racial and gender equity, community access, and institutional complicity in the Vietnam War. See Julia Bryan-Wilson, *Art Workers: Radical Practice in the Vietnam War Era* (Berkeley: University of California Press, 2009).

4   Jack Burnham, "Systems Esthetics," *Artforum* 7, no. 1 (1968): 35.

5   William H. Whyte, *The Organization Man* (New York: Simon and Schuster, 1956).

6   Systems thinking is a central concern of Pamela M. Lee, *Chronophobia: On Time in the Art of the 1960s* (Cambridge, MA: MIT Press, 2004), 62.

7   Lee extends her use of systems theory, in particular the social-systems theory of Niklas Luhmann, in her analysis of Nancy Holt's work. See Pamela M. Lee, "Art as a Social System: Nancy Holt and the Second-Order Observer," in *Nancy Holt: Sightlines*, ed. Alena J. Williams (Berkeley: University of California Press, 2011), 58.

8   James Nisbet, *Ecologies, Environments, and Energy Systems in Art of the 1960s and 1970s* (Cambridge, MA: MIT Press, 2014), 12.

9   Lisa Tickner, *Hornsey 1968: The Art School Revolution* (London: Frances Lincoln, 2008), 51.

10 See Bruce Clarke, "From Information to Cognition: The Systems Counterculture, Heinz von Foerster's Pedagogy, and Second-Order Cybernetics," *Constructivist Foundations* 7, no. 3 (2012): 197. Besides Clarke, a rich body of literature has emerged over the past two decades around the intersection of systems theory, cybernetics, and postwar counterculture. See also Ron Eglash, "Cybernetics in American Youth Subculture," *Cultural Studies* 12, no. 3 (1998): 382–409; and the work of Fred Turner, *From Counterculture to Cyberculture: Stewart Brand, the Whole Earth Network, and the Rise of Digital Utopianism* (Chicago: University of Chicago Press, 2006) and *The Democratic Surround: Multimedia and American Liberalism from World War II to the Psychedelic Sixties* (Chicago: University of Chicago Press, 2013). In addition, two exhibitions, 2013's *The Whole Earth* at

the Haus der Kulturen der Welt, curated by Diedrich Diedrichsen and Anselm Franke, and 2015's *Hippie Modernism: The Struggle for Utopia*, curated by Andrew Blauvelt, were both accompanied by extensive catalogs that demonstrate the extent and variety of this systems counterculture. For instance, see Hugh Dubberly and Paul Pangaro, "How Cybernetics Connects Computing, Counterculture, and Design," in *Hippie Modernism: The Struggle for Utopia*, ed. Andrew Blauvelt (Minneapolis, MN: Walker Art Center, 2015), 126–41.

11 See Bruce Clarke, "John Lilly, the Mind of the Dolphin, and Communication Out of Bounds," *communication+1* 3, no. 1 (2014): article 8. Clarke presented on Lilly's "cosmic weirdness" on the Weird Systems panel at the Society of Literature, Science, and the Arts 30th Annual Meeting in Atlanta, Georgia, November 2016. The panel was convened by Timothy Stott. The other panelists were Philip Thurtle and Francis Halsall.

12 See Stafford Beer, *Brain of the Firm* (London: Penguin, 1972).

13 Gloria Sutton, "Between Enactment and Depiction: Yayoi Kusama's Spatialized Image Structures," in *Yayoi Kusama: Infinity Mirrors*, ed. Mika Yoshitake (New York: Prestel, 2017), 140–57.

14 George Nelson, "The Enlargement of Vision," in *Problems of Design* (New York: Whitney, 1957), 71. See Justus Nieland, "Happy Furniture," *Places Journal*, January 2020, https://placesjournal.org/article/happy-furniture/.

15 See Skrebowski, in this volume. Ramsden first used the phrase in a talk, "Remembering Conceptual Art," at the conference Who's Afraid of Conceptual Art (March 19, 1995, Institute of Contemporary Arts, London), 9–10. The phrase has been widely cited since, including by Charles Harrison, *Conceptual Art and Painting: Further Essays on Art & Language* (Cambridge, MA: MIT Press, 2001), 27; and as the epigraph to Steve Edwards, "Art & Language's Doubt," in *Art & Language in Practice*, vol. 2, *Critical Symposium*, ed. Charles Harrison (Barcelona: Fundació Antoni Tàpies, 1999), 249. However, in a later interview Ramsden expressed his regret, stating, "We wish we'd never said this," adding that the expression was intended to point to Conceptual art as a "disorder" within the history of modernism. See Ann Stephen, "Some More Questions: Interview with Mel Ramsden," *1969: The Black Box of Conceptual Art* (Sydney: University Art Gallery, University of Sydney, 2013), 81. Thanks to J. Myers-Szupinska for helping us unravel this genealogy.

16 Our use of *nervous* echoes the title of anthropologist Michael Taussig's book *The Nervous System*, a collection of essays that pursue a Frankfurt school–inspired critique of capitalist modernity and control society. Evoking an appositely conspiratorial worldview in which everything is connected, Taussig characterizes modernity as "a System, all right, switchboard of the commanding heights, delicate in the power of its centrality. But there was no System. Just a Nervous System, far more dangerous, illusions of order congealed by fear—an updated version of what the poet Brecht had written in the 1930s, obsessed with ordered disorder, the exception *and* the rule." Michael Taussig, *The Nervous System* (New York: Routledge, 1992), 2.

17   See Edward Shanken, "The House That Jack Built: Jack Burnham's Concept of 'Software' as a Metaphor for Art," *Leonardo Electronic Almanac* 6, no. 10 (1998), http://www.artexetra.com/House.html; and Edward Shanken, "Reprogramming Systems Aesthetics: A Strategic Historiography," *UC Irvine: Digital Arts and Culture 2009*, http://escholarship.org/uc/item/6bv363d4. Shanken has also authored a textbook survey, *Art and Electronic Media* (London: Phaidon, 2009), and a reader, *Systems* (Cambridge, MA: MIT Press; and London: Whitechapel, 2015).

18   See also Etan J. Ilfield, "Contemporary Art and Cybernetics: Waves of Cybernetic Discourse within Conceptual, Video, and New Media Art," *Leonardo* 45, no. 1 (2012): 57–63.

19   Judith Rodenbeck, "Poeisis in Bali: Notes on Feedback," *Media-N: Journal of the New Media Caucus* 10, no. 3 (2014), http://median.newmediacaucus.org/art-infrastructures-information/poeisis-in-bali-notes-on-feedback/.

20   Michel Foucault, "Nietzsche, Genealogy, History," in *Michel Foucault: Aesthetics, Method, and Epistemology*, ed. James D. Faubion (London: Penguin, 2000), 371. Originally published as Michel Foucault, "Nietzsche, la généalogie, l'histoire," in *Hommage à Jean Hyppolite*, ed. Suzanne Bachelard (Paris: Presses universitaires de France, 1971), 145–72.

21   See, for instance, Lee, *Chronophobia*; Pamela M. Lee, *Think Tank Aesthetics: Midcentury Modernism, the Cold War, and the Neoliberal Present* (Cambridge, MA: MIT Press, 2020); Francis Halsall, *Systems of Art: Art, History and Systems Theory* (Oxford: Peter Lang, 2008); Eve Meltzer, *Systems We Have Loved: Conceptual Art, Affect, and the Antihumanist Turn* (Chicago: University of Chicago Press, 2013); and Christine Filippone, *Science, Technology, and Utopias: Women Artists and Cold War America* (New York: Routledge, 2017).

22   Mitchell Whitelaw, "1968/1998: Rethinking a Systems Aesthetic," *ANAT Newsletter* 33 (May 1998): n.p. Marga Bijvoet makes a similar point in *Art as Inquiry: Toward New Collaborations between Art, Science, and Technology* (Bern: Peter Lang, 1999), 7.

23   John Corbett, "Brothers from Another Planet," in *Extended Play: Sounding Off from John Cage to Dr. Funkenstein* (Durham, NC: Duke University Press, 1994), quoted in Kodwo Eshun, "Further Considerations on Afrofuturism," *CR: The New Centennial Review* 3, no. 2 (2003): 295. See Mark Dery, "Black to the Future: Interviews with Samuel R. Delany, Greg Tate, and Tricia Rose," in *Flame Wars: The Discourse of Cyberculture*, ed. Mark Dery (Durham, NC: Duke University Press, 1994), 179–222.

24   Eshun, "Further Considerations," 292.

25   See Marleen Barr, ed., *Afro-Future Females: Black Writers Chart Science Fiction's Newest New-Wave Trajectory* (Columbus: Ohio State University Press, 2008).

26   The art historian T. J. Demos has written extensively on Akomfrah's *Vertigo Sea*. See Demos, "From the Postcolonial to the Posthumanist: Moving Image Practice in Britain and Beyond," in *Artists' Moving Image in Britain since 1989*, ed. Erika Balsom, Lucy Reynolds, and Sarah Perks (New Haven, CT: Yale University Press, 2019), 31–50.

27 Lawrence Alloway, introduction to *Systemic Painting* (New York: Solomon R. Guggenheim Foundation, 1966), 19. See also Clement Greenberg, "The Case for Abstract Art," *Saturday Evening Post*, August 1959, republished in Clement Greenberg, *Clement Greenberg: The Collected Essays and Criticism*, vol. 4, *Modernism with a Vengeance*, ed. John O'Brian (Chicago: University of Chicago Press, 1993), 80–81.

28 Alloway, *Systemic Painting*, 17.

29 Dore Ashton, "Marketing Techniques in the Promotion of Art," *Studio International* 172, no. 884 (1966): 270.

30 This history is helpfully summarized by Fred Turner in *The Democratic Surround*.

31 Norbert Wiener, *Cybernetics: Or Control and Communication in the Animal and the Machine* (Cambridge, MA: MIT Press, 1948), 11.

32 Alongside Wiener, another early theorist of cybernetics was the Austrian American scientist Heinz von Foerster, who defined first-order, linear, and predictable systems as "trivial machines," which maintain equilibrium through negative feedback and can be predicted due to the determinate relation between input and output. By contrast, second-order cybernetics examines "nontrivial" or historical machines, which are highly sensitive to changes in their internal states and to their environment, and which include other systems. The distinction between first- and second-order cybernetics is influentially detailed in N. Katherine Hayles, *How We Became Posthuman: Virtual Bodies in Cybernetics, Literature, and Informatics* (Chicago: University of Chicago Press, 1999). Other important scholarship on cybernetics includes Charles François, "Systemics and Cybernetics in a Historical Perspective," *Systems Research and Behavioral Science* 16 (1999): 203–19; Steve Heims, *Constructing a Social Science for Postwar America: The Cybernetics Group, 1946–1953* (Cambridge, MA: MIT Press, 1991); Ronald Kline, *The Cybernetics Moment: Or Why We Call Our Age the Information Age* (Baltimore, MD: John Hopkins University Press, 2015); Andrew Pickering, *The Cybernetic Brain: Sketches of Another Future* (Chicago: University of Chicago Press, 2010); and Stuart Umpleby, "A History of the Cybernetics Movement in the United States," *Journal of the Washington Academy of Sciences* 91 (2005): 54–66.

33 Bruce Clarke and Mark B. N. Hansen, "Introduction: Neocybernetic Emergence," in *Emergence and Embodiment: New Essays on Second-Order Systems Theory*, ed. Bruce Clarke and Mark B. N. Hansen (Durham, NC: Duke University Press, 2009), 6.

34 See Ludwig von Bertalanffy, *Lebenswissenschaft und Bildung* (Erfurt, Germany: Stenger, 1930); Ludwig von Bertalanffy, "Untersuchungen über die Gesetzlichkeit des Wachstums, I. Teil: Allgemeine Grundlagen der Theorie; Mathematische und physiologische Gesetzlichkeiten des Wachstums bei Wassertieren," *Wilhelm Roux Archiv für Entwicklungsmechanik der Organismen: Organ für d. gesamte kausal Morphologie* 131, no. 4 (1934): 613–52; and Ludwig von Bertalanffy, "An Outline of General System Theory," *British Journal for the Philosophy of Science* 1, no. 2 (1950): 134–65.

35 John Bednarz, "Complexity and Intersubjectivity: Towards the Theory of Niklas Luhmann," *Human Studies* 7, no. 1 (1984): 57.

36 Ludwig von Bertalanffy, *General System Theory: Foundations, Development, Applications* (London: Allen Lane, 1971), 31.

37 Von Bertalanffy, *General System Theory*, 36.

38 Von Bertalanffy, *General System Theory*, vii.

39 Peter Galison, "The Ontology of the Enemy: Norbert Wiener and the Cybernetic Vision," *Critical Inquiry* 21, no. 1 (1994): 228–66. In one relevant example of such dissemination, in a lecture given at the ICA, London, in April 1960, titled "Art and Communication Theory," the British psychiatrist and cybernetician W. Ross Ashby discussed the advantages of cybernetics for understanding art. W. Ross Ashby, transcript of the lecture "Art and Communication Theory," delivered at the ICA, April 7, 1960, Tate Gallery Archives 955/1/7/30, London.

40 Gregory Bateson, "Style, Grace, and Information in Primitive Art," first presented at the Wenner-Gren Conference on Primitive Art, Burg Wartenstein, Austria, 1967; reprinted in Gregory Bateson, *Steps to an Ecology of Mind* (Chicago: University of Chicago Press, 1972), 145–47.

41 Sim Van der Ryn, quoted in "Advertisements for a Counter Culture," *Progressive Architecture* 51, no. 6 (1970): 72.

42 Christopher Alexander, "Systems Generating Systems," in *Systemat* (Berkeley, CA: Inland Steel Products Company, 1967).

43 Michael J. Apter, "Cybernetics and Art," *Leonardo* 2, no. 3 (1969): 257.

44 Hans Haacke, "Untitled Statement" from "Information 2," in *Conceptual Art and Conceptual Aspects*, exhibition catalog, ed. Donald Karshan (New York: New York Cultural Center, 1970), 32.

45 Burnham, "Systems Esthetics," 31. See also Luke Skrebowski, "All Systems Go: Recovering Hans Haacke's Systems Art," *Grey Room*, no. 30 (2008): 54–83; and Caroline A. Jones, "Hans Haacke 1967," in *Hans Haacke 1967* (Cambridge, MA: MIT Press, 2011), 6–27.

46 Jack Burnham, *Beyond Modern Sculpture: The Effects of Science and Technology on the Sculpture of This Century* (London: Allen Lane, 1968), 369.

47 Burnham, *Beyond Modern Sculpture*, 369.

48 Burnham, "Systems Esthetics," 32; and Burnham, "Real Time Systems," 49. See Mathew Rampley, "Systems Aesthetics: Burnham and After," *vector* 12 (2005), http://www.virose.pt/vector/b_12/rampley.html.

49 Cildo Meireles, *Cildo Meireles* (Valencia, Spain: IVAM Centre del Carme, 1995), 174.

50 Discussion between Mary and Reyner Banham and Magda Cordell and John McHale, in *Fathers of Pop* (dir. John McHale, 1979).

51 Quoted in David Robbins, ed., *The Independent Group: Postwar Britain and the Aesthetics of Plenty*, exhibition catalog (London: Institute of Contemporary Arts, 1990), 87.

52 See María Fernández, "Detached from HiStory: Jasia Reichardt and *Cybernetic Serendipity*," *Art Journal* 67, no. 3 (2008): 6–23; and Timothy Stott, "When Attitudes Became Toys: Jasia Reichardt's *Play Orbit*," *Art History* 41, no. 2 (2018): 344–69.

53 Roy Ascott, "Behaviourist Art and the Cybernetic Vision" (1966–67), in *Telematic Embrace: Visionary Theories of Art, Technology, and Consciousness*, ed. Edward

Shanken (Berkeley: University of California Press, 2003), 111. Originally published in two parts: "Behaviourist Art," *Cybernetica: Journal of the International Association for Cybernetics* 9 (1966): 247–64; and "The Cybernetic Vision in Art," *Cybernetica: Journal of the International Association for Cybernetics* 10 (1967): 25–56.

54 Ascott, "Behaviourist Art and the Cybernetic Vision," 110. See also Nick Lambert, "The Cybernetic Moment: Roy Ascott and the British Cybernetic Pioneers, 1955–1965," *Interdisciplinary Science Reviews* 42, nos. 1–2 (2017): 42–53.

55 Reichardt, *The Computer in Art* (London: Studio Vista, 1971), 35.

56 See Filippone, *Science, Technology, and Utopias*.

57 See Jorge Glusberg, *El Grupo de los trece en arte de sistemas* (Buenos Aires: Centro de arte y comunicación, 1971).

58 Frank Popper, *Art Action Participation* (London: Cassel and Collier Macmillan, 1975), 7–9.

59 Lev Nusberg, "Cybertheatre," *Leonardo* 2, no. 1 (1969): 61.

60 Margareta Tillberg, "You Are Now Leaving the American Sector: The Russian Group *Dvizhenie*, 1962–1978," in *Place Studies in Art, Media, Science and Technology: Historical Investigations on the Sites and the Migration of Knowledge*, ed. Andreas Broeckmann and Gunalan Nadarajan (Weimar: VDG, 2008), 147.

61 Tillberg, "You Are Now Leaving the American Sector," 158.

62 Enzo Mari, quoted in Emanuel Quinz, "From Programme to Behaviour: The Experience of Art Programmata in Italy 1958–1968," in *Practicable: From Participation to Interaction in Contemporary Art*, ed. Samuel Bianchini and Erik Verhagen (Cambridge, MA: MIT Press, 2016), 95.

63 Bruno Munari, quoted in Lindsay A. Caplan, "Open Works between the Programmed and the Free: Art in Italy 1962–1972" (PhD diss., City University of New York, 2017), 69, emphasis added. Original quotation from "Arte Programmata," in *Arte Programmata: Kinetic Art*, exhibition catalog, ed. Bruno Munari and Riccardo Musatti; trans. Lindsay A. Caplan (Milan: Officina d'Arte Grafica A. Lucini; Washington, DC: Smithsonian Institution, 1964), n.p.

64 Caplan, "Open Works," 69.

65 We are indebted to Gráinne Coughlan for these insights. See Gráinne Coughlan, "An Organisational Analysis of Participatory Art in Art Institutions" (PhD thesis, Dublin School of Creative Arts, Technological University Dublin).

66 Nicolas Bourriaud, *Relational Aesthetics* (Paris: Les Presses du réel, 2002), 14. First published in French as *Esthétique Rélationnel*, Bourriaud's text focuses primarily on a group of mostly male European artists that includes Gabriel Orozco, Rirkrit Tiravanija, Félix González-Torres, Pierre Huyghe, Liam Gillick, and Maurizio Cattelan.

67 Nicolas Bourriaud, "Modelized Politics," *Flash Art* 26, no. 171 (1993): 142–43.

68 Francis Halsall has noted the compatibility of systems and relational aesthetics, which both work to "radically [reconceive] the purposes and effects of art practice. . . . This reconceived understanding locates art in a system of relationships between art and its environment; its viewers and art discourse." Halsall, *Systems of Art*, 121.

69 Claire Bishop, "Antagonism and Relational Aesthetics," *October*, no. 110 (2004): 51–79.

70 Beyond the gallery-based "relational" works that Bourriaud promotes, we identify a contemporary systems aesthetics in art practices that are durational, quasi-ethnographic, and/or infrastructural. Here, the "social turn" gives way to an "organizational turn," meaning a turn to large-scale experiments in collaborative organization initiated and managed by artists. To take only one example, systems thinking informs the "co-creation" methodology of Artway of Thinking, the nonprofit arts organization founded in Venice in 1992 by Stefania Mantovani and Federica Thiene, which develops and implements creative strategies for social engagement and collaboration. See Artway of Thinking, "Co-Creation Methodology," accessed at http://www.artway.info/.

71 Dipesh Chakrabarty, "The Climate of History: Four Theses," *Critical Inquiry* 35, no. 4 (2009): 222.

72 Filippone, *Science, Technology, and Utopias*.

73 Agnes Denes, "The Dream," *Critical Inquiry* 16, no. 4 (1990): 920.

74 Giampaolo Bianconi, "Agnes Denes in the 1970s: Toward the Hologram," in *Agnes Denes: Absolutes and Intermediates*, ed. Emma Enderby (New York: The Shed, 2020), 166.

75 Bianconi, "Agnes Denes," 167.

76 T. J. Demos, *Decolonizing Nature: Contemporary Art and the Politics of Ecology* (Berlin: Sternberg, 2016), 26.

77 Demos, *Decolonizing Nature*, 216–20.

78 Demos, *Decolonizing Nature*, 220.

79 Lee, *Chronophobia*, 67.

80 Pamela M. Lee, *Forgetting the Art World* (Cambridge, MA: MIT Press, 2012), 3.

81 Lee, *Forgetting the Art World*, 21.

82 Lee, *Forgetting the Art World*, 21.

Systems Aesthetics to Systems Politics

Jack Burnham Redux

Reappraising Systems Aesthetics

LUKE SKREBOWSKI

In 1969 Robert Morris recommended that artist Patricia "Patsy" Norvell, then his graduate student in sculpture at Hunter College, interview the Chicago-based educator, critic, and theorist Jack Burnham (1931–2019) in connection with her master's thesis on an emergent conceptual art. At the time Burnham was an associate professor of art at Northwestern University and was best known for his recently published *Beyond Modern Sculpture: The Effects of Science and Technology on the Sculpture of This Century* (1968)—in which he charted the evolution of sculpture's ontological ground from "object" to "system" on the model of a Kuhnian paradigm shift—and for his *Artforum* articles "Systems Esthetics" (1968) and "Real Time Systems" (1969), in which he generalized his analysis of recent sculpture to contemporary "unobject" art as a whole.[1]

Norvell was unable to interview Burnham but raised the question of the significance of his theory of systems aesthetics with several of the artists she spoke to, including Dennis Oppenheim, Robert Barry, Sol LeWitt, Robert Smithson, and Morris himself. Most responded favorably to Burnham's work, except for Smithson and LeWitt. Smithson's evaluation was the most detailed and the most critical:

> I don't see the trace of a system anywhere. That's a convenient word. It's like "object." It's another abstract entity that doesn't exist. . . . There are

things like structures, objects, systems. But, then again, what are they? I think that art tends to relieve itself of those hopes. Like, last year we were in an object world and this year we're in a system world. . . . Jack Burnham is very interested in going beyond and that's a kind of utopian view. The future doesn't exist, or if it does exist, it's the obsolete in reverse. . . . I see no point in utilizing technology or industry as an end in itself or as an affirmation of anything. That has nothing to do with art. They're just tools. So if you make a system you can be sure that the system is bound to evade itself. So I see no point in pinning your hopes on a system. It's just an expansive object, and eventually that all contracts back to points.[2]

Smithson criticized Burnham's purported technophilia ("I see no point in utilizing technology . . . as an end in itself"), teleological orientation ("Like . . . this year we're in a system world"), and utopianism ("Burnham is very interested in going beyond"). An astute and perceptive critic, Smithson's negative assessment anticipated both the terms and the tone of subsequent judgments about the character and value of Burnham's theoretical oeuvre by influential art historians. Rosalind Krauss derogates Burnham's work as "technocratic"; Benjamin H. D. Buchloh deprecates "the limitations of a systems-aesthetic viewpoint"; and Thierry de Duve disparages Burnham as a pot-smoking "utopianist of art's dissolution into life."[3]

As a result, Burnham long eluded mainstream art historical acceptance, and his major works are no longer in print. What, then, might be gained by revisiting Burnham's work today? Such a question, while always historiographically pertinent, follows the publication of a collection of Burnham's writing—*Dissolve into Comprehension: Writings and Interviews, 1964–2004* (2016)—edited by Melissa Ragain in MIT's prestigious "Writing Art" series.[4] This republication reflects the fact that Burnham's systems aesthetics has gained more favorable critical attention from scholars in recent years, principally because of its pioneering embrace of systems theory and cybernetics as productive discourses for the interpretation of art (as discussed by Sabeth Buchmann, Michael Corris, Francis Halsall, Pamela M. Lee), its anticipation of new media art (as Charlie Gere and Edward Shanken have focused on), and in relation to the influence of Burnham's systems thinking on Hans Haacke's work (an issue treated by Caroline A. Jones, Lee, and in my own earlier writing).[5] Yet in the introduction to *Dissolve into Comprehension*, Ragain argues for the significance of Burnham's work as a whole, noting that "his visionary theoretical ideas have only become more relevant" and consequently that it is important to "restore his rightful place in art criticism and theory."[6] How, then, might we assess his "rightful place"?

In what follows I argue that, in order to evaluate Burnham's work and to assess the principal charges leveled against it, we need to reconstruct its intellectual development and deepen our understanding of its major terms, specifically its aesthetic character, in ways that go beyond the reception it has received to date. Burnham's work unquestionably suffers from an awkward elision of humanistic and scientific traditions of thought, and his later writing is characterized by an esotericism that disqualifies it from conventional academic validity.[7] Yet his attempt to think the humanities and the sciences alongside each other in a politicized manner (informed by Marcuse's critique of technocracy) was highly prescient. And his later turn to esoteric thinking resulted from the profound challenges involved in such a syncretic approach, challenges that remain politically instructive (even as esotericism as a solution does not).

Burnham also discussed a range of issues in his writing on the contemporary art of the late 1960s that remain live today. These include his attention to the fraught relationship between art and technology (a major fault line in contemporary culture, echoing in the highly contested debates around contemporary art's relationship with the outmoded, new media art, postinternet art, and retro-technofetishism); his pioneering consideration of the use of artificial intelligence and biological engineering in and as art (even if we are no longer persuaded by his idea that these engagements would define art's telos); the artistic relevance of systems theory and cybernetics (both in the historicization of late modern art and for contemporary art theory, particularly in light of the general ecological turn); and the need for a coherent ontology of contemporary art (addressed in ongoing debates about the "postmedium condition" and the emergence of "the contemporary" as a critical category to replace postmodernism). These issues all crystallize in his postformalist systems aesthetics, the genealogy and aesthetic character of which I reconstruct and reassess in detail in what follows, the better to evaluate its legacy.

The True Art Critic Helps the World by Revealing Mystic Truths?

Though best known as a theorist, Burnham started his career as an artist. He trained at the Boston Museum School of Fine Arts, beginning in 1953, majoring in commercial design and silversmithing, with minors in sculpture and painting. While in Boston he struck up an influential friendship with Naum Gabo, who was then teaching at the Graduate School of Design at Harvard. Burnham also trained as an engineer, in this respect explicitly resembling his mentor Gabo: Burnham's studies at the Boston Museum School divide into two phases, 1952–54 and 1956–57, and during the intervening two years (1954–56) he studied for an engineering associate's degree in architectural construction at the Wentworth Institute in Boston (then, as now, a vocationally oriented college). Burnham subsequently went on to study at the Yale School of Art, taking a Bachelor of Fine Arts in 1959 and a Master of Fine Arts in 1961. Burnham's training was thus distinctively hybrid, combining art and the (applied) sciences, the practical and the fine arts.

Burnham worked as an artist from 1954 to 1968 but supported his practice by a mixture of full- and part-time employment as an architectural draftsman and designer (1957–58), as a corporate sign fabricator and painter (1956–68), and as an educator (1959–68). Although Burnham had five one-man shows from 1965 to 1969 and participated in several group shows from 1957 to 1978 (with most concentrated in the years 1965–70), none of his solo shows (and only one of his group shows) were in New York, and his career as an artist did not take off. He began teaching as an assistant professor of art at Northwestern University in 1964, having previously served as an instructor at Yale, Wesley College, and Northwestern from 1959 to 1964. Burnham subsequently worked principally as an art educator, theorist, and critic, holding a contributing editorship at *Artforum* (1971–72), an associate editorship at *Arts* (1972–76), and a contributing editorship to *New Art Examiner* (1976–83), while progressing from assistant to associate professor of art at Northwestern in 1969 and to full professor by 1974, before transferring to the University of Maryland as chair of the art department in the 1980s, where he taught until his retirement.[8]

Burnham's oeuvre comprises two book-length monographs, *Beyond Modern Sculpture: The Effects of Science and Technology on the Sculpture of This Century* (1968) and *The Structure of Art* (1971); several catalog essays (including short monographic studies on Hans Haacke, Marcel Duchamp, and Vitaly Komar and Alexander Melamid); a theoretical monograph on Herbert Marcuse published as the pamphlet *Art in the Marcusean Analysis* (1969); and numerous articles, interviews, and reviews published from 1964 to 1990 (with the great majority appearing from 1964 to 1981) in magazines including *Artforum, Arts, New Art Examiner*, and *Art in America*, or as chapters in collections (a selection of these articles, written up to 1973, were anthologized

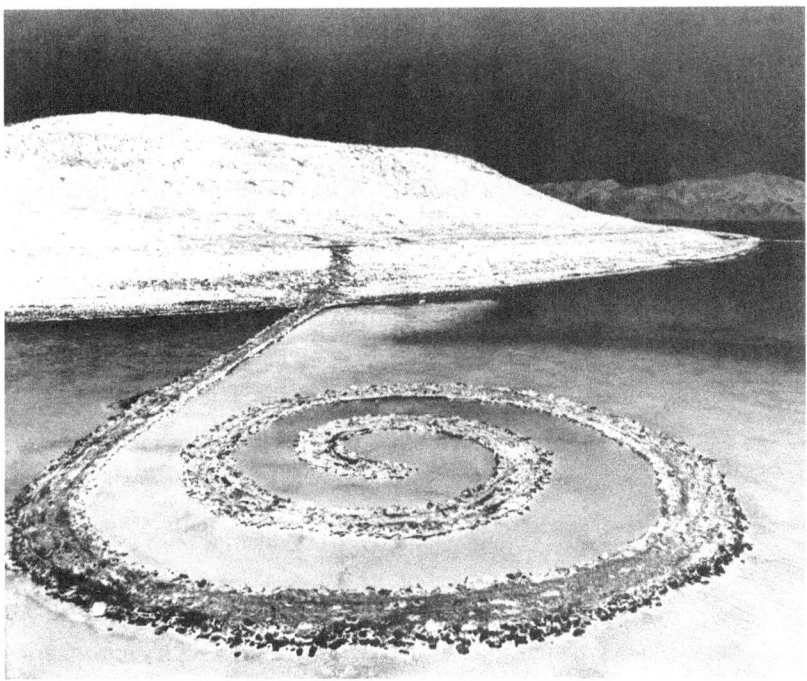

great western salt works
essays on the meaning of Post-Formalist art

FIGURE 1.1. Jack Burnham, cover of *Great Western Salt Works: Essays on the Meaning of Post-formalist Art*, 1974.

in Burnham's 1974 book *Great Western Salt Works: Essays on the Meaning of Post-formalist Art*).[9] Beginning in 1973, Burnham also worked on a projected monograph interpreting the art and writings of Duchamp. Although unfinished in his lifetime, it was outlined in a series of articles on Duchamp written from 1971 to 1973 for various art magazines (some of which were collected in *Great Western Salt Works*). The prolific period of Burnham's career as a theorist was thus relatively compressed, running from the mid-1960s to the mid-1970s. Burnham's intellectual career can be schematized into four distinct moments that are marked by three significant theoretical turns:

1 A History and Theory of Modern Sculpture (1964–67). In *Beyond Modern Sculpture* (1968), Burnham provided a materialist, avowedly technologically determinist history of modern sculpture from the 1870s to the 1960s. His account was teleological, distinguishing between an earlier and residual conception of "sculpture as object" and a later, still-emergent, conception of "sculpture as system." He predicted that sculpture would eventually evolve into a living system (thus collapsing the separation between the representation and the production of life), in concert with the broader emergence of a posthuman future in which synthetic life would dominate organic life.

2 An Account of Contemporary Art (1967–70). In "Systems Esthetics" (1968) and his other essays on the topic of systems and aesthetics—including "Systems and Art" (1969), "Real Time Systems" (1969), *Art in the Marcusean Analysis* (1969), "The Aesthetics of Intelligent Systems" (1970), and "Notes on Art and Information Processing" (1970)—Burnham generalized his earlier claims about sculpture to art in general (hence systems *aesthetics*) while simultaneously dropping the teleological aspects of *Beyond Modern Sculpture*, insisting that another paradigm would likely supersede systems aesthetics.

3 A Theory of Modern Art (1970–72). In *The Structure of Art* (1972), written as a thoroughgoing response to criticisms leveled at *Beyond Modern Sculpture* and in light of the failure of his exhibition "Software: Information Technology; Its New Meaning for Art" (1970) to convincingly demonstrate systems aesthetics in practice, Burnham converted to structuralism to more effectively clarify the ontology of modern art, now understood as an overarching signifying system. Here, Burnham combined structural anthropology and semiological analysis (both derived from Saussurean structural linguistics) in an account of the underlying, synchronic, structural logic of modern art (1840s–1970s). Burnham modeled his new approach on Claude Lévi-Strauss's exploration of the underlying logic of myth in traditional cultures but translated it to an analysis of "Western art" (thereby also challenging anthropology's Eurocentrism).

4 A Hermetic Theory of Art (1972–2019). In his work on the structural logic of modern art, understood to be in an endgame, Burnham came to regard Duchamp's work as exemplary, finding in the *Large Glass* and the readymades the logical semiotic structure of *all* forms of art. Burnham also became convinced that Duchamp was a hermeticist who had covered up the true meaning of his art. Burnham

consequently sought to reveal the meaning of Duchamp's work, and thus of art *tout court*, by engaging with various esoteric traditions as interpretative methodologies, principally Kabbalah. Burnham combined these esoteric readings with structuralism in the remainder of his work, which is characterized by an arcane mysticism that did not find a ready audience. Representative texts of this phase include "The Semiotics of 'End-Game' Art" (1972) and the three-part "Duchamp's Bride Stripped Bare" (1972), "The True Ready-Made" (1972), and "Voices from the Gate" (1972).

As can be seen from this schematization, Burnham's thought was apparently uneven and mercurial, starting in scientific rationalism and ending in esoteric irrationalism. Dealing with the issue of why his thought underwent such significant theoretical turns in short order is a necessary propaedeutic to any evaluation of the contemporary value of his work. I argue that Burnham's eventual mysticism was a result of the persistent frustration of his syncretism. By the time of writing the introduction to *Great Western Salt Works* in 1974, Burnham openly acknowledged his own "psychological metamorphosis" and the apparently jarring contrasts that characterized his theoretical project: "Given the quasi-scientific rationalism implicit in the first few systems essays, the gradual transition toward high magic in cabalism and alchemy appears to be a complete inversion."[10] Yet Burnham explained the links connecting the theoretical turns in his thought: "The systems view of reality, with its theory of hierarchies and fusion of living and nonliving structures, is not inconsistent with hermetic philosophy."[11] But he also clarified what he took to be the limitations of systems theory for constructing a theory of art, noting that its "utilitarianism and obsession with efficiency leave much about organic relationships misunderstood. Ultimately systems theory may be another attempt by science to resist the emotional pain and ambiguity that remain an unavoidable aspect of life."[12] In *Great Western Salt Works*, Burnham projected a new iteration of his project, inspired by his work on Duchamp, that would involve developing a full-blown "hermetic theory of art."[13]

Burnham thus produced a coherent, if not necessarily persuasive, rationale for the evolution of his thought. His embrace of irrationalism should not, therefore, simply be dismissively pathologized (or passed over in quiet embarrassment) as an example of what Michel Foucault describes in *Madness and Civilization* as "reason dazzled" (Burnham's writing on nonmystical topics in articles written after his esoteric turn is perfectly lucid).[14] Here I agree with Ragain, who asserts that for full comprehension of Burnham's work "historians [should] no longer efface the mystical turn of Burnham's later career."[15] Yet her claim that the turn can be addressed "as an *extension* of the self-organizing and determining nature of systems and their not-so-distant relation to historical notions of 'spirit' or 'mind'" is less convincing since it fails to register sufficiently Burnham's self-avowed break with his earlier systems theoretical work and it elides the highly contested issue of the conceptual relationship, or nonrelationship, between autopoiesis and the dialectic (and the organization of biological versus social systems).[16]

I argue that it is principally the second, "systems aesthetics" phase of Burnham's work that proves to be generative today because of the way that it helps us to think the relational ontology of contemporary art that was inaugurated in the 1960s. Nonetheless, this second phase needs to be contextualized in light of the full development of his thought. In particular, the final phase of Burnham's thought should not be dismissed as a case of New Age burnout (however unrewarding its artistic readings might appear to noninitiates). Rather, it was an attempt to reconcile the tensions that marked his artistic and theoretical project, which sought to fuse art and technology and thereby resist the "disenchantment of the world"—as diagnosed by Max Weber via Friedrich Schiller—effected by modernity.

Becoming "Jack Burnham"

Burnham's work was shaped by the deradicalized "Cold War constructivism" propagated by Gabo (to employ Benjamin H. D. Buchloh's insightful coinage) as well as by a broader engagement with the reformulated postwar terms of the historic avant-gardes as influentially disseminated in the United States via the New Bauhaus, refounded in Chicago.[17] Burnham records that "a design course" he had taken in the early 1950s "under one of Kepes' and Moholy-Nagy's protégés at the Chicago Bauhaus" proved "extremely influential" for his developing "interest in luminous art and Russian Constructivism."[18] Later, in 1957, after he had completed his studies in architectural engineering at the Wentworth Institute, Burnham states that he attended a "seminar on emitted light as an art form" given by György Kepes himself to architectural students at MIT and that this "gave me things to ponder."[19] Burnham also notes that he went through Josef Albers's "Bauhaus pedagogy" at Yale.[20]

Although Burnham did not take any of his degrees from the New Bauhaus itself, his formation was very much in the spirit of its reformed US *Vorkurs*, incorporating specialized scientific and technical training alongside more traditional instruction in art and design. Burnham's *Bildung* was then distinctively

New Bauhausian, in both its Moholy-Nagian design institute and Albersian liberal arts inflections.[21] This determined the artistic problems he addressed in his early practice as a kinetic sculptor.

What has not been discussed elsewhere in the existing scholarship on Burnham, as far as I am aware, is the fact that after graduating from high school in 1949 Burnham spent four years in the US Army at Fort Belvoir (1949–52), in the drafting school of the Corps of Engineers. Although Burnham did not serve in the Korean War (1950–53), he nonetheless undertook military service at the inception of the Cold War, under the then recently announced, newly interventionist Truman Doctrine, which promised to provide American economic and military assistance to any democratic nation threatened by authoritarianism.

Burnham's professional formation thus began within, and proceeded through, a full set of constituent institutions of a nascent US military-industrial (-educational) complex, friendly to radical innovation in the means of production but hostile to any corresponding innovation in its social relations— and still more so to any change in the mode of production. Burnham's early exposure to, and engagement with, the "Bauhaus and related ideals" under the Cold War pressure of political neutralization profoundly shaped the subsequent development of his artistic practice and thinking.

Yet while Burnham was manifestly formed in and by the postwar technocracy, to consider his intellectual work as if it were completely overdetermined by its context would be a mistake. Caroline A. Jones has adeptly traced how "Clement Greenberg" was constructed as a subject, but also was constructed himself, as in relation to the development of a particular version of modernism (understood in terms of the sensory priority of vision) and modernity (conceived in terms of a bureaucratization of the senses). I want to begin to explore a similar critical history of Burnham's subjective formation in relation to modernism (understood in terms of a New Bauhausian attempt to reconcile scientifico-technical and artistic culture under US capitalism) and modernity (understood in terms of the ramifications of technocracy).[22]

Burnham was subjected to technocracy, but he also molded his artistic and intellectual subjectivity in complex forms of negotiation with it, both in terms of negation as well as of affirmation. By the time he undertook a one-year fellowship at the Center for Advanced Visual Studies (CAVS) at MIT under Kepes in 1968, Burnham was, by his own retrospective account from 2004, "trying to get away from the Constructivism of Naum Gabo" and also "in full revolt against Kepes's 'New Bauhaus' philosophy."[23] One of the principle points of contention for Burnham was Kepes's failure to engage with the advanced, computerized technology of a dawning second machine age: "Except for those areas of scientific research that produced stunning photographs. . . . Kepes had a strange aversion to direct involvement with sophisticated technology, particularly anything to do with the computer sciences."[24] In failing to keep pace with its latest developments, Kepes, for Burnham, automatically sacrificed the possibility of technology's progressive reorientation.

In direct contrast to Kepes, Burnham spent his time at CAVS in conversations with two computer scientists (Oliver Selfridge and Jack Nolan) and "working on an essay on the use of computers in art making" (which would be published as "The Aesthetics of Intelligent Systems").[25] Burnham also focused on his own artistic practice, making a "light environment involving programmed electronics and computer components" that employed "electroluminescent tapes" predominantly used by the military for "instrument panels, safety lights, and temporary helicopter landing beacons in Vietnam" that Kepes had secured via an "alliance with Sylvania Corporation."[26]

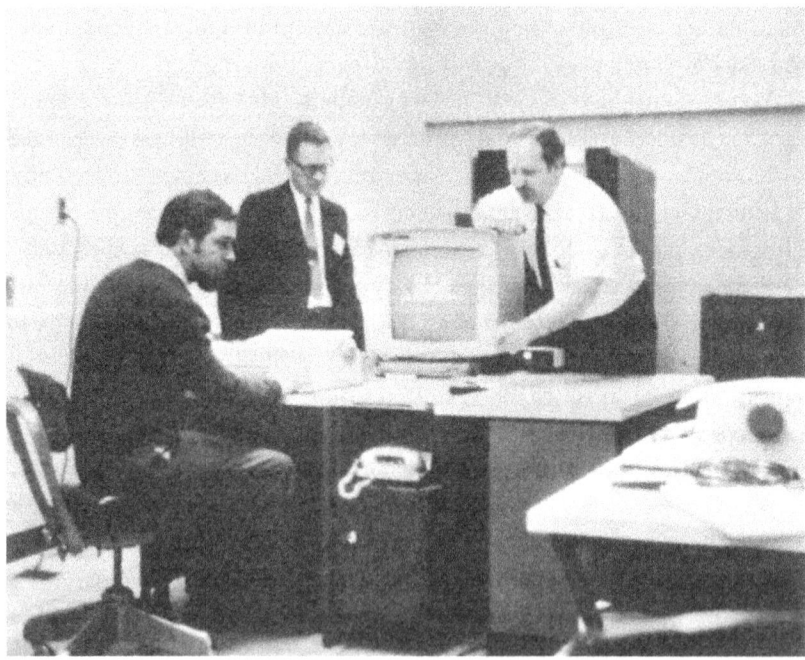

FIGURE 1.2. Jack Burnham (*left*) at Lincoln Laboratory, Massachusetts Institute of Technology, Lexington, Massachusetts, 1968. The image is from Burnham's "The Aesthetics of Intelligent Systems," and no credit information is supplied in the original.

The Sylvania tape works were, however, awkward constructions that did not gain sufficient critical purchase on their *matériel* and therefore fetishized technology and were technocratic in a reactionary sense. Consequently, we might question how successful Burnham's self-declared "revolt" against Kepes's and broader New Bauhaus principles actually was at the level of his practice. Yet the significance of these works within Burnham's oeuvre inheres in their lack of success as meaningful art and their failed reception, acknowledged by Burnham himself: "I could not give the systems works away, much less sell them."[27] In fact, the Sylvania tape constructions that Burnham worked on at CAVS represent not only the concluding moment of his electroluminescent work (begun in 1966) but of his artistic career as a whole.[28] After his CAVS placement, Burnham stopped making art.

Burnham's cessation of his artistic practice gives us insight into the stakes of his historical and theoretical writing. *Beyond Modern Sculpture*, completed in 1967 but not published until 1968, can and has been read as a pioneering attempt to articulate a history of the development of modern sculpture in relation to technological change. Yet the book also contextualized the artistic problems that Burnham attempted to deal with in his own art practice. This can be inferred from Burnham's inclusion of a brief description of his own work within this history, under the heading of "Recent Use of Light in American Art":

> In 1954 the author began to use incandescent light as back lighting for various wood and cardboard reliefs. The author's first experiments with neon light were begun in 1955, partly as a result of Kepes's example. The work shown is one of a series of hanging constructions using neon created during the 1950s. . . . Subsequent projects, beginning in 1959, have included experiments in photo-kinetics, or light motion phenomena. These include light walls using the principles of apparent motion, color-modulating consoles using fiber-optic wires (i.e., light-transmitting wires), and programmed constructions using electroluminescent Tape-Lite.[29]

A single image of his 1956 work *Atom* illustrated this modest, descriptive paragraph. Nonetheless, it demonstrates the coterminous character of Burnham's artistic and intellectual work in the early part of his career. After his CAVS fellowship, and in light of his recognition of the limitations of his own practice (as well as in response to the criticisms leveled at *Beyond Modern Sculpture* that came in from 1968 onward), Burnham broke decisively with teleological conceptions of advanced art as well as with what he described as the "romanticization of technology" marking the New Bauhausian project.[30]

After ceasing to make art of his own, Burnham turned in his "systems essays" to a concerted attempt to theorize successful contemporary art. In so doing he continued to pursue the same artistic problems he had previously directly worked on by the proxy means of his writing and teaching practice. Burnham combined systems theory and Marcusean critical theory in a post–(New) Bauhausian project, to explain contemporary art that resisted a reactionary technocracy while not shying away from the implications he believed the dawn of informational technology would hold for art.

Systems Aesthetics

Burnham developed systems aesthetics as a *general* theory of contemporary art, avoiding movement-specific categorization. As he writes, "The notion of a 'Systems Esthetics' appeared to have validity as momentum built up for Earth Art, Ecological Art, Body Art, Video Art, and the multitudinous forms of Conceptualism."[31] Although scholars have addressed the "systems" aspect of Burnham's systems aesthetics, almost nothing has been made of its specifically *aesthetic* claims, claims that I will argue are central to appreciating the political stakes and significance of his work. Burnham's notion of a systems aesthetic involved more than just an investment in then-current forms of systems thinking (systems theory, cybernetics, and information theory). Rather, it held an explicitly aesthetic character in the strong philosophical sense of the term, one derived from Burnham's adoption and adaptation of Marcuse's neo-Schillerian rethinking of the possible relation between aesthetic and technocratic reason.

While Theodor Adorno refused utopian speculation, Marcuse proposed an aestheticization of technique as a socially transformative response to the dialectic of enlightenment and the domination of technocratic reason. This is precisely what Burnham took from Marcuse's work. Rejecting Greenberg's and Fried's formalist aesthetics, he attempted to produce a reformulated account of the vanguard art of the late 1960s *as aesthetic*. Melissa Ragain productively recovers the facts surrounding the composition and publication of "Systems Esthetics" in her introduction to *Dissolve into Comprehension*. As she notes, Burnham had originally planned to give "Systems Esthetics" a different title—"Towards a Post-formalist Aesthetic"—but was persuaded by Philip Leider, then editor of *Artforum* (and also at that point a strong ally of Fried's), to amend his title and to cut substantial parts of his opening polemic against formalist aesthetics.[32] While it is not clear that Burnham's systems aesthetics fully succeeded in grounding the ontology of the art that it purported to specify, his postformalist move to embrace systems theory was highly prescient, anticipating the methodological diversity of the new art history as well as of postconceptual art. In "Systems Esthetics" Burnham called upon Ludwig von Bertalanffy's work to furnish a definition of art as a system, a "complex of components in interaction." Even though this was a relatively loose claim, disqualifying nothing more than the minimalist "specific object" and art made in the traditional mediums, it was also highly ambitious, setting out to grasp the nature of nascent forms of post-object-specific art in the expanded field (particularly performance and installation). Indeed, Burnham's systems aesthetics attempted to define "unobject" art by way of a relational ontology thirty years before Nicolas Bourriaud's claims about art exhibiting a relational aesthetic. As Burnham put it: "The specific function of modern didactic art has been to show that art does not reside in material entities, but in relations between people and between people and components of their environment"; "conceptual focus rather than material limits define the system."[33]

Burnham's theory of systems aesthetics is often read only as it was articulated in his 1968 essay "Systems Esthetics," but his project for a postformalist aesthetics was in fact articulated across all of his systems essays and developed in dialogue with his artistic practice and teaching.[34] "Systems and Art" (1969) recounts Burnham's experience giving an art and systems course at Northwestern.[35] His course principles derived from the frustrations he had found when previously trying to teach students to make kinetic art (his own métier as a luminist artist). Burnham insisted that "the essential task lies in defining the aesthetic implications of a technological world" and noted that the Bauhaus-derived, but politically neutered, industrial-era pedagogical methods that were then being used in the United States were not up to the task.[36] Burnham instead seized upon the "systems analysis and design approach to problem solving" as an alternative methodology that could be applied to his teaching.[37] Although he recognized that systems analysis was tainted by its association with the military-industrial complex (he referred to it as being understood to possess an "icy Pentagon-esque logic"), Burnham was nevertheless convinced that "the systems approach" seemed to be "the one technique which can embrace an understanding of the span of present-day technology and its consequences" and noted its contemporaneous application in pacific fields, including "conservation, pollution control, and human ecology."[38]

Burnham's broader pedagogical aim was, he wrote, to achieve a "future rapproachment [sic] between art and technology" but his malapropism here—conflating the opposed senses of the French *rapprocher* ("to bring [something] closer") and the English reproach ("to express disapproval")—functions as a Freudian slip disclosing the tensions that marked his theoretical project.[39]

Rather than define art, Burnham's systems aesthetics argued for its *dissolution*: "In an advanced technological culture," Burnham claimed, "the most important artist best succeeds by liquidating his position as artist vis-à-vis society."[40]

This ambition to dissolve the distinction between art and technology led Burnham to Marcuse's work. In *Art in the Marcusean Analysis* (1969) Burnham comments in detail on his reading of Marcusean critical theory, and from this text we can trace the influence that Marcuse exerted on his work.[41] *Art in the Marcusean Analysis* consists of an extended exegesis and critical commentary on Marcuse's thought up to 1968, largely focused on his aesthetics.[42] Burnham not only drew on Marcusean theory but also attempted to remedy what he considered to be its deficiencies. To this end, Burnham took up Marcuse's insight about art's resistance to technological rationality and its possible role in effecting an aestheticization of technique, but turned it into his own stronger and more deterministic claim that "art *will* become an important catalyst for remaking industrial society."[43] Burnham correctly observes that "the emergence of an *artistic technology* rather than the emphasis on *technical art*" is "the essence of Marcuse's hopes," yet he also objects that "somehow Marcuse, a master of the dialectic, never consciously comes to the conclusion that newer media are the critical instruments of social liberation."[44]

Here Burnham reveals his own hopes, claiming that "a fusion of artistic and technical reason" was "inevitable" once art ceased "to function as illusion and ideal appearance."[45] Yet in making such a claim Burnham misunderstands Marcuse's speculative, neo-Schillerian claims for the potential *sublation* of technological rationality by aesthetic rationality, mistakenly arguing for the possibility of *synthesis* between incompatible rationalities under actually existing postwar capitalism: "His [Marcuse's] most subtle speculation is directed towards the traditional antipathy between art and technology. . . . The dialectical synthesis becomes a technology based on esthetic values."[46] Optimistically venturing the critique that "Marcuse fails to recognize . . . that cultural forces of assimilation are just as often assimilated by forces which they have sought to engulf," Burnham misses, or chooses to ignore, Marcuse's clear-eyed recognition that "'art as a form of reality' means not the beautification of the given, but the construction of an entirely different and opposed reality. The aesthetic vision is part of the *revolution*."[47]

Burnham thus deradicalizes, wittingly or not, Marcuse's political claims and misunderstands his aesthetic ones. He argues for a process of social reform, rather than revolution, and thinks this might be achieved by the *fusion* of "artistic and technical reason" in a "technology based on esthetic values."

Nonetheless, Burnham's work engages an important tradition of Left technocracy, stemming from Karl Marx's fragment on the machines in the *Grundrisse* and developed by Marcuse in the United States (a tradition that has also inspired more recent attempts to rethink the possibility of a shift to "postcapitalist" production).[48] Thus Burnham's systems aesthetics, despite its theoretical shortcomings, offers suggestive resources for attempts to rethink the possible relations between art and technology in a progressive manner.

Burnham compounded these misunderstandings in the exhibition he curated at the Jewish Museum in 1970, sponsored by the American Motors Corporation: *Software: Information Technology; Its New Meaning for Art.* Here he presented advanced art and advanced technology within the same institutional and conceptual frame—his curatorial rationale was inspired by the same attempted fusion of Marcuse and systems theory that underlay his theory of systems aesthetics. As he wrote in his catalog essay, "Notes on Art and Information Processing," "Software makes none of the usual qualitative distinctions between the artistic and technical subcultures. At a time when esthetic insight must become a part of technological decision-making, does such a division still make sense?"[49]

Burnham's attempt to prevent his theory of systems aesthetics from being conflated with the ideology of an increasingly marginalized tech art was also an undercurrent that informed the show, in part inflamed by a spat he had entered into in *Artforum* in 1969 with the critic Terry Fenton, who had accused Burnham's position of amounting to little more than a rehash of (postwar) constructivism's misguided technoscientific enthusiasms.[50] Burnham's response was telling: "Again and again I have stressed the need not for TekArt—that new hobgoblin of the critics—but for *a technology based on aesthetic considerations.* Where the latter exists the art impulse will take care of itself."[51] Burnham insisted in his catalog essay, "*Software* is not technological art; rather it points to the information technologies as a pervasive environment badly in need of the sensitivity traditionally associated with art."[52] Still, he struggled to convey the coherence and the validity of his curatorial premise, and his show met with considerable controversy, being widely panned and accused of complicity with the military-industrial complex.

Reflecting on the negative reception of "Software" in an interview with Willoughby Sharp later in 1970, Burnham reserved some sharp words of his own for the hypocrisy of much of the New York art world: "In the last few years, Maurice Tuchman, Kepes at MIT, and myself among others have used money from visible outside sources, electronics companies and such. So the artist is put in the compromising position of making pieces with money whose

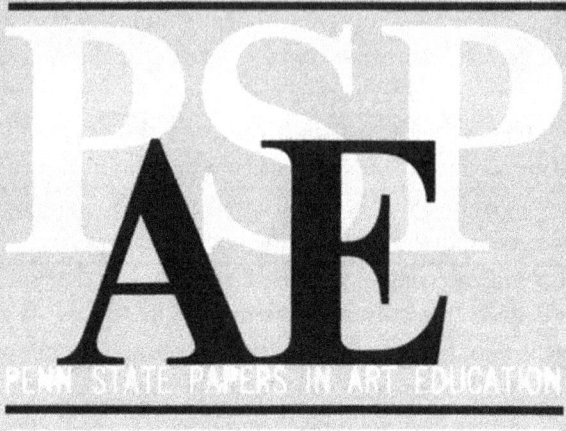

FIGURE 1.3. Jack Burnham, cover of *Art in the Marcusean Analysis*, 1969.

source he knows. Somehow the fact that the Guggenheim Foundation's grant come [*sic*] from the copper mines of South America doesn't bother artists half so much as openly working with American Motors."[53] Yet the major problem with Burnham's show was not compromised ethics, as many critics charged (Burnham had a valid rejoinder to make about the art world's sources of institutional funding), but rather its voluntarism. He attempted to simply produce (or, on a more charitable interpretation, agitate for) his hoped-for fusion of aesthetic and technological reason by juxtaposing cutting-edge art and bleeding-edge technology, without recognizing the impossibility of his hope for the resolution of the contradictions between their competing rationalities under actually existing social conditions.

This fundamental aporia in his thinking shortly led Burnham to jettison the philosophically inspired project of his systems aesthetics altogether. His interest in systems thinking continued, but he turned to structuralism in his second book, *The Structure of Art* (1972), which announced the third phase of his theoretical project, an attempt at a unified, general theory of modern art (with art's underlying, synchronic, structural logic understood by analogy with myth): "Esthetic doctrines once proclaimed that art was 'beauty,' 'the search after truth,' or 'significant form'; what passes for esthetics today—that lingering element which makes art *art*—is no more helpful. Like the patient who repeatedly relocates the cause of his neurosis while being careful never to divulge its underlying origins, redefinition diverts us from the structure of art. . . . Our purpose [is] a structural definition of art."[54]

Burnham's second book is an unpersuasive text, beset by its project to equate modern Western art with myth and hobbled by an attempt to apply the same unconvincing structural schema across a wide array of sharply divergent case studies, from J. M. W. Turner's *Rain, Steam and Speed* (1844) to Daniel Buren's *Photographic Souvenir of One of the Pieces Executed in Kyoto, Japan* (1970). In short order—inspired by his work on putatively hermetic aspects of Duchamp's work that emerge in his chapter on the artist in the book—Burnham began to supplement the limited interpretive schema he mobilized in *The Structure of Art* with categories drawn from Kabbalah and other esoteric sources.

This final turn inaugurated the fourth and concluding phase of Burnham's intellectual project, wherein he set out to produce a hermetic theory of art via his projected book on Duchamp as an esoteric key to the logical semiotic structure of *all* forms of art. I am not able to comment on the accuracy of Burnham's work drawing on esoteric traditions, but the deeply unpersuasive readings of particular artists and works that they advance militate against according them historical value. Rather, I propose that Burnham's late hermeticism is best understood as symptomatic; it is a reaction to, and a final attempt to resolve, the fundamental aporia that marked his work and that he did not resolve by attempting to mythify modern art in *The Structure of Art*.

Support for this argument can be found in Burnham's important late essay "Art and Technology: The Panacea That Failed" (1980), which qualifies his esoteric turn as an attempt at a mystical re-enchantment of the world, which Burnham had failed to achieve in his earlier Marcuse-inspired project to reconcile aesthetic and technological rationality. In "Art and Technology," Burnham explores the reasons why "science has spawned a wealth of technical gadgetry, while ... modern visual artists have been notoriously unsuccessful in utilizing much of it in the making of socially acceptable art."[55] Burnham begins his argument by reflecting on the limited number of exceptions to the broad failure of art and technology. These include Alexander Calder's and George Rickey's kinetic sculpture, the "unexotic fluorescent fixtures" of Dan Flavin's "luminous sculpture," Haacke's "water boxes," Takis's *Signals*, and Jean Tinguely's "fantastic robots and constructions."[56] Burnham then assesses five major art and technology projects initiated in the 1960s: Billy Klüver and Robert Rauschenberg's Experiments in Art and Technology, Jasia Reichardt's *Cybernetic Serendipity* exhibition, Burnham's own *Software* exhibition, CAVS, and the Los Angeles County Museum of Art's Art and Technology initiative.

Burnham has incisive, local points to make about aspects of these projects, all of which he considers limited. His conclusion about the overall failure of art and technology–based practice, however, is particularly revealing: "Have they failed as art because of technical or esthetic incompetency, or because they represent some fundamental dissimilarity as systems of human semiosis? Although it is clear that technical incompetency is partly to blame, I would suspect the latter is a more fundamental explanation."[57] Burnham here reveals the tensions that mark his own thought as much as any fundamental truth about the relationship between art and technology (compare, for example, the ambiguity of *techné*, and its entanglement with *poiesis*, for Martin Heidegger in "The Question concerning Technology").[58]

He then narrates his turn to myth as an alternative explanatory schema adequate to "systems of human semiosis" (here glossed with reference to Roland Barthes's book *Mythologies*, originally published in 1957 but first published in English translation in 1972). Burnham remarks on the challenges he found in attempting to transpose Barthes's semiology to art, noting that it offered "insufficient insight into the dynamic vicissitudes of ... more complex phenomena."[59] He concludes the essay by commenting on the metaphysical insights about art to which this recognition of semiology's limitations led: "Western art . . . contradicts Barthes' everyday mythic invisibility because art by its very paradoxical nature (its near perfect resistance to economic, psychological, or sociological interpretation), openly signifies an apparent mystery concerning the fusion of spirit and matter. So at the highest level, secrecy and a code of concealment are imperative for its cultural survival."[60]

In "Art and Technology: The Panacea That Failed," Burnham narrates how the fundamental aporia that characterizes his artistic and intellectual work—the tension between art and technology, and between aesthetic and technological rationality—came to be "resolved" by his later-career recognition that art was a set of secret codes that conceal its "fusion of spirit and matter." This mystical understanding of art led Burnham to turn to esoteric interpretation, inspired by a new faith in an ability to reenchant the world by revealing veiled truths.

Modernism's (Other) Nervous Breakdown

Revisiting the criticisms of Burnham's work as *technocratic, teleological,* and *utopian,* first leveled by Smithson in 1969 and echoed by leading art historians since then, we can see that they hold equal measures of truth and inaccuracy. Burnham's technophilia was tempered by his critique of reactionary technocracy. He produced a teleological account in *Beyond Modern Sculpture* in 1968 but had renounced this aspect of his work by the time he published "Systems Esthetics" later that same year (thus Smithson's critique of Burnham's teleological thinking was already inaccurate at the time it was made). The charge of utopianism is perhaps most apposite—and certainly more forgivable, indeed potentially laudable—but Burnham's secular political hopes for a fusion of art and technology were displaced into an otherworldly mysticism and were thus also a passing aspect of his project.

The character and value of Burnham's work does not come, therefore, from any one coherent methodological approach or theoretical position. Rather it issues from his prescient and determined commitment to produce a postformalist account of the ontology of art and its associated, highly creative, although often problematic, theoretical syncretism. Haacke, a long-standing friend and interlocutor of Burnham, accurately captures both aspects: "Jack's was not the kind of art criticism based exclusively on an art historical and humanist foundation. Instead, his interdisciplinary approach drew from a wide range of disparate fields that were normally not connected. It opened a new understanding of that peculiar, socially negotiated phenomenon referred to as 'art,' and it explicitly challenged the formalist doctrine, which held considerable sway at that time."[61] The legacy of Burnham's work comes from the specific theoretical syncretism and the innovative postformalist aesthetics represented by the second phase of his work; namely, the account of the ontology of contemporary art as articulated in relationship to technology and offered by his systems aesthetics.

Burnham was among the first to attempt a substantive critique of Greenberg's and Fried's formalist position in the US context (innovatively mobilizing methodologies taken from outside the humanities to do so) as well as the first to venture a comprehensive theoretical alternative to it, anticipating the antiformalism of artistic postmodernism. His postformalist aesthetics tried to combine Marcuse's neo-Schillerianism with systems theory and cognate disciplines, but the structural contradictions of this project proved intractable, resulting in a failed syncretism that exerted its own psychic cost.

Systems aesthetics might thus be historicized as the "nervous breakdown" of the new Bauhausian modernist tradition that Burnham failed to extend for an age of advanced technology.[62] As a result, Burnham might now look like a transitional figure in the history of ideas. Yet his project (if not its specific methodological articulation) is relevant again today because it throws into relief the narrowly anti-aesthetic and often technophobic shortcomings of its principle successor. Postmodernist accounts of art were deeply overdetermined by (the breakdown of) Greenberg's narrow, aesthetically formalist conception of modernism, as Jones and Peter Osborne discuss and Hal Foster himself has acknowledged.[63] Artistic postmodernism was constructed for the most part—notwithstanding the importance of John Cage's "minor" (in the Deleuzean sense) aesthetics—as the refutation of Greenbergian formalist modernism.[64] Even when Greenberg was disavowed, he was affirmed. The postmodern "anti-aesthetic," as propounded by Foster in the introductory essay to his highly influential edited volume of the same name, was—despite considering the wider "adventures of the aesthetic" as "one of the great narratives of modernity" (and in the process touching on both Walter Benjamin's and Adorno's work)—ultimately an anti-*Greenbergian* anti-aesthetic.[65] In this sense it was also, as Foster reflects in retrospect, "parochial."[66]

This anti-aesthetic critical conjuncture has been to the detriment of a more sustained and historically self-reflexive engagement with other accounts of modernism—and indeed of the philosophical critique of (technocratic) modernity more broadly, such as that elaborated by Adorno and Marcuse, as well as the longer German aesthetic tradition (beginning with Schiller's critique of Immanuel Kant) to which these thinkers belong. All this has begun to become clear with the waning of the postmodern theory of a

French poststructuralist stripe that usurped Greenberg, along with the concomitant rise of a renewed attention to aesthetics in the theoretical humanities (which has sought to interrogate the philosophical heritage of debates in postmodern theory).[67] Here, Burnham's postformalist "systems" aesthetics—with its ambition to think the relational ontology of distributed, post-object-specific art in the expanded field and its associated commitment to accounting for the relations between art and technology—finds itself once again rooted in the present.

NOTES

An earlier version of this chapter was published as Luke Skrebowski, "Jack Burnham Redux: The Obsolete in Reverse?," *Grey Room*, no. 65 (2016): 88–113. © 2017 by Grey Room, Inc., and the Massachusetts Institute of Technology, published by the MIT Press.

1   Jack Burnham, *Beyond Modern Sculpture: The Effects of Science and Technology on the Sculpture of This Century* (New York: George Braziller, 1968); Jack Burnham, "Systems Esthetics," *Artforum* 7, no. 1 (1968): 30–35; Jack Burnham, "Real Time Systems," *Artforum* 8, no. 1 (1969): 49–55.

2   Patricia Norvell, "Interview with Robert Smithson, June 20, 1969," in *Recording Conceptual Art*, eds. Alexander Alberro and Patricia Norvell (Berkeley: University of California Press, 2001), 133.

3   Rosalind Krauss, *Passages in Modern Sculpture* (Cambridge, MA: MIT Press, 1981), 212; Benjamin H. D. Buchloh, "Hans Haacke: The Entwinement of Myth and Enlightenment," in *Hans Haacke: "Obra Social,"* ed. Walter Grasskamp (Barcelona: Fundació Antoni Tàpies, 1995), 49; and Thierry de Duve, *Kant after Duchamp* (Cambridge, MA: MIT Press, 1996), 285–86.

4   Jack Burnham, *Dissolve into Comprehension: Writings and Interviews, 1964–2004*, ed. Melissa Ragain (Cambridge, MA: MIT Press, 2016).

5   My list of scholars working on Burnham's work is indicative rather than exhaustive and based on those whose work I have engaged with and found most productive. For a regularly updated record of the scholarship on Burnham, see Robert Horvitz's diligently maintained online resource, "A Node for Jack Burnham," http://mujweb.cz/horvitz/burnham/homepage.html.

6   Burnham, *Dissolve into Comprehension*, front cover, inside flap.

7   On the relationship of the academy to esoteric traditions of thought, see Wouter Hanegraaf, *Esotericism and the Academy: Rejected Knowledge in Western Culture* (Cambridge: Cambridge University Press, 2014).

8   Burnham reflects on the fraught editorial politics of the New York magazines of the period in his article "Criticism in the Provinces" (1978), in Burnham, *Dissolve into Comprehension*, 237–40.

9   A list of Burnham's publications can be found online at Robert Horvitz's website, "A Node for Jack Burnham," http://mujweb.cz/horvitz/burnham/homepage.html; and a list of pre-1981 publications and a CV is reprinted in Burnham, *Dissolve into Comprehension*, 290–96.

10   Jack Burnham, *Great Western Salt Works: Essays on the Meaning of Post-formalist Art* (New York: George Braziller, 1974), 11.

11   Burnham, *Great Western Salt Works*, 11.

12   Burnham, *Great Western Salt Works*, 11.

13   Burnham, *Great Western Salt Works*, 12.

14   Michel Foucault, *Madness and Civilization: A History of Insanity in the Age of Reason*, trans. Richard Howard (London: Routledge, 2001), 101.

15   Melissa Ragain, introduction to Burnham, *Dissolve into Comprehension*, xiii.

16   Ragain, introduction, xiii, emphasis added.

17   See Benjamin H. D. Buchloh, "Cold War Constructivism," in *Formalism and Historicity: Models and Methods in Twentieth-Century Art* (Cambridge, MA: MIT Press, 2015), 375–408.

18   Burnham, "Joan Brigham Interviews Jack Burnham," in *Dissolve into Comprehension*, 244.

19   Burnham, "Joan Brigham Interviews," 244.

20   Burnham, "Joan Brigham Interviews," 244.

21   Burnham did not, however, engage with the Dada-inflected strand of this tradition that proved so fertile at Black Mountain and that would later spread to New York, inspired by the college's teaching and summer courses.

22   Caroline A. Jones, *Eyesight Alone: Clement Greenberg's Modernism and the Bureaucratization of the Senses* (Chicago: University of Chicago Press, 2005).

23   Burnham, "Joan Brigham Interviews," 241, 244.

24   Jack Burnham, "Art and Technology: The Panacea That Failed," in *The Myths of Information: Technology and Postindustrial Culture*, ed. Kathleen Woodward (Madison, WI: Coda Press, 1980), 208.

25   Burnham, "Joan Brigham Interviews," 243.

26   Burnham, "Joan Brigham Interviews," 241, 244.

27   Burnham, "Joan Brigham Interviews," 241.

28   Burnham's artistic career began with incandescent light construction in 1954, moved on to constructions with neon tubing in 1955, programmed light environments in 1959, programmed luminous constructions in 1962, and programmed light boxes with fiber-optic wires and chemical filters in 1964, before first using Sylvania tape in 1966. This schematization of Burnham's practice comes from the CV reproduced in Burnham, *Dissolve into Comprehension*, 284.

29   Burnham, *Beyond Modern Sculpture*, 302.

30   Burnham, "Joan Brigham Interviews," 244.

31   Jack Burnham, "Steps in the Formulation of Real-Time Political Art," in Hans Haacke, *Hans Haacke: Framing and Being Framed* (New York: New York University Press, 1975), 132–33.

32   Ragain derives this claim from a letter from Philip Leider to Michael Fried in which Leider relates his editorial intervention, among other matters. Ragain, introduction, xvii–xix. Ragain's inclusion of Burnham's original draft version of the article ("Towards a Post-formalist Aesthetic") in the new volume, albeit abridged, is particularly valuable).

33   Burnham, "Systems Esthetics," in *Great Western Salt Works*, 16–17.

34 See Skrebowski, "The Artist as Homo Arbiter Formae: Art and Interaction in Jack Burnham's Systems Essays," in *Practicable: From Participation to Interaction in Contemporary Art*, ed. Samuel Bianchini and Erik Verhagen (Cambridge, MA: MIT Press, 2016), 39–54.

35 Jack Burnham, "Systems and Art," *Arts in Society* 6, no. 2 (1969): 194–203.

36 Burnham, "Systems and Art," 195.

37 Burnham, "Systems and Art," 195.

38 Burnham, "Systems and Art," 196.

39 Burnham, "Systems and Art," 197.

40 Burnham, "Systems Esthetics," 16.

41 The text was originally written as a lecture in September 1968 but was not presented until January 1969 at Pennsylvania State University, where it was subsequently published as a pamphlet. Marcuse's intellectual influence on Burnham has been little discussed. Melissa Ragain includes a heavily excerpted version of Burnham's *Art in the Marcusean Analysis* in *Dissolve into Comprehension* and discusses it relatively briefly in her introduction to the volume. For the only significant exception I am aware of to this general oversight (of which my own earlier work is also guilty), see Michael Corris, ed., *Conceptual Art: Theory, Myth, Practice* (Cambridge: Cambridge University Press, 2004), 195, 271. Burnham himself had effectively encouraged such oversight by not acknowledging the philosopher's influence on "Systems Esthetics," despite the fact that the article was published in September 1968 and was thus contemporaneous with the composition, if not the delivery, of his lecture on Marcuse and demonstrably indebted to it. Burnham references Marcuse in "Real Time Systems," but the reference is to *Eros and Civilization: A Philosophical Inquiry into Freud* (1955) and does not touch on his more significant debt to *One-Dimensional Man: Studies in the Ideology of Advanced Industrial Society* (1964). Burnham also quotes Marcuse on the back jacket of *Beyond Modern Sculpture*, but not inside, perhaps suggesting that he began reading Marcuse after the main text was completed in 1967.

42 Burnham's interpretation of Marcuse concentrates on *One-Dimensional Man* and "Art in the One-Dimensional Society" (1967). Burnham's analysis also broaches Marcuse's earlier works *Eros and Civilization* and *Soviet Marxism: A Critical Analysis* (1961).

43 Jack Burnham, *Art in the Marcusean Analysis* (University Park: Pennsylvania State University Press, 1969), 3, emphasis added.

44 Burnham, *Art in the Marcusean Analysis*, 7–8.

45 Burnham, *Art in the Marcusean Analysis*, 9.

46 Burnham, *Art in the Marcusean Analysis*, 8–9.

47 Herbert Marcuse, "Art as a Form of Reality," in *On the Future of Art*, ed. Edward Fry (New York: The Viking Press, 1970), 133.

48 J. Jesse Ramirez productively insists on Marcuse's US-specific development of his own "heretical" strand of Frankfurt School thought, elaborated in dialogue with Left Technocracy. See J. Jesse Ramirez, "Marcuse among the Technocrats: America, Automation, and Postcapitalist Utopias, 1900–1941," *Amerikastudien/ American Studies* 57, no. 1 (2012): 34–35.

49 Jack Burnham, "Notes on Art and Information Processing," in *Software: Informa-tion Technology; Its New Meaning for Art* (New York: Jewish Museum, 1970), 14.

50 I discuss this exchange in more detail in my essay, "All Systems Go: Recovering Hans Haacke's Systems Art," *Grey Room*, no. 30 (2008): 54–83.

51 Jack Burnham, "Jack Burnham, Terry Fenton: An Exchange," *Artforum* 7, no. 8 (1969): 60, emphasis added.

52 Burnham, "Notes on Art," 14.

53 Burnham, *Dissolve into Comprehension*, 255–56.

54 Jack Burnham, *The Structure of Art* (New York: George Braziller, 1971), 7.

55 Burnham, "Art and Technology," 200.

56 Burnham, "Art and Technology," 200–201.

57 Burnham, "Art and Technology," 211–12.

58 Martin Heidegger, "The Question concerning Technology," in *Martin Heidegger: Basic Writings*, trans. D. F. Krell (San Francisco: HarperCollins, 1977), 283–317.

59 Burnham, "Art and Technology," 214.

60 Burnham, "Art and Technology," 215.

61 Hans Haacke, preface to *Dissolve into Comprehension*, x.

62 Mel Ramsden, discussing conceptual art's effect on Greenbergian formalism, refers to "Modernism's nervous breakdown." Mel Ramsden, cited in Charles Harrison, *Conceptual Art and Painting: Further Essays on Art & Language* (Cambridge, MA: MIT Press, 2001), 27.

63 See Peter Osborne, "Aesthetic Autonomy and the Crisis of Theory: Greenberg, Adorno, and the Problem of Postmodernism in the Visual Arts," *New Formations* 9 (Winter 1989): 31–50; and Caroline A. Jones, "Postmodernism's Greenberg," in *Eyesight Alone*, 347–86. Foster states, "It's true: the version of postmodernism pre-sented by the nefarious *October* group was an attempt to break with one model of Modernism, that associated with Greenberg above all others, but also to recover other models, ones displaced by the prestige of Greenberg." See James Elkins and Harper Montgomery, eds., *Beyond the Aesthetic and the Anti-aesthetic* (University Park: Pennsylvania State University Press, 2013), 27.

64 For treatments of Cage's significance and influence, see Branden W. Joseph, *Be-yond the Dream Syndicate: Tony Conrad and the Arts after Cage; A "Minor" History* (New York: Zone, 2008); and Liz Kotz, "Post-Cagean Aesthetics and the Event Score," in *Words to Be Looked At: Language in 1960s Art* (Cambridge, MA: MIT Press, 2007), 59–98.

65 Hal Foster, introduction to *The Anti-aesthetic: Essays on Postmodern Culture*, ed. Hal Foster (New York: New Press, 1998), xvii.

66 Elkins and Montgomery, *Beyond the Aesthetic*, 49.

67 See, for example, Elkins and Montgomery's anthology *Beyond the Aesthetic*, as well as Armen Avanessian and Luke Skrebowski, eds., *Aesthetics and Contemporary Art* (Berlin: Sternberg, 2011); and Francis Halsall, Julia Jansen, and Tony O'Connor, eds., *Rediscovering Aesthetics: Transdisciplinary Voices from Art History, Philoso-phy, and Art Practice* (Stanford, CA: Stanford University Press, 2009).

2

The Artist as "Weatherman"

Hans Haacke's Critical Meteorology

JOHN TYSON

Weather boxes *seemingly* have nothing to do with sociopolitical situations; however, even on the superficial level of figure of speech, there are many similarities. . . . More important . . . on a conceptual level, physical and biological phenomena have their equivalents in the social and behavioral sphere. . . . These are not correspondences due to an imaginary language, but are based on specifiable isomorphisms. . . . *Physical and biological systems are per se political.* —Hans Haacke, "Provisional Remarks"

With these words, Hans Haacke introduced the multiple, editioned work that is today titled *Condensation Cube* (1963–67).[1] These geometric plexiglass volumes each contain a small amount of water that assumes different states over time. The liquid unceasingly evaporates and condenses in response to its environment. Institutional surroundings and gallerygoers nourish the artwork. The artist intended the shape and materials of his container to be unremarkable, as he hoped spectators would pay attention to the ongoing processes that were partially framed by his plastic cubes. He believed "water in all its states" to serve an indexical function similar to a sensory device such as a photoelectric cell, which "registers and processes certain information from its environment."[2] With their palimpsest of dripped lines through steamy planes, which accrue over time, his vessels challenge gallerygoers to become aware of normally invisible systems: the broader meteorological patterns inside art institutions.[3]

The artist intended audiences to consider his "weather boxes" as political on multiple levels: on one hand, they constitute demonstrations of real phenomena, art spaces' material conditions (a mode of analysis with Marxist overtones). And, on the other, they are metaphorically charged; their "specifiable isomorphisms" spark a consideration of "social and behavioral" climates too. The cubes are not just aestheticized barometers measuring humidity, pressure, and temperature. The foggy indexes of Haacke's boxes signal the effects of institutional lighting as well as the costly climate control in place, which respectively mark and protect and preserve the valuable class of things known as "art." Depending on the potency of the heating and cooling systems, *Condensation Cube* also registers the presence of warm, moist bodies of spectators, who have no choice but to become collectively implicated performers in its production. The work teaches lessons about the ecology of the system of privileged objects that galleries and museums host: weather conditions in art institutions are not natural, but they are naturalized. The atmosphere of the museum also depends on the flows of capital and power in economic and political systems.

Thus, *Condensation Cube*, and the entirety of Haacke's projects with weather, should be considered some of the earliest instances of institutional critique; such artworks mark and investigate the meteorology (both actual and metaphorical) of the sites that frame them. Indeed, the environments of art institutions are in some sense a medium that mediates between Haacke's artistic critiques and his interest in systems thinking and climates. As Luke Skrebowski has explored, recuperating Haacke's interest in systems implies revised and expanded understandings of conceptual art to include systematic artworks championed by Haacke's friend and interlocutor, the artist and critic Jack Burnham.[4] Skrebowski correctly traces concerns for systems forward in Haacke's oeuvre post-1969. I propose we encounter politics further back. This essay argues that his artworks with a systems aesthetic always investigate systems of politics.

Haacke produced numerous meteorological projects that critically reflect on their environments, equally physical and cultural: *Rain Tower* (1962), *Condensation Floor* (1967), and *Condensation Wall* (1967); works with refrigerated coils, like *Ice Stick*, that convert water in the surroundings into a solid state; *Wind in Water: Snow, December 15, 1968* (1968), with weather and weather maps employed as ready-mades; works consisting of sprayed mist and its effects (*Fog, Swamp, Erosion* [1969]); assorted projects with fans, such as *Wind Room* (1968–69); weather balloons in *Sky Line* (1967), which was realized in Central Park and at MIT, and *Sphere in Oblique Air Jet* (1964–67); and institutional climates in *Recording of Climate in Art Exhibition* (1970) and *Weather, or Not* (a 2009–10 installation in which the gallery space was not climate controlled). Drawing on period discourse to develop close readings, I analyze and historically contextualize *Wind in Water, Sky Line, Recording,* and *Weather, or Not.*

The April 4, 1968, assassination of Martin Luther King Jr. prompted Haacke to take stock and reassess the political efficacy of art (see Gosse and Stott's introduction to this volume).[5] He wrote to Burnham, following King's murder: "Art is unsuited as a political tool. . . . I have known that for a number of years. All of a sudden it bugs me. I am also asking myself, why the hell I am working in this field at all. . . . I still have no answer, but I am no longer comfortable."[6] Although the tragedy shook his faith in the truck of "political" art, he kept working.

Haacke's resolution for overcoming the impasse was to expand his analysis of systems.[7] His "weatherworks" provided one clear path. Looking back on his career, Haacke told Cecilia Alemani, "I understood weather as a prototypical system of interactive physical components—with metaphorical materials."[8] He began such projects before King's murder and continued to concentrate on weather in works made in the especially charged atmosphere following the tragedy.[9] Meteorological thinking evidently remained highly relevant to him for understanding complex systems. Taking what he described in February 1969 as a meteorological "attitude" would "lead to working strategies that could expose the functioning and consequences of . . . interdependent processes."[10] Additionally, for the era's "tuned in" visitors, artworks dealing with meteorology might well have evoked political sentiments of the counterculture. His projects could provoke reflection on—following Bob Dylan's lyrics in "Subterranean Homesick Blues"—"which way the wind blows" inside art institutions and, because of his concern for exploring connections that transcend their bounds, outside them as well.[11] Certainly, at this time, Dylan's brand of folk was understood as central to the soundtrack of American leftwing radicalism, as evidenced in Stephen Shames's 1970 photograph of Black Panther Huey Newton listening to Dylan's *Highway 61 Revisited* (1965). Haacke hoped those engaging with his art would take the "hint to the double meaning of the word 'climate'" and consider ethics as well as aesthetics.[12]

Understanding the ways that weather has been inscribed into systems of culture, politics, and language helps account for the meteorological bent of Haacke's output. It seems no coincidence that ideas about weather systems, environments, and ecology increasingly shaped understandings of the world at the same moment that he was developing his first systems artworks. Walter Benjamin, a critical thinker, like Haacke, concerned with material conditions, muses in *The Arcades Project* about the nature of weather, penning the following fragment: "Of the double meaning of the term *temps* in French [both time and weather]."[13] Haacke strove to make explicit "something which experiences, reacts to its environment . . . which reacts to light and temperature changes, is subject to air currents . . . which lives in time and makes the 'spectator' experience time"; hence, his works can be seen to physically embody Benjamin's two significances of *temps*.[14] Weather surely appealed to the artist as material and metaphor precisely because of multivalent range of connections and associations it engenders.

The history of meteorology confirms Haacke's comprehension of weather as physical phenomena that must always be understood as entangled in social systems. Meteorology as a science developed most forcefully in the nineteenth century. Some of the first US weather maps and reports were produced by the US Army Signal Corps, the entity that oversaw weather observation from circa 1819 until the 1890s, when the US Weather Bureau, the precursor of the National Weather Service, took over operations.[15] The Division of Telegrams and Reports for the Benefit of Commerce and Agriculture was the name of the section that oversaw the collection and communication of meteorological data, revealing that the weather was not solely entangled with national security but also with the economy and new technologies.[16] Beginning in 1853, the Smithsonian Institution published weather reports in the *Washington Evening Star*.[17] In the UK, Sir Francis Galton's *Meteographica* gathered and systematized data on climate conditions in 1863. In addition, Galton made weather maps available to the general public for the first time on April 1, 1875. His chart graphically representing the previous day's weather appeared in the London *Times*.[18] About a year later, American readers began to regularly encounter such maps in US dailies.[19]

A concern for the environment and the ways weather systems intersected with one another was an increasingly urgent issue in Western society that accelerated in the mid-twentieth century. In the 1940s, new theories of meteorology developed from within the milieu of the Institute for Advanced

Study in Princeton, New Jersey, simultaneously with advances in computer programming, game theory, and cybernetics, involving figures such as John and Klára Dán von Neumann.[20] John von Neumann's better-known collaborator Norbert Wiener also discusses meteorology briefly in his *Cybernetics: Or Control and Communication in the Animal and the Machine* (1948). He notes that meteorology enables a rethinking of what to the layperson may seem like concrete objects, such as clouds. He argues that a "topologically inclined meteorologist might perhaps define a cloud as a connected region of space in which the density of the part of the water content in the solid or liquid state exceeds a certain amount and would at most represent an extremely transitory state."[21] Similarly, artworks consisting of weather phenomenon might provoke a similar ontological realignment, prompting spectators to focus on art as part of systems in flux, rather than timeless objects in rarefied surrounds.

From the late 1960s onward, political activism related to environmentalism was concretized by *The Environmental Handbook* (1970) and the associated radical pedagogical actions, the National Teach-In on World Community (October 25, 1969) and the Environmental Teach-In at Columbia University on April 22, 1970, which from that point on became known as Earth Day. Members of the New Left group Students for a Democratic Society (SDS), most notably Tom Hayden and Mark Rudd, orbited within the solar system of environmental activism; both Hayden and Rudd would go on to form part of the most radical wing of SDS: the Weathermen. The Museum of Modern Art also participated in the first Earth Day celebrations. An ecological film series linked the museum to other events held throughout New York, such as a teach-in and banning of traffic on a large section of 14th Street.[22]

Haacke's interest in weather systems should be understood as part of a wider environmental and ecological turn in art, commencing with Allan Kaprow's environments (in 1957) and continuing into land art and to present-day explorations of ecology by the likes of Mark Dion (who had been exposed to Haacke's works and teachings while a participant in the Whitney Independent Study Program).[23] In Europe, artists important for a young Haacke dealt with decidedly low-tech or no-tech depictions of natural phenomena. Members of ZERO circulated depictions of wind, water, and light in the group's eponymous *ZERO 3* (July 1961). The publication juxtaposes water in different states both as liquid and as snow. ZERO's demonstrations evoked both the scientific and political sense of the term "weather." Nonetheless, a concern for ludic interaction was the prime motivator for these carnivalesque, costumed group performances. The demonstrations expanded art to the air and streets by the inclusion of processions with participants holding numerous balloons or inflatable sculpture.

By the late 1960s, Jack Burnham and the curator Willoughby Sharp insisted that society was no longer "object-oriented." Instead, art with what Burnham importantly dubs a "systems esthetic" was the result of a network of interactions.[24] "The art of the future, like the most advanced art of the present, will be environmental," Sharp declared in 1968.[25] Given the importance of living spectators as part of systems works (as is the case for Haacke's artworks), we should think that many of these environmental projects were necessarily ecological. Suggesting a further conflation was acceptable to period thinking, weather was also understood as part of this field of inquiry: Haacke contributed meteorological systems art to initiatives organized by Burnham and Sharp. His works with weather were compatible with various emerging tendencies. Meteorological projects by Haacke featured in exhibitions that would be recognized to be of major importance for the respective development of systems aesthetics, conceptual art, and tech art: Jan van der Marck's *Art by Telephone* (1969) at the MCA-Chicago; Lucy Lippard's *557,087* (1969) at the Seattle Art Museum; Donald Karshan's (with Joseph Kosuth and Ian Burn) *Conceptual Art, Conceptual Aspects* (1970) at the New York Cultural Center; Pontus Hulten's *The Machine as Seen at the End of the Mechanical Age* (1968) at MOMA; and Experiments in Art and Technology's *Some More Beginnings* (1968) at the Brooklyn Museum.

In her introduction to the catalog *557,087*, which consists of ninety-five index cards, Lippard argues that Haacke's works with "frost, condensation, evaporation, snow, mist, grass," are ecological.[26] She links Haacke's projects with natural processes to other contemporaneous artistic engagements with "urban ecology," such as Ed Ruscha's photobook *Every Building on the Sunset Strip* (1966) and Daniel Buren's striped posters. Similarly, Haacke's explorations of the built environment, such as his famous real-estate ownership profiles, *Shapolsky et al. Manhattan Real Estate Holdings, a Real-Time Social System, as of May 1, 1971* (1971; dated to coincide with May Day as well as the largest Vietnam War protests then to date), should also be viewed as related to his meteorological interventions; all are born under the sign of ecology.

By the late 1970s, it was not just artists (and activists) who thought explicitly about the system of art institutions and climate conditions, which the presence of spectators' bodies impacted. Haacke's projects with condensation anticipated directions that museums themselves would increasingly consider. Environmental thinking entered the mainstream with Garry Thomson's *The Museum Environment* (1978). Thomson, conservator and research chemist of the National Gallery, London, embraced the utility of conceiving institutions as environments. His text discusses, among other issues, ways of mitigating the damaging effects of humidity, light, and temperature—precisely the elements that are the requisite lifeblood of Haacke's meteorological artworks.

Reframing Weather to Liberate Science

For *Wind in Water: Snow, December 15, 1968* (figure 2.1), Haacke used an official weather map and corresponding data juxtaposed with documentation of the actual conditions of the climate (as the tautological title, which he determined after observing the precipitation, underscores).[27] *Wind in Water* was in part a performance of art-world conventions. He advertised it using a postcard invitation mimicking those of commercial galleries. In a kind of studio visit gone wrong, he took groups of visitors upstairs, out of the heated work space, past a wall label, and through a doorway that opened onto the stage of the cold rooftop of his Bowery studio.[28] The wall-mounted labels he produced with the text "Wind in Water: Snow" have standardized, bold sans serif font, connoting institutional officiality. Once outside, guests encountered water in different states, solid and liquid, on the rooftop—as well as the wider environment of Lower Manhattan and the New York skyline.

Wind in Water updates the tactics of Marcel Duchamp in order to analyze various kinds of frames.[29] According to Edward Fry, the curator who organized Haacke's canceled Guggenheim show, *Wind in Water* "represented Haacke's most extreme extension of the Duchampian readymade."[30] He continues, "[Haacke] has in effect signed a phenomenon of nature without having in any way intruded upon it, the only interference with natural processes being their identification and isolation through the selection of a given day."[31] However, it was not just natural systems that were articulated with Haacke's artwork; the project also demonstrates the way climates are culturally conditioned. The work subsequently existed as photographic documentation accompanied by visualized data, a weather map with the day's forecast, apparently sourced from a newspaper.

The actions of *Wind in Water* were not entirely absurdist (despite consisting of a bizarre visit to a snowy roof rather than to an artist's studio). Haacke forced a contemplation of real weather, rather than a representation—scientific or artistic—abstracting it. Furthermore, by de- and recontextualizing everyday data (the weather map) as art, Haacke charged spectators with gazing on every detail, including the words crediting the weather's first author: the US Department of Commerce. With his framing and reframing, Haacke implicitly

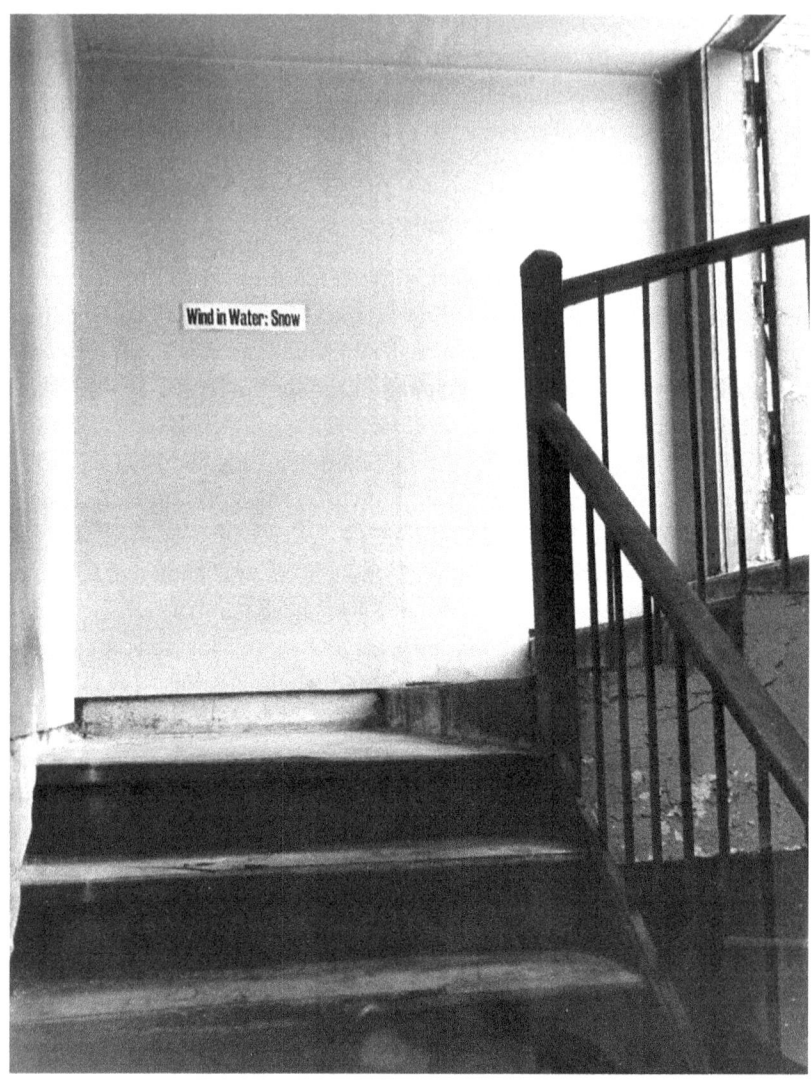

FIGURE 2.1. Hans Haacke, *Wind in Water: Snow, December 15, 1968*, 1968. © Hans Haacke/ Artists Rights Society (ARS).

staked a claim on the weather and prompted those who participated in his action (or contemplated its documentation) to train their attention on normally invisible meteorological systems—as well as on their links to economics.

Haacke's project resonates with Herbert Marcuse's call for "a science and technology released from their service to destruction and exploitation, and thus free for liberating exigencies of the imagination."[32] Marcuse, a Frankfurt school political theorist and philosopher, was at the time a central figure for the American Left. Moreover, his ideas correlated with emerging citizen science initiatives. This movement had countercultural resonances, as it attempted to decentralize data collection, taking science from the hands of laboratories ensconced in the military-industrial complex. *Wind in Water: Snow*, then, was a comparable attempt to wrest the environment—or at least its measuring and visualization—from the rationalizing and commercial control of the Department of Commerce.[33]

As with *Wind in Water*, a number of Haacke's artworks from the ensuing year called for the collection of scientific data in the name of art—a move that anticipates his better-known polling pieces, typically understood to be the artist's earliest instance of institutional critique (the first of which was conducted in November 1969). Turning amateurs into authorities and potentially further activating an audience outside of the art world, in September 1969 Haacke developed a project for Willoughby Sharp's *Place and Process*, which saw Dan Graham depositing one hundred bottles with messages in the Saskatchewan River. The bottled text asked that, in four languages, whomever encountered them return the paper with an account detailing the location and time of the find.[34] Haacke contributed other instances of art as science to Lucy Lippard's *557,087* (and later to *955,000*); in *Precipitation Minus Evaporation* (September 1969) nonspecialists similarly became authorities. A tube was implanted in the ground and a recorder marked and signed the water levels each day. A collaborative, multiply autographed line drawing on the plastic cylinder where the measurements were taken emerged over the course of the shows. In sum, the performances of citizen science that Haacke threaded though the art system constitute a meteorological face to the critique of institutions.

Climate Data as Pedagogy

Haacke produced *Recording of Climate in Art Exhibition* (1969–70) for *Conceptual Art, Conceptual Aspects* (April 10–August 25, 1970). His project consisted of functional ready-mades. He employed the instruments commonly found in gallery spaces: a thermograph, barograph, and a hydrograph, as well as the numerous paper printouts charting the environmental history of the exhibition. Rather than insert an alien component (as in *Condensation Cube*) into the space of art, here Haacke refunctioned elements of the museum apparatus and made them his own. He converted the institution into a medium. While less frequently encountered today, instruments measuring climate conditions (weather over time) were common at the time of his project's execution.

As Haacke's work supplements and doubles the institution's data, serving to monitor the museum, it questions the totalizing authority of the host. With its mechanized, real-time drawing, the "scientistic" artwork imagines alternative functions for scientific technology. Moreover, *Recording* investigates the conditions of the museological frame beyond simply representing the weather. Haacke asserts that "it was a site-specific ironic comment . . . to the rarified, super-controlled environments in which art works are exhibited . . . their commodity/insurance values and white glove treatment."[35] *Recording* was particularly ironic given the fact that the majority of the artworks that accompanied Haacke's project in the galleries moved away from preciousness toward what Lippard famously termed "dematerialization."[36] Nevertheless, by "mimetic exacerbation," *Recording* draws attention to the continuation of museum practices used for the conservation of "old media" art.[37] Especially given that the mechanically drawn charts are part of the artwork, he also signals the way that institutions can return materiality even to conceptual artworks, turning them or their documentation into something valuable. Working with and within the system of exhibition, Haacke reprograms the gallery's already extant extra-art element. He prompts the instruments to teach lessons about links between institutional conservation and the production of art commodities.

Weather as Antimonument and Antiwar

For two days in 1967, one in the spring and one in fall, visitors to Central Park were greeted with an abnormal sight: *Sky Line* (figure 2.2), a 1,280-foot chain of white balloons flitting in the wind. These curious weather balloons were strung one after another, ascending into the atmosphere above Observatory Pond and Sheep Meadow—parts of the park that hosted antiwar protests the same year. The fragile, temporary work, which lasted only a few hours, was shown twice for a two-part exhibition organized by Sharp titled *Kinetic Environment* (again underscoring a link between avant-garde art and ecology).[38]

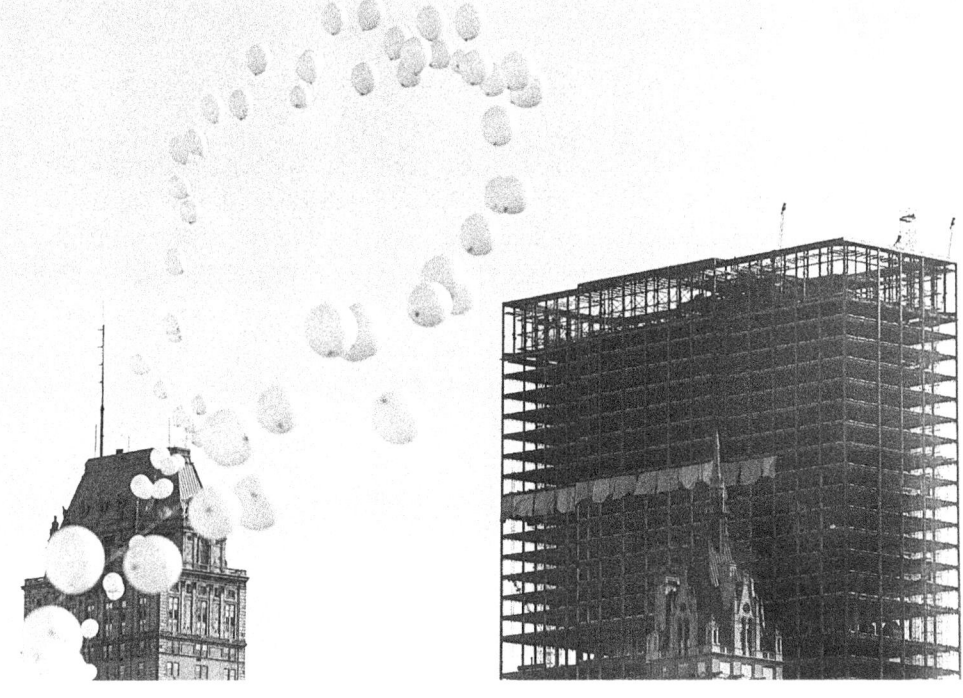

FIGURE 2.2. Hans Haacke, *Sky Line*, 1967. Balloons and fishing line, as installed in *Kinetic Environment II*. © Hans Haacke/Artists Rights Society (ARS).

The New York City Department of Parks and Recreation press release states that it would "attempt to break the barriers between art and nature."[39] *New York Times* critic Grace Glueck affirms that *Kinetic Environment* altered Central Park, rendering it a "wondrous toy."[40] Glueck's interpretation reinforces the notion that the park's program could be played with using art.

Notably, at this juncture in the antiwar movement, balloons formed part of the iconography of protest (and would continue to do so through the early 1970s). As early as December 1966, the activist Bread and Puppet Theater released balloons attached to streamers emblazoned with "Peace, Vietnam, Napalm, War" in Grand Central Station.[41] Distributing balloons was part of the broader Yippie strategy; hence, spring 1967 antiwar rallies in New York and San Francisco saw demonstrators holding these playful orbs.[42] Perhaps most strikingly, protesters lying prostrate as if dead released black and white balloons symbolizing Vietnam War casualties in the 1969 "lie-in" in Central Park.[43] Furthermore, the balloon chain and balloon drops are features of more mainstream democratic politics, appearing since the mid-twentieth century at party conventions in relation to presidential elections.[44] Given all these uses of balloons (and parks), *Sky Line* surely resonated with some spectators as more than just a demonstration of the forces of the wind.[45]

Haacke created a version of the balloon chain, MIT *Sky Line*, for his 1967 exhibition at the Massachusetts Institute of Technology. It, too, altered the standard behavior of its collaborators. In a collective action with the artist, students paraded the balloons across the campus prior to their flight into the air of Cambridge. He effectively imported the form of the ZERO demonstration to a changing climate. It is notable that at precisely the moment Haacke occupied the campus, student (and faculty) activism was beginning to brew on the banks of the Charles River. In the 1960s, a significant percentage of the university's funding came from the Pentagon, a fact that increasingly divided the school.[46] In February 1967, Noam Chomsky, then a freshly radicalized MIT linguist, published an article in the *New York Review of Books* questioning American involvement in Vietnam and calling on intellectuals to resist.[47] Concurrent with Haacke's exhibition, on November 6, members of SDS confronted a recruiter from Dow Chemical (the manufacturer of napalm), who was visiting the campus to conduct interviews. Later, MIT would organize a colloquium related to the debate that followed, "Napalm, Vietnam and the University."[48] Hence, Haacke's October ludic and civic action could be read as one of various "improper" manifestations of bodies in space that autumn.

In her essay for the 2011 (re)exhibition of Haacke's 1967 show at MIT, Caroline A. Jones views Haacke's parade in more aesthetic than political terms. She asserts, "This choreography left the Beaux-Arts columns of the old MIT behind, aiming for the new postwar 'functionalist' architecture linked to technology and engineering."[49] Nevertheless, Haacke's ever-shifting artwork contrasts sharply with the Brutalist student center as well as with the massive, rounded exteriors of the Saarinen edifices that placed this institution of higher learning at the center of the military-industrial complex. With MIT *Sky Line*, Haacke implicates the campus in his work as support. The lyrical qualities of the bobbling, flitting balloons to some degree flew in the face of the gravity of the edifices to which they were attached. MIT *Sky Line* was an ephemeral parasite—neither architecture nor sculpture—that slightly altered the meaning of the architectonic host, sucking out some of its gravitas. The student center from which the line was strung was declared an "unmitigated failure" by one undergraduate writing to the editor of the university paper in 1965, as it functioned solely as a space of commerce that did not transcend the grind of everyday MIT activities.[50] Haacke's project resists the former function at the very least (as a work that could not easily be sold), but it too was, to a certain extent, a failure, as the climate of Massachusetts limited its life span.

However, obsolescence was part of Haacke's plan in creating an antimonument. His artwork was quickly taken by the wind and slammed against the host's walls; the effects of entropy began almost immediately, as several of the balloons detached from the chain and flew away. The work continued to be tied to the roof of the student center for the rest of the day, where wind gusts sent it flopping back and forth.[51] As the Cambridge skyline is fairly modest and free of obstacles, Haacke's artwork was likely visible to numerous observers—although many people may not have understood the chain of balloons to be art. The remains of the artwork were later taken to MIT's Hayden Gallery and allowed to float to the ceiling, where the balloons again interfaced with the interior of the architecture, mapping themselves onto the architectural support, and hanging pendulously like a clutch of eggs deposited by an enormous insect.

Equally engaging with its environment, the New York *Sky Line* was a momentary break in the tight, timeless choreography of Frederick Law Olmsted's rolling greens and rambling woodlands, artfully changing the nature of the public park—and emphasizing temporality and process. In some ways a literal title, *Sky Line* can also be understood as a pun, referring to the iconic view of the silhouette of a city's architecture.[52] Haacke's project is a multivalent intervention in the skyline of Manhattan. Depending on the location of the viewer and the direction of the wind, the line might be turned into a slash, striking out elements of the architecture on the horizon. Given that users of Central Park generally circumambulate the green space or pathways, distinct buildings would be crossed out as spectators, deliberately and inadvertently, made their way through the park.

Relevant to Haacke's piece, the urbanist Paul D. Spreiregen has described skylines as "a physical representation [of a city's] facts of life . . . a potential work of art . . . its collective vista."[53] The work is a nonarchitectural intrusion into the skyline, which constantly shifts in response to the weather conditions and lasts only for a short time. It is a gesture that could be understood to mark the artificial urban horizon, underscoring the instability of the representation of the city (it iconically symbolizes). Taking weather balloons, normally tied to data collection, and converting them into a weathervane, the work always indicates its invisible referent in the present tense.[54]

The engagement with the skyline using transitory, antimonumental materials locates Haacke's project at the vanguard of urban public sculpture at that historical juncture. Following the critic Gregory Battcock (who along with Haacke was a core member of the radical collective the Art Workers' Coalition), in an essay penned a few years after *Sky Line*: "The notion of monument in art has been subverted, and it's about time."[55] *MIT Sky Line* anticipates other site-specific outdoor artworks created for noncommercial exhibitions that occupied college campuses, like the temporary outdoor installations at Windham College organized by Seth Siegelaub (1968) and Sharp's *Earth Art* at Cornell University (1969), for which Haacke created a subtle site- and time-specific weather intervention; he stretched a rope across a waterfall and allowed nature to take its course in *Spray of Ithaca Falls: Freezing and Melting on Rope, Feb 7, 8, 9, 1969* (1969).

The question of how to compete with architecture typically led artists to advance large-scale public projects, which would become a presence on the skyline. Otto Piene's solution to the issue of scale was to advance the creation of artworks the size of skyscrapers. Haacke's friend and fellow conceptual artist Sol LeWitt, albeit with his tongue in his cheek, suggested encasing the Empire State Building in concrete.[56] Sharp considered *Sky Line* a challenge to the costly (phallic) demonstrations of capitalist potency, calling it "a successful attempt to build a structure higher than the Empire State Building (1250 ft.) for less than $50."[57] Unlike LeWitt and Piene's overblown proposals, Haacke's work deftly negotiates the interface with the built environment without reproducing old forms. No longer creating sculpture but "real" contingent systems, Haacke implicitly acknowledges the state of art Battcock identified.[58]

Monuments often express nationalistic sentiments and regularly commemorate war heroes or military conquests. As I have posited, new varieties of art were not just comprehended as reactions to prior artistic traditions. For their audiences, they signified new ways of thinking and acting. Betraying parallel beliefs, the curator Kynaston McShine saw painting as politically impotent and unviable in 1970. He wrote in the catalog for *Information* (an exhibition that included Haacke's *MOMA Poll* [1970]): "If you are living in the United States, you may fear that you will be shot at, either in the universities, in your bed or more formally in Indochina. It may seem too inappropriate, if not absurd to get up . . . and apply dabs of paint from a little tube to a square of canvas."[59] Hence, by creating unmonumental, environmental work in a fluctuating, nontraditional artistic medium freed from the constraints of a gallery, Haacke questioned the belief system that buoyed late capitalism and accepted the waging of the Vietnam War—resonances that are largely lost on audiences today. He saw the embrace of the law of change in his (meteorological) artworks as a mode of resisting the current order of things.[60]

Furthermore, Haacke's artworks arguably teach subversive modes of thinking. One of their lessons is that other kinds of systems can be identified, named, and disrupted. His artworks thus align with contemporary prescriptions by the SDS member Paul Potter, given in a speech criticizing the war in Vietnam that was presented on the National Mall on April 17, 1965, as part of the March against the Vietnam War. Potter states: "We must name it, describe it, analyze it, understand it, and change it. For it is only when that system is changed and brought under control that there can be any hope for stopping the forces that create a war in Vietnam today or a murder in the South tomorrow. . . . How do you stop a war then, if the war has its roots deep in the *institutions* of American society?"[61] Haacke opposed the war and was sympathetic toward SDS's practices, emulating some himself in other works and in activities related to the Art Workers' Coalition. Even if he was not aware of the precise details of Potter's speech, the artist would have been familiar with some of the rhetoric. In statements published in the *Conceptual Art, Conceptual Aspects* catalog, he closely echoes Potter's sentiments. Haacke holds that his mode of working was based on "think[ing] in terms of systems; the production of systems, the interference with and the exposure of existing systems."[62] A certain "isomorphism" exists between the artworks and other contemporary expressions of dissent.[63] It seems no coincidence that the connection between weather and politics was also explored by the radical splinter group of SDS, who in 1969 took the Bob Dylan–inspired nom de guerre the Weathermen, later the Weather Underground Organization.[64] As an artist occupying institutions and working with meteorological phenomena, Haacke, too, could be considered a kind of weatherman in the art system.[65] Haacke's interventions attempt to blow up the status quo and blow winds of change into this sector of the public sphere (despite its corporate funding and direction by private individuals).

Haacke's fragile, whimsical *Sky Line* opposes another far more horrific technological absurdity of the age, death from the air in Operation Rolling Thunder. This was the sustained bombing campaign in North Vietnam throughout 1965–68. Rolling Thunder also capitalizes on a weather metaphor, serving both to convey power and to obfuscate what is really happing on the ground. While napalm and Agent Orange had horrific consequences on human bodies, their official purpose was optical: the defoliation of the dense Vietnamese jungles, a strategy aimed at augmenting the destructive capacity of aerial vision. Environmental artworks, though also in a sense ecological interruptions, should be seen as the obverse of the destructive chemical ecocide inflicted on the biomass of Vietnam. Although potentially visually appealing, they do not privilege retinal spectatorship and instead try to peacefully show the imbrication of living beings and their surrounds.

Haacke was not the only creator to mount meteorological resistance in 1967. Performance artist Carolee Schneemann also produced works that attempted to stir up sentiments against American aggression in Vietnam by engaging weather and the war. Produced for Angry Arts Week, her *Snows* (1967) consisted of five films, most famously *Viet-Flakes*, in which she juxtaposes images of wintery environs with depictions of atrocities from the hot war in South Asia in order to show that war was a condition as "randomized" and "constant as weather."[66]

Nevertheless, in his April 10, 1968, letter to Burnham cited above, Haacke expressed his frustrations with events like Schneemann's in the wake of the King assassination: "All the shows of Angry Arts will not prevent a single Napalm bomb from being dropped."[67] He suggests that representation alone is insufficient. The most effective projects produce real changes to the institutional systems in which they intervene.[68] He would go on to nuance his position, advocating for the value of transmitting political messages in an art context: "It would be dangerous if there were only the option to be an artist or a politician."[69]

Today's Forecast: *Weather, or Not?*

Confounding ideas about a rupture in his methods between his early and late career, Haacke has returned to meteorological critique in recent projects.[70] Making decisions about climate usually left up to conservators, he left the windows open for the duration of *Weather, or Not* (2009–10) at the X-Initiative in New York.[71] The artist also took over curatorial duties, as *Weather, or Not* was both an exhibition and an installation. Haacke showed new projects alongside historic works. Because the exhibit was held in the middle of winter, cold air chilled the Chelsea galleries. The audience and artworks were immersed in the same weather system—as was the rest of Manhattan. Haacke's moves to occupy the art space with weather were pedagogical—a kind of climatic teach-in: the cold snap provided a sufficiently sharp contrast to typical museological conditions that it was hard not to reflect on the difference between X-Initiative's climate and standard institutional environments. He underscored this point by reprising *Recording of Climate in Art Exhibition*, lit prominently and displayed on a plinth, adjacent to three open windows (figure 2.3).

In addition, he included a series of fans paired with a large, black, flashing light box emblazoned with the word BONUS in orange, powered by the electric outlets in the gallery. Titled BONUS-*Storm* (2009), the work consists of almost exactly the same components as an installation from 1968 to 1969,

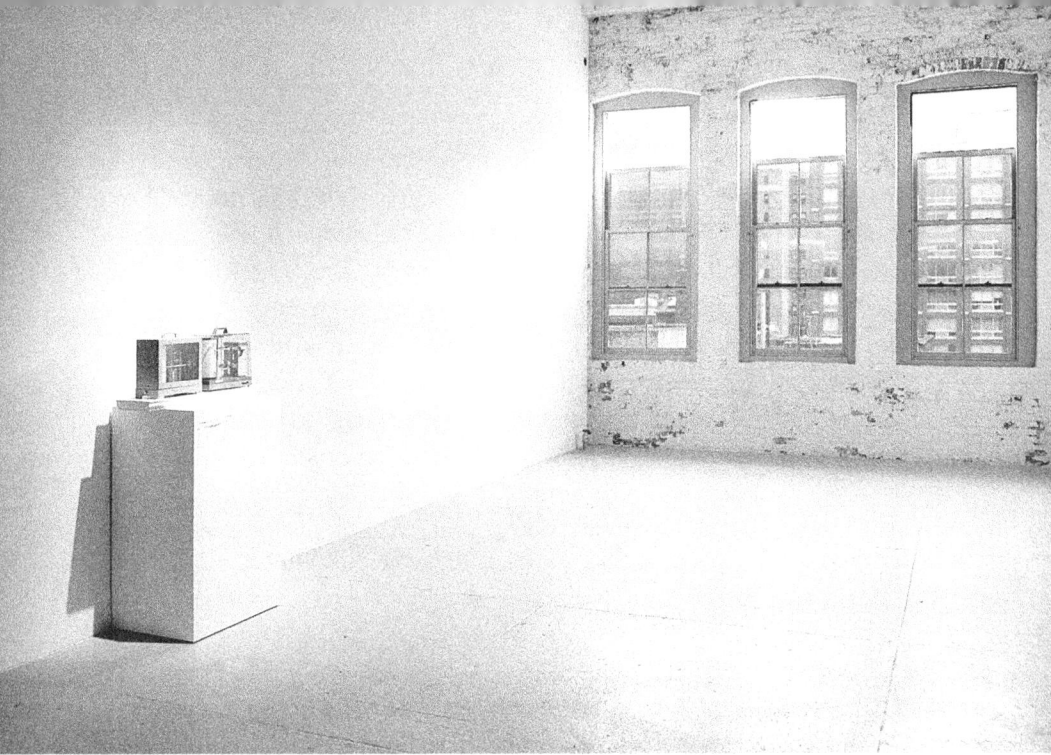

FIGURE 2.3. Hans Haacke, *Recording of Climate in Art Exhibition*, 1970–2009. As installed in solo exhibition, *Weather, or Not*, X-Initiative, New York, 2009. © Hans Haacke/Artists Rights Society (ARS).

Wind Room; the only real difference is the textual appendage. Updated for the current circumstances, Haacke's tactics in the recent work are largely the same as in its historical double. Like *Wind Room*, BONUS-*Storm* really intervenes in its environment. But Haacke does not just use fans to blow air: to paraphrase his words from the epigraph, the work's components and literal operations must be understood to always possess a metaphoric charge as well. By his captioning, he points spectators to the fact that—just like the winter climes that joined and blurred inside and outside at X-Initiative—economic forces are at play within and beyond art institutions, that the art world is part of the world.[72] While 2009 marked a low point in prosperity for many as a result of the global financial crisis, a selection of executives continued to be handsomely paid. In some cases, public funds seemed to flow quite directly into their pockets. For instance, top employees at American International Group (AIG) received nearly $165 million in bonuses after the government spent $170 million to bail out the firm.[73]

    Weather, or Not was one of the final nonprofit exhibitions held in the building at 548 West 22nd Street, which was converted into a venue for parties, trade shows, and art fairs months later. The chilling relation between art and real estate development, and the sense that culture might soon be left out in the cold, also preoccupied the artist. Indeed, a further index of the neoliberal climate came in the fate of the building where he had staged *Wind in Water*; it is now the location of a branch of the upmarket grocer Whole Foods Market.[74] Occupying the institution of art, Haacke raised questions about the fate of the host of his exhibition. Like so many other projects by this artist as weatherman, *Weather, or Not* was a meteorological installation, a barometric indicator of the current state of economic affairs, and a call to take ethical and political stands to interrogate the status quo. As with the ecological investigations of sites of display performed by his weatherworks from the 1960s and 1970s, Haacke's twenty-first-century intervention maneuvered systems aesthetics into systems politics.

NOTES

1   Hans Haacke, "Provisional Remarks" (1971), in *Institutional Critique: An Anthology of Artists' Writings*, ed. Alexander Alberro and Blake Stimson (Cambridge, MA: MIT Press 2011), 120, emphasis added. For more on the cancellation of the exhibition see Jack Burnham, "Hans Haacke's Cancelled Show at the Guggenheim," *Artforum* 9, no. 10 (1971): 67–71; and John A. Tyson, "The Context as Host: Hans Haacke's Art of Textual Exhibition," *Word and Image* 31, no. 3 (2015): 213–32.

2   Hans Haacke, "Untitled Talk at Annual Meeting of Intersocietal Color Council, New York, April 1968," in *Working Conditions: The Writings of Hans Haacke*, ed. Alexander Alberro (Cambridge, MA: MIT Press, 2016), 24.

3   I reference Jack Burnham's ideas from his "Systems Esthetics," *Artforum* 7, no. 1 (1968): 30–35. Here Burnham argues that Haacke focuses on "the invisible components of systems" (35).

4   See Luke Skrebowski, "All Systems Go: Recovering Hans Haacke's Systems Art," *Grey Room*, no. 30 (2008): 54–83. Like Skrebowski's, my account revises Benjamin H. D. Buchloh's version of conceptual art. Buchloh considers Haacke's *Condensation Cube* as a merely "proto-conceptual" work on a path that leads to the critique of institutions in 1969; see Benjamin H. D. Buchloh, "Conceptual Art 1962–69: From the Aesthetic of Administration to the Critique of Institutions," *October*, no. 55 (1990): 134.

5   See Hans Haacke, letter to Jack Burnham, April 10, 1968, reproduced in Jack Burnham, "Steps in the Formulation of a Real-Time Political Art," in *Hans Haacke: Framing and Being Framed* (Halifax: Press of the Nova Scotia College of Art and Design, 1975), 130.

6   Hans Haacke, letter to Jack Burnham, April 10, 1968.

7   See Burnham, "Steps in the Formulation," 130.

8   Hans Haacke, "Interview with Cecilia Alemani," in *Working Conditions: The Writings of Hans Haacke*, ed. Alexander Alberro (Cambridge, MA: MIT Press), 237.

9   For more on the intersections between the politics of race, climate, and conceptual art, see Ellen Tani, "Black Conceptualism and the Atmospheric Turn, 1968–2008" (PhD diss., Stanford University, 2015).

10   Hans Haacke, "Statement, New York, February, 1969," reprinted in Caroline A. Jones, *Hans Haacke 1967*, exhibition catalog (Cambridge, MA: MIT Press, 2011), 51.

11   Bob Dylan, "Subterranean Homesick Blues," in *Bringing It All Back Home* (Columbia Records, 7-inch vinyl record, January 1965).

12   Haacke, "Interview with Cecilia Alemani," 242.

13   Walter Benjamin, *The Arcades Project*, trans. Howard Eiland and Kevin McLauglin (Cambridge, MA: Belknap Press of Harvard University Press, 1999), 106, quoted in Shep Steiner, "It Must Be the Weather: Today's Forecast—Again, Mainly Capitalism," *Afterall* 2 (2000): 77.

14   Hans Haacke, "Untitled Statement, '. . . Make Something Which Experiences . . .'" (1965), in *Working Conditions: The Writings of Hans Haacke*, ed. Alexander Alberro (Cambridge, MA: MIT Press), 5.

15   See NOAA, "Surface Weather, Signal Service and Weather Bureau," National Centers for Environmental Information, November 5, 2018, https://data.nodc.noaa .gov/cgi-bin/iso?id=gov.noaa.ncdc:C01214.

16   See US Congress, House of Representatives, *Report of the Board on Behalf of the United States Executive Departments at the International Exhibition* (Washington, DC: Government Printing Office, 1884), 985.

17   US Congress, House of Representatives, *Report of the Board*, 985.

18   See Francis Galton, *Meteographica, or Methods of Mapping the Weather* (London: Macmillan, 1863), reproduced online at Galton.org, accessed December 21, 2018, http://galton.org/books/meteorographica/galton-1863-meteorographica-color .pdf.

19   R. de C. Ward, "The Newspaper Weather Maps of the United States," *American Meteorological Journal* 11 (July 1894): 97–99.

20   Thank you to Maibritt Borgen for making me aware that these investigations occurred simultaneously. For more on this, see Paul Edwards, *A Vast Machine: Computer Models, Climate Data, and the Politics of Global Warming* (Cambridge, MA: MIT Press, 2013).

21   Norbert Wiener, *Cybernetics: Or Control and Communication in the Animal and the Machine* (Cambridge, MA: MIT Press, 1948), 32.

22   See Museum of Modern Art, "Films on Ecology to Be Shown at Museum," press release, April 22, 1970, https://www.moma.org/momaorg/shared/pdfs/docs/press _archives/4443/releases/MOMA_1970_Jan-June_0040_41.pdf.

23   For more, see James Nisbet, *Ecologies, Environments, and Energy Systems in Art of the 1960s and 1970s* (Cambridge, MA: MIT Press, 2014); and Janine Randerson, *Weather as Medium: Toward a Meteorological Art* (Cambridge, MA: MIT Press, 2018).

24   Burnham, "Systems Esthetics," 31.

25 Willoughby Sharp, *Cinetismo: Systems Sculpture in Environmental Situations* (Mexico City: UNAM Press, 1968), 14.

26 Lucy R. Lippard, "Introduction to *557,087*" (1969), in *Conceptual Art: A Critical Anthology*, ed. Alexander Alberro and Blake Stimson (Cambridge, MA: MIT Press, 1999), 181.

27 The variety of precipitation that day (snow) determined the final title. See Edward Fry, "Introduction to the Work of Hans Haacke" (1971), in Caroline A. Jones, *Hans Haacke 1967*, exhibition catalog (Cambridge, MA: MIT Press, 2011), 36.

28 Haacke describes the work as "staged on the roof of 95 East Houston Street," in Caroline A. Jones, *Hans Haacke 1967*, exhibition catalog (Cambridge, MA: MIT Press, 2011), 37.

29 See Craig Owens, "From Work to Frame: or, Is There Life after 'The Death of the Author'?," in *Beyond Recognition: Representation, Power, and Culture*, ed. Scott Bryson, Barbara Kruger, Lynne Tillman, and Jane Weinstock (Berkeley: University of California Press, 1992), 122–39.

30 Fry, "Introduction," 37.

31 Fry, "Introduction," 37.

32 Herbert Marcuse, *An Essay on Liberation* (Boston: Beacon, 1969), 31.

33 See Dan McQuillan, "The Countercultural Potential of Citizen Science," *Media/Culture Journal* 17, no. 6 (2014), https://doi.org/10.5204/mcj.919/.

34 See Willoughby Sharp, "Place and Process," *Artforum* 8, no. 3 (1969): 48.

35 Haacke, "Interview with Cecilia Alemani," 241.

36 See Lucy R. Lippard, *Six Years: The Dematerialization of the Art Object from 1966 to 1972* (New York: Praeger, 1973).

37 "Mimetic exacerbation" is Hal Foster's phrase describing Dada's and pop's critical multiplications. See Foster, *Bad New Days: Art, Criticism, Emergency* (London: Verso, 2015), 122, 124, 127–29, and 194.

38 See Jones, *Hans Haacke 1967*, 8.

39 Department of Parks, City of New York, "An Environment of Kinetic Art for the Central Park Festival," press release no. 347, July 18, 1967, accessed December 17, 2018, http://nyc.gov/html/records/pdf/govpub/42611967_press_releases_part3 .pdf.

40 See Grace Glueck, "The Great Big Park Was a Wondrous Toy," *New York Times*, July 24, 1967.

41 See Marty Jezer, *Abbie Hoffman: American Rebel* (New Brunswick, NJ: Rutgers University Press, 1992), 99.

42 See Jezer, *Abbie Hoffman*, 102. Various reporters comment on the balloons at protests. See S. J. Micciche, "Antiwar Rally Largest Ever," *Boston Globe*, April 25, 1971.

43 See Lawrence Van Gelder, "Lie-In Held in Central Park to Symbolize the Dead in Vietnam: Attendance in Schools Drops Markedly Here," *New York Times*, November 15, 1969.

44 Erin Blakemore, "Watch Historic Footage of Seven Consequential (and Cringeworthy) Convention Moments," *Smithsonian Magazine*, July 18, 2016, https://www.smithsonianmag.com/smart-news/watch-historic-footage-of

-seven-consequential-and-cringeworthy-convention-moments-180959827
/#2kLy1ck1sBSwrFxX.99.

45   In "Luminism and Kineticism," Willoughby Sharp argues that *Sky Line*, as well
       as other projects made to "activate" Central Park, changed the order of things
       (358). While he does not propose specific connections to antiwar activism, Sharp
       affirms that such works helped spectators to become "acclimated to the rapidly
       changing kinetic climate of our age" (318). He further adds that "there is a strong
       feeling of confidence in the ability of the new art to reconstruct the world kinet-
       ically" (358). Willoughby Sharp, "Luminism and Kineticism," in *Minimal Art: A
       Critical Anthology*, ed. Gregory Battcock (New York: E. P. Dutton, 1968), 317–58.

       The editor and critic Jean Clay published a Haacke special, the November–
       December 1967 issue of *Robho* (which included a long discussion of *Sky Line*).
       Clay argues that Haacke's oeuvre "s'agit d'une démarche exemplaire par son radi-
       calisme et par les multiples questions qu'elle sugiere sur les rapports de l'art et du
       réel" [is an exemplary approach for its radicalism and for the multiple questions it
       suggests about the relations between art and reality]. Jean Clay, "Art Signe et Art
       Piege," *Robho* 2 (November–December 1967): n.p.

       August Heckscher, the Parks Commissioner at the time of the project's execution,
       was particularly sympathetic to antiwar protests and the arts. See Eric Pace, "August
       Heckscher, 83, Dies; Advocate for Parks and Arts," *New York Times*, April 7, 1997.

46   Stuart W. Leslie, *The Cold War and American Science: The Military-Industrial-
       Academic Complex at* MIT *and Stanford* (New York: Columbia University Press,
       1993).

47   Noam Chomsky, "A Special Supplement: The Responsibility of Intellectuals," *New
       York Review of Books*, February 23, 1967.

48   "SDS Sits In on Dow Recruiter," *Tech*, November 7, 1967, 1.

49   Jones, *Hans Haacke 1967*, 8.

50   Leonard Levin, "Letter to the Editor," *Tech*, November 17, 1965, 4.

51   Bobbi Lev, "Haacke Sculpture Popular in Hayden Gallery Exhibit," *Tech*, Octo-
       ber 27, 1967, 11.

52   The title could equally evoke Lewis Mumford's eponymous column published in
       the *New Yorker* until 1963.

53   Paul D. Spreiregen, *Urban Design: The Architecture of Towns and Cities* (New
       York: McGraw-Hill, 1965), quoted in James A. Clapp, *The City: A Dictionary of
       Quotable Thoughts on Cities and Urban Life* (New Brunswick, NJ: Rutgers Univer-
       sity Press, 1984), 223.

54   Roland Barthes, "Rhetoric of the Image" (1964), in *Image, Music, Text*,
       trans. Stephen Heath (New York: Hill and Wang, 1977), 44, quoted in Carrie
       Lambert-Beatty, "Moving Still: Mediating Yvonne Rainer's *Trio A*," *October*,
       no. 89 (1999): 107.

55   Gregory Battcock, "An Experiment with Art in Education," in *New Ideas in Art
       Education*, ed. Gregory Battcock (New York: Dutton, 1974), 283.

56   Alexander Alberro, *Conceptual Art and the Politics of Publicity* (Cambridge, MA:
       MIT Press, 2003), 65.

57   Willoughby Sharp, "Earth Art: The Untold Story," May 5, 1995, p. 20, box 2, "WS
      CUNY TALK Nov. '94" Folder, Willoughby Sharp Papers, 2016.M.16, Getty Re-
      search Institute, Los Angeles.

58   Haacke, "Untitled Statement," 1967," n.p., Hans Haacke Artist File, box 16, folder
      250, Records of Howard Wise, 1954–1989, SC 17, Harvard Art Museums Archives,
      Cambridge, MA.

59   Kynaston McShine, "Introduction to *Information*" (1970), in *Conceptual Art: A
      Critical Anthology*, ed. Alexander Alberro and Blake Stimson (Cambridge, MA:
      MIT Press, 1999), 212.

60   Hans Haacke, quoted in Jeanne Siegel, *Artwords: Discourse on the '60s and '70s*
      (Ann Arbor, MI: Da Capo, 1985), 214.

61   I refer here to Potter's call to "name the system" in 1965. The speech was given
      during "A March on Washington D.C. in Protest of the War in Vietnam in
      Washington D.C. Organized by Students for a Democratic Society," April 17, 1965,
      transcribed online in "'Naming The System' Speech," Students for a Democratic
      Society (SDS) Document Library, accessed on April 1, 2021, https://www.sds
      -1960s.org/sds_wu0/sds_documents/paul_potter.html.

62   Hans Haacke, "Untitled Statement" in "Information 2," in *Conceptual Art and
      Conceptual Aspects*, exhibition catalog, ed. Donald Karshan (New York: New
      York Cultural Center, 1970), 32. This exhibition was actually "authored" by Joseph
      Kosuth. See Fionn Meade, "Joseph Kosuth," *Artforum* 47, no. 6 (2009): 189–90.

63   See Haacke, "Provisional Remarks," 123.

64   The Weathermen formed in June 1969 from the Revolutionary Youth Movement
      within SDS. The name is drawn from the lyrics of Bob Dylan's 1965 "Subterra-
      nean Homesick Blues": "You don't need a weatherman to know which way the
      wind blows." See "You Don't Need a Weatherman to Know Which Way the Wind
      Blows," reprinted from *New Left Notes*, June 18, 1969, accessed November 17, 2015,
      http://ia600409.us.archive.org/27/items/YouDontNeedAWeathermanToKnowWh
      ichWayTheWindBlows_925/weather.pdf.

65   Revealing that such sentiments were not foreign at the time, Robert Smithson de-
      scribed his and Mel Bochner's *Domain of the Great Bear* (1966) as "a bomb in the
      art system." See Yve-Alain Bois, "What If . . . ," in Mel Bochner, *Solar Systems and
      Restrooms: Writings and Interviews 1965–2007*, ed. Roger Conover (Cambridge,
      MA: MIT Press, 2008), xi–xvi.

66   Carolee Schneemann, "II. Recent Work," in *Early and Recent Work* (New Paltz,
      NY: Max Hutcheon Gallery–Documentext, 1983), n.p.

67   Hans Haacke, letter to Jack Burnham, April 10, 1968.

68   Despite the fact that Angry Arts seemed politically impotent to Haacke at that
      nadir, art sales under its auspices raised money to help protesters who had been
      arrested. See Grace Glueck, "Coming in on the Beam," *New York Times*, Novem-
      ber 5, 1967.

69   Hans Haacke, in Tony Brown, "Artist as Corporate Critic: An Interview with
      Hans Haacke by Tony Brown," first published in *Parachute* 23 (Summer 1981):
      12–17; reprinted in *Hans Haacke*, vol. 2, *Works, 1978–1983*, exhibition catalog
      (London: Tate Gallery; and Eindhoven: Van Abbemuseum, 1984), 104.

70 Benjamin H. D. Buchloh, "Hans Haacke: Memory and Instrumental Reason," in *Neo-Avantgarde and Culture Industry: Essays on European and American Art from 1955 to 1975* (Cambridge, MA: MIT Press, 2000), 205.

71 This exhibition formed part of the gallerist Elizabeth Dee's yearlong series of exhibitions for X-Initiative, a temporary institution, which was located in the former Dia Art Center in Chelsea in 2009–10. Dia could not afford renovations and sold the building in 2007.

72 This last phrasing is a paraphrase of comments Haacke has made to me in conversations over the course of 2019–2020.

73 Because of the new legislation created in response to the announcement of these bonuses, some of the money was recouped in taxes. See Edmund Andrews and Peter Baker, "A.I.G. Planning Huge Bonuses after $170 Billion Bailout," *New York Times*, March 14, 2009.

74 Haacke suggested I add this detail. Hans Haacke, email to author, April 27, 2020.

3

Desalineación

Open Systems as Social Transformation in Tucumán Arde

CHRISTINE FILIPPONE

Circuits of information in 1960s Argentina were entwined with Europe and the United States for good or ill. Following the ouster of President Juan Perón by the military in 1955 for his populist policies and full-throated support of the union movement, Argentina contended with a series of fragile social-liberal presidential administrations. The most consequential, that of President Arturo Frondizi (1958–62), established strong ties to the United States. Cultivating foreign investment, Frondizi hosted a state visit by President Dwight Eisenhower, who presented his economic objectives in starkly anti-Soviet, Cold War terms: "When freedom, democracy and national sovereignty are in jeopardy in any country, they are to some degree in jeopardy in all free countries of the world. This is one strong reason why the United States is vitally interested in the development of the general well-being of all free nations."[1] "General well-being" for Eisenhower meant economic and industrial development, with which the United States was happy to assist. The cultural sphere in Argentina had a similarly internationalist agenda. Foundational funding for the prestigious Torcuato di Tella Institute, a leading center for avant-garde art founded in 1958, was raised using the US model of corporate financing, along with grants from the Ford and Rockefeller Foundations.[2] But relations between Latin America and the United States began to falter at the onset of the Cuban Revolution. The rise of the military dictatorship of Juan Carlos

Onganía in 1966, coupled with mistrust of imperialist US policies culminating in the assassination of Fidel Castro's comandante—Ernesto "Che" Guevara, from Rosario, Argentina—by the CIA, came to define Argentine political radicalism. The assassination of Che, along with the Vietnam War, and the US invasion of Santo Domingo, inspired a series of collective exhibitions in Buenos Aires between 1966 and 1968, including *Homage to Vietnam* and *Homage to Che*. The art historian Ana Longoni asserts that the artists understood these exhibitions "as political events inserted into the artistic atmosphere."[3] Retaining those political aims, Longoni claims that Tucumán Arde (Tucumán is burning) was the beginning of a different type of conceptual art related to radical, political preoccupations.[4] Described in their project manifesto as "an overinformational circuit that disrupts or disorganizes (*desalinea*) the straight linear circuit of mass media coverage," the artists conceived of Tucumán Arde as a "political-cultural action," in which art was dissolved "into the social."[5]

This chapter argues that the concept of open systems was essential to the development of art as social action in Tucumán Arde, and to explicitly political conceptual art globally. The primary objective of the process-based performance and installation Tucumán Arde, undertaken in the Argentine cities of Rosario and Buenos Aires in 1968, was to open up the closed mass-media circuits of *dis*information that had been set in motion by the authoritarian military dictatorship. Countering a media campaign initiated by the government to cover up the joblessness and rising poverty in the agricultural province of Tucumán, Grupo de artistas de vanguardia de Rosario (the Rosario Group) collaborated on site with sociologists, local workers, and union groups to collect accurate information, which they infused back into the media cycle, juxtaposing empirical data against the government's false narrative. The collected information was then installed for the public, plastered from ceiling to floor in the union halls in Rosario and Buenos Aires, intentionally outside of the art institution and within the context of labor (figure 3.1).[6] The photograph in figure 3.1 captures the entrance to the installation in Rosario whose walls feature the word TUCUMAN repeated in orderly, horizontal columns, mimicking the stacks of abandoned sugar sacks photographed by the artists in Tucumán. The words VISIT TUCUMAN, GARDEN OF MISERY festooning the threshold announce the reality of the workers and their families, witnessed firsthand by the artists, while also countering the government's false media campaign that celebrated "Tucumán, Garden of the Republic." Tucumán Arde was meant to burst open the closed political systems of power with an explicitly open, social, and political art generated and

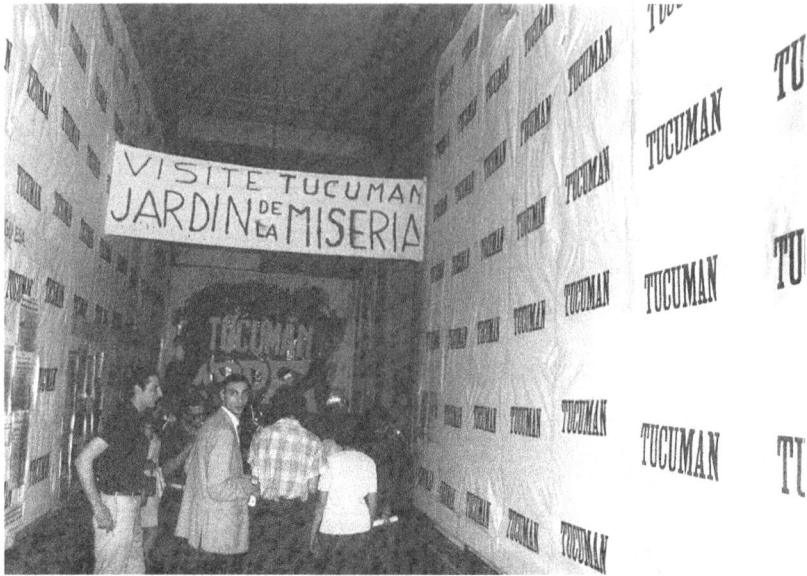

FIGURE 3.1. Rosario Group, *Tucumán Arde: Phase 3*, Exhibition in CGTA, Rosario, Argentina, November 1968. Image of the hallway leading to the exhibition. Photo by Carlos Miletello. Archive of Graciela Carnevale, Rosario, Argentina.

amplified by multiple voices. Open systems provided an empirical description and heuristic model for process-oriented, multisensory, collaborative works that not only engaged but infiltrated social and political contexts in the midst of dictatorship. My analysis of Tucumán Arde extends beyond its consideration as conceptual, performance, and/or cybernetics-inspired media art, to encompass its roots in open systems, understood by the artists as inextricable from social and political systems as well as from the real bodies—those of the workers and their families in Tucumán—subject to those systems.

I want to briefly extend this argument to assert that "open systems" was, as concept and methodology, central to the insurgence of social and political art globally in the late 1960s.[7] Here I seek to emphasize its role in the development of institutional critique as a strategy reaching beyond the art system to address social, economic, and political contexts.[8] In Tucumán Arde's engagement with various publics—unions, agricultural workers, economists, sociologists, and consumers of mass media (citizens)—to subvert the military government in Argentina, to shape media discourse, and to engender democratic change, the project represented the earliest and most profound example of institutional critique. The art historian Ana Longoni notes that Tucumán Arde has long been canonized as the foundation of ideological conceptualism, a variant of institutional critique, and "the mother of all political art."[9] American accounts of institutional critique typically begin with Hans Haacke's work of 1969 and later, but Tucumán Arde, created a year prior, shatters that origin story.

Furthermore, my analysis of Tucumán Arde demonstrates that open systems was a progenitor of institutional critique, which, according to art historian Blake Stimson, was "a child of 1968."[10] The art historian Alexander Alberro characterizes institutional critique as work that calls attention to the "objective relations" that "structure it." He identifies these works as ones that form connections between heretofore disparate realms of thought, noting "relations" between the otherwise discontinuous realms of experience (politics, publics) that comprise and structure it. Alberro describes examples of institutional critique as those "that provocatively *linked* previously unconnected spheres of public experience together in unexpected knots, in unexpected combinations of trajectories."[11] In fact, connection between various spheres of social experience is the definition of open systems. As put forth by the biologist Ludwig von Bertalanffy in the 1930s, an open system is a complex of interacting elements that is open to, and interacts with, its environment.[12] All biological organisms, all living systems that exchange matter or information with their environment, are open systems—including social systems. Thus, open systems inhere in Alberro's definition of institutional critique: those works that create "links" among unconnected spheres of experience. Alberro further emphasizes the "unexpected" connections, the "unexpected combinations of trajectories" foregrounding unpredictable futures and an openness of possibility. Unpredictability—as with all flexible, open, living systems that grow and increase in complexity—is at the core of open systems. In his book *General System Theory* (1968), von Bertalanffy defined open systems for a generation of American artists whose names would become synonymous with institutional critique. Open systems offered artists a metaperspective on society—concepts and principles applicable to all forms of knowledge, a way of thinking about the various spheres of human activity (governments, industries, workers) in constant, dynamic (and often economic) relationship to one another. Artists Martha Rosler and Hans Haacke, for example, have consistently pointed to the importance of von Bertalanffy's open systems for the origins of their own institutional critique.[13]

Alberro located the core of historical institutional critique in the art institution or museum, but the scope of Tucumán Arde's aims was much broader.[14] Alberro identifies the museum, or art institution, as the locus of what he calls "historical institutional critique," pointing to the practices of Daniel Buren, Julio Le Parc, Marcel Broodthaers, Haacke, and Rosario Group cofounder Eduardo Favario, who all, in the late 1960s, refused to comply with the dictates of the art institution. But Tucumán Arde effectively circumvented the museum altogether, representing instead a refusal or negation of traditional art structures, albeit one that foresaw alternatives enmeshed with the social structure. The Rosario Group understood that if only they "resisted" the dictatorship's efforts to mislead the public at the expense of workers, radical change might yet result.

The Rosario Group's understanding of systems stemmed from structural linguistics and from communication and information theories including those of Marshall McLuhan, the anthropologist Gregory Bateson, and the writer Umberto Eco, all of whom claimed mathematician Norbert Wiener as an important influence.[15] In his book *The Human Use of Human Beings* (1950), Wiener theorized that closed systems are isolated systems prone to gradual decay or disorganization—in short, increased entropy. In contrast, some open systems, like human beings, communities, and ecosystems, grow and increase in complexity over time, exchanging energy, matter, or information with their environment.[16] The Rosario Group's understanding of art as open system was informed by Umberto Eco's *Opera aperta* (*The Open Work*), a short treatise on aesthetics published in 1962 in which Eco connected notions of aesthetic "openness" to mathematical theories of information.[17] During the mid-1960s, the leading Buenos Aires–based artists Roberto Jacoby, Eduardo Costa, and Raúl Escari participated in a reading group led by the writer Oscar Masotta and attended by the sociologist Eliseo Verón. Masotta and Verón introduced the artists to key authors on structuralism, semiology, and cybernetic communication theory, including Eco.[18] Masotta prized Eco's semiological analysis over Marshal McLuhan's, arguing that Eco offered a deeper structural analysis of communication informed by Marxism. Masotta wrote, "Where North American reflection on communication and the culture of the masses sinks in calm waters of unsatisfactory methodology, Eco has the virtue of bringing us back into the field of Marxist reflection."[19]

Eco's treatise on the "open" artwork argued that contemporary art has no fixed form but rather an open one in which the constituents are left to the viewer or to chance, thereby offering generative interpretation. Eco was affiliated with international art and technology movements in the early 1960s, including the art and technology collective Groupe de Recherche d'Art Visuel (GRAV). Cofounded by Argentine artist Julio Le Parc, a staunch supporter of

Tucumán Arde, GRAV's objective was to involve viewers directly in works of art, providing a phenomenological sensory experience.[20] Eco and GRAV collaborated on the exhibition *Arte programmata* in 1962, for which Eco wrote an essay hailing kaleidoscopic kinetic sculpture for its process of "becoming while we watched it." Eco celebrated artists whose work realized "the richness of chance and disorder" and reflected awareness of "the reevaluation—made by scientific disciplines—of random processes" that can occur in "fields of events." He described open works as those that present "a dialectic between chance and program, between mathematics and accident, the possibility of formative patterns, which do not negate spontaneity, but rather enlarge its boundaries."[21] The art historian Lily Woodruff has adeptly characterized Eco's influence on GRAV's concept of participatory connection, noting, "Openness of permanent transformation would produce a social openness with democratic potential."[22] Indeed, Le Parc's 1963 essay for GRAV titled "No More Mystifications" used the language of cybernetics to announce the collective's disgust over the separation between artistic creation and the public whereby "the current circuit of art remains closed." An 'opening' is necessary."[23] Le Parc understood the opening of the circuit as the creation of an "open work," in itself a political and social act.

The creators of Tucumán Arde associated open systems with participatory democracy, interdisciplinary collaboration, the concept of indefinite completion, and a disruption of the status quo yielding a greater quantity of information capable of generating new perspectives. Open systems provided an antidote to the mechanism of a repressive military regime defined by clockwork precision and rigid hierarchal relationships. Indeed, the artists—including Graciela Carnevale, Eduardo Favario, León Ferrari, Roberto Jacoby, Juan Pablo Renzi, Noemí Escandell, and Norberto Púzzolo, as well as the writers Nicolás Rosa and María Teresa Gramuglio—equated closed systems with the art establishment represented at the time by Torcuato di Tella Institute in Buenos Aires. Under pressure from the regime, the di Tella Institute had sought in 1968 to alter artists' work to eclipse social commentary and conform to the standards of decency mandated by the government. The dictatorship staunchly defended "Christian and Western values" as national values in its fight against communism.[24] One contentious example was León Ferrari's six-foot tall sculpture *La civilización occidental y cristiana* (Western and Christian civilization; figure 3.2), made in protest of the Vietnam War and featuring a plastic crucifix on a US fighter plane. Christ's bloodied arms stretch over the wings of the plane, and each palm is nailed to a bomb. With

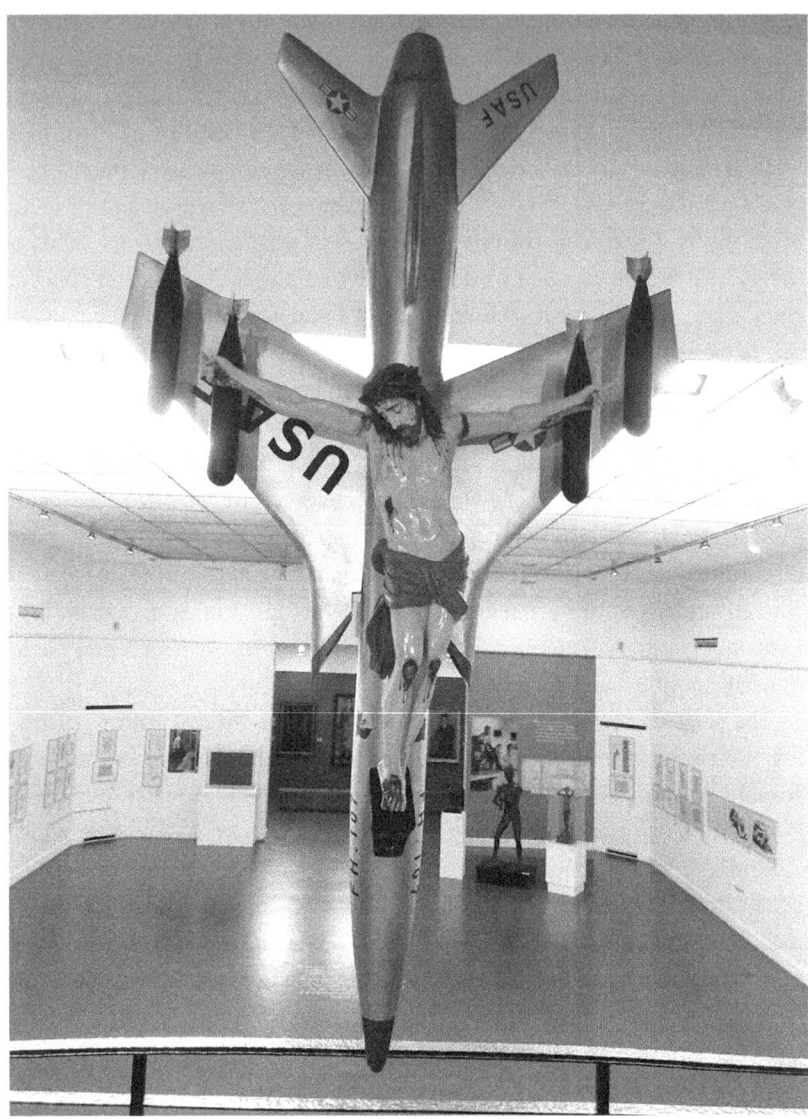

FIGURE 3.2. León Ferrari, *La civilización occidental y cristiana* (Western and Christian civilization), 1965. Polyester, wood, cardboard, and plaster. 6 ft. © FALFAA-CELS, Fundación Augusto y León Ferrari Arte Acervo—Centro de Estudios Legales y Sociales. Courtesy of Sicardi, Ayers, Bacino. Photo by Marisa Pereyra.

nose to the ground, the jet seems destined for impact with its precious cargo. Ferrari's sculpture foregrounds the relationship between the US military and the Catholic Church, both supportive of Onganía's dictatorship. Onganía adhered to the National Security Doctrine, the raison d'être of the military regimes in Latin America, by which he/they understood that the military dictatorship was the only entity that could guarantee security, economic prosperity, and national values in the fight against communism.[25] In 1969 Onganía dedicated the country to the Immaculate Heart of Mary.[26]

To openly express their disdain for an art system seeking to censor their work, the artists convened the First National Meeting on Avant-Garde Art in August 1968 in the city of Rosario. In their manifesto, "We Must Always Resist the Lures of Complicity," they declared, "because our NONPARTICIPATION in this event is but a small expression of a greater will to NOT PARTICIPATE in any act (official or apparently nonofficial) that signifies complicity with . . . the cultural mechanism that the bourgeoisie has put in place to absorb any revolutionary process."[27] Their target was a complacent bourgeoisie and the art institution it utilized as a tool of cultural control. The artists also created a series of experimental artworks informed by the participatory performances known as Happenings. For her work *Lock Up Action*, Graciela Carnevale invited her opening night audience into an empty room and unexpectedly locked them inside. Bursting with gallerygoers the small glass-fronted room at first remained calm as its occupants spoke quietly to one another, waiting for something to happen. Anxiety mounted over time while the confined participants (Were they still "participants"?) began searching for an exit. Carnevale wrote in an accompanying statement, "There is no possibility for escape, in fact the spectators have no choice, they are obliged, violently, to participate."[28] After an hour a passerby broke the glass and helped the audience out, at which time they received a handout asking them to consider their incarceration in light of the abusive policies of the military government. Linking the closed artistic establishment to the dictatorship, Carnevale wrote in her statement, "Through an act of aggression, the work intends to provoke the viewer into awareness of the power with which violence is enacted in everyday life."[29] Her work seeks to force the presumably bourgeois audience to act against forms of cultural oppression enforced by the government, in part to make them conscious of their complicity but also as a means to demonstrate the radical action required to break free.

An important context for the violence Carnevale sought to redress was the notorious Noche de los Bastones Largos (Night of the Big Sticks) of July 29, 1966, when Onganía ordered police to invade the Faculty of Sciences at the

University of Buenos Aires. Seeking to unilaterally revoke hard-won academic freedoms gained by student activists earlier in the century, police beat students, graduates, and professors with long police batons and arrested more than four hundred people. In discussing her work, Carnevale later explained, "When confronting an act of violence, you cannot be passive. You have to exert violence yourself."[30] It is well-documented that many of the Rosario Group abandoned their art practices after Tucumán Arde to pursue political activism. Indeed, not all of the artists survived. Eduardo Favario, a good friend of Carnevale's, entered the military wing of the leftist activist group Partido Revolucionario del Pueblo (PRP) at the conclusion of Tucumán Arde.[31] He was among many young activists who were systematically "annihilated" under the subsequent rightwing authoritarian regime of Isabel Perón.

In the throes of a coercive military dictatorship, the Argentine artists fully grasped the threat of repressive, mechanistic societies described by the philosopher Herbert Marcuse. Their works were a response to a closed technological society in which the military and its communications apparatus embodied the system, perpetuated its ideals of control, and remained frustratingly invisible to the larger populace.[32] Similarly, Marshall McLuhan's endeavor to reveal the way the content of a message "blinds us" to the character of any medium or technology in his familiar thesis "the medium is the message" resonated with the artists. He argued that the content of the message is irrelevant. It is the means of communication that embeds itself in the message and shapes "the scale and form of human association and action."[33] McLuhan described the press as the successor to the book that instead possesses a participatory nature lending it a mosaic form. He claimed, "The mosaic is the mode of the corporate or collective image and commands deep participation. This participation is communal rather than private, inclusive rather than exclusive."[34] McLuhan explained that the mosaic form of the press facilitates participatory democracy, a point suggestive to the artists seeking appeal to broad publics.[35]

The artists began to apply communication theory to Happenings which, despite their interactive nature, still largely reached a limited audience. The result was the group Arte de los medios de comunicacíon de masas (Art of Mass Communication Media), which called for the construction of art within the mass media, or more specifically the dissolution of art into the media. Jacoby's first mass media work was a response to the Happening whose success in Argentina the artists believed stemmed from mass media overreporting about the works, creating a sense of anticipation. Jacoby's

Happening for a Dead Boar (1966), effectively an anti-Happening, consisted in the announcement of a Happening via the mass media. But the event was never held. The work existed solely in the false press accounts as a form of information created in and by the media. The work foregrounded the role of the media, which in its relentless pursuit of the story of the Happening, effectively hunted down and killed it, like a dead boar. Jacoby described the false media report as follows: "a closed universe that neither describes nor deforms" but instead creates its own unique language replete with slipping signifiers that "deceive and distort" as a matter of course. The positive influence of the media depends on its adherence to "the truth and reality."[36] While the media could be used to deceive and distort, Jacoby noted that its information circuits could also be applied to the utopian purpose of creating "an enlarged life," one capable of reaching a mass audience so as to transform critical and political consciousness.[37] For Art of Mass Communication Media, communications technology offered a new "liberating energy," the diminishing physical materiality of which offered more direct communication and a new expressive potential.[38]

The dematerialization of art was a means of social and political liberation. Dematerialization meant freedom, a loosening of artistic and social strictures that had led to atomization, yielding instead an "enlarged life."[39] Masotta equated the terms "dematerialization" with "liberated energy" in 1966. He also declared that the avant-garde work should be an "open work" that yields a new range of aesthetic possibilities but at the same time negates something.[40] Jacoby's essay for his planned work *Closed Information Circuits* (1966) indicates how he understood the distinction between closed and open systems. He sought to create a closed loop of information, for which he postulated two distinct rooms: one containing the audience and a separate, distant room. The audience shares its room with a teletype receiver and a TV. The distant room contains a teletype transmitter and a TV camera. In the distant room, the camera records the transmitter as it sends its message to the audience. Thus, the audience simultaneously perceives the two ends of the communication process—the televisually recorded moment of transmission and the message itself. The artist described this closed (mass mediatic) information work as markedly different from his previous information works and anti-Happening, which he believed possessed a decidedly more open, participatory flavor: "Unlike my previous information works, these are closed, rather than societal events. In the information works set in a social context, the mass consumer was surrounded by mass media. . . . In this case, only a small audience can witness the work, but it will have an idea of the totality: the information process."[41] Here, Jacoby indicates his understanding of the open work of art as a societal event, set in a social context, relating the open circuit to a social system.

Jacoby used the term "open work" to describe the Happening that achieves communication with as little mediation as possible, reflecting the open work whose central concern is the role of the viewer in receiving and making meaning of a message.[42] Similarly, Verón conceived of the Happening as "a poetics of social action" and saw media art as the opening up of the "poetics of mass media," which leaves open the "possibilities of works intended to displace the organizational methods of mass media."[43] Eco's analysis of open-ended systems as a means to inculcate participation and social connection was formative for the Rosario Group and complemented McLuhan's notion that mass media could facilitate a participatory democracy. Jacoby believed the Happening was ultimately too individualistic and exclusive but euphorically declared, "Today we can imagine an art, collective in its creation and its reception, of the mass communication media."[44] Indeed Eco's notion of openness argued that the solution to a conflict must come "from the collective enterprise of the audience."[45] He also saw contemporary art as political and equated the open work with acts of "conscious freedom."[46] Eco's and McLuhan's interpretations of systems and their relationship to social democracies, considered in the context of the government's false narrative about the status of Tucumán's state-owned sugar plantations, then in the process of privatization, prompted the artists to conceive of ways to infuse the mass media with factual information that reflected the lived experience of individuals.

The *dis*information media circuit initiated by the government of Juan Carlos Onganía promoted the myth that Tucumán was a paradise. Accompanied by idyllic posters of well-fed children and the slogan "Tucumán: The Garden of the Republic," the media campaign covered up the widespread hunger and unemployment wrought by privatization measures that were funded, in large part, by the United States. The Rosario Group's project manifesto read as follows: "'Operation Tucumán,' devised by government economists, aims to disguise this blatant aggression against the working classes with the fiction of economic development based on the creation of new or hypothetical industries financed by U.S. capital."[47] The artists also charged (accurately) that the dictatorship intended to break up worker groups and dissolve the substantial union movement underway in northwest Argentina in order to mitigate the impact of unions elsewhere in the country. Finding common interest with these workers, the artists collaborated with them to realize the work. Tucumán Arde was conceived as an open process in four phases: a preliminary, stealth publicity campaign; the collection and analysis of accurate information; the showcasing of that information in two exhibitions; and the publication and archiving of the information together with documentation of the exhibitions. Elements of each phase were looped back into prior phases, and the results were carried forward into subsequent ones, creating an ongoing, always open circuit of information where (factual) information could be continually (re)inserted.

The second phase comprised research of the situation through two research trips to Tucumán, which were a collective process. Before their first trip, in September 1968, the artists gathered an exhaustive amount of press coverage, subjecting it to critical analysis "to measure the degree of manipulation and distortion." They then brought their data to Tucumán where they verified the social situation for themselves. Together with union workers, sociologists, economists, students, and technicians, the artists collected data on-site: taking photographs of abandoned factories, settlements, and hospitals; and conducting preliminary interviews with local workers, union representatives, and cultural organizations. Reminiscent of 1930s Farm Security Administration (FSA) documentary photographs, many of these photos feature workers and their families set in their impoverished circumstances. In one photograph (figure 3.3), young boys line the sidewalk, the first with his arm outstretched, seeking work as shoe shiners to make money for their families. During the second trip, in October 1968, interviews with the local working population were taped and filmed. The artists then gathered local journalists for a press conference where they presented their findings, which "publicly and vehemently repudiated" the government's account issued through the media, whose role in disseminating the disinformation was also called to account.[48] Thus the media became the conduit for both accounts, the dictatorship's propaganda and the reality presented by the artists.

Through the press conference, the artists disrupted the media cycle of disinformation by inserting empirical evidence, creating an *over*informational circuit meant to saturate the public with facts, while exposing the previous reports as lies. By their presentation of the facts, the artists "publicly denounced [the poverty and hunger in] Tucumán and the complicity of the mass media with the official discourse."[49] The artists' deliberate "disordering" of the predictable linear narrative of the government's account produced an open work.[50] Their "controlled disorder" violated the government's pattern of information, yielding a "dialectical tension," in Eco's words, that they hoped would generate "new perspectives and a greater quantity of information" for the public, thus performing "a liberating role."[51] The solution to a conflict of unresolved problems, according to Eco, must come "from the collective enterprise of the audience."[52] Openness is based on the theoretical, mental collaboration of the participant.

The third phase consisted of two "exhibition-condemnations" that presented all of the information gathered on the situation and the artists' actions in Tucumán. Both exhibitions were held at CGTA headquarters, explicitly outside the official art institutions: the first, in Rosario in November 1968, was preceded by an anonymous, performative ad campaign consisting of posters plastered around Rosario and a graffiti campaign, arguably the first use of street art.[53] In the iconic photograph, the words TUCUMAN ARDE, scrawled in enormous letters on the side of a building in Rosario, punctuated by a woman walking toward them in full stride, are purely provocative, meant to stimulate interest rather than reveal details about the upcoming exhibition. The second exhibition was held at union headquarters in Buenos Aires and was open for barely a day due to warnings from government security forces threatening to break in. The exhibition in Rosario included the products of information and publicity: news reports, leaflets, the artists' audiotaped interviews with displaced Tucumán workers, films, the documentary photographs of emaciated workers and child laborers, and diagrams revealing the economic relationships between private corporations (including US multinational corporations like Monsanto and Sears Roebuck) and the government officials responsible for the closure of the sugar refineries.[54] Images and information covered all surfaces from floor to ceiling in a cacophonous and confrontational barrage, while the taped interviews played simultaneously. Guests were served bitter black coffee without sugar, and the lights flickered in a rhythm that indicated the child mortality rate. The artists also looped the media coverage of their own press conference in Tucumán into this subsequent phase of the information circuit.

The unpredictable, participatory nature of the exhibitions inspired by Happenings also epitomized the open work. Intentionally installed according to a collage (kaleidoscopic mosaic) aesthetic, it allowed the viewer to constantly reevaluate their relationship to its messages and, implicitly, to the state. As Eco noted, listeners must place themselves amid an infinite network of relationships "within a field of possibilities" to determine meaning.[55] The

FIGURE 3.3. Rosario Group, *Tucumán Arde: Phase 2: Artists' Trip to Tucumán*, October 1968. View of child shoe shiners. Photo by Rosario Group. Archive of Graciela Carnevale, Rosario, Argentina.

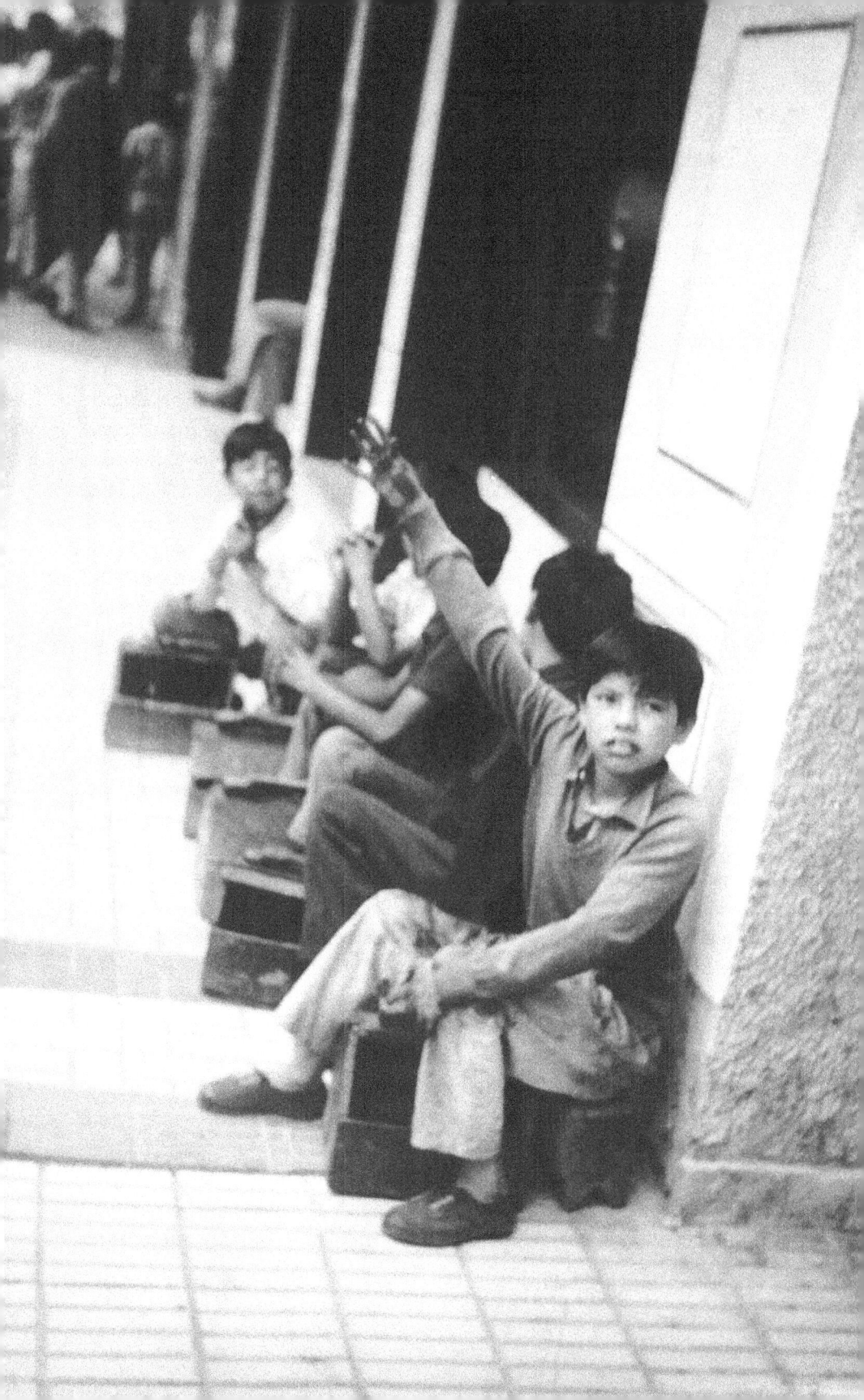

open work is comprised of "a complex interplay of motive forces . . . a configuration of possible events, a complete dynamism of structure."[56] Indeed, the crediting of individual artists was not intended: remaining true to the collective nature of the project, the artists' names had not been meant to appear. Artist Norberto Púzzolo explained to me that the artists deliberately chose to withhold their names at the outset and agreed that none should specify another in a given task. "The artist as individual should disappear."[57]

The fourth phase was a planned compilation and analysis of all collected documents, intended for publication. The archive was meant to "record the process of conceiving and performing the work, along with all documentation and a final evaluation."[58] Graciela Carnevale had assembled the archive, which remained unfinished when the group was dispersed, fearing arrest. Today, it remains open and subject to change as Carnevale continues to incorporate documentation of the project. She is the archive's gatekeeper, facilitating access by describing each document and offering context. She explained to me that she sees her role as "socializing the archive." Carnevale said, "I kept these items for affective reasons. These were some of my best friends." She references here the affective nature of the archive, the feelings she has for her friends who participated in Tucumán Arde, suggesting a reading of the project through affect theory. Of course, the affective turn itself is an outgrowth of open systems, representing "an engagement with the complexity of open systems."[59] Carnevale's physical presence and accounts provide a point of mediation between dry, material documents and her own personal, lived experience.[60] The artist's recollection offers not only firsthand testimony but also access to her subjective memory. She explained to me why the artists conceived of the archive as an essential component of Tucumán Arde: "We had the consciousness to write about ourselves because we knew nobody would write about us, about the project, because we were outside the institution."[61] Thus the archive is testament to the radical nature of Tucumán Arde as institutional critique, a project conceived wholly outside of the art institution and in defiance of the national government. The artists understood the importance of preserving the critical, social function of their work.

Desalinear, which I have characterized here as the artists' goal—to disrupt or disorder the linear circuit of media coverage that furthered the aims of the dictatorship—means literally to disrupt the straight line, to *des-alinear* or dis-align.[62] How can the artists' objective to disorder—ostensibly, to foster entropy—be squared with their aim to clarify and communicate facts? If entropy is the measure of disorder in a message, how can disorder foster a message's organization and meaning? The answer lies in Eco's interpretation of the *opera aperta*. Eco claimed that it is the work of art's "deliberate disorder" that makes it so much more informative. "We then confront a message that deliberately violates or, at least, questions the very system, the very order—order *as system of probability*—to which it refers. In other words, the ambiguity of the aesthetic message is the result of the deliberate 'dis-ordering' of the code, that is, of the order that, via selection and association, had been imposed on the entropic disorder characteristic of all sources of information."[63] Applying Wiener's information theory to linguistics and works of art, Eco differentiated the open work from ordered information conveyed using expected linguistic structures. For Wiener, the order of a message is proportional to the quantity of information it contains, which Eco understood to mean: the more information conveyed, the more meaningful information is also conveyed.[64] But Eco also made an important distinction between information and meaning.[65] He argued that expected types of information transmitted in predictable ways from predictable sources add little that is new and meaningful. Using poetry as his example, he asserted instead that it is the originality of organization that conveys meaning, an uncommon piece of information that violates the laws governing language. "This sort of information would, of course, be connected not to a state of order but to a state of disorder."[66]

Eco equated disorder with open systems and with freedom. The artists presented elements of disorder in violation of the established code of the government's erroneous message distributed through the media, thus introducing a form of greater organization and meaning akin, I would argue, to *negentropy*, a term used by von Bertalanffy to mean the negative of entropy. Entropy characterizes closed systems, whereas open systems can be characterized by greater organization. The factual information the artists inserted into the noise of the dictatorship's predictable information resulted in a very particular form of disorder that increased the probability that the public would learn the facts, while drawing attention to the ways in which the government manipulated the media, the structure that conveyed its message. Eco equated this disorder to a poetics of openness and to freedom. "This tendency toward disorder, characteristic of the poetics of openness, must be understood as a tendency toward controlled disorder, toward a circumscribed potential, toward a freedom."[67] Rather than mere noise, the artists' infusion of statistical information into the media cycle was meant to bring awareness to the government's misuse of the complicit media. Where people may have been indifferent to information qua information, the artists' intention was to generate meaning.[68] Proposing to "construct works within the media itself," Jacoby understood the creation of media work as a process of "aesthetic shaping."[69] Similarly, León Ferrari insisted that the artists organized their aesthetic materials around their meaning, which lay in "the efficacy of their transmission, their persuasive power, their clarity, and their inescapability."[70] Tucumán Arde was meant to demonstrate for the larger populace the ability of a collective to shape social discourse despite severe repression.

Eco saw the openness of art that disorders, that "violates patterns and schemes," in dialectical relationship to the predictable, preexisting linguistic codes. He noted that such elements of disorder were in "dialectical tension" with the established order (code), and that this dialectic would generate new perspectives and a greater quantity of information. He suggested that this art fulfills a liberating role, concluding, in soaring language, that "it would come to represent modern man's path to salvation, toward the reconquest of his lost autonomy at the level of both perception and intelligence."[71] At the heart Eco's open work is a liberating energy with the potential to bring about social transformation, "modern man's path to salvation," the means to disrupt or disorder.

The purpose of Tucumán Arde was to juxtapose the reality of the factual situation in Tucumán with the unreality of the false media reports, to countercirculate messages through which new values would be disseminated to participants.[72] Jacoby had described the intent of mass media art in ways strikingly similar to the (now) current US media cycle: the intention of the works of mass media art is to refer to "a play between the reality of things and the unreality of information, between the reality of information and the unreality of things, with the materialization, through mass media art, of imaginary facts."[73] The artists noted in their manifesto, "The media is a powerful, mediating force, susceptible to being loaded with various content; its positive influence on society depends on its adherence to the truth and reality."[74]

The creation of a collective work of art, made by artists, union workers, sociologists, and economists, indicates an open system in which the work is shaped by a network of voices. The collective work of art, of course, has roots in social protest but also in the art and technology movements of the 1950s like GRAV. The incorporation of multiple voices from various sectors of society undermines the traditional notion of a work imbued with definitive, authorial meaning, making it instead an open work. The artists explained in their manifesto, "The collective aggressive action . . . destroys the system of official culture, replacing it with a subversive culture that incorporates the process of change, establishing a truly revolutionary art."[75] Seeking a transformation of social structures, "a transforming art," the work itself is a process subject to disruption, to feedback. The emphasis in the quote is on the act of disruption, the opening of a closed system through a collaborative, artistic act through which truth is intentionally, forcefully reinserted into public discourse. It was precisely through the application of open systems to specific, lived social and political experience that yielded the artists' insight into their indissoluble interconnectedness.

NOTES

Millersville University of Pennsylvania provided necessary sabbatical leave in support of research for this project, and Faculty Grants provided important funding. I am grateful to Marisa Pereyra, Nils Jacobsen, Mónica Amor, Bradley Filippone, Dennis Summers, and Roger Rothman for their feedback on early drafts, and to editors Johanna Gosse and Tim Stott, as well as the Duke University Press reviewers, for their very helpful comments.

1   "Eisenhower Flies to Andes Resort after Cordial Reception in Mar del Plata; Eisenhower's Speeches; Toast at Dinner," *New York Times*, February 28, 1960.

2   The nonprofit Torcuato di Tella Institute in Buenos Aires was founded to promote research in the interest of scientific, cultural, and artistic development in Argentina. Luis Eduardo Herrera offers a fascinating account of the origins of the di Tella Institute as the product of interconnected business leaders in the United States and Argentina who understood artistic modernism as inseparable from economic developmentalism (capitalist modernization). Luis Eduardo Herrera, "The CLAEM and the Construction of Elite Art Worlds: Philanthropy, Latinamericanism and Avant-Garde Music" (PhD diss., University of Illinois, Urbana-Champaign, 2013).

3   Ana Longoni, *Vanguardia y revolución: Arte e izquierdas en la Argentina de los sesenta-setenta* (Buenos Aires: Editorial Paidós SAIF, 2014), 183; all translations from Spanish in this chapter, unless otherwise noted, are by Marisa Pereyra. In 1968 the artist Juan Pablo Renzi and a group of other artists interrupted a talk by di Tella director Jorge Romero Brest with the statement, "The life of Che Guevara and the actions of the French students are greater works of art than most of the rubbish hanging in the thousands of museums throughout the world. . . . Death to all institutions. Long live the art of the Revolution!" Originally reproduced in Guillermo Fantoni, *Arte, vanguardia y política en los años '60: Conversaciones con Juan Pablo Renzi* (Buenos Aires: El Cielo por Asalto, 1998), 104. Quoted in Oscar Terá, "Culture, Intellectuals, and Politics in the 1960s," in *Listen Here Now! Argentine Art of the 1960s: Writings of the Avant-Garde*, ed. Inés Katzenstein (New York: Museum of Modern Art, 2004), 272.

4   Ana Longoni and Mariano Mestman, *Del Di Tella a "Tucumán Arde": Vanguardia artística y política en el 68 Argentina* (Buenos Aires: EUDEBA, 2010), 172.

5   Maria Teresa Gramuglio and Nicolás Rosa, "Tucumán Arde Manifesto," in *Desinventario: Esquirlas de Tucumán Arde en el archivo de Graciela Carnevale*, ed. Graciela Carnevale, Marcelo Exposito, Andre Mesquita, and Jaime Vindel (Santiago,

Chile: Ocho Libros, con la colaboración del Museo Nacional Centro de Arte Reina Sofía, 2015), 140–43. See also Roberto Jacoby, "Message in the di Tella," in *Listen Here Now! Argentine Art of the 1960s: Writings of the Avant-Garde*, ed. Inés Katzenstein (New York: Museum of Modern Art, 2004), 288. Several scholars of Latin American art have noted the political character of Latin American art in this period: Jane Farver, ed., *Global Conceptualism: Points of Origin, 1950s–1980s* (New York: Queens Museum, 1999), 67; Claire Bishop, *Artificial Hells: Participatory Art and the Politics of Spectatorship* (London: Verso, 2012); Andrea Giunta, *Avant-Garde, Internationalism, and Politics: Argentine Art in the Sixties* (Durham, NC: Duke University Press, 2007); and Luis Camnitzer, *Conceptualism in Latin American Art: Didactics of Liberation* (Austin: University of Texas Press, 2007).

6   Julia Bryan-Wilson discussion of the context of labor in Tucumán Arde is brief, but important. Julia Bryan-Wilson, *Art Workers: Radical Practice in the Vietnam War Era* (Berkeley: University of California Press, 2009), 134.

7   I have argued elsewhere for the role of systems theory in the origins of feminist art in the United States. Christine Filippone, *Science, Technology, and Utopias: Women Artists and Cold War America* (London: Routledge, 2017).

8   Luke Skrebowski's characterization of institutional critique as strategy with systems thinking as its origin, rather than as a period, is particularly useful here. Luke Skrebowski, "Systems, Contexts, Relations: An Alternative Genealogy of Conceptual Art" (PhD diss., Middlesex University, 2009), 249.

9   Longoni, *Vanguardia y revolución*, 64. Longoni also recites the art historiography of Tucumán Arde as "the foundation of ideological conceptualism," a term first coined by Marchan Fiz in 1972 (67n5).

10   Blake Stimson, "What Was Institutional Critique?," *Institutional Critique: An Anthology of Artists' Writings*, ed. Alexander Alberro and Blake Stimson (Cambridge, MA: MIT Press, 2011), 21.

11   Alexander Alberro, "Institutions, Critique, an Institutional Critique," in *Institutional Critique: An Anthology of Artists' Writings*, ed. Alexander Alberro and Blake Stimson (Cambridge, MA: MIT Press, 2011), 4, emphasis added.

12   See Ludwig von Bertalanffy, *Lebenswissenschaft und Bildung* (Erfurt, Germany: Stenger, 1930); and Ludwig von Bertalanffy, "Untersuchungen über die Gesetzlichkeit des Wachstums, I. Teil: Allgemeine Grundlagen der Theorie; Mathematische und physiologische Gesetzlichkeiten des Wachstums bei Wassertieren," *Wilhelm Roux Archiv für Entwicklungsmechanik der Organismen: Organ für d. gesamte kausal Morphologie* 131, no. 4 (1934): 613–52. Bertalanffy began publishing his theory of open systems in English in the late 1940s and early 1950s. See, for example, Ludwig von Bertalanffy, C. G. Hempel, R. E. Bass, and H. Jonas, "General System Theory: A New Approach to Unity of Science," *Human Biology* 23, no. 4 (1951): 30–27.

13   Filippone, *Science, Technology, and Utopias*, 65; Martha Rosler, "The System of the Postmodern in the Decade of the Seventies," in *The Idea of the Post-modern: Who Is Teaching It?*, ed. Lawrence Alloway, Donald B. Kuspit, Martha Rosler, and Jan van der Marck (Seattle: Henry Art Gallery, University of Washington, 1981),

25, 27, 31; Martha Rosler, "Video: Shedding the Utopian Moment," in *Decoys and Disruptions: Selected Writings, 1975–2001* (Cambridge, MA: MIT Press, 2004); Hans Haacke, foreword to *Dissolve into Comprehension: Writings and Interviews by Jack Burnham*, ed. Melissa Ragain (Cambridge, MA: MIT Press, 2015), ix; Jack Burnham, "Steps in the Formulation of Real-Time Political Art," in Hans Haacke, *Hans Haacke: Framing and Being Framed; 7 Works, 1970–75* (Halifax: Press of the Nova Scotia College of Art and Design; New York: New York University Press, 1975), 31.

14 Jane Farver, Luis Camnitzer, and Rachel Weiss, foreword to *Global Conceptualism: Points of Origin, 1950s–1980s*, ed. Jane Farver (New York: Queens Museum, 1999), ix.

15 Interview with Roberto Jacoby, Buenos Aires, June 25, 1993, in Longoni and Mestman, *Del Di Tella a "Tucumán Arde,"* 346.

16 Norbert Wiener, *The Human Use of Human Beings: Cybernetics and Society* (New York: Avon, 1967), 52.

17 Umberto Eco, *Opera aperta: Forma e indeterminazione nelle poetiche contemporanee* (Milan: Bompiani, 1962). I want to extend Francis Halsall's important call for a consideration of systems aesthetics as a retrospective critical discourse prior to that of Burnham, which would include that of Eco. Francis Halsall, *Systems of Art: Art, History and Systems Theory* (Oxford: Peter Lang, 2008), 114.

18 Ana Longoni and Mario Mestman, "After Pop, We Dematerialize: Oscar Masotta, Happenings, and Media Art at the Beginnings of Conceptualism," in *Listen Here Now! Argentine Art of the 1960s: Writings of the Avant-Garde*, ed. Inés Katzenstein (New York: Museum of Modern Art, 2004), 170n4. For Verón's engagement with cybernetics and systems theory, see Eliseo Verón, *Conducta, estructura y comunicacion* (Buenos Aires: Editorial Jorge Álvarez, 1968).

19 Quoted in Oscar Masotta, *Conciencia y estructura* (Buenos Aires: Eterna Cadencia Editora, 2010), 305.

20 Darko Fritz, "The Notion of Program in 1960s Art: Concrete, Computer-Generated and Conceptual Art," paper presented at the conference Art-Oriented Programming 2 (Programmation orientée-art 2) at the Amphithéâtre Richelieu of the Sorbonne, Paris, October 20, 2007. Published in David-Olivier Lartigaud, ed., *Art++* (Orléans: Editions HYX, 2011), 26–39. See also Larry Busbea, "Kineticism, Spectacle, Environment," *Grey Room*, no. 144 (2013): 98.

21 Umberto Eco, untitled text, in *Arte programmata: Arte cinetica, opere moltiplicate, opera aperta*, exhibition catalog, ed. Umberto Eco and Bruno Munari (Milan: Officina d'arte grafica A. Lucini, 1962), n.p.

22 Lily Woodruff, "The Groupe de Recherche d'Art Visuel against the Technocrats," *Art Journal* 73, no. 3 (2014): 21, 22.

23 Julio Le Parc/GRAV, "No More Mystifications!" (1963), in *Listen Here Now! Argentine Art of the 1960s: Writings of the Avant-Garde*, ed. Inés Katzenstein (New York: Museum of Modern Art, 2004), 56, internal quotation is Le Parc's. Estrellita Brodsky noted that Le Parc met Graciela Carnevale and other Argentine artists during his retrospective at the Torcuato di Tella Institute in 1967. Estrellita

Brodsky, "Latin American Artists in Postwar Paris: Jesús Rafael Soto and Julio Le Parc, 1950–1970" (PhD diss., New York University, 2009), 338.

24 Guillermo Sagen Gil, *La CGT de los Argentinos en Rosario, 1968–69* (Rosario, Argentina: Universidad Nacional de Rosario, 2005), 45.

25 Sagen Gil, *La CGT de dos Argentinos*, 49.

26 "La Patria consagrada al Inmaculado Corazón Hace: 43 años era oficialmente consagrada a los pies de la Virgen de Luján" (The Fatherland consecrated to the Immaculate Heart: 43 years since the official consecration at the feet of the Virgin of Luján), *Página Católica*, November 30, 2012, http://pagina-catolica.blogspot .com/2012/11/la-patria-consagrada-al-inmaculado.html.

27 Osvaldo Mateo Boglione, Aldo Bortolotti, Graciela Carnevale, Rudolfo Elizalde, Noemí Escandell, Eduardo Favario, Fernández Bonina, Carlos Gatti, Emilio Ghilioni, Martha Greiner, José M. Lavarello, Lia Maisonnave, Rubén Naranjo, Norberto Púzzolo, Juan Pablo Renzi, and Jaime Rippa, "We Must Always Resist the Lures of Complicity," in *Listen Here Now! Argentine Art of the 1960s: Writings of the Avant-Garde*, ed. Inés Katzenstein (New York: Museum of Modern Art, 2004), 294.

28 Graciela Carnevale, "Project for the Experimental Art Series," in *Listen Here Now! Argentine Art of the 1960s: Writings of the Avant-Garde*, ed. Inés Katzenstein (New York: Museum of Modern Art, 2004), 299.

29 Carnevale, "Project for the Experimental Art Series," 299.

30 "Tucumán Arde: Color Natal," video, dir. Cecilia Vallina, 2011, accessed January 10, 2019, https://www.youtube.com/watch?v=-MgjwIHthew.

31 Graciela Carnevale, interview with the author, Rosario, Argentina, August 7, 2019.

32 Carnevale, interview with the author, August 7, 2019; León Ferrari, "Artist's Response," in *Listen Here Now! Argentine Art of the 1960s: Writings of the Avant-Garde*, ed. Inés Katzenstein (New York: Museum of Modern Art, 2004), 280. See also Herbert Marcuse, *One-Dimensional Man: Studies in the Ideology of Advanced Industrial Society* (Boston: Beacon, 1964); Martin Heidegger, *The Question concerning Technology, and Other Essays,* trans. D. F. Krell (New York: Garland, 1977); Jacques Ellul, *The Technological Society*, trans. John Wilkinson (New York: Knopf, 1964); and Lewis Mumford, *The Myth of the Machine*, 2 vols. (New York: Harcourt, 1967).

33 Marshall McLuhan, *Understanding Media: The Extensions of Man* (New York: McGraw Hill, 1964), 24.

34 McLuhan, *Understanding Media*, 189.

35 The notion of modern participatory democracy goes back at least to Alexis de Tocqueville if not to the Iroquois. My thanks to the historian Nils Jacobsen for pointing this out to me.

36 Longoni and Mestman, "After Pop, We Dematerialize: Oscar Masotta, Happenings, and Media Art at the Beginnings of Conceptualism," 167.

37 Longoni and Mestman, "After Pop, We Dematerialize: Oscar Masotta, Happenings, and Media Art at the Beginnings of Conceptualism," 157. First published in an interview with Roberto Jacoby, "Via Libre," *La Nacion* (Buenos Aires), May 21, 1998.

38 Oscar Masotta, "After Pop, We Dematerialize," in *Listen Here Now! Argentine Art of the 1960s: Writings of the Avant-Garde*, ed. Inés Katzenstein (New York: Museum of Modern Art, 2004), 208–9.

39 Masotta, "After Pop," 209.

40 Masotta, "After Pop," 213.

41 Roberto Jacoby, "Closed Information Circuits," in *Listen Here Now! Argentine Art of the 1960s: Writings of the Avant-Garde*, ed. Inés Katzenstein (New York: Museum of Modern Art, 2004), 251.

42 Roberto Jacoby, "Against the Happening," in *Listen Here Now! Argentine Art of the 1960s: Writings of the Avant-Garde*, ed. Inés Katzenstein (New York: Museum of Modern Art, 2004), 232.

43 Longoni and Mestman, "After Pop, We Dematerialize: Oscar Masotta, Happenings, and Media Art at the Beginnings of Conceptualism," 167.

44 Jacoby, "Against the Happening," 232.

45 Umberto Eco, *The Open Work*, trans. Anna Cancogni (Cambridge, MA: Harvard University Press, 1989),11. Eco here draws on Bertolt Brecht.

46 Eco, *The Open Work*, xv, 4.

47 María Teresa Gramuglio and Nicolás Rosa, "Tucuman Is Burning: Statement of the Exhibition in Rosario," in *Listen Here Now! Argentine Art of the 1960s: Writings of the Avant-Garde*, ed. Inés Katzenstein (New York: Museum of Modern Art, 2004), 321.

48 Gramuglio and Rosa, "Tucuman Is Burning," 321.

49 Maria Teresa Gramuglio and Nicolas Rosa, "Tucuman Arde Manifesto," in Carnevale et al., *Desinventario*, 142.

50 Maria Teresa Gramuglio and Nicolas Rosa, "Tucuman Arde Manifesto," in Carnevale et al., *Desinventario*, 143.

51 Eco, *The Open Work*, 64, 83.

52 Eco, *The Open Work*, 12.

53 The artists collaborated with the radical union faction, Confederación general del trabajo de la república de los Argentinos, led by Raimundo Ongaro. In 1968, the faction split from the CGT, which was allied with the military junta.

54 Graciela Carnevale, Tucumán Arde Archive, Rosario, Argentina.

55 Eco, *The Open Work*, 11, 13.

56 Eco, *The Open Work*, 14.

57 Norberto Púzzolo, email communication with the author, October, 2018. Púzzolo told me that he has often observed the paradox that Tucumán Arde was art without artists.

58 Gramuglio and Rosa, "Tucuman Is Burning," 322.

59 Patricia Ticineto Clough and Jean Halley, eds., *The Affective Turn: Theorizing the Social* (Durham, NC: Duke University Press, 2007).

60 Cecilia Macón, *Sexual Violence in the Argentinean Crimes against Humanity Trials: Rethinking Victimhood* (Lanham, MD: Lexington, 2017), 42.

61 Carnevale, interview with the author, August 7, 2019.

62 The art historian Mónica Amor has also discussed Venezuelan artist Gego's consideration of the line in her *Reticulárea* series, which aims "to order and derange its mechanical and organic association, its freedom, and its potential to embody opposites." Mónica Amor, "On the Contingency of Modernity and the Persistence of Canons," in *Antinomies of Art and Culture: Modernity, Postmodernity,*

Contemporaneity, ed. Terry Smith, Okwui Enwezor, and Nancy Condee (Durham, NC: Duke University Press, 2008), 83–96; and Mónica Amor, "Another Geometry: Gego's *Reticularea, 1969–77*," in *Theories of the Nonobject: Argentina, Brazil, Venezuela, 1944–1969* (Oakland: University of California Press, 2016), 172–217.

63   Eco, *The Open Work*, 66–67, emphasis in original.

64   Eco likely understood the relationship between information and meaning in Wiener from the following: "In control of communication we are always fighting nature's tendency to degrade the organized and to destroy the meaningful; the tendency, as Gibbs has shown us, for entropy to increase." Wiener, *Human Use of Human Beings*, 26.

65   Eco, *The Open Work*, 57. Eco affirms, "Information must not be confused with meaning."

66   Eco, *The Open Work*, 55.

67   Eco, *The Open Work*, 64–65.

68   N. Katherine Hayles, "Narrating Consciousness: Language, Media, and Embodiment," *History of Human Sciences* 23, no. 3 (2013): 134.

69   Longoni and Mestman, "After Pop, We Dematerialize: Oscar Masotta, Happenings, and Media Art at the Beginnings of Conceptualism," 164.

70   León Ferrari, "The Art of Meanings," in *Listen Here Now! Argentine Art of the 1960s: Writings of the Avant-Garde*, ed. Inés Katzenstein (New York: Museum of Modern Art, 2004), 316.

71   Eco, *The Open Work*, 83.

72   Mari Carmen Ramírez, "Tactics for Thriving on Adversity: Conceptualism in Latin America, 1960–1980," in *Global Conceptualism: Points of Origin, 1950s–1980s*, ed. Jane Farver (New York: Queens Museum, 1999), 57.

73   Quoted in Longoni and Mestman, "After Pop, We Dematerialize: Oscar Masotta, Happenings, and Media Art at the Beginnings of Conceptualism," 167.

74   Gramuglio and Rosa, "Tucuman Is Burning," 321.

75   Gramuglio and Rosa, "Tucuman Is Burning," 319.

Nervous Interfaces

4

The Irresolutions of Charles Gaines

KRIS COHEN

The Black Arts movement that immediately preceded Charles Gaines's career actively debated the blackness of abstraction.[1] In these debates, abstraction was framed as a choice, and the very capacity to exercise that choice was at the heart of those debates.[2] These were also debates, therefore, about personhood seen in relation to work—the labor of art making, of self-elaboration, of testing out some ways of working that were ways of living in and with blackness, of challenging and elaborating it.

But all the while, a certain other kind of abstraction was coming, one that did not so much exercise personhood as shape it. The particular source of abstraction I am concerned with here is the graphical display of the personal computer (graphical user interface, or GUI)—we can think of it, provisionally, as an abstraction of the body, although really its ambition was to be an abstraction of white personhood. To be involved with modes of abstraction, including with conceptualism and systems art (usually considered to be the genres that best fit Gaines's practice), was therefore necessarily to be involved with this coming abstraction, like it or not. Gaines's gridwork confronts this torquing of personhood and the forms it had taken under the impress of the graphical field—if not exactly head on, then certainly with a committed persistence. Systems aesthetics was the ground on which he met it; it was his starting point for creating a zone of nonexpressive art within the delimited confines of the artwork as system. This was to be a homeopathic aesthetic, pitting the systematicity of computing's bodily abstractions against that of systems art, both set within the frame of a long history of racial violence. The effect was to force open the smallest space for movement between the framing of black abstraction as a choice, as a certain kind of freedom, and the coming abstraction that wanted to generate a feeling of freedom as its object—its product, really. Freedom was to be the key problem, both in its implications for black personhood and in the relatively new promises being made by the graphical field for personal computing.

Research into systems, into cybernetics, into information theory, both in state-funded efforts and in the art world, intervenes directly in the relationship between labor, technology, and personhood.[3] While only ever glancingly acknowledged in most art histories, many Black artists have participated in, challenged, or quizzically inhabited this territory: Alma Thomas, Jack Whitten, Adrian Piper, Howardena Pindell, Peter Halley, Ed Clark, Romare Bearden, Tom Lloyd, William T. Williams, Melvin Edwards, Julie Mehretu, Louis Cameron, Jacolby Satterwhite, Aria Dean, American Artist, Martine Syms, Caitlin Cherry, Sondra Perry, Adrienne Gaither . . .[4] I make no distinction in such a list, partial as it is, between artists who employ systems in the making of their work (most of the above do not) and those who work with what appear to be traditional media in order to materialize some aspect of systems logic. All these artists offer significant, sustained, and uncommon thinking on the collision between human and machine in postwar US history and the reverberations of that collision within histories of personhood and labor. Taken together, their work offers up a reimagination and a slantwise retelling of the impact of systems logics on labor generally and on art as a specific form of labor.

The works that I am concerned with most are what the Studio Museum has called Gaines's "gridworks." And while the grid is their most basic visual referent, the period in which they were made (from the 1970s to the present), their contiguity within an overall system, and Gaines's abiding interest in related questions of work and personhood render that referent not so much a grid as a raster. This is a grid put to a kind of use. And it is a system that is often not taken to be a system at all so much as an image technology: the raster-based computer screen (see figure 4.1).[5] In its form as a graphical user interface, the graphical screen aspired to invent a form of labor best performed by a human who was to be augmented by the new forms of freedom, often pitched as a loosening of constraint, to be generated by the graphical screen itself.[6] In Gaines's investigations of that form of the screen, this technocratic

FIGURE 4.1. Charles Gaines, *Faces: Men and Women Set #9, "Pam Criswell,"* 1978. Photograph, ink on paper, three sheets. Each 24×20×1.5 in / 60.96×50.8×3.81 cm; overall 24×64×1.5 in / 60.96×162.56×3.81 cm. © Charles Gaines. Courtesy of the artist and Hauser and Wirth.

promise of augmenting the human lingers as a kind of broken promise, given flesh or form in a constrained, divested personhood that Gaines referred to as "contiguity."[7] Gaines's systematizations of personhood, collectivity, and creative labor need to be seen in this context, and not just in the universalizing history—the white history—of the twentieth century that has provided the implicit or explicit background for most histories of conceptual art, process art, and systems art.

Rasterworks

In the early 1970s, as a recent graduate of the MFA program at the Rochester Institute of Technology (its first Black graduate), Charles Gaines stopped painting and started to produce the work that indissociably connected him with systems and process-based work: work that the Studio Museum, in its major 2014 survey, titled *Charles Gaines: Gridwork 1974–1989*. This body of work has been a through line of his prolific and varied practice—much of which deals with music, with quotation, and with a history of black protest, as well as with signification, metaphor, and metonymy—extending from the early 1970s to the present. Here's how, in a letter to Carol and Sol LeWitt, Gaines explained this transition from painting to systems: "I dropped painting in 1972. . . . The problem is the associated discourse surrounding gesture, that is, gesturing was a material manifestation of emotive or expressive intent.

And I didn't care for that idea."[8] He did not care, perhaps, for the fantasy of autonomy that was encouraged by the discourse of gesture, the feeling that expressivity could be an analogue to something like human spirit or unbounded imagination. More broadly, Gaines seems to reject any easy coincidence or relay between the laboring body, that body's interiority, and the product of that body's labor. Gaines often called the work that followed from this rejection "systems work," a common enough idiom at the time, although here put to some unexpected uses. Most unexpected, perhaps, is the fact that systems do not, in Gaines's work, constitute an antinomy or opposition to gesture and expressive intent, even if they do work to escape the gravity of those subjective emanations.

One of the most approachable of Gaines's early systems works, *Faces* (1978–79)—a work he would revisit for his 2018 exhibition at Paula Cooper and 2021 exhibition at Hauser and Wirth in London—employs a transposition system like all of his other gridwork, moving from one imaging system to and through others.[9] The full series from 1978 to 1979 comprises sixteen triptychs. Each of the individual images (forty-eight in total) is 23 by 19 inches. The triptychs all follow the same transpositional pattern, each triptych a kind of process in itself: in the first or left-most image, a photograph; next, its outline in negative; and finally, a composite image that gathers and overlays each of the previous outlines from the second image onto the same image plane. In the first triptych, then, the right-most image contains only one outline, one face; in the right-most image of the sixteenth triptych, there are sixteen superimposed outlines. Each individual triptych is titled with the legal name of the subject photographed, friends and associates of Gaines's, most of whom were not widely known. The fourth triptych, for instance, is called *Faces: Men and Women Set #4, "Stephen W. Walls."* It pictures a young Black man, photographed frontally and close-up. It arrays the face for study but also, in its immobilized frontality, can't not evoke a long historical tradition of surveillance, incarceration, and criminalization. In this sense, Gaines's system here moves in at least two directions: back along this violent trajectory that wants to inscribe identity onto the body of its victims but also along speculative trajectories that want to free the body from such compulsions to speak, to be legible, to be fungible precisely in its identifiability. Both of these are black histories.

As if to immediately announce the project's intention to tarry with some protocols of representation, the first image of every triptych in the series is a black and white portrait photograph—a close-up with the face arrayed frontally, as though for "our" examination (the work makes that collective pronoun possible, if not equally inhabitable for everyone). It invokes a kind of overseeing collectivity precisely in its frontality and the history of penality that it evokes. Because of this, the photographs reference technologies of identification, technologies for even more indelibly inscribing identity onto body. But in the second image, the face, first given in extreme, even forensic photographic detail, now becomes an outline hollowed out of a fully activated raster—as though its representational protocols are starting to fray, or to become something else. That is, into each of the grid squares, Gaines has inscribed numbers in black ink, leaving empty squares to articulate the face's barest outline. This use of the activated or unactivated raster to materialize an image is why many refer to Gaines's images as "pixelated."[10]

The numbering, too, is systematized. It begins with zero in the exact center of the image plane, with zeroes written in a vertical line extending from top to bottom of the image. From this center line and extending horizontally out to the sides of the image, the numbers ascend to sixty-six. Gaines stops this numbering system one column short of the leftmost column. In that column, he has used the letters of the English alphabet to give coordinates to the grid squares, this time starting from the bottom at A and extending to the top at 7M, cycling through the alphabet six and a half times. So, this is not just a grid space but a coordinate space. I call a grid square with a number inscribed in it *activated* and an empty square *unactivated*, but this is arbitrary. The language of *activated* and *unactivated* I think is accurate to the raster display system employed here, but there is nothing in the logic of that system to say that one state is "on" and the other is "off." In fact, as Gaines's images show quite clearly, there are really only two states of "on," and the contrast is between those two states. The second image, then, presents the body in negative (but here, too, the language of *negative* and *positive* is a heuristic, an artifact of photographic technologies that are actually *not* the historical precursors of the raster display system used here); it presents the body schematized, mathematicized for configuration on *this* particular surface, a raster that seems designed to block any fantasy of free movement, gestural or expressive, through the body of the artist or the space of the image while at the same time decidedly manifesting an image out of the traces of labor visible in the handwritten numbers.

In the third or rightmost image, the numbers themselves (not the spaces left in their absence) articulate the outline of the head and face. Here, the face appears as the barest outline with the surrounding raster left empty. In the final accumulation and intercalation of faces in the raster of the third image, the different colors in which Gaines has written the numbers of each outline allow one to distinguish individual faces, but barely and only with difficulty. Otherwise, accumulation moves toward indistinction, with facial features clustering in rough zones (evoking not the surveillance technology of photography but of facial recognition). This precise effect is repeated in Gaines's *Faces 1: Identity Politics* series, this time extending across the twelve artworks of the series so that, in the final artwork, the faces of twelve thinkers—Aristotle, Maria W. Stewart, Karl Marx, W. E. B. Du Bois, Malcolm X, Jacques Lacan, Dolores Huerta, Michel Foucault, Luce Irigaray, Edward Said, Molefi Kete Asante, and bell hooks—overlap, intercalate, and gather in interference and irresolution along jagged lines of what is nevertheless a kind of contiguity.

While so much like Gaines's other gridworks, the objects of his system here are human faces, many of them black or brown, and this has allowed commentators to discuss *Faces* in the context of identity politics.[11] As one might imagine, there is far less talk about race or identity politics in Gaines's other gridwork: *Regression* (1973–74), *Calculation of a Numerical Equation* (1975), *Walnut Tree Orchard* (1975–2014), *Color Regression* (1978), *Falling Leaves* (1979), *Incomplete Text* (1978–79), *Shadows* (1978–80), *Motion: Trisha Brown Dance* (1980–81), and *Numbers and Trees* (1986–present). So maybe the first kind of work that systems have performed in Gaines's oeuvre is to erect an obstacle to talking about race or identity. This is understandable, but it's also a mistake, reliant on the assumption that race is primarily a technology of representation.[12] Race is not that in Gaines's work, nor is that what it becomes in graphical systems, though representational forms can be easily overlaid onto graphical systems. This, in fact, is one of the reasons why graphical screens have been so attractive, have felt so usable, for so many people. Rather than a negotiation with a computer, the graphic interface lets the user engage with their own creative instincts such that the work produced in that space can serve as a self-representation. "Work different," as Apple almost never said. While Gaines was likely *not* thinking about this precise articulation of freedom, he *was* interested in harnessing graphical systems to engage a rhetoric of freedom in relation to raced personhood, as we will see.

Most of what I have written about systems so far is commonplace for the field this volume inhabits. But writing about systems (like abstraction and conceptualism) often suffers from a lack of precision. It is too often deployed as a totalizing framework, collapsing significant political and aesthetic distinctions under the sign of technology—precisely what this volume attempts to remedy. Nizan Shaked's work has also been an important part of a broad reconsideration of the ways that systems aesthetics and conceptualism actively take up, rather than avoid, the particular and the political. Shaked tracks the movement in conceptualism from, as she puts it, art about art (Joseph Kosuth) to "art about political art" (Adrian Piper); that is, from conceptualism to a politicized conceptualism that explicitly takes up identity politics. But the parallel movement, occurring in the development of the computer screen and centrally concerned not just with systems but with subject formation, makes it clear that all systems aesthetics are concerned with identity politics. The questions are, What sort? In service of what?[13] Gaines's work tracks not just systems art's involvement with identity politics but the involvement of computer systems with identity politics and the machinery of subject formation. Like Gaines's gridworks, the raster-based graphical display system for computer screens is also a system for image transposition—not, primarily, an image or representational space.[14] This transpositional system generates—as Gaines's work hints that it would—a space that resituates the labor of gesture, creativity, expression, and subjecthood itself.

Labor in the Graphical Field

Though first imagined in a variety of forms in the 1960s and 1970s at computer graphics labs around the United States, the graphical form of the computer screen—manifest in the raster of the cathode ray tube (CRT) monitor and now the encompassing environment for basically all facets of life accommodated and actively solicited by the computer—took shape in the years immediately following World War II. The GUI now ships with almost every personal computer. At its simplest (and it has been designed to appear simple so its user can appear fulsome and autonomous) the GUI consists in an overall desktop metaphor, with icons representing units of work, all organized within a space that one can navigate through the prostheses of mouse and cursor. My interest, however, is not in a design history of the GUI, a story that has been told elsewhere, but in a history of personhood as it was reimagined for and then by the graphical screen.[15]

In the postwar decades that saw the development of the graphical interface, questions of nationalism, knowledge, and personhood were at the center of a massive multidisciplinary effort, spanning public and private realms, to imagine, bring into being, and then parade globally a form of distinctively American subjectivity that would be resistant to authoritarianism of the sort that so concerned governments, corporations, and critical theorists alike.[16] There is a line that can be drawn within this scattered field—not a straight one, for sure—between Douglas Engelbart's research at the Stanford Research

Institute and Apple Computer's eventual mass marketing of the graphical user interface. Engelbart's research wasn't isolated or singular, but he plays a central role here because he, of all the others working on computer displays across the country, most clearly articulated the stakes of this research, which he called, tellingly, the augmented human intellect project.

Engelbart believed that digital computers would eventually circulate scientific information through a global network that would repair the postwar world by converting war machines into human-machine hybrids designed to produce not death but knowledge.[17] The labor performed by these new human-computer dyads, joined in and by the graphical interface, Engelbart called "knowledge work"—presciently, as it turns out.[18] As first demonstrated to a scientific public in 1968, the graphical interface was an open expanse whose finite dimensions could be infinitely expanded with windows, each containing discrete but connectable types of work. The user's hand could touch down anywhere in this open field via the proxemics of the mouse that Engelbart invented precisely to foster this feeling of openness and freedom of movement.[19] In his words, Engelbart aimed to grant the user "considerable freedom as to the positions and circumstances under which he can operate" computers.[20] "We want to develop new communication means that allow a human to control or make use of machines (especially information-handling machines) with minimal interference in other physical activities associated with his primary tasks."[21] A particular organization of the computer screen, an open field accessed prosthetically through the mouse and cursor, would become the means to this end. "Considerable freedom" was to be a primary objective of that screen form.[22] The graphical screen—for Engelbart, a minor implementation of his larger and more ambitious research efforts—was to be the answer to this question of how to retrain the human worker for the coming age of computers. "The system we want to improve can thus be visualized as a trained human being together with his artifacts, language, and methodology."[23] Labor, newly organized in the graphical field of the computer screen that Engelbart prototyped and there reimagined as knowledge work, was to be the crucible of this new subject's formation, its proving ground. The graphical screen itself made this labor and this form of the subject possible. As computer historian Jacob Gaboury's work shows, this form of freedom wasn't just artifactual, something made out of the graphical screen. It was a constitutive, even ontological feature of the graphical interface designed for a CRT monitor. The pixels of the bitmapped screen, for instance, act as a form of memory, a "memory location," allowing what Gaboury calls "random access" to whatever image or image environments the screen displays.[24]

In "random," hear echoes of Engelbart's "freedom," as well as a hint as to how "freedom" was to be understood in this context: namely, expressed as and in the quiddity of the individuated self, the self set free within the individuated person form—free not because autonomous or sovereign (though those might well manifest themselves as effects, as feelings) but because augmented, bolstered by a system that wasn't immaterial or invisible so much as fully in the service of the human user's creative instincts. The nonrepresentational nature of the graphical interface was key to the kind of freedom Engelbart imagined; it is what allowed the user to feel that the system was not a product so much as a manifestation, a transposition of the user's own creativity.

Although Engelbart had other aims, his work on the graphical screen formed the acknowledged basis of Xerox PARC's creation of the first fully-implemented graphical user interface. And Xerox PARC's work made Apple Computer's own work possible. These histories are well documented.[25] Perhaps the most significant contribution that Xerox and later Apple would make to this history was to inflect Engelbart's somewhat ambivalent conceptualization of the individual—free, yes, but also highly malleable, trainable—toward the kind of idealized creative type that Apple dreamed into being with slogans like "Think Different," and "The Power to Be Your Best." At the most obvious level, Engelbart and later Apple proffer freedom from the command-line interface, from having to interact with a computer on a computer's own terms. Beyond this, and especially in Apple's later technical and marketing schemes, freedom would come to mean creative freedom generated by a screen that wasn't just an interface to a computer but was, in effect, the computer itself. Subsuming the computer, and in this sense erasing it, the contemporary graphical screen allows a user a far more "considerable freedom": freedom to manipulate everything, to place herself anywhere in the field of the screen, to physically move objects rather than issue commands in another language.[26] In Fred Turner's terms, this particular modality of freedom partook of the larger postwar interest in a form of democratic personhood that was free to make choices within a constrained field of options, a freedom to feel as though one's choices are one's own, so that those very choices come to define one's individuality.[27] The crowd or the mass or the audience are thereby defused as threats to individual autonomy because they come to exist most strongly within the ambit of this individuality, in service to it, a way to set it off, to mark its distinction.[28]

What matters most for my purposes is that we see the graphical interface—alongside contemporary art, the postwar labor milieu, the home, and the commodity market—as an environment for a significant reimagining of the individual, but an individual now seen in relation to (individuated on the basis of) the world reimagined as a vast information-sharing network. What emerges then, at the end of this history if not quite at the beginning, is a vision of the individual powerfully isolated by their own creative capacity and by the standard of competition (for status, for raises, for personal computers on desks) that was to be the ultimate inheritance of this history of American individualism.[29] The graphical screen of the personal computer has been one of the most important sites for the elaboration of this version of the self, which has become so integral to the workplace, to citizenship, and to contemporary personhood more broadly.

In other words, the creators and salespeople of the graphical screen had found a way to make systems—graphical, computational—sit in the service of an American ideal of autonomy, creativity, expressivity. Already, then, when Gaines started working with systems in the 1970s, they were not, as the rhetoric of conceptual art often frames it, antithetical to those ideals.[30] The system of the graphical screen was an environment and engine of this change.

Individuality, Fungibility, Contiguity

So it is striking—especially within this larger history of how the raster and its arrayed pixels have played such a central role in the augmentation of the self—that Gaines's gridworks are each interested, in a few distinct ways, in forms of de- or nonindividuated life, life tethered and contiguous. In *Faces*, as in all of Gaines's other gridwork, the third image in the triptychs of his series gathers up previous images, accumulating silhouettes of the bodies of people or objects. In a sense, the third image simply gathers each of the individual images from the second image in one place, on one plane. But the third image also performs a counting function: counting off the number of bodies in the series up to that point. The series *Faces* accumulates silhouettes of faces. *Falling Leaves* accumulates the total leaves fallen from a single tree over time. *Motion: Trisha Brown Dance* accumulates outlines of single images extracted from the flow of a dance, bodies frozen in space, although retaining a (nonindexical) trace of movement in their ultimate accumulation. *Faces 1: Identity Politics* (2018) collects the outlines of faces of recognized thinkers, from Aristotle to bell hooks, so that by the twelfth image the famous identities intermingle nearly to indistinction. In his move to systems, Gaines was not just siding against expression, as is often said; he was moving away from, or at least working to radically expand our sense of and the possibilities of the individual—whether an individual pixel or the singular user. A gathering, something always just more than one, veering away from *one* but not toward more defined forms of the collective, a collective that is contiguous but never unified: this is where Gaines's transpositions from one representational system to another, his system aesthetics, most insistently and consistently lead.

Falling Leaves consists of sixteen sets of triptychs (figure 4.2). The driving idea, the system that structures the work, is to document the rate at which leaves fall from the same tree. In the series, each triptych's first image gives color photographs of the tree documented in successive states of abscission. The second image transposes that photograph into a line drawing of the tree that proceeds mostly heedless of the grid. Grid squares are activated by Gaines's familiar numbering system but here represent leaves on the tree—one number to one leaf—rather than component parts of a drawing. In the final image is the same line drawing of the tree, but the activated grid squares now graph where the leaves have fallen from the tree over time, with colors articulating vertical strata of leaves, but also documenting the intervals at which Gaines visited the tree. The final image of the triptych, in other words, aggregates leaves as a function of time (figure 4.3).

But in all the gridwork series, including *Faces* and *Falling Leaves*, there is a different kind of collectivity implied in the second image. The first image, a photograph, pictures a specific face or tree: that very one. But the system

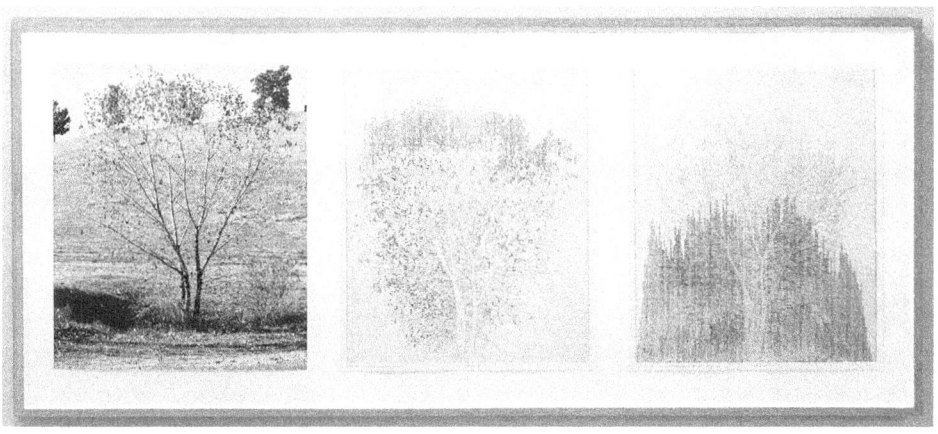

FIGURE 4.2. Charles Gaines, *Falling Leaves: Set #12*, 1979. Photograph, ink on paper, three sheets. Framed 30 × 70 in / 76.2 × 177.8 cm. © Charles Gaines. Courtesy of the artist and Hauser and Wirth.

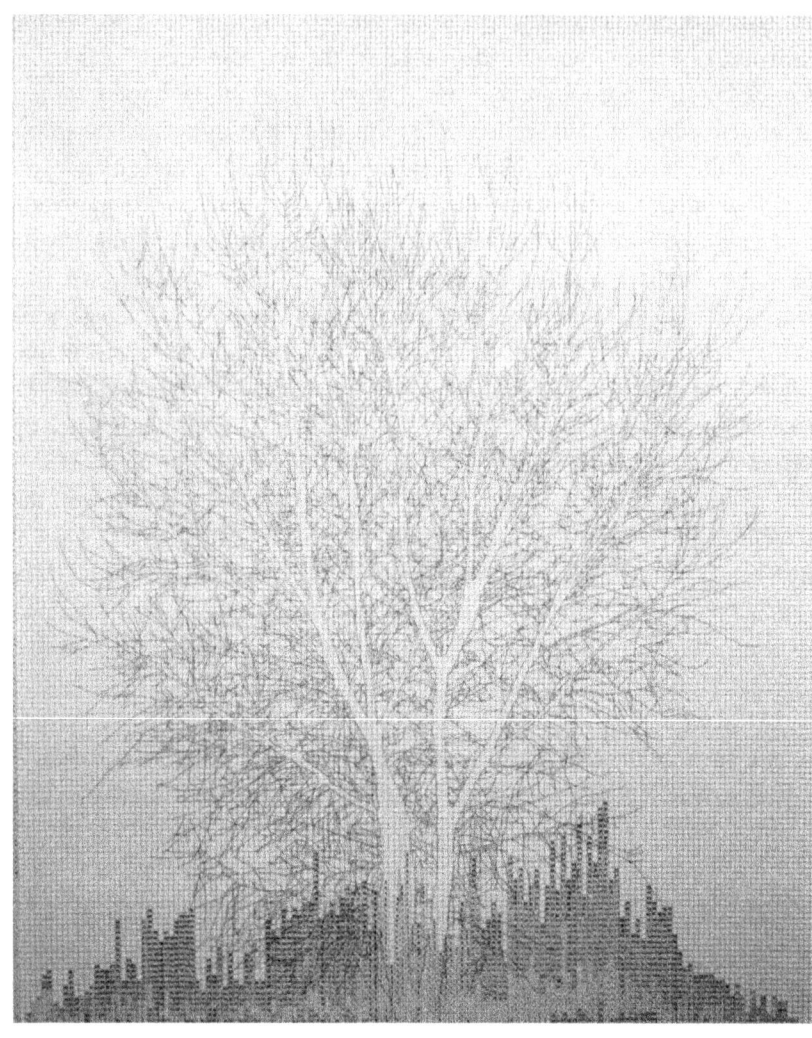

FIGURE 4.3. Charles Gaines, *Falling Leaves: Set #6* (detail), 1979. Photograph, ink on paper, three sheets. © Charles Gaines. Courtesy of the artist and Hauser and Wirth.

for producing subsequent images of *that* person, that tree, for transposing that image from a photograph to a numerical tabulation within an enabling raster, could equally well produce such an image of any person or thing. The system, in a sense, is designed to perform just this function—that is precisely its systematicity. In this way, the tree and the singular face, seen in and for their particularity, generate a collective, are already collectives once they enter the system of Gaines's gridworks. This means that the action of the system on personhood (or thinghood) here is not to render it anonymous or faceless as in the Adornian nightmare of modernity—Gaines graphs the particular shape of *that* tree, *that* branch, *that* nose, *that* hair—but fungible. In other words, systems thinking here manifests as a way of materializing bodies and objects that recognizes their individuality—even documents and underscores it, in the *Faces* series' reference to mugshots—but does so in a form constituted precisely to let anyone, anything, anybody step into that space (the mugshot performs the same function). While the graphical computer screen would aim to cater to the singular individual, set free into an unconstrained field and feeling of her own subjective expression, Gaines's graphical fields interpolate anyone whatsoever, a fact that is as true of their production (once the system is established, anyone could, in the theory of the system itself, replicate it) as it is of their subjects.

Both of these previous forms of collectivity—that of the aggregated pixel field and that of the fungible object—are both produced and encompassed by a third form: what Gaines called contiguity.[31] He entrains the images in each series by way of a thematic or morphological unit (trees, faces), and the images in each triptych by way of a numericized part/whole extension that starts with the source photo and circuits its way through to the final image, in which all the images in the series up to that point get aggregated. In this way, Gaines makes his systems generate accumulation, contiguity, or in a different but related langue, indebtedness. The point of his transpositional systems often seems to be these contiguities themselves more than any image produced.

Motion: Trisha Brown Dance doesn't conform to the patterned three-part structure of the triptych, but there is nonetheless the same accumulative procedure, slowly dissolving the named body into a system, a motion study that records the dancer's (Brown's) movements but that could equally well record any movements whatsoever once the system is established. To initiate the work, Gaines took a photograph every three seconds of Trisha Brown performing one minute of her *Son of Gone Fishin'* (1981).[32] Gaines then asked Brown to select images from the larger set for inclusion in the final work.

There are two registers of images in each set of the sixteen-set series of *Motion*: twenty-four smaller, rastered images proceeding horizontally across the top and four larger images across the bottom. In the lower register, the two leftmost images are color photographs chosen "algorithmically" from the complete set: the rightmost image is a plotted enlargement—or, as given in Gaines's title, a "blow up"—of one of the small drawings on top, and the gridded image to that image's left is another accumulative window, with figures adding up over the course of the series of sixteen.[33] Again, the rastered images are composed of numbers recorded into grid squares (although this time, the numbering system that orders the smaller pages proceeds from 1 to 52 moving left to right and from A to 2P bottom to top). Colors code the different poses as they gather. As in many of Gaines's works, bodies accumulate across the rastered upper register, culminating in the final image to the far right.

Here the accumulation doesn't follow the linear logic of the system's transpositional procedure. Instead, it takes its form from two interlinked sets of choices: Brown's selections from the total set of photographs, and Gaines's ordering of those selections according to the chronology of the dance. So while bodies accumulate, both layered and intercalated, in the rightmost image of the upper register, they do so in some relation to Brown's selections, themselves constrained and enabled by Gaines's photographs. Choice, a kind of subjective emanation and constituent part of individuality, finds a place within the terms that shape the work's form, but is never far from a set of constraints—invoking Turner's democratic subject and seeming to cancel that subject at the same time. Brown chooses, but only after Gaines has made his photographs. Gaines photographs, but only at predetermined intervals. The system here, and in all of Gaines's gridwork, seems less about making systems antithetical to expression and more about producing a series of enchainments where no part floats free (as generator or product, author or final artwork), where all parts move in contiguity with those that proceed and follow.

Unlike in other of Gaines's gridworks, the bodies here are all Brown's, recorded in different states of movement. In a sense, Gaines's system renders Brown's performance, and Brown herself, as the generator of that performance, as so many overlapping windows, each a unit of movement, of arrest, seeming in the end to consolidate the self projected into that graphical environment, unifying that body's varied permutations only in and through multiplicity. Here, among all of Gaines's gridworks, the graphical screen with its accommodation and aggrandizement of the individual, its division of the self into units of labor all of which appear to be emanations of that self's expressive interiority, its use of windows as a way expanding the space in which work can happen, seems perhaps most disconcertingly near.

The machinery of aggregation in all of Gaines's gridwork flirts with the danger felt by so many in the 1960s and 1970s, documented in Turner's work and elsewhere, of the human-turned-automaton, a true, mimetic product of mechanized factory labor and early IBM-style corporatism.[34] This is sometimes expressed as a fear of anonymity, of becoming nameless.[35] But given Gaines's commitment to transposing the quiddity of his objects, anonymity is not the threat that looms in Gaines's work. In the lamination of systems to the threat of fungibility, Gaines's work forces a reconsideration of the longer histories of white anxiety that coursed beneath various postwar efforts to reassemble personhood inside the new universalism of systems thinking. Taken on its own and somewhat ahistorically, the fungible self has been called a neoliberal modality, in which selves become interchangeable within an overall atmosphere of shared inequality, which in turn makes competition into society's dominant collectivizing force.[36] This, in fact, is exactly why some queer theorists have found in fungible personhood a source of cautious optimism, a new politics of negativity in which proprietary individuality might be dissolved in a solution of general equivalence.[37] But seen within a longer history of commoditized labor, fungibility isn't just about a general equivalence. It also involves an asymmetrical structure of intersubjectivity in which white subjects are marked as white by their endowed capacity to inhabit the subject position of the other, the Black American—a capacity that is just as available to avowed racists as it is to liberal sympathizers.[38] Saidiya Hartman documents this component of fungibility in relation to human subjects traded as commodities.[39] Key to this quietly brutal mode of subjectivization is to deny all points of contact, of touch, between subject and other: whether existential, ontological, or political. The violent intersubjectivity of human fungibility does not violate this sequestration; it enforces it. In order to inhabit someone's subject position, whether through violence or sympathy, one has to feel oneself utterly separate from them, linked, in fact, only by the fickle bonds of sympathy, which is not a linking at all but a delinking, fully asymmetrical, a denial of contiguity at a deep, even ontological level.[40]

Putting it this way helps us to see another fear being warded off by and in the graphical field of the computer screen and elsewhere. Beyond the fear of authoritarianism (Turner's focus and the express focus of so much liberal postwar anxiety across public and private sectors) or the anonymity of the crowd (an early modern fear recast by Turner in the postwar period as a fear of the brainwashed crowd, the subjects of authoritarian aesthetics), this specter of the fungible human hearkens not to the white shirt and blue tie of the IBM worker, a context of subsumed individuality, but to slavery, a context of stolen life.[41]

As Frank B. Wilderson III stresses, to have one's individuality subsumed is to have already been granted, in a framework of universal rights, the privilege of individuality.[42] One's individual rights can be violated only because they existed in the first place, having been granted a priori to some, precisely as a way to differentiate those who were to be included in universal personhood and those whose exemption (not exclusion, not alienation) from it was to set off and define those rights for their bearers. In its focus on the augmented individual intellect—the creative self working within, but not subsumed by, informational networks—the graphical field should therefore be seen as one part of a far larger and longer defense against what Hartman calls "the fungibility of the captive body."[43] The fungibility of the commodity makes the captive body an abstract and empty vessel vulnerable to the projection of others' feelings, ideas, desires, and values; and, as property, the dispossessed body of the enslaved is the surrogate for the master's body since it guarantees his disembodied universality and acts as the sign of his power and dominion.[44]

Turner, in his two books on the relationship between twentieth-century media and American democracy, tells the history of what are, in effect but also by design, efforts to build spaces to foster the creation of a strong (and, we can now see more clearly, white male) individuality as a bulwark against certain strong forms of collectivity: against the authoritarian mass, yes, but also—lying entirely outside of Turner's history and transforming its terms—against the feared and projected fungibility of blackness. The computer's graphical interface was one of these spaces of retreat and defense. But to remove the assumption of universal personhood in this history is to radically change the valence of attempts to set the individual against the collective within the context of systems and the systematization of life. This is why Gaines's arrangement of the raster for and against the assembly of a fungible collective is important. The raster of the graphical field, like those of Gaines's gridworks, reconfigures creative labor in its relation to personhood and the possibilities of the creative self. The graphical field was designed to produce a form of the individual that was, on the one hand, well adapted to navigating a world turned into an information network, while on the other, able to forge a strong mode of individuality precisely in those spaces. Abetted by the proxemics of the mouse and cursor, set free within the seemingly open fields of the graphical display—its raster transforming the apparently undemocratic rigidity of the command line interface into the democratic playground of the graphical display's open spaces—the ideal subject of graphical display systems forged a mode of creative individuality not sapped but buoyed by the vastness of an information network.[45]

In Gaines's denaturing of this graphical field, a kind of constraint is emphasized, and into that constrained opening comes an assembly, bodies arrayed together, mutually interfering, indistinct. It was as if Gaines saw the dangers of a certain renewed rhetoric of freedom, ascendant both in civil rights movements and in new technocultures—saw it, perhaps, as a technologized version of what Hartman calls "burdened individuality," referring to the freedoms that were granted to enslaved people after emancipation precisely in order to extend their subjugation, this time under the yoke of personal responsibility.[46] In the wake of emancipation and its vaunted freedoms, Hartman says, "the exercise of free will, quite literally, was inextricable from guilty infractions, criminal misdeeds, punishable transgressions, and an elaborate micropenality of everyday life."[47] Call it burdened or call it augmented, this false promise of freedom, transformed but never abated, has left a deep scar across the present tense.[48]

The history of black life in the United States reveals the lie behind both sides of the antimony often constructed to make sense of systems in general and computational contexts in particular: on the one side, the system, the machine, the inhuman, all of which have been used to entrap, incarcerate, and immiserate black life from the Atlantic slave trade until now; on the other, freedom, the human, the subjective, the expressive, all of which have also long been used—often by people who feel themselves sympathetic to equality and civil rights—to circumscribe and burden black life by trapping it within the form of the expressive individual, thereby erasing, even seeming to solve the structural history of racism.

This progressive freedom as manifest in the freedom of the artist's hand set loose from social norms, the freedom of the blank canvas or the blank graphical screen, the trained freedom of the postwar knowledge worker, the authorial freedom of the conceptualist working in service of the idea—Gaines wanted none of it. But neither could he simply reject it. The threats to freedom were real, both intra- and interpolitically, among his fellow Black artists as well as within various technocratic think tanks that established the political milieu for his thinking about labor and its environments.[49] If freedom imagined a particular form of collectivity built around, on the one hand, autonomy galvanized in opposition to the threat of alienation, and, on the other, the threat of homogenization, Gaines would make his graphical fields produce forms of collectivity based in indebtedness, contact, contiguity; in indistinction and accumulation.[50] Within the long history of false promises and "burdened individuality," these qualities of Gaines's collectives need not be understood as states of subjection chosen nihilistically or pessimistically, but as tactics for standing down, for ceasing the escalation of the human into more and more powerful technocracies of freedom, self-possession, control.

Gaines's systems are a machine for producing contiguity more than they are an imposed logic or depersonalizing structure. Contiguity, in this sense, short-circuits—rather than negates or opposes—or more simply, just doesn't believe in the smooth interior-to-exterior relay of expressivity: what Gaines, echoing Kant, has called the "free play of meanings."[51] Gaines reorganizes the field of his images as rasters, as subtly deformed graphical interfaces, precisely in order to emphasize and extend contiguity, contact, and self-limitation.[52] The selves and things that show up in Gaines's rasters, via system or the projections of viewership, do so as tethered, indebted. Everything that appears in one of Gaines's gridworks owes its existence, in precisely that form, to another image in the series or the triptych. Key here, especially for the ways in which Gaines's work addresses racial politics after expressivity and its associated modes of representational politics, is the fact that this contiguity is how Gaines supplements—deforms but doesn't negate or erase—the fungibility one sees in the way his systems dissolve the singularity of particular selves. The move here isn't the dramatic one from fungibility to freedom, as though any form of individuality were going to defend against ongoing forms of racializing violence, as though individuality in all of its updates, including the graphical one, hasn't been the very instrument of that violence. Gaines makes the quieter move to contiguity, an avowed collective form that sees selfhood as the problem, not the solution, and so stresses contact without communication, indebtedness without (self-)possession, transposition without representation. Fungibility-contiguity is a different problem than alienation-individuality. Gaines wrests both Conceptualism and the graphical interface out of the latter to show their entanglements with the former. The latter is a white history in search of a new universalizing principle; the former is a black history, which is to say, an American history. If the new subjects of the graphical computer screen were to evade (and so invoke) the threat of fungibility in their exercise of a renewed form of creative freedom, Gaines's graphical systems would raise that threat, not to overturn it exactly but to show the role that a certain enabling rhetoric of individuality and freedom has always played in both the racializing violence of fungible personhood as well as in white, predominantly liberal attempts to define itself against those threats.

NOTES

1 Margo Natalie Crawford, *Black Post-blackness: The Black Arts Movement and Twenty-First-Century Aesthetics* (Champaign: University of Illinois Press, 2017).

2 Romare Bearden chaired a public conversation among older and younger prominent Black artists at just this historical crux: Romare Bearden, Sam Gilliam Jr., Richard Hunt, Jacob Lawrence, Tom Lloyd, William Williams, and Hale Woodruff, "The Black Artist in America: A Symposium," *Metropolitan Museum of Art Bulletin* 27, no. 5 (1969): 245–61. Darby English's book on 1971 reflects on this juncture. Darby English, *1971: A Year in the Life of Color* (Chicago: University of Chicago Press, 2016).

3 Alexander G. Weheliye, "Engendering Phonographies: Sonic Technologies of Blackness," *Small Axe* 18, no. 2 (2014): 180–90; Katherine McKittrick, "Mathematics Black Life," *Black Scholar* 44, no. 2 (2014): 16–28; Bernard Stiegler, *Technics and Time 1: The Fault of Epimetheus*, trans. Richard Beardsworth and George Collins (Stanford, CA: Stanford University Press, 1998); and Bernard Stiegler, *Technics and Time 2: Disorientation*, trans. Stephen Barker (Stanford, CA: Stanford University Press, 2008).

4 I want to acknowledge here especially the work of American Artist. American Artist, "Black Gooey Universe," *Unbag*, no. 2 (January 2018), http://unbag.net/issue-2-end/black-gooey-universe/; and Kris Cohen, "Abstraction, the Irreconcilable: An Interview with American Artist," *Open Set*, January 2019, http://www.open-set.com/krcohen/essay-clusters/abstraction-the-irreconcilable-an-interview-with-american-artist/.

5 *Gridwork* is the Studio Museum's term. Naima J. Keith, ed., *Charles Gaines: Gridwork 1974–1989* (New York: Studio Museum in Harlem, 2014).

6 The circular logic here is an artifact (probably direct, certainly indirect) of cybernetic thought. See N. Katherine Hayles, *How We Became Posthuman: Virtual Bodies in Cybernetics, Literature, and Informatics* (Chicago: University of Chicago Press, 1999); and Seb Franklin, *Control: Digitality as Cultural Logic* (Cambridge, MA: MIT Press, 2015).

7 Charles Gaines, "Reconsidering Metaphor/Metonymy: Art and the Suppression of Thought," *Art Lies: A Contemporary Art Journal*, no. 64 (2009).

8 Charles Gaines to Sol and Carol LeWitt, 1988, in Keith, *Charles Gaines*, 155–56.

9 The titling convention for Gaines's gridworks used here is to italicize the individual works in a series (there are sixteen in *Faces*), as well as the name Gaines gives to the series itself. Here, *Faces* (1978–79) is the series name, and the sixteen triptychs that compose that series are each given titles in italics.

10 See the exhibition literature for *Charles Gaines* at Paula Cooper Gallery (May 3–June 23, 2018); and Ellen Tani, "The Face Is a Politics," in Keith, *Charles Gaines*, 57–63.

11 See, for instance, Tani, "The Face Is a Politics."

12 Stephen Best, *None Like Us: Blackness, Belonging, Aesthetic Life* (Durham, NC: Duke University Press, 2018); Cedric J. Robinson, *Black Marxism: The Making of the Black Radical Tradition* (Chapel Hill: University of North Carolina Press, 2000).

13 Nizan Shaked, *The Synthetic Proposition: Conceptualism and the Political Referent in Contemporary Art* (Manchester: Manchester University Press, 2017), 17.

14 Jacob Gaboury stresses, rightly I think, that computer graphics are broadly nonrepresentational, not fundamentally based in images or pictures. I take up this important claim only obliquely here. Jacob Gaboury, "The Random-Access Image: Memory and the History of the Computer Screen," *Grey Room*, no. 70 (2018): 24–53.

15 For more design-oriented approaches that are far more attentive to the particularities and metaphorics of the graphical user interface, see Brenda Laurel and S. Joy Mountford, *The Art of Human-Computer Interface Design* (Reading, MA: Addison-Wesley, 1990); and Helen Armstrong, *Digital Design Theory: Readings from the Field* (New York: Princeton Architectural Press, 2016).

16 Fred Turner, *From Counterculture to Cyberculture: Stewart Brand, the Whole Earth Network, and the Rise of Digital Utopianism* (Chicago: University of Chicago Press, 2006); Fred Turner, *The Democratic Surround: Multimedia and American Liberalism from World War II to the Psychedelic Sixties* (Chicago: University of Chicago Press, 2013).

17 Douglas C. Engelbart, "Special Considerations of the Individual as a User, Generator, and Retriever of Information," *American Documentation* 12, no. 2 (1961): 121–25.

18 Douglas C. Engelbart, "Toward High-Performance Knowledge Workers," OAC '82 *Digest: Proceedings of the* AFIPS *Office Automation Conference* (April 1982): 279–90.

19 This demonstration was performed at the Association for Computing Machinery and the Institute of Electrical and Electronics Engineers (ACM/IEEE) Computer Society's Fall Joint Computer Conference, December 9, 1968, San Francisco. It can be viewed at "Firsts: The Demo," Doug Engelbart Institute, accessed January 24, 2019, http://www.dougengelbart.org/content/view/209/448/.

20 Douglas C. Engelbart, "Introducing Our Thinkpiece on Man-Machine Communication Means and Automatic Physical Skill Training" (March 22, 1961), box 17, folder 7, Douglas C. Engelbart Papers, 1953–2005, Stanford University, Stanford, CA.

21 Engelbart, "Introducing Our Thinkpiece," 1.

22 Wendy Chun, *Control and Freedom: Power and Paranoia in the Age of Fiber Optics* (Cambridge, MA: MIT Press, 2006).

23 Douglas C. Engelbart, "Augmenting Human Intellect: A Conceptual Framework" (October 2, 1962), Summary Report, Stanford Research Institute, on Contract AF 49(638)-1024.

24 Gaboury, "The Random-Access Image," 34–35.

25 Thierry Bardini, *Bootstrapping: Douglas Engelbart, Coevolution, and the Origins of Personal Computing* (Stanford, CA: Stanford University Press, 2000).

26 For a kind of Frankfurt school critique but with optimism for the computer as a utopia, if only it is used correctly, see Neal Stephenson, *In the Beginning . . . Was the Command Line* (New York: Avon, 1999).

27 Turner, *The Democratic Surround.*

28 Chun, *Control and Freedom.*

29 I'm referring here to the literature on the emergence of the neoliberal subject. See, for instance, Wendy Brown, *Undoing the Demos: Neoliberalism's Stealth Revolution* (Cambridge, MA: MIT Press, 2015); and Michel Foucault, *The Birth of Biopolitics: Lectures at the Collège de France, 1978–1979*, trans. Graham Burchell (New York: Picador, 2008).

30 Shaked also works to dispel this misconception about Conceptual Art. Shaked, *The Synthetic Proposition.*

31 Gaines, "Reconsidering Metaphor/Metonymy."

32 *Son of Gone Fishin'* premiered on October 16, 1981, at the BAM Opera House, Brooklyn. This was Brown's first musical collaboration, with original music by Robert Ashley.

33 *Algorithmic* is Shaked's term, which she uses to distinguish Gaines's procedures from something random, which, in a mathematical sense, human actions can never be. Shaked, *The Synthetic Proposition*, 232.

34 Turner, *The Democratic Surround*; Andrew Ross, *No-Collar: The Humane Workplace and Its Hidden Costs* (New York: Basic Books, 2003); and Alan Liu, *The Laws of Cool: Knowledge Work and the Culture of Information* (Chicago: University of Chicago Press, 2004).

35 For a very different take on the anonymity that so vexed modernists of all stripes, see John Paul Ricco, "The Commerce of Anonymity," *Qui Parle: Critical Humanities and Social Sciences* 26, no. 1 (2017): 101–42.

36 See Aihwa Ong, *Neoliberalism as Exception: Mutations in Citizenship and Sovereignty* (Durham, NC: Duke University Press, 2006); and Lisa Duggan, *The Twilight of Equality? Neoliberalism, Cultural Politics, and the Attack on Democracy* (Boston: Beacon, 2003).

37 See Tom Roach, "Becoming Fungible: Queer Intimacies in Social Media," *Qui Parle: Critical Humanities and Social Sciences* 23, no. 2 (2015): 55–87; and Shannon Winnubst, "The Queer Thing about Neoliberal Pleasure: A Foucauldian Warning," *Foucault Studies* 14, no. 14 (2012): 79–97.

38 This asymmetrical structure is what Fred Turner's books never consider. See Orlando Patterson, *Slavery and Social Death: A Comparative Study* (Cambridge, MA: Harvard University Press, 1982); Saidiya V. Hartman, *Scenes of Subjection: Terror, Slavery, and Self-Making in Nineteenth-Century America* (New York: Oxford University Press, 1997); and Frank B. Wilderson III, *Red, White and Black: Cinema and the Structure of U.S. Antagonisms* (Durham, NC: Duke University Press, 2010).

39 Hartman, *Scenes of Subjection.*

40 On racializing ontologies, see Calvin L. Warren, *Ontological Terror: Blackness, Nihilism, and Emancipation* (Durham, NC: Duke University Press, 2018).

41 Fred Moten, *Stolen Life* (Durham, NC: Duke University Press, 2018).

42 Wilderson, *Red, White and Black.*

43 Hartman, *Scenes of Subjection*, 19.

44 Hartman, *Scenes of Subjection*, 19. Of course, white subjects have never been truly subject to such fungibilty. But part of the very structure of fungibility being described by Hartman is the ever-present capacity to project oneself into the subject position of the Black other, to feel what they feel, to fear what they fear, to fear becoming what they are—a liberal subject position that purchases empathy at the cost of obliterating the actual subjectivity of blackness, of rendering it utterly useless, even for its own uplift.

45 Alexander Galloway, *The Interface Effect* (Cambridge: Polity, 2012).

46 Hartman, *Scenes of Subjection*, 115–24.

47 Hartman, *Scenes of Subjection*, 125.

48 Christina Sharpe, *In the Wake: On Blackness and Being* (Durham, NC: Duke University Press, 2016).

49 Derek Conrad Murray, *Queering Post-Black Art: Artists Transforming African-American Identity after Civil Rights*, International Library of Modern and Contemporary Art 30 (London: I. B. Tauris, 2016); and Darby English, *How to See a Work of Art in Total Darkness* (Cambridge, MA: MIT Press, 2007).

50 Gaines's terms for the freedom he wanted to resist was metaphor; the contiguity he set out to produce he called metonymy. Gaines addresses this metonymy/metaphor distinction most directly in Gaines, "Reconsidering Metaphor/Metonymy."

51 Gaines, "Reconsidering Metaphor/Metonymy."

52 For a different take on the raster as a mode of picture making, see Richard Shiff, "Photographic Soul," in *Where Is the Photograph?*, ed. David Green (London: Gardners, 2003), 95–112.

5

Light and Space as Institutional Critique

DAWNA SCHULD

In 1971, the Los Angeles County Museum of Art mounted *Art and Technology*, the culminating exhibition of a five-year, multipronged program of the same name. The museum had a limited collection and a brief history, having been established only in 1961, but its board of trustees represented the film, plastics, aerospace, and defense industries that had defined midcentury Los Angeles and propelled its economy.[1] Recognizing that the present strengths of the institution rested more in its administration than with its collections, the curator Maurice Tuchman proposed a project that would "provide the necessary meeting ground for some eminent contemporary artists with sophisticated technological personnel and resources."[2] To promote collaboration between art and industry (and absent any concrete notion of what the ensuing art might look like), Tuchman relied on the social status of his supporters on and off the board (most importantly that of arts advocate Dorothy Chandler, wife of *Los Angeles Times* publisher Otis Chandler); on the reputations of the artists; and, lastly, on the museum's authority as a public arts establishment. By the time the exhibition opened, however, few of the artists associated with the program had work to show, many had dropped out entirely, and criticism of the entire endeavor was mounting. The project's most forceful contemporary critics concerned themselves first with its corporatization of art (one critic calling the entire venture a "fascist game" and a "boondoggle") and second with the glaring exclusion of women and artists of color.[3] These criticisms were warranted and timely, and they raise an important question: To whom is a public museum administration accountable? To the critics, control presumably resided with the program's industrial sponsors, while artists had little agency apart from deciding whether to participate and choosing a collaborator. Members of the museum-going public—mentioned only in passing—were merely unsuspecting accessories to an "experiment in patronage."[4]

For his part, Jack Burnham offered a more nuanced, insider's assessment, noting that most critics had overlooked the curator's (positive) role as facilitator. He observed that "Tuchman's strategies for meeting some tricky sociopolitical situations" amounted to the most interesting aspect of the project, and he described the curator as the program's "most skillful technologist."[5] Burnham's reference to "strategies" is revealing: one does not strategize with art objects but with people. Tuchman was a close reader of Burnham's writings and a systems aesthetics advocate. He recounted his own nimble coordination of disparate interests—the board of trustees, corporations, and artists—in his introduction to the exhibition "catalog," in reality a "report" that reveals in documentary detail the false starts, missteps, and miscommunications that characterize such an ambitious project but that are seldom aired in public.[6] Burnham deemed the published report the second most interesting aspect of the project after the curator's machinations, and the exhibition a distant third. On this last point Tuchman agreed; if he had been acting strategically, however, the strategy was an open-ended one. Indeed, the curator did not and could not anticipate what he himself recognized as the program's most significant achievements: these were neither his own, nor the publication's, but the somewhat intangible outcomes of a program-sponsored collaboration between the Los Angeles–based artists Robert Irwin and James Turrell, and Ed Wortz, a psychologist subcontracted to the National Aeronautics and Space Administration.[7]

Assistant curator Jane Livingston called the collaboration "the preeminent example under Art and Technology of an endeavor based on a directly systems-conscious premise."[8] If that is the case, then systems-consciousness is primarily a biological concern, a proposition elided in technocentric critical and historical accounts of the Art and Technology project.[9] The trio produced no art objects for the 1971 exhibition; rather, they conducted a series of psychological tests pertaining to the perceptual fringes of sensory deprivation that involved soundless anechoic chambers, undifferentiated light fields—or *Ganzfelds*—and alpha conditioning.[10] Unquestionably, these "technologies of experience" emerge from the system so despised by Art and Technology's critics and evoke associations with mind-control tactics and paranoiac fantasies of administrative collusion.[11] But the experiments did not take place in the museum and they produced no official findings, so there was little about them to attract public interest, let alone criticism.[12] Absent specific goals on the part of the principal investigators, questions of personal agency came to the fore, namely, can self-awareness be fostered through perceptual conditioning; and what is to be gained in examining our own perceptions, in seeing ourselves seeing? For such an ill-defined project, the effects were immediate and far-reaching: the Art and Technology experiments prompted a multidisciplinary symposium on habitability in the built environment in 1970 and, significantly, advanced a phenomenological turn in California minimalism already under way. Tuchman's sociopolitical maneuverings— not only regarding the Irwin-Turrell-Wortz collaboration, but for most of the Art and Technology projects—took place mostly behind the scenes and were made public only after the fact and in narrative form (via the report, which he edited). It remained for others elsewhere to manage the pitfalls and consequences of implementing technologies of experience not as loosely-framed psychological experiments but as art exhibited within establishment institutions such as the Museum of Modern Art in New York and the Tate Gallery in London.[13] New to both the concept and the reality of art as environment (or environment as art), visitors to these museums became unwitting test subjects; they occupied a shared physical space, but they embodied social differences, with disparate, even conflicting expectations. Provoked into self-consciousness by the disorientations of perceptual art, visitors were unable and unwilling to remain passive observers; a newly participatory role lent them an agency that relied only on perception rather than on social or economic status. At the same time, their willingness to submit to such disorientations depended on accepting the museum's authority to arbitrate artistic significance and to ensure bodily safety. This chapter examines the paradoxical outcomes of raising body awareness within an art institution constrained by behavioral custom and aesthetic ideals.

As early as 1966, James Turrell and Doug Wheeler were experimenting with the perceptual effects of projected and distributed light in enclosed spaces, while Robert Irwin and Larry Bell were each manufacturing ethereal objects whose salience depended on the contingencies of light and, most importantly, viewer perception and attention. Commonly referred to as "light and space" art, this work is more aptly referred to as "phenomenal art" so as to foreground the embodied, situated nature of the work—being and circumstance in tandem.[14] These early projects doubtless motivated Irwin's and Turrell's interest in the Art and Technology program. Since the artists sought to control the physical conditions of exhibition (through lighting, surface color and texture, sound-proofing, and so on), they needed a resourceful curator who was not only able to procure materials and oversee fabrication but who could also act as liaison between diverse parties involved in the work's realization and mainte-nance. In other words, they required what Burnham saw in Tuchman: some-one with a comprehensive familiarity with the sociopolitical mechanisms of the art institution and a willingness and ability to challenge, circumvent, or subvert them. In 1970, at the Tate Gallery in London, Michael Compton volunteered for the part when he organized an exhibition of environmental works by Irwin, Wheeler, and Bell.

There is little to suggest that the light and space artists sought to raise po-litical awareness with their work; rather, they aimed to foster perceptual self-awareness and, by extension, viewer agency. Through careful preparation of the gallery environment, they could anticipate how visitors might respond intuitively to the work but, like behaviorist psychologists, they were loath to prescribe a specific course of action, as this could contaminate results. Herein lies the latent anarchy in phenomenal art: the "purity" of the experience de-pends on a refusal to signify, but this also means that interpretation is left to individual participants. Nested together in this situation are two orders of systems consciousness: a first-order awareness of playing a physical, percep-tual role within the open system of the artwork, along with a freedom to in-terpret its meaning; and a second-order awareness of how the closed system of the institution comprises multiple roles performed by diverse bodies in a shared space. This second-order consciousness of the conscious awareness of others, as Compton would discover, has the potential to reinforce systemic integrity—but also to disrupt it. The pristine minimalism of the work belied its potential to upend accepted norms for administrative jurisdiction and vis-itor behavior. One can either preserve the integrity of the system or the purity of the experience, but not both. The curtailment of disruption necessitates a form of systems hygiene, akin to the protocols imposed in scientific labora-tories but eschewed by Irwin, Turrell, and Wortz during the Art and Tech-nology experiments in favor of openness. In a museum context, exhibition essays, wall signs, and audio tours instruct visitors in the "correct" manner of behavior, while ropes, guards, and entry fees ensure that only the "correct" visitors enter.

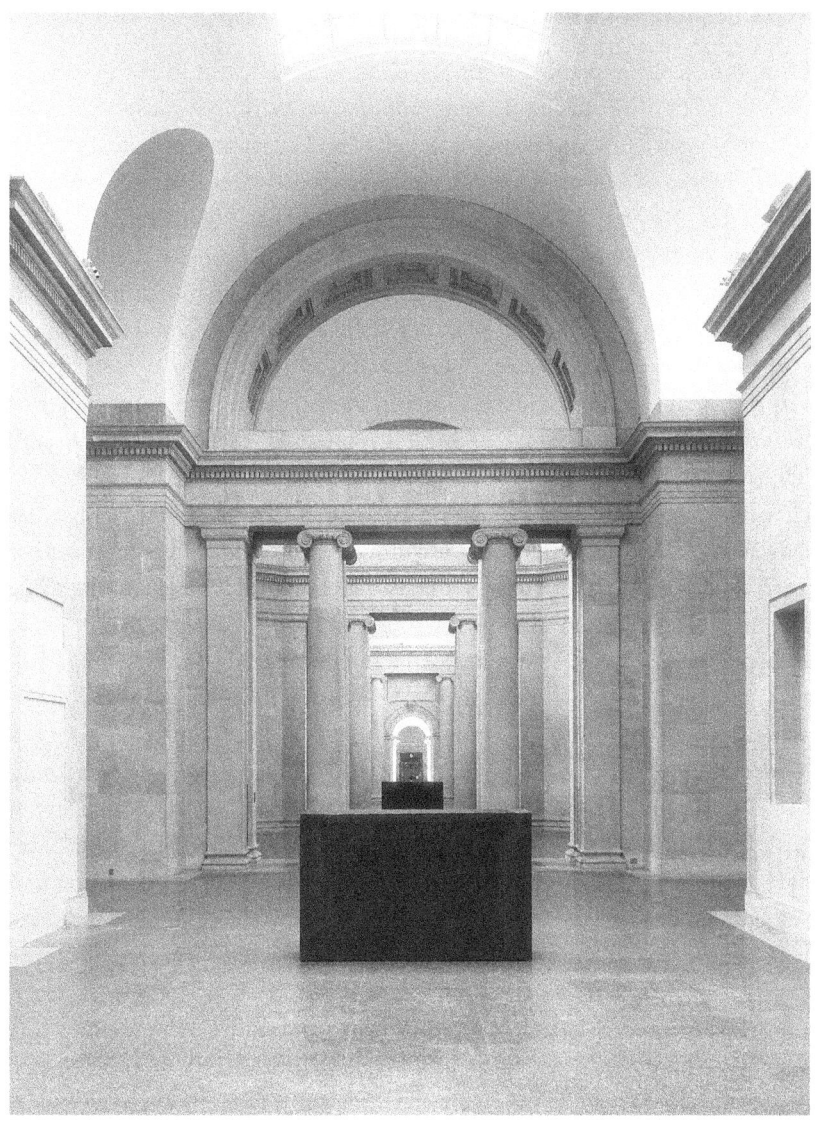

FIGURE 5.1. Duveen Gallery, Tate Britain, London, 2014. Photo © Tate.

Three Los Angeles Artists

Compton's skills as a socio-technologist were already put to the test in the process of finding space for contemporary art within a conservative institution. As a non-American, nationally funded institution, the Tate was relatively free of associations with the corporate system that drew such ire toward the Art and Technology program, but the art establishment in London had history and entrenched class consciousness on its side. In 1968, Compton, newly appointed to run the contemporary exhibitions program at the Tate Gallery, had received a Churchill Fellowship to spend three months traveling in the United States. There, he was introduced to Walter Hopps, former curator at the Pasadena Museum of Art, where James Turrell's projection pieces had been exhibited the previous year.[15] The projections were light-formed geometrical illusions that dissolved the dimensionality of architectural space by merging it with perceptual contingency.[16] Though the Tate board of trustees did not approve his proposal to purchase of one of Turrell's artworks, Compton was nonetheless committed to exhibiting these and other American environmental sculptures in the gallery.[17] In late 1969, he approached Turrell, along with contemporaries Irwin and Bell, to participate in an exhibition of their work—in what was an unforeseen gap in the exhibition schedule, in May 1970—that would be titled *Three Artists from Los Angeles*.[18] Turrell backed out of the project almost immediately, and Doug Wheeler was substituted, so that the three Los Angeles artists became Irwin, Bell, and Wheeler. Compton's arrangement for the exhibition in such a hasty and seemingly extemporary manner is a subtle comment on the uncertain status of contemporary art in the Tate Gallery's exhibition program and revelatory of his own systems awareness. He later confessed that much of the more experimental work he brought in during this period would not have survived the approval process with the board of trustees and that therefore he occasionally put forward appealing and overly ambitious exhibition proposals, expecting them to fall through so as to free up time, funds, and space for contemporary work.[19] Contemporary art exhibitions were a relatively new aspect of the gallery's remit and were considered an ancillary concern relative to the development and maintenance of the permanent collection. As Compton put it, contemporary art was seen by several members of the board as both "contaminating and contaminable."[20] In keeping with this viral metaphor, the temporary exhibitions were quarantined by means of false walls, which allowed for flexibility in staging diverse exhibitions but which also obscured the stately stone columns of the Duveen Gallery and segregated the canonized permanent collection from the not-yet-sanctioned work of living artists.[21] Because of the nature of the work included in the *Three Artists* installation, some segregation was also necessary: all three men were working with light, meaning that each installation required its own distinct space, separated by passageways and chicanes to keep the light in one area from interfering with that of another. Moreover, by embodying the effects of experiential art, visitors become its carriers, so that these encounters shaped their visit overall and those of others, whether positively, negatively, or even unconsciously. As Bell acknowledged in a later interview: "The truth is—a piece is never resolved—you know? A crucial aspect of any project is the fact that if the exhibition is of a transitory nature—the concept will be a transitory concern."[22]

Three Artists was the Tate Gallery's first presentation of art as experience. By manipulating and controlling dissolute, numinous, and elusive light, the artists produced a series of disorienting and perceptually provocative immersive experiences.[23] Accordingly, the project complicated the curator's traditional role as collections keeper. Engaging such work for a Tate exhibition significantly extended the gallery's purview as "National Gallery of the future" to exhibit, collect, and house significant objects by noteworthy artists.[24] Light and space art was speculative, dematerializing, untested, and open-ended. Though not completely unknown to London audiences, the reputations of Bell, Irwin, and Wheeler were hardly well-established. Viewers were both exhilarated and enervated by the physical challenges the works presented, especially those by Bell and Wheeler. Spectators no more, visitors occupied and embodied the work, so that their physicality, both threatened and threatening, became the focus of institutional safekeeping. The previously inviolable art object was now subject to alteration, damage, and even demolition. The numerous complaints and compromises that Compton negotiated before and during the exhibition—as revealed in written exchanges with the artists, museum authorities, and members of the public, as well as between museum staff and outside contractors—offered a preview of the subsequent debacle in 1971 when Robert Morris chose to stage new participatory work in lieu of a traditional retrospective.[25] The circumstances engendered by both exhibitions raised questions about the Tate's institutional mandate and responsibilities, the curator's accountability to the artist's vision, the presumptive age, class, education level, and responsibilities of museum visitors, and their personal comfort and safety.

For practical and ideological reasons, no installation shots were taken of any of the work. The accompanying publication—explicitly *not* a catalog

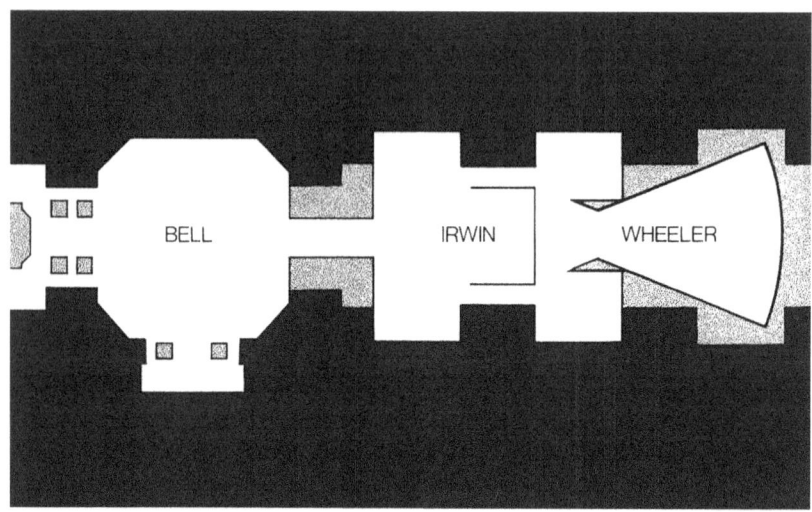

FIGURE 5.2. Exhibition plan for *Three Artists from Los Angeles*, May 5–31, 1970. Published in Michael Compton, *Larry Bell, Robert Irwin, Doug Wheeler* (London: Tate Gallery, 1970), n.p.

according to Compton—explains: "The exhibition will comprise three spaces in which three artists will have made their art. At the moment of writing we are not sure exactly what they will do—and we cannot know how what they will do will appear to us. Therefore we cannot attempt to help you to perceive it."[26] To further underscore this emphatic privileging of the viewer's immediate experience, no photos were taken during the exhibition either, and even Compton's publishing of the exhibition plan alongside the text was achieved under protest from the artists. In the words of Irwin (who was most adamant on this score), "Reproducing [the] plan is to give it value."[27] Irwin's concern with this detail reflects a broader distrust of information and its capacity for misdirecting attention and infecting innate, embodied knowledge. Compton was similarly wary of information's capacity to contaminate experience, and he offered only a curatorial caveat by way of guidance for the visitor. Noting that what he had written was not an introduction but "an attempt to think around my reaction to these artists and their work," Compton emphatically stated: "*It is not intended to be read until you have seen the exhibition.*"[28] This was neither elucidating nor reassuring, and the visitor who committed the unintended error of perusing the text beforehand was thus faced with the implicit and paradoxical directive to unlearn what she had just read. Given the constraints of Compton's ad hoc exhibition schedule and the contingent nature of the work itself, neither the curator nor the artists knew precisely how the work would appear, nor how much it would cost, let alone how it would be received. Having conceded the role of interpreter to the visitor, Compton set in motion a series of events that would shift how the institution's responsibility vis-à-vis both artist and viewing public was understood—from a position of tacit authority to one of active negotiation.

The exhibition was navigated in sequence, beginning with Bell's installation, moving through the Irwin gallery, ending with Wheeler's environment, and then revisited in reverse to exit. Bell was (and is) best known for a series of cubes (1964–69) made of glass treated with vaporized metals in a vacuum chamber. Minimal in presence and form, they are also perceptually inconstant, being at once transparent and reflective. But by 1970, Bell was in a more experimental mood. He had participated in a group study of "applied perception" under the aegis of a NASA-sponsored project, an offshoot of Irwin and Wortz's Art and Technology collaboration with Turrell, that culminated in the First National Symposium on Habitability of Environments in May 1970 in Venice Beach, California.[29] In that context, Bell expanded his interest in the spatial contingencies of visual perception, building out environments in his studio that were intensely disorienting, such as, for example, a shadowless room. In one such experiment, instantiated as part of the 1969 *Spaces* exhibition at the Museum of Modern Art (MoMA) and a precursor to the Tate installation, Bell wanted to create a "light trap."[30] *New York Times* art critic Grace Glueck described the experience as one where the visitor "can lose his spatial perception completely."[31] The Tate situation was similarly disorienting and elusive. A spiral-shaped pathway filled the gallery, which was darkened and sound-dampened by black cloth that covered the floor, walls, and ceiling. The space was entirely unlit, apart from aluminized Pyrex tubes suspended above the fabric ceiling that caught light projected from outside the space and then refracted it at oblique angles, so that as the viewer negotiated the darkened labyrinth she might begin to detect filtered lines of light floating before and above her. As Bell recalled: "The idea was that you stepped into the room, and when your eyes accustomed themselves somewhat to the darkness, the only thing you'd see was the line way at the back. As you stepped in and moved toward the line, you were moving away from the light source—so the line appeared to keep moving away from you in direct proportion to how far away you were from the light source."[32] Both the habitability symposium and the *Spaces* exhibition provide insight into the quietly disruptive force of Bell's work in 1970 and contradict problematic readings (contemporary and retrospective) of light and space art as perceptually active but socially and politically indifferent. As I have noted elsewhere, the symposium presented Bell, Irwin, and their collaborators with an opportunity to promote social awareness through spatial and perceptual conditioning.[33]

The habitability symposium took place in a depressed area of Venice Beach, where the artists had their studios, and exposed participants to variances in light, space, and social interaction. Subject to daily changes imposed by the artist-hosts, the meeting space was incrementally transformed from an insulated academic cocoon into a public forum, ultimately open to the "drunks and beach bums and young kids" who populated the neighborhood.[34] This "second openness"—not only self-awareness but a self-consciousness prompted by exposure to the Other through a recognition of shared space and shared experience—was also what made the Tate environments so liberating for some and so discomfiting for others.[35] The *Spaces* exhibition similarly aimed to challenge viewers' presumptive disinterest through reconditioning, with "art that undermines our autonomy over personal terrain."[36] In 1969, the New York MoMA, perhaps the most visible and influential modern art institution in the world, was under considerable pressure from politicized groups like the Art Workers' Coalition to consult with living artists regarding how their work was maintained, installed, and reproduced, and to reach out to the greater, diverse public through its collecting and exhibition programs and through waiving entrance fees at least once a week.[37] The works installed for *Spaces* necessitated greater openness on both counts: in collaborative efforts with the artists (Bell's installation, for example, was radically different from the glass-paneled environment first envisioned[38]) and in accommodating members of the public, who were given the uncommon encouragement to (literally) kick off their shoes and stay a while.[39] The immersive nature of the work ensured, as Carter Ratcliff described, that "participation [was] automatic, denied to no one."[40] The nature and extent of that participation, however, depended on the individual's level of awareness. For many, the funhouse vibe contributed to the work's (and the museum's) accessibility, while for others this was its fundamental weakness.[41] To the establishment, the work was populist pandering, while for the Art Workers' Coalition, the exhibition was problematically dependent on corporate collaboration and sponsorship.[42]

Like Bell's, Irwin's career was also at a critical juncture in 1970. After participating in the Art and Technology experiments and cohosting the habitability symposium, he had arrived at a point where he felt he had nothing left to make. He was unsure of art's relevance in the world, and doubly unsure of the art establishment: "On what conditions, I started wondering, do we operate with art as a confined element in the world, in others words, an object or a painting as an isolated event in this world, surrounded by the world but somehow not totally or directly attached to it, actually somehow superior to it? It's a highly developed, raised rationale that this art object exists in."[43] Though this mindset is not well represented in the work he chose to show in London, it likely dampened his interest in the project. Irwin opted to exhibit three of his disc paintings in concert, each an ephemeral acrylic hemisphere, spotlit by four lamps that blurred the boundary between wall and object and produced an aureole effect of light and shadow. They were lovely and effective—insofar as light and shadow, wall and painted object, appeared to merge—but by 1970 Irwin had moved past the discs and was experimenting with what he called conditional art, including work such as *Fractured Light—Partial Scrim Ceiling—Eye Level Wire*. For that project, he took over an empty gallery at MoMA serendipitously made available by curator Jennifer Licht, which he transformed into an environment that induced perceptual awareness at the fringes of consciousness. Depending on their level of attention, visitors were nonplussed or indifferent.[44] In comparison, the decision to show the discs at the Tate was surprisingly conservative. Correspondence between Irwin and Compton suggests that the artist did not feel he had the time to personally supervise an installation in London and therefore chose a less potentially problematic route.[45] That said, the installation was in keeping with asserting the primacy of perception in the way that the discs contravene notions of object autonomy.

The most ambitious of the three environments was Wheeler's, a dizzying white space that expanded in height and depth toward what appeared to be a forty-foot cyclorama of light along the far wall.[46] He achieved this with the aid of Hollywood-trained plasterers, who created a seamless, curved surface lit on all sides by hidden fluorescent bulbs. In addition, the room was sound-dampened with white carpeting on the floor and a white scrim stretched across the ceiling. "It was a real illusion," stated Wheeler, "because people were afraid of falling over the edge—as if there were an edge to fall over! . . . What I was after was a Ganzfeld effect in which you couldn't trust your own vision. . . . Everybody is always looking at things from the standpoint of an anchor, and they're always anchored in one place . . . and if there isn't anything hard-edged around, then they start becoming conscious of things they've always overlooked before, so that it's also a kind of insecure feeling because there is this feeling of being drawn into the void."[47] As one reviewer described it: "The wall had forsaken its substances and turned into white space."[48]

Visitors to the exhibition were therefore first plunged into darkness while finding their way through Bell's maze, then given a temporary reprieve in front of Irwin's discs before confronting Wheeler's white void, and then renegotiated the darkness on the way out. There appear to have been generational differences in viewer reactions to such perceptual overload. Although several older visitors were dismayed and discomfited, younger visitors were often emboldened to act out in various ways, some declaring the whole experience a "very good trip" (and there is a fair amount of anecdotal evidence indicating that the phrase was not merely metaphorical).[49] Bell's dark space in particular presented significant challenges—or opportunities, depending on your perspective—and the exhibition archive is revealing on this score. For example, a complaint from a certain Mrs. Mason of Grosvenor Square, was brought to Compton's attention, in which she stated that "if she wanted to be frightened, she would go to Battersea Fun Fair, but this sort of thing was not suitable for the Tate . . . [and] that at least there should be some warning about what effect this room can have on people."[50] In response to such grievances, Compton had the light levels raised and the requested warning sign was installed. Furthermore, despite Compton's apparent protest, the administration "insisted that one of the emergency lights be left on" after visitors reported that they had been "tripped up by kids lying on the floor."[51] All of these interruptions and interventions distracted from the work's capacity to effect perceptual awareness. As one observer later remarked, "The word 'exit' did have a certain impact."[52]

In an object-oriented system, the curator's role is clear: preservation of the work of art is paramount, and intellectual distance between it and the viewer is sustained through physical separation. Maintaining systems hygiene in this model is uncomplicated: the curator is keeper. But phenomenal art collapses the distance between the work and visitor, forcing the curator into a managerial role, wherein he or she may even compromise the work of art to maintain systemic integrity. Letters in the Tate archive indicate that on several occasions Compton asked both Bell and Wheeler to alter their initial plans, sometimes to a considerable degree. Bell's maze, for economic reasons, was built as an octagon rather than with curved walls, which radically affected the way the space was navigated. Compton also altered the tone of the walls in Wheeler's installation from white to a light gray "after watching the orientation of people in the side rooms."[53] In light of his cautionary note in the catalog about the misleading potential of the written word (from curators or critics), the addition of a warning notice was no small concession. Yet Bell, who approached the project as part of an ongoing investigation into the limits of perception, seems to have been fairly sanguine about these changes,[54] whereas Wheeler, who was much more precise in his plans, balked at Compton's many requests for changes, including the suggestion—later abandoned—of adding a bench to the space, protesting that his art had become "riddled with compromise." Ultimately, Wheeler resignedly saw the whole process as a worthwhile, if failed, experiment: "I hope enough remains of what I was attempting not to be too much of a disappointment to you and those who come to see," he wrote to Compton.[55]

Social Body Consciousness

If viewer experience is integral to phenomenal art, the question then arises: Whose experience? Historical accounts, including Burnham's, tend to describe a relationship between a singular learned and attentive viewer (modeled after the artist himself) and the work of art or artistic environment. This seems very much in keeping with Wheeler's aim, which was to afford the individual viewer a specific kind of self-reflexive experience: "They start becoming conscious of things they've always overlooked before" (first-order systems consciousness). Similarly, Irwin's choice to exhibit only the discs was an expedient means of exerting control over the conditions of viewing. In opening up the work to fulfillment by and through a participating public, however, these artists and a complicit curator introduced a situation wherein viewers are made manifestly aware not only of the phenomenology of the art but of the presence and behavior of each other (second-order systems consciousness). In retrospect, it appears that they found one another wanting. Claire Bishop has referred to such participatory events as "artificial hells" (invoking the popularized existential observation, "Hell is other people!"), noting that the maintenance of aesthetic standards does not mix well with promoting participatory freedom.[56]

A key distinction between Wheeler's response and Bell's lies in the different systems these artists saw themselves engaging—one physiological, the other social. While both artists aimed to disorient the viewing public, Bell's work was the more disruptive, calling into question not only visitors' physiological relationships to the environment but, significantly, to each other. In fact, Compton attempted to curtail this early on, writing to Bell: "While I imagine that a certain degree of social and physical as well as sensory disturbance is a calculated part of your idea, I wonder whether this situation is not too much."[57] Too much for whom? As Jan Butterfield has noted, one of the most intriguing aspects of Bell's environmental experiments during this period is that "they raise [the question of] whether a public museum or gallery should be used for untried experiments."[58] Indeed, Bell was also challenging the authority of a moribund institution—the modern art museum—that had prematurely defined and confined him as a maker of specific objects, namely, glass cubes.[59]

Bell's early successes with the cubes (he was twenty-six when his work was included in the seminal 1966 *Primary Structures* exhibition at the Jewish Museum in New York) tend to overshadow his environmental work, which is also more difficult to stage and maintain. In contrast, the institutional critique of Michael Asher—Bell's contemporary and a fellow Californian—is inextricably linked to his situational practice. To be fair, this aspect of Asher's work emerged more forcefully in subsequent years. But in the 1970s, both artists were producing environmental works that tested administrative and perceptual conditions for viewership. Asher had been staging immersive environments, similar to those created by Bell and Wheeler at the Tate, that seemed at once devoid of content but were perceptually and conceptually open. Describing his 1969 *Spaces* installation to Grace Glueck (and sounding very much like Compton), Asher commented that people shouldn't have preconceptions about what they were about to encounter but, rather, should "bring a terrific amount of innocence" to the occasion.[60] Kirsi Peltomäki notes how such openness contributes to Asher's ability to "disable the day-to-day functioning of the host institution."[61] Regarding a 1974 intervention in Los Angeles, where he removed the partitioning wall between the administrative and public spaces at the Claire Copley Gallery, Asher remarked: "In the same way that gallery personnel seemed to become increasingly aware of their activities, viewers also became more aware of themselves as viewers."[62]

In the present context, it is worth (re)examining the relationship between perceptual and critical responses. Events surrounding *Three Artists* and the subsequent Morris retrospective at Tate Gallery point to viewer awareness as the driving force of institutional critique rather than the result of it (the inverse of Asher's later observations in Los Angeles). The uneasy spaces produced by Bell and Wheeler foregrounded viewers' bodily awareness to such a degree that gallery personnel were compelled to respond. The work necessitated more than maintenance; it needed constant managing. By installing the work in the central gathering space of a national gallery, the artists and curator compelled a reckoning with the bodies that comprise an art institution—its administrators and its visitors—and their disruptive potential. Like Asher, Bell aimed to promote a heightened sense of self-awareness, and in so doing made it impossible to negotiate his Tate installation with un-self-conscious grace. The Mrs. Masons of the world were at best disoriented and disconcerted. At worst, loitering "kids" might startle or even trip up visitors groping through the darkened meander, but, real or imagined, such circumstances significantly curtailed the achievement of reflective visuality that Bell that was seeking. The curators, charged now with the realization and sustenance of an artistic idea rather than the care and keeping of the art object, saw a need to intervene. Paradoxically, every intervention further detracted from the pure experience envisioned by the artist in his studio (where visitors were likely to be supportive and select). While the exit sign rendered the reflected lines of light in the ceiling less salient, it also loudly declared the presence and role of the museum administration. Even before the sign was introduced, Mrs. Mason's discomfort made her aware of this invisible hand, if only in its failure to protect her from her own anxiety. Indeed, she prefaces her complaint with the declaration that "Normally I am not frightened."[63] By forcing that hand, Bell produced an Asher-like exposure of institutional bias, in this case one that privileges the expectations of one class and generation over another.

If *Three Artists from Los Angeles* appeared to contravene institutional protocols for acceptable behavior, those issues came to a head with the 1971 Robert Morris exhibition, which infamously closed after only five days of participatory upheaval. Though there was a retrospective section of the exhibition which displayed objects from Morris's earlier career, the main attraction was a collection of objects, ramps, and ropes that turned the Duveen gallery into an adult playground legitimated as art by the explicit authority of the museum.[64] The individuals who wielded that authority, in turn, expected a degree of decorum on the part of the public. This was not to be. The self-consciousness that plagued some individuals encountering the *Three Artists* exhibition fell away at the Morris exhibition, where there was a clear imperative to act, if not to act out. Like Irwin, Wheeler, and Bell, Morris was averse to providing a written explanation, but he was nevertheless willing to provide instructions for the work by means of "how to" photographs showing Tate employees and family members (including Compton's own daughters) engaging the various apparatuses (figure 5.3). These were provided, said Compton, because it was presumed that otherwise "the British public would be too inhibited to play with the works freely."[65]

But, as he later admitted, he "had miscalculated the public."[66] Aiming at an anti-aesthetic and likewise concerned with keeping costs down, Morris chose to build the interactive parts out of inexpensive, recyclable materials. Most of the constructed pieces were made from raw plywood and scrap metal. This

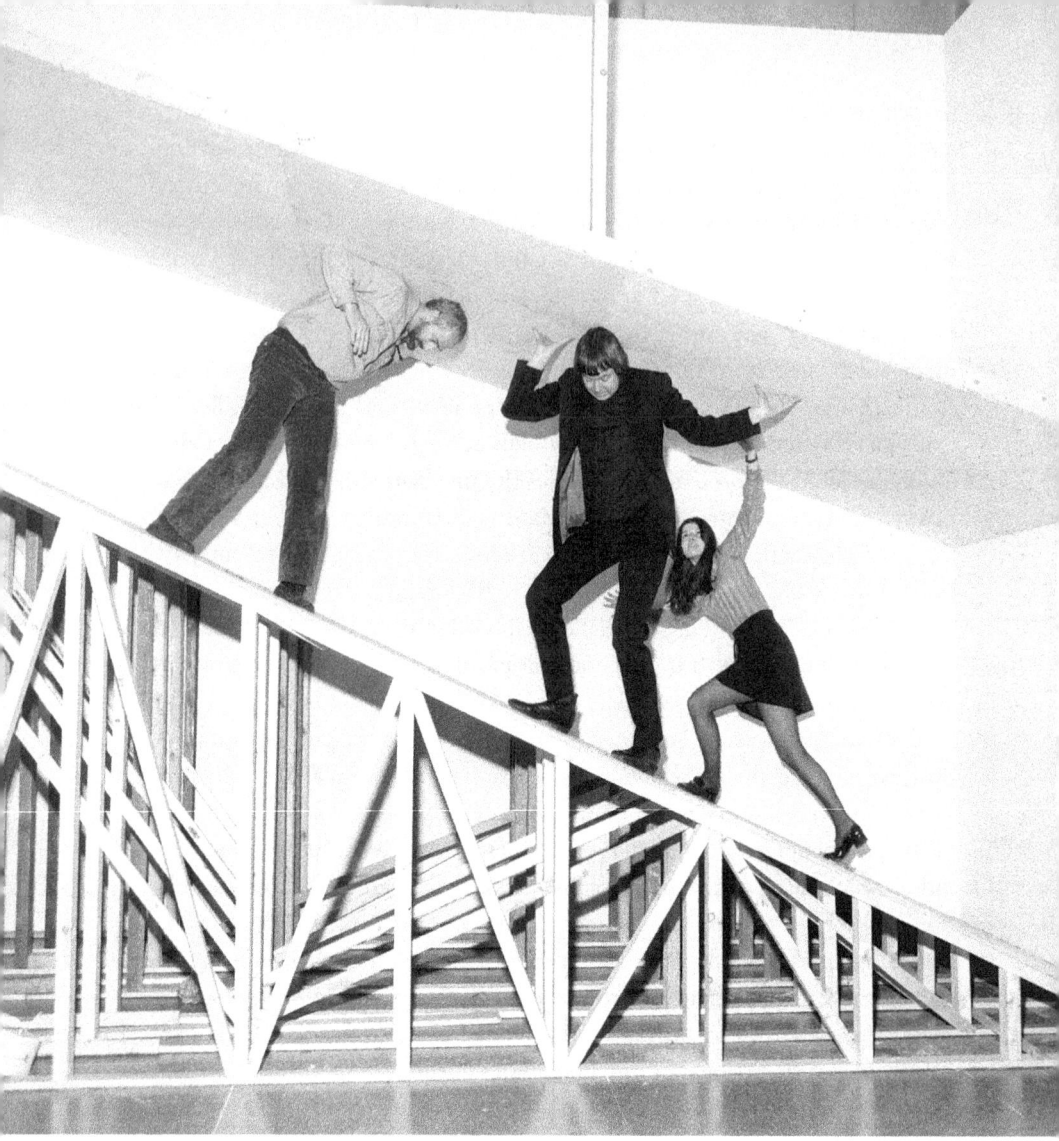

FIGURE 5.3. Robert Morris, *Bodyspacemotionthings*, Tate Gallery, London, April 28–June 6, 1971. Installation photo, April 28, 1971. Photo © Tate.

decision had several unforeseen side effects: the plywood gave off splinters, snagging hosiery and resulting in several minor injuries; and, when struck or walked on, the materials were noisy, and this in turn encouraged more noise making. People became less and less inhibited, risking their safety—but also engaging one another. The critic Reyner Banham wrote, "By the end of the private viewing the place was a bedlam in which all rules of decorum had been abandoned as liberated aesthetes leaped and teetered and heaved and clambered and joined hands with total strangers."[67] For the first time, the Tate was obliged to staff a first aid room for its visitors.[68]

Five days after *bodyspacemotionthings* opened, Compton and the Tate director Norman Reid decided to close the exhibition, since there seemed to be no clear way of inducing the public to behave responsibly, let alone in a dignified manner. It reopened briefly some days later with a more traditional retrospective in place. Maurice Berger has written that Morris presented the museum with a "challenge to [its] repressive hierarchies" that it was in no position to accept, but as Jon Bird has pointed out, there is little evidence that Morris knew the work had such potential for provoking anarchy.[69] Indeed, Morris, like Compton, had been more concerned that visitors might *not* overcome the inhibitions trained into them from years of respectful contemplative viewing.[70] Morris, who had studied as a dancer, "wanted a situation where people could use their bodies as well as their eyes."[71]

Writing in June 1970 about *Three Artists from Los Angeles* for *Studio International*, Compton stated, "The artists control the situation not by symbols or by extrinsic abstractions but by the perceptual equipment of the viewer. . . . I believe it permits a new kind of freedom from cultural pressure and pre-determination both for the artist and the viewer."[72] Compton's description of freedom through control is positively cybernetic in nature, with the artist occupying the position of steersman, and it usefully extends the discussion beyond language-based systems to account for body-based systems. On the other hand, he does not acknowledge his own role as facilitator, nor the institutional constraints (such as exit signs) that served to protect certain types of actors over others. In this, he is no different from the artists, who envisioned idealized viewers like themselves, ready and willing to observe themselves observing in a civilized manner. Likewise, Morris had expected an orderly response. The distinction (invoking Pierre Bourdieu) between a society of the studio and public participation was made plain. Critiquing Morris's latent "classicism," Banham wrote, "If Morris thinks the public still thinks that way, in 1971, he's got to be joking. Show us an end of rope and we'll swing for the hell of swinging, not to meditate on the precession of the pendulum."[73] But the Morris debacle did not stop the Tate or any other museum from producing large-scale participatory works, far from it. As Andrea Fraser would later clarify in her analysis of museum service economies: "By early 1970, Jack Burnham could write that the fact that gallery and museum exhibitions were 'increasingly planned . . . on the basis of submitting proposals' was a *reason* for the emergence of conceptual art rather than a response to it."[74] As Compton himself admitted, it was an expedient and economical way to introduce the general public to new work without having to commit the institution to making a purchase, while simultaneously acknowledging the artists' increased reluctance to have their artwork "hanging around becoming permanent."[75]

By introducing the art-going British public to the perceptual and social ambiguities of the *Three Artists* and *bodyspacemotionthings* exhibitions, Compton inadvertently raised previously unconsidered questions about the degree of control the museum may exert upon the artist as they are creating the work, the conflicting needs and desires of the viewing public, and the institution's role in ensuring their security. Perhaps participants in both exhibitions "acted out" because the work provoked a heightened sense of bodily awareness, but they were also made less aware of their responsibility for that awareness by the tacitly paternalistic maneuvers of the Tate establishment. In response, that authority has been made more explicit. At both exhibitions, the imperative to "use their bodies as well as their eyes" not only encouraged visitors to contemplate the physiological nature of aesthetic experience; their doing so brought the physical authority of the museum under scrutiny from the inside. If viewing remained a purely ocular endeavor, institutional order could be maintained at a semantic level and visitors would not need to be protected from their own impulses or from each other.

Considering its long association with computing, systems theory has a way of reducing everything to disembodied information. But "systems consciousness" is embodied by human actors, whose behavior is rather less predictable than that of numbers. Looking at early installations of light and space environments, it appears that curators and museums were simply not prepared to deal with the social and economic consequences of a shift from "pure form to pure experience."[76] Providing a pristine environment for the safeguarding of objects is one thing; ensuring a quality of art as experience is another, the latter necessitating reconsideration of the respective roles of the visitor, the curator, the museum administration, and the critic. Certainly, the degree of participation and interactivity in museum exhibitions has increased dramatically since 1970. But this does not mean that museums willingly invite chaos; rather, safety concerns have become paramount. As artists and exhibiting institutions become increasingly susceptible to lawsuits, these circumstances inevitably raise barriers, both physical and legal, between the artwork and visitors—the very figures purported to be fulfilling art's experiential potential.[77] A restaging of Morris's installation in the Turbine Hall at the Tate Modern in 2009 used less injurious materials situated on or near carefully placed rubber mats, with participants watchfully supervised by museum employees. Meanwhile, an untitled 1971 environmental glass work by Larry Bell in the Tate collection is shown with the following gallery label: "In 1968 . . . [Bell] began to experiment with works of an environmental character and to create a space which people could walk around and into, and at the same time see through. *However, in the interests of safety visitors must keep behind the barriers.*"[78] The phrasing implies that it is not the work that needs safekeeping as much as its visitors require safeguarding, the currency of their trust given priority. This troubling paternalism reinforces systemic constraints while eliding systems consciousness, troubling not because it is imposed but because it is expected.

NOTES

1   Some of the museum's collections had previously been housed in the Los Angeles Museum of History, Science, and Art, which was founded in 1910. Tuchman's interdisciplinary initiative was therefore not only current but also in keeping with the museum's prior mandate. In 1961, the art-based institution known as LACMA was established, with a new building at its current location in 1965. See "History," lacma.org, accessed January 20, 2021, https://www.lacma.org/about?tab=history#history.

2   Maurice Tuchman, *Art and Technology: A Report on the Art and Technology Program of the Los Angeles County Museum of Art 1967–1971* (Los Angeles: Los Angeles County Museum of Art, 1971), 11.

3   Max Kozloff, "The Multimillion Dollar Boondoggle," *Artforum* 10, no. 2 (1971): 72–76.

4   Kozloff, "The Multimillion Dollar Boondoggle," 72.

5   Burnham was well-positioned to know, since he was navigating similar terrain as curator of the 1971 *Software* exhibition at the Jewish Museum. Jack Burnham, "Corporate Art," *Artforum* 10, no. 2 (1971): 66–71; reprinted in Jack Burnham, *Dissolve into Comprehension: Writings and Interviews, 1964–2004*, ed. Melissa Ragain (Cambridge, MA: MIT Press, 2015), 184–92.

6   Tuchman, *Art and Technology*.

7   Wortz worked for Garrett Airesearch, where he headed the life sciences division. Tuchman, *Art and Technology*, 128.

8   Jane Livingston, "Thoughts on Art and Technology," in Tuchman, *Art and Technology*, 46.

9   As Anne Collins Goodyear has noted, criticism was driven by the technophilia of early enthusiasts and later by the technophobia of Vietnam-era protests. In either case, the historical record skews toward a concern with corporate conduct rather than artistic interests (let alone those of the viewing public). Anne Collins Goodyear, "From Technophilia to Technophobia: The Impact of the Vietnam War on the Reception of 'Art and Technology,'" *Leonardo* 41, no. 2 (2008): 169–74.

10 Tuchman, *Art and Technology*, 127–41.

11 See also Dawna Schuld, *Minimal Conditions* (Berkeley: University of California Press, 2018), 34. The phrase *technologies of experience* was coined by musicologist Phil Ford, who applies it much more broadly to various coordinated forms of aesthetic experience. Phil Ford, "Everythingology," paper presented at the Technologies of Experience symposium, Department of the History of Art and the Jacobs School of Music Department of Musicology, April 4–6, 2013, Indiana University, Bloomington.

12 As late as 2005, documents pertaining to the Wortz collaboration were kept in an unlocked file drawer in the LACMA curatorial offices. More recent interest in Art and Technology is outlined in this volume's introduction. The 2011 Getty Research Institute initiative *Pacific Standard Time: Art in L.A. 1945–1980* considerably revived interest in the program and surrounding events. See "Past Initiatives," getty.edu, accessed March 30, 2021, https://www.getty.edu/foundation /initiatives/past/pst/index.html.

13 This is not to say that the *Art and Technology* exhibition included no environmental work, but it tended to make a spectacle of the technology, rather than raise awareness of the perceptual experience. As Max Kozloff wrote in his review: "The laser beams of Krebs, the strobes of Mefferd, and the mirror projections of Robert Whitman were as imaginatively pointless as they were physically disembodied." Kozloff, "The Multimillion Dollar Boondoggle," 75.

14 Robin Clark and Hugh Davies, eds., *Phenomenal: Light, Space, and Surface* (Berkeley: University of California Press, 2011); and Robert Irwin, *Being and Circumstance: Notes toward a Conditional Art* (Culver City, CA: Lapis Press, 1985).

15 Michael Compton, "Artists' Lives: Michael Compton 1927–2013," oral history, British Library Archives, C466/198, July 14 to September 22, 2005, Oxted, UK, Part 55: Tape 28. During his tenure at the Pasadena Art Museum and through the Ferus Gallery, which he had cofounded, Hopps was instrumental in bringing attention to the contemporary Los Angeles art scene in the 1950s and 1960s, but he left the museum in 1967. John Coplans was the curator of record for the exhibition in question: *Jim Turrell*, Pasadena Art Museum, 1967.

16 It's not precisely clear where Compton encountered the projection pieces, but Turrell first exhibited them in Pasadena in 1967 and subsequently in his Santa Monica studio in 1968.

17 Simon Wilson, "Michael Compton: A Tate Eminence," typescript of unpublished remembrance, October 2013, Tate Museum, London.

18 "Three Artists from Los Angeles: Larry Bell, Robert Irwin, Doug Wheeler," exhibition archive, Tate Gallery Archives, London, TG 92/228/1, September 10, 1969, to July 27, 1981.

19 Compton, "Artists' Lives."

20 Compton, "Artists' Lives."

21 Canonical or "classical" status could not, by definition, be conferred on avant-garde art, but at least as late as 1963 it was still very much the expectation that work added to the collection would in the future "become 'classical'" and so merit permanent residence in the national collection. Sir John Rothenstein, *A Brief History of the Tate Gallery* (London: Pitkin Pictorials, 1963), 21.

22 Larry Bell, "Larry Bell: A Statement," 1976, typescript, Santa Barbara Museum of Art, Santa Barbara, CA, reprinted in Jan Butterfield, *The Art of Light and Space* (New York: Abbeville Press, 1993), 185.

23 Compton, "Artists' Lives."

24 Rothenstein, *A Brief History*, 1.

25 "Three Artists from Los Angeles," exhibition archive.

26 Michael Compton, *Larry Bell, Robert Irwin, Doug Wheeler* (London: Tate Gallery, 1970), 5.

27 This was a persistent concern for Irwin but was also in keeping with an emphasis on phenomenological immediacy in the work of Bell and Wheeler during the same period. Robert Irwin, Letter to Michael Compton, February 27, 1970, in "Three Artists from Los Angeles," Tate Gallery Archives, London, TG 92/228/1: 29; Robert Irwin, "Statement on Reproductions," *Artforum* 3, no. 9 (1965): 23.

28 Compton, *Larry Bell, Robert Irwin, Doug Wheeler*, 5, emphasis in original.

29 Ed Wortz, ed., *First National Symposium on Habitability*, 4 vols. (Venice, CA: Garrett Airesearch Manufacturing Company, 1970).

30 Larry Bell, conversation with the author, Venice, CA, February 6, 2018.

31 Grace Glueck, "Museum Beckoning Space Explorers," *New York Times*, January 2, 1970, 34.

32 Larry Bell, quoted in Butterfield, *Art of Light*, 181.

33 Dawna Schuld, "Beyond Method and without Object," in *Hybrid Practices*, ed. David Cateforis, Steven Duval, and Shepherd Steiner (Berkeley: University of California Press, 2018), 85–86.

34 Ed Wortz, quoted in Lawrence Weschler, *Seeing Is Forgetting the Name of the Thing One Sees* (Berkeley: University of California Press, 2008), 136.

35 "The other's gaze on the things is a second openness." Maurice Merleau-Ponty, *The Visible and the Invisible*, trans. Alfonso Lingis (Evanston: Northwestern University Press, 1968), 59.

36 Jennifer Licht, *Spaces* (New York: Museum of Modern Art, 1969).

37 "13 Demands," submitted to Mr. Bates Lowry, Director of the Museum of Modern Art, by a group of artists and critics, January 28, 1969. Art Workers' Coalition, *Documents 1*, digital facsimile, 2008, accessed January 20, 2021, http://www.primaryinformation.org/product/art-workers-coalition-documents-1/.

38 The exhibition catalog describes glass panels "in the architectural domain." Though Bell was certainly producing work of this nature at this time, the final installation was more radically perceptual in nature and less overtly architectural. Licht, *Spaces*, n.p.

39 Julie Reiss, *From Margin to Center* (Cambridge, MA: MIT Press, 1999), 99.

40 Carter Radcliff, "New York Letter," *Art International* 14, no. 2 (February 1970): 78.

41 Reiss, *From Margin to Center*, 98.

42 Glueck, "Museum Beckoning."

43 Robert Irwin, quoted in Weschler, *Seeing Is Forgetting*, 151.

44 Weschler, *Seeing Is Forgetting*, 153–58.

45 Robert Irwin to Michael Compton, February 5, 1970, in "Three Artists from Los Angeles," Tate Gallery Archives, London, TG 92/228/1: 21.

46 Compton, "Artists' Lives."

47 Doug Wheeler, in conversation with Jan Butterfield, transcribed in Butterfield, *Art of Light*, 123.

48 Robert Melville, "Bare Walls at the Tate," *New Statesman*, May 15, 1970, 709.

49 Compton, "Artists' Lives."

50 Letter forwarded to Michael Compton (reply dated May 13, 1970), in "Three Artists from Los Angeles," Tate Gallery Archives, London, TG/92/228/1: 90.

51 Michael Compton to Larry Bell, May 13, 1970, in "Three Artists from Los Angeles," Tate Gallery Archives, London, TG 92/228/1: 87.

52 Donald Hankey, conversation with the author, London, October 2, 2014. Lord Hankey was the architect of record for the temporary galleries in 1970.

53 Michael Compton to Doug Wheeler, May 13, 1970, in "Three Artists from Los Angeles," Tate Gallery Archives, London, TG 92/228/1: 86.

54 More recently, Bell has indicated that he saw the project as part of an ongoing experiment about visual experience rather than as a discrete work of art. Larry Bell, conversation with the author, Venice, CA, February 6, 2018.

55 Doug Wheeler to Michael Compton, March 17, 1970, in "Three Artists from Los Angeles," Tate Gallery Archives, London, TG 92/228/1: 45.

56 Claire Bishop, *Artificial Hells* (London: Verso, 2012), 190; Jean-Paul Sartre, *No Exit*, trans. Stuart Gilbert (New York: Vintage International, 1946), 45.

57 Michael Compton to Larry Bell, January 30, 1970, in "Three Artists from Los Angeles," Tate Gallery Archives, London, TG 92/228/1: 16.

58 Butterfield, *Art of Light*, 183.

59 Larry Bell, in conversation with Jan Butterfield, in Butterfield, *Art of Light*, 182.

60 Glueck, "Museum Beckoning."

61 Kirsi Peltomäki, *Situation Aesthetics* (Cambridge, MA: MIT Press, 2010), 5.

62 Michael Asher, *Writings, 1973–1983, on Works, 1969–1979*, ed. Benjamin Buchloh (Nova Scotia: Press of the Nova Scotia School of Art and Design; Los Angeles: Museum of Contemporary Art, 1983), 96.

63 "Three Artists from Los Angeles," Tate Gallery Archives, London, TG 92/228/1: 90.

64 Regarding the relationship of play to governance in this work, see also Timothy Stott, *Play and Participation in Contemporary Arts Practices* (New York: Routledge, 2017), 118–19, 125–29.

65 Compton, "Artists' Lives," C466/198, Part 56, Tape 29.

66 Compton, "Artists' Lives," C466/198, Part 57, Tape 29.

67 Reyner Banham, "Art in London: It Was SRO—and a Disaster," *New York Times*, May 23, 1971.

68 Compton, "Artists' Lives," C466/198, Part 57, Tape 29.

69 Maurice Berger, *Labyrinths* (New York: Icon, 1990).

70 Jon Bird, "Minding the Body," in *Rewriting Conceptual Art*, ed. Michael Newman and Jon Bird (London: Reaktion Books, 1999), 88–106.

71 Robert Morris, interview with Simon Grant, September 1, 2008, http://www.tate .org.uk/context-comment/articles/simon-grant-interviews-robert-morris/.

72 Michael Compton, "UK Commentary," *Studio International* 179, no. 923 (June 1970): 269–70.

73 Banham, "Art in London."

74 Andrea Fraser, "What's Intangible, Transitory, Mediating, Participatory, and Rendered in the Public Sphere, Part II," in Andrea Fraser, *Museum Highlights: The Writings of Andrea Fraser*, ed. Alexander Alberro (Cambridge, MA: MIT Press, 2005), 69.

75 Banham, "Art in London."

76 Jack Burnham, *Beyond Modern Sculpture* (New York: George Braziller, 1968), 172–81.

77 In 1982, for example, James Turrell and the Whitney Museum were sued when a visitor became disoriented, fell, and injured her wrist in one of his installations. Grace Glueck, "Whitney Sued over 1980 'Light Show,'" *New York Times*, May 4, 1982. In contrast, visitors were required to sign a waiver, noting that they were willing to risk "serious injury, including without limitation partial or total disability, paralysis, death, and severe social and economic losses" to gain entrance to one of Turrell's "perception cells" at the Los Angeles Museum of Art in 2013. Waiver and release of liability for *Light Reignfall*, May 3, 2013, Los Angeles County Museum of Art.

78 Gallery label for Larry Bell, *Untitled* (1971), August 2004, accessed January 20, 2021, http://www.tate.org.uk/art/artworks/bell-untitled-t01473/, emphasis added. The image of the artwork shown to an online public—safely positioned behind another barrier/screen—shows it in a pristine state, in reproduction uncompromised by either a barrier or the public.

6

One among Many

Experiencing Complexity in
Participatory Art Systems

CRISTINA ALBU

Over the last two decades, we have become enchanted with visual maps of complexity, whether related to the global use of the World Wide Web, the swarm behavior of bacterial colonies, or the tracking of weather fronts. These mesmerizing images often capture a mere snapshot of the intricacy of systems evolving at different scales and tempos. Composed of numerous entities—human, animal, or technological—complex systems defy predictability as their components develop new patterns of behavior in relation to changes in communication and environmental variables.[1] Despite the sense of wonder that the visualization of this interconnectivity inspires, representations of such systems usually fail to convey that we are not mere voyeurs of complexity but we are in fact deeply immersed in its webs. Attuned to these limitations in perception, several contemporary artists have created participatory environments that unveil our bodily entanglement in such systems, thus complicating the vision of the modern subject as an autonomous agent. Gina Czarnecki, Mariko Mori, and Tomás Saraceno design sensitive environments that channel participants' attention both inward and outward by signaling complex processes of communication that evolve across bodily confines. They elicit awareness of otherwise imperceptible material relations and encourage participants to sense the ongoing transformation of biological and cognitive systems.

In terms of stylistic approaches, the works of Mori, Czarnecki, and Saraceno share limited affinities. A Japanese artist espousing a sci-fi aesthetic, Mariko Mori is primarily known for creating performances and installations that reflect the transcendence of selfhood through reliance on technological and spiritual means. Embracing a much more minimalist approach to art making, the Argentinian artist Tomás Saraceno anchors his installation practice around issues of habitability inspired by the geometry of large systems such as constellations, as well as by ethereal small-scale formations such as soap bubbles or spider webs. Equally enthusiastic about gathering knowledge from mutating systems, yet more prone to connecting abstraction to visual representation, Gina Czarnecki designs works that test the relations between biotechnology and cultural beliefs. Different as their visual languages and thematic pursuits may be at first glance, these three artists are similarly concerned with issues of entanglement, whether at the level of spiritual oneness in Mori's work, planetary interdependence in Saraceno's environments, or biological contingency in Czarnecki's practice. Their works might not reveal insightful formal analogies when examined in comparative pairs, but as part of a triad engaged with issues of system dynamics, they set in motion related inquiries into how complex entanglements can be experienced both physically and cognitively.

This chapter examines how Mori's *Wave UFO* (1999–2002), Czarnecki's *Contagion* (2008), and Saraceno's *In Orbit* (2013–ongoing) generate an embodied understanding of different degrees of agency and reciprocal influences among participants interacting with and within complex systems. I have specifically chosen to focus on works representative of different systems—neural, social, and viral—to emphasize their similar dynamics and the different challenges they pose to experiencing complexity through aesthetic means. While Mori's *Wave UFO* invites viewers to join a voyage into the intricacy of the human mind, Czarnecki's *Contagion* and Saraceno's *In Orbit* signal the complexity of the outward world that brims with vitality whether one considers the rapid evolution of viruses or the slow but inevitable transformation of the planet. Notably, these artists ask us to consider exchanges across systems that are nested within each other and forfeit the presumably rigid boundaries between distinct types of biological and non-biological entities.

In this chapter, I connect Mori, Czarnecki, and Saraceno's installations with Jack Burnham's prescient theory of "systems esthetics" from the 1960s in view of their capacity to instigate "psychic preparedness" while calling attention to social and environmental variables.[2] I show that Burnham's critique of ocular bias as an impediment to ecosystemic awareness resonates with recent views of new materialist and affect theorists who argue that our reliance on visual evidence prevents us from sensing less easily perceptible forms of communication and material changes. Conscious of how optical engagement can sometimes overshadow reflection on system relations, Mori, Czarnecki, and Saraceno promote more intuitive ways of connecting to ecological principles such as interdependence. They render physical entanglement across multiple systems more palpable by disclosing both the limits and potential of perceptual observations in facilitating attunement to environments.

These contemporary artists' inquiries into visible and invisible interconnections that transcend bodily thresholds resonate with the conceptual and aesthetic goals of the originators of the systems-oriented art tendency identified by Jack Burnham in the late 1960s. According to the art critic, artists such as Hans Haacke and Les Levine created process-oriented works that encouraged participants to connect to their physical surroundings through intuitive movement rather than through sight. In Burnham's view, art could prompt individuals "*not* to look at the 'skin' of objects, but at those meaningful relationships within and beyond their visible boundaries."[3] Moreover, it could prime participants to embrace change instead of focusing on attaining control over evolving system coordinates. Mori, Czarnecki, and Saraceno expand the turn against the primacy of visuality and human agency advocated by Burnham's systems esthetics by conceiving affective environments that elicit multisensory engagement and reveal the complex communicative processes that unfold beneath the visible surface of systems. As ecological concerns have mounted and notions of distributed agency have gained ground since the turn of the twenty-first century, these artists have created interactive models that dismantle long-standing binaries between the social and the biological underpinnings of human behavior. In what follows, I show that their focus on enmeshed, coevolving systems does not free art participants from experiencing a sense of responsibility. On the contrary, these artists' works demand a critical reconsideration of such presumed binaries as singularity and difference, autonomy and interdependence. In the context of heavily imbricated physical and information networks, which are bound to become even denser in the age of the internet of things, it becomes imperative to account for fluctuating degrees of agency and to discern interconnections between biological, social, and technological systems at different spatial and temporal scales.

Inward and Outward Complex Systems

Mori's *Wave UFO*, Czarnecki's *Contagion*, and Saraceno's *In Orbit* sensitize participants to the porosity of material boundaries and the vibrancy of the space between ourselves and others. They bring them near each other to trigger a visceral experience of their involvement in systems that evolve both beneath their skin and outside their bodies. These environments encompass not just living systems that temporarily affect their space but also "meaning systems," which can extend beyond the physical site in which interactions take place. In Bruce Clarke's view, such metabiotic systems are composed of psychic and social systems which develop their own operational integrity as ideas develop, mutate, and coalesce into new forms of knowledge.[4] Significantly, contemporary artists such as Mori, Czarnecki, and Saraceno establish analogies between the dynamics of the human body and mind and the self-organization of ecological, social, and viral systems. They elicit speculation on the communication that occurs across system thresholds and its impact on the overall balance of the environment.

Mariko Mori conceived *Wave UFO* as a space in which participants can register both the complexity of their own brain wave oscillations and the complexity of their neural ties to others. The opalescent surface of her sci-fi sculptural object transforms through fluid shifts in color depending on the viewer's vantage point. Participants enter its space in groups of three through a small sliding door that resembles an eye. Once inside, they are fully isolated from the exterior and wear electrodes on their heads while reclining on flexible Technogel seats that take the shape of their bodies (figure 6.1). As participants contemplate the activity of their brains on the capsule's domed ceiling via a dynamic graphic representation, the plasticity of their surroundings presents an analogy with the plasticity of the human mind. By observing a network of colored lines and circular shapes corresponding to different brainwave frequencies, individuals become aware of their psychic state and note its fluctuations in conjunction with the neural dynamics of two co-participants. Red hues signal high-frequency beta waves corresponding to states of agitation, blue hues indicate alpha waves corresponding to "relaxed wakefulness," and yellow hues show the presence of theta waves produced when one transitions into unconsciousness. Moreover, pairs of silver spheres represent the activity of the left and right hemispheres of each individual and yellow lines oscillate in relation to the movement of eyes, face, and body.[5] Thus, bodily motion is conjoined with otherwise invisible psychic changes. Participants can note contingent relations between their neural oscillations

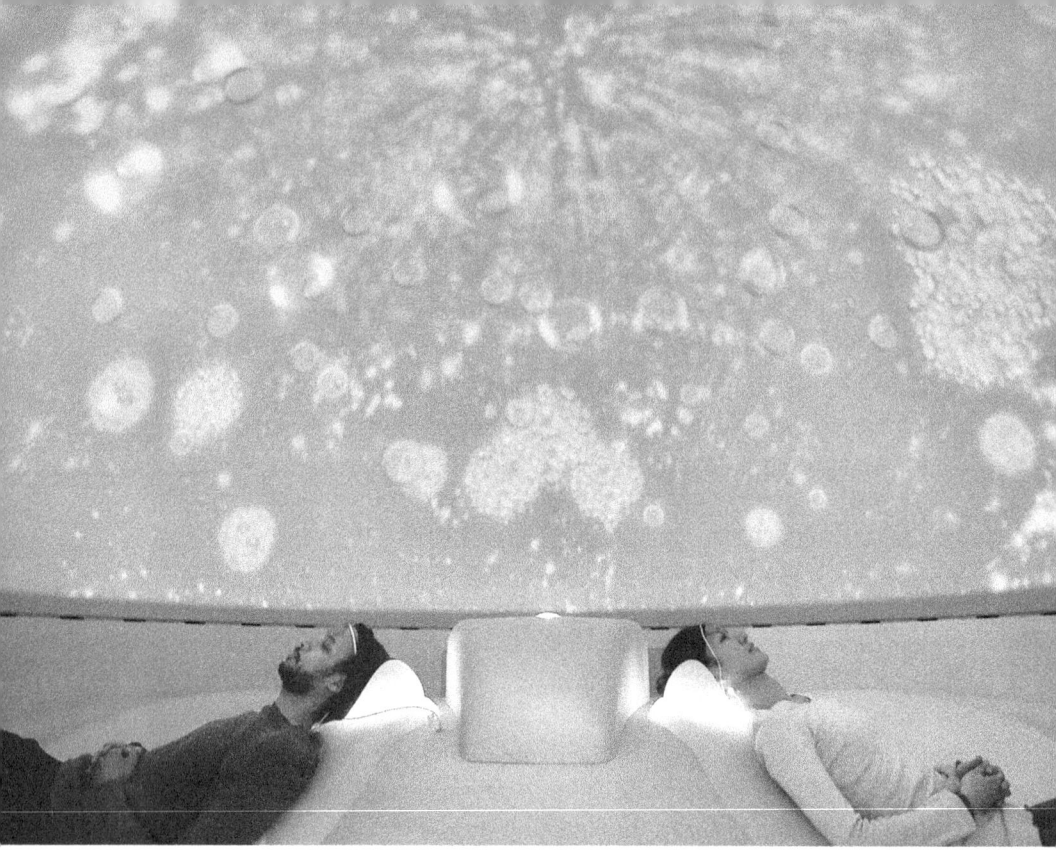

FIGURE 6.1. Mariko Mori, *Wave UFO* (detail), 1999–2003. Brainwave interface, Vison Dome projector, computer system, fiberglass, Technogel®, acrylic, carbon fiber, aluminum, magnesium, 493 × 1134 × 528 cm. The artwork's participants are monitored by a brain wave–tracking apparatus while they watch projected images on hemispherical overhead screens. All rights reserved. Photo by Tom Powel. Courtesy of Mariko Mori and Sean Kelly, New York. ©2020 Mariko Mori, Member Artists Rights Society (ARS), New York.

and induce variations in their dynamics in a conscious manner. If synchronization between the left and right brain hemispheres occurs, the silver spheres converge. This synchronization can reach even a higher level: if participants' neural oscillations become increasingly attuned, they can witness the formation of a ring on the dome, evoking a state of psychic oneness.

To the holism of the individual body, Mori juxtaposes the emergent unity of interconnected psychic systems that temporarily synchronize despite material boundaries. Following this three-minute interval of psychic attunement, the artist shifts the analogy between converging spherical shapes and participants' minds to a more abstract level at which the distinctions between systems become blurrier. Over three and a half minutes, participants watch a video animation that features mutating cellular shapes evocative of complex interconnectivity between microcosm and macrocosm. Titled *Connected World*, the animation enhances the disorder within the system and triggers the emergence of new neural and cognitive connections, which are no longer charted on the dome surface. It indicates that systems cannot be perpetually closed off to external influences and are bound to undergo changes as they correlate with other systems. According to Mori, *Wave* UFO enables spectators "to share in a feeling of a multi-dimensional world that exists inside our consciousness."[6] In this, she draws on Tibetan Buddhist beliefs about the oneness of the world and on scientific research concerning neural modulation. In her view, mental interdependence is a sign of connectivity not only between human beings but also between the earth and the cosmos.

If Mori enables participants to experience the complexity of neural systems, the British artist Gina Czarnecki invites them to ponder the permeable boundaries of their bodies and minds repeatedly exposed to "contamination" with both viruses and mass media information. In collaboration with experts in epidemiology, she designed *Contagion* as an open system that models the spread of diseases and information through color, sound, and video footage.[7] Participants enter a fairly dark environment in which they encounter a red circular perimeter on the gallery floor (figure 6.2). This zone communicates with what seems to be a telescopic lens that frames visual projections on the wall. What may first appear to be a view onto a world found at a remote spatial or temporal distance is a real-time presentation of the actual gallery space intertwined with multiple layers of mass media images and a visual model of the air spread of the SARS virus.

As participants overstep the boundaries of the red disc on the floor, a surveillance camera tracks their movements from above and turns them into colorful plumes that float across grainy images encapsulated into the video projection on the wall. Different hues are ascribed to individuals based on the area through which they have accessed the perimeter of contagion. These colors are far from stable, mutating over the course of time as they intersect with each other. Human bodies turn into fuzzy substances that appear to compete or collaborate with each other. Crosshairs mark the presence of viruses within this system. When participants come near them, the colorful plume corresponding to their movements turns to gray and a time and date stamp renders visible the point of contagion. The epidemiological map overlaps video data that is accessed each time the disease is passed on. The images range from representations of biological processes such as the growth of a fetus to iconic recordings of violent conflicts and popular culture symbols. They emerge not only within the lens-like zone of contagion but also at the periphery of it, in different areas of the wall. Not always easily perceptible, the images have a pixelated appearance indicative of their deterioration through repeated acts of conversion into other formats. Thus, the work points to the spread and mutation of biological matter, as well as to the decay of information even when it is encrypted digitally. Comparing viral threats to the potentially disruptive effects of mass media information on cognitive processes, Czarnecki indicates the permeability of both living and metabiotic systems. In the context of the COVID-19 pandemic, these correlations between the spread of a viral disease and the distribution of media information about its effects have become even more poignant.

Contagion is characterized by a greater degree of complexity than *Wave UFO*, given its openness to the presence of multiple participants who can enter and exit its space independently of a schedule.[8] It also has a memory of past interactions because it temporarily stores within the system fading visual traces of sites and times of contamination. The work provokes intense sensations since visitors inevitably feel that what might constitute a virtual health threat associated with a devastating epidemic may indicate actual risks of viral infection from which we are never completely free. After all, the work's public includes both human actants and invisible microorganisms spreading within and across individual bodies without immediately perceptible effects. The analogies established by Czarnecki between the extensive influence of viruses and the effect of mass media on the construction of knowledge signals the extension of biological and cognitive systems beyond the confines of individual bodies. Unlike Mori, who equates the operations of psychic systems with those of cellular and cosmic bodies, Czarnecki does not picture a complete merger of systems of different types at the level of abstract visual language. While their representations are superimposed, the systems remain distinct, interconnected yet operationally closed. Both viral and cognitive systems function in relation to living bodies. They thrive on them, but they are not restricted to their material thresholds.

FIGURE 6.2. Gina Czarnecki, *Contagion*, 2008. Interactive video installation, on view at the Blue Coat, Liverpool, in 2011. Photo by Jon Barraclough. Produced by Forma. Supported by the Wellcome Trust Sci-Art Award. Courtesy of Gina Czarnecki and Jon Barraclough.

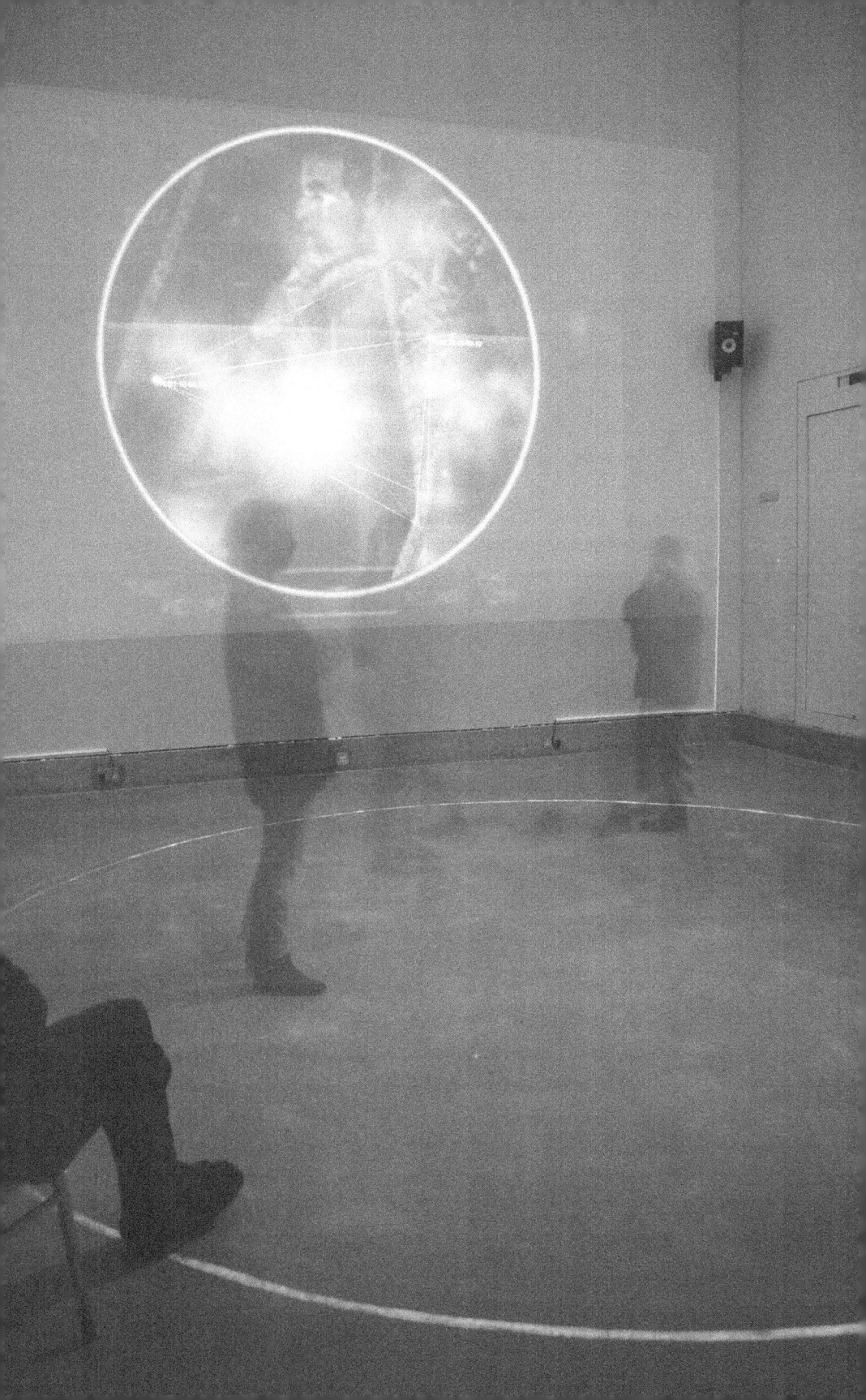

Tomás Saraceno is equally interested in triggering analogies between the behavior of biotic and metabiotic systems. Embracing collaborative research, he has explored the complexity of spider webs, constellations, and ecosystems in an attempt at developing models for alternative habitats that can ensure survival under environmentally precarious circumstances. *In Orbit* is a suspended structure formed out of a steel wire net interspersed with six air-filled PVC spheres, whose upper level lies 66 feet above the ground floor of the K21 Ständehaus in Düsseldorf (figure 6.3). Up to ten participants are allowed within its space at a time. They tentatively walk across the vibrating web while observing the transparent and reflective spheres that offer a promise of provisional shelter in a variable environment. Whether they are near each other or not, participants sense each other's presence via vibrations in the net. The systemic qualities of this overly sensitive environment direct attention to the fragility of social ties that ensure the integrity of a community. The contingent relations immediately established among them pinpoint the inherent interdependence between all beings sharing an ecosystem. *In Orbit* asks participants to envision their roles not only in an insular habitat restricted to human activity but also in a planetary system encompassing dynamic processes that eschew observation from a unique vantage point. The tensile forces in the net evoke such invisible transformations. Saraceno's installation bespeaks what Bruce Clarke calls the "planetary imaginary," a mode of self-observation in relation to systemic operations that surpass human abilities of visualization and control.[9] As participants enter the space of *In Orbit*, they engage both in a highly tenuous kinetic experience and in a process of speculative inquiry into the possibilities and limits of their capacity to influence ecosystems.

Saraceno has also designed pneumatic environments that place visitors in an even more precarious position by making their behavior and the plasticity of the support structure contingent on shifting air pressure.[10] He generally avoids providing any guidelines to participation within such systems in order to stimulate self-organization and emergent behavior. Saraceno asserts that embodied cognition offers more possibilities for developing efficient survival strategies in a communal space than didactic principles that restrict the range of behavioral approaches: "If you explain in advance the rules of the game they [participants] behave very badly and even irresponsibly. . . . Quite strangely, when I do not explain anything there is a lot of solidarity from the beginning because you do not know what will happen."[11] Nonetheless, K21 Ständehaus in Düsseldorf found it necessary to establish safety rules and appointed a team of safety instructors who informed audience members how

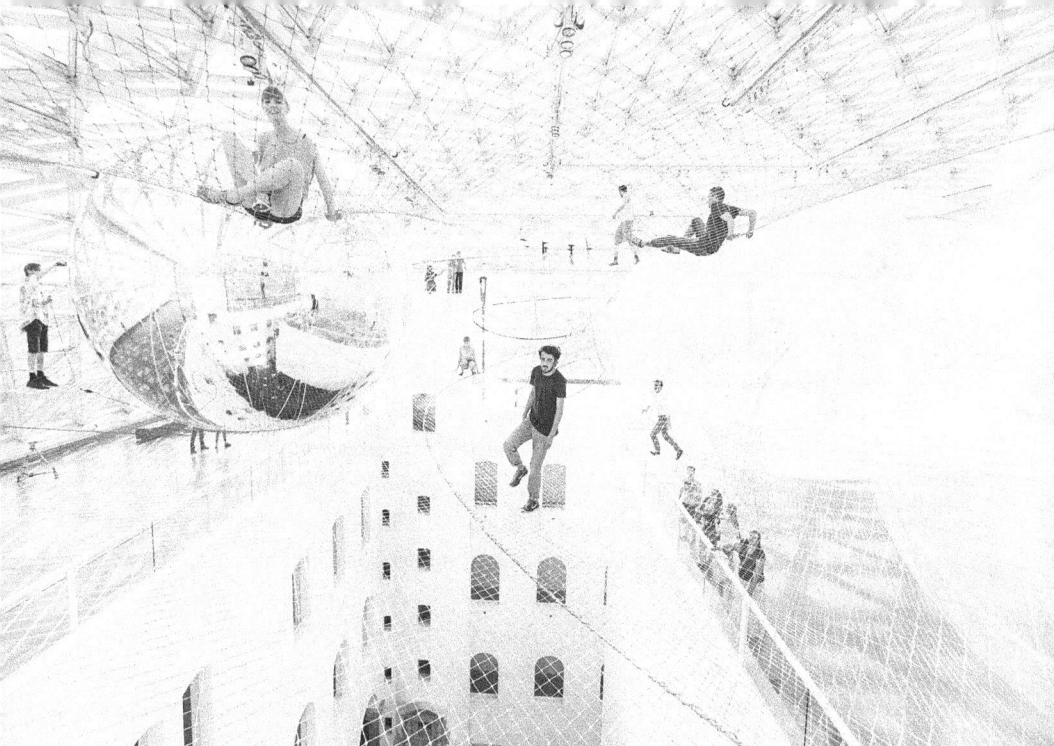

FIGURE 6.3. Tomás Saraceno, *In Orbit*, 2013–ongoing. Installation view at Kunst-sammlung Nordrhein-Westfalen, κ21 Ständehaus, Düsseldorf, Germany. Curated by Marion Ackermann and Susanne Meyer-Büser. Courtesy of the artist; Andersen's, Copenhagen; Ruth Benzacar, Buenos Aires; Tanya Bonakdar Gallery, New York/Los Angeles; Pinksummer contemporary art, Genoa; Esther Schipper, Berlin. Photo © 2013. Studio Tomás Saraceno.

to "negotiate" the work.[12] A contractual relationship was thus established that implied trust in the museum, as long as one abided by the imposed rules of conduct. Mori's *Wave* UFO called for similar assistance and norms, thus underlining the heterotopic quality of art institutions even when unpredict-ability constitutes a core concept of the artwork.

In Orbit simultaneously embodies order and disorder. The edges of the net suggest a rational grid structure, which would normally guarantee con-trol and facilitate predictions. Yet, once participants step onto its surface, it becomes more heavily subjected to tensile forces that hint at the inevitable entropy nestling even within rigorously organized structures. The environ-ment is the epitome of a multicentered system in which relations between participants are contingent on physical laws that defy individual control. The participatory scenario Saraceno proposed for *In Orbit* is closer to that set up by Czarnecki in *Contagion* because it inspires a heightened sense of physical threat that is only partially evident in Mori's *Wave* UFO. The latter triggers more concerns about psychic manipulation than anxieties over the sustainability of the system one enters. Nonetheless, all three installations prompt awareness of both universal patterns and ongoing transformations that impede the possibility of fully predicting the evolution of biological and social systems solely based on observations of their most characteristic behavior. They enable an embodied experience of "distributed agency," a concept formulated by Jane Bennett to explain that a singular subject is not necessarily "the root cause of an effect" and that interrelations between actants, whether human or nonhuman, are "porous, tenuous and . . . indirect."[13] At an aesthetic level, systems thinking is rendered intelligible not simply through the translation of abstract ideas into visual information but though the enactment of sensory and behavioral scenarios that open up the potential for unpredictable relations. Defying the logic of discursive exchanges which can be mapped out based on syntactic rules, the three works set in motion affective responses and competing conjectures concerning the evolution of systems. They intensify the experience of dynamic transformations and hinder facile assumptions about individual capacities to model relations in isolation from others or apart from environmental variables. Neither of the three participants in *Wave* UFO can willfully shape the connections between the neural oscillations on her own, nor can visitors of *Contagion* put a stop to the virtual spread of viruses by exerting personal control over the flow of images. By the same token, individuals orbiting the space of Saraceno's environment cannot bring the vibration of the net beneath their feet to a halt. The fact that participants constitute *one among many* key sources of disorder within these works signals the end of modern dichotomic modes of thinking that align humanity with rationality and nature with chaos, while concomitantly drawing sharp distinctions between the mind and the body, the individual and the collective.

Making the Invisible Perceptible

Directing participants' attention to subtle transformations in consciousness and bodily motion, *Wave* UFO, *Contagion*, and *In Orbit* stimulate embodied experiences of complexity. In addition to inviting inward observation in connection with changes in one's environment, these works have an undeniably spectacular character because they conspicuously set the stage for observing other exhibition visitors' responses. On the face of it, this aspect seems somewhat at odds with the undermining of visuality in Burnham's systems esthetics. Yet this voyeuristic form of spectatorship exposes another layer of participants' systemic entanglement by pointing out how overt and covert social relations shape one's self-perception and behavior. Participants find themselves in a double bind that enhances the affective potential of the works: they are noting changes in their bodily signals while concomitantly watching others engage in similar or disjunctive physical and cognitive processes. At this level, the installations reflect the core principles of second-order cybernetics, which posit that an observer's presence impacts a system. Enhancing consciousness of copresence, they hint at the varying degrees of openness of systems and the interdependent ties formed with or without an individual's deliberate choice.

Visitors waiting in line to enter *Wave UFO* observe both the scintillating surface of the unfamiliar object lying in front of them and the facial expressions of those who are exiting its space. Similarly, *Contagion* engenders observation of participants from the exterior and interior of the red circle delimiting the area of interaction with the image projections. *In Orbit* also triggers the formation of a secondary audience that watches the behavior of participants who have chosen to walk in the net suspended above their heads. Through the multiple vantage points these installations offer onto their fluctuating components, they trigger the formation of affective ties among copresent viewers who grasp the limited degree of autonomy they have in relation to complex systems. Discussing the aesthetics of experience triggered by such works, art historian Caroline A. Jones argues that they may evoke the submission to spectacle but also establish bonds among participants that can trigger reflection and agency. She affirms, "If experience is always at risk of commodification, it is also in some sense all we have to build our communities of action and contemplation."[14] *Wave UFO*, *Contagion*, and *In Orbit* call attention to the affective exchanges among participants who model their systems. They enable participants to sense that communication is established between them not only via an exchange of words or gazes but also via inconspicuous means such as neural wiring and biochemical processes. A heightened systems consciousness is thus acquired not through an omniscient perspective on a set of relations observable from afar but through an embodied experience of material ties that are not always visible.

The three installations suggest that individual bodies cannot be fully contained from one another and that the space between them is subject to extensive dynamic transformations. In *The Transmission of Affect*, philosopher Teresa Brennan argues that hormonal and electrical changes are contingent on individual biology as well as on the social environments in which people act. She underlines the erroneous view of unidirectional cause-and-effect relations between living beings and their surroundings and contends that we regularly shape the space between us through affective exchanges that defy the presumably insulating boundaries of our bodies.[15] Participants in *Wave UFO* are made visually aware of their interconnected minds even when they are not facing each other. Their bodies are oriented toward the dome where projections of their neural oscillations may eventually converge in a harmonious whole. The intensity of the experience stems from the close bodily proximity of the participants, which enables the neural communication and emphasizes the social underpinnings of perception and cognition. Czarnecki's *Contagion* similarly enhances the acuity of participants' awareness of copresence. The perimeter in which viral infection seemingly occurs is only visually contained by the red circle projected on the floor. What is implied is that the actual spread of airborne diseases may defy physical containment. The movement and color of the plumes indexical of human presence, along with the dramatic musical composition accompanying the interaction, heighten the experience of impossible insulation from other entities. Saraceno's *In Orbit* also confirms that reciprocal influences among participants in a system are not only the effect of direct contact or conscious manipulation but can be triggered by intuitive responses to each other's actions and their impact on the shared environment.

The multisensory art practices associated by Jack Burnham with "systems esthetics" anticipated more recent scientific findings about neural and biological entrainment. Expressing his concern that visuality in art diminishes the ability of individuals to sense the contingent relations between themselves and their environment, he emphasized that "in a systems context, invisibility, or invisible parts, share equal importance with things seen."[16] Teresa Brennan also suggests that by prioritizing visual information over data received via other sensorial registers, we become more and more inclined to disregard social contingency and to privilege individualism. She remarks that "sight . . . is the sense that renders us discrete, while transmission breaches individual boundaries."[17] Mori, Czarnecki, and Saraceno share this concern about reliance on visual information as the ultimate source of facts. In *Wave UFO*, visitors recline in seats that are positioned with their backs against each other to prevent visual focus on the presence of coparticipants. Since synchronization between neural oscillations primarily occurs when individuals close their eyes and produce alpha brainwaves upon entering a restful state, participants may not actually be able to catch a glimpse of the ring formed on the dome when their neural systems grow in sync with each other. *Contagion* prompts a similar realization that systems consciousness does not necessarily originate in the observation of visible ties. Ultimately, there is no reliable visual evidence of the moment of contamination with SARS viruses even if the work may strive to render it noticeable. *Contagion* indicates that information can make an inconspicuous entrance within a system and gradually lead to its reconfiguration. The haptic quality of the grainy video footage emerging in the margins of the circular disc makes viewers strive to identify its content based on analogies with memories of events they experienced in person or via mass media representations. What is vaguely perceptible can ultimately fuel more attention than what is immediate. It can also stimulate a greater activation of the higher-order processing of information to derive meaning and adopt a critical position on what one senses. In Burnham's words, "By rendering the invisible visible through systems consciousness, we are beginning to accept responsibility"[18] for our limited, yet salient, agency in the equilibrium of relations.

While visual cues for aesthetic experience and behavior are still quite prominent in visitors' interactions with *Wave UFO* and *Contagion*, once inside *In Orbit*, participants need to respond promptly to changes in the system by relying on proprioception. They attempt to maintain their balance on the steel wires by adjusting their bodily posture, yet every slight change in the pressure applied by just one participant to the net is bound to trigger a reverberation under the feet of other coparticipants. Burnham's notion that "sight analysis" becomes less dominant in systems-oriented art practices, whereas "kinaesthesis" rises in significance, is evident in Saraceno's environment. *In Orbit* places heavy constraints on participants' mobility and visual assessment of their position in space. They gradually acquire an acute sense of changes in tension in the steel nets and intuitively learn to adjust their muscle tension in response.

Kinetic acuity is significant in participants' encounters with all three installations. Mori enables viewers to visualize their neural activity as well as the easily perceptible movement of their eyes and limbs. The quivering of the body is indelibly intertwined with the flow of consciousness. If at first sight *Wave UFO* may be interpreted as an artwork that privileges the mind over the body, it is actually consonant with Mori's beliefs that the spiritual and the corporeal are heavily entangled.[19] Kate Mondloch explains that this environment acts as a foil for neuroscientific modes of recording brain activity in isolation from other bodily processes and the social context of experience. She argues that *Wave UFO* offers a "creative repurposing of neuroimaging" and reveals "the condition of embodied cognition—that is, the fundamental entanglement of body, brain and environment."[20] What may appear as abandonment to a state of passive surrender by witnessing representations of one's neural activity is in fact a call for considering the enactment of the mind in conjunction with shifting social and biological parameters.

Czarnecki's *Contagion* also proposes a recalibration of attention based on participants' enhanced multisensory acuity. Within its space, they realize that what they sense is ultimately the result of their movement in space and their contact with others. The lack of a visual index of the virus on the screen until contagion ultimately occurs and the fuzzy formations corresponding to human presence acquire a grayish hue further suggests that invisible biological entities that exist in the space between participants can be health hazards. Movement constitutes both a necessity for survival and a potential threat to subsistence within the red perimeter of contagion. Sean Cubitt astutely remarks that *Contagion* makes evident the failures of individual or mass control of a system. He signals the limitation of biopolitics in the context of dynamic systems: "If the biopolitical mind that manages populations is a database, the near involuntary jostlings of people . . . are the database's unconscious, the material reality of gesture which escapes its plan."[21] Participants follow pathways that are not necessarily congruous with a predictable pattern that is thought out in advance. Since *Contagion* is an open system, it is always liable to expand in complexity as other visitors join its space.

Saraceno's *In Orbit* similarly exposes the chaotic interdependency inherent in the system of nets and spheres in which participants act. How one moves does not depend merely on the vibrations triggered by the movements of another participant but also on the relations established among multiple participants and the elasticity of the sensitive web, which resonates as an instrument collectively played by an improvising orchestra. In Saraceno's view, one must adapt almost instinctively, being deprived of the ability to pause and consider multiple options for how to behave. The work challenges the self-centered inclination to overlook physiological entanglement in heavily interconnected systems and become immersed in processes of subjective projection that imply a rigid separation of oneself from the environment. If the participants cling too closely to controlling their individual role in the web of *In Orbit*, they risk losing their balance. The material parameters of the work undergo rapid changes and push participants to experience the limits of personal control viscerally. Saraceno is interested in identifying a faster mode of communication through the body that would enable us to adapt in a more fluid manner to transformations instead of strictly abiding by behavioral rules that lose their validity as relationships change. Embracing an ecosystemic approach, Saraceno posits: "We have to try to activate a process of re-actualization in relation to ever changing contexts, to therefore find a feedback for a faster process of communication, capable of imagining more elastic and dynamic rules."[22] Hence, it becomes apparent that a systems-oriented approach to art making necessitates not only a turn outward to the social construction of experience, but also a concomitant turn inward, toward the materiality of the body and its relationship to other biological and nonbiological entities.

Sensing System Instability

Wave UFO, *Contagion*, and *In Orbit* carry metaphorical associations with both protective, womb-like spaces and with environments that offer no promise of a fully insulated shelter. They suggest that individual containment is a myth, both in terms of the biochemistry of human bodies and the impossible separation of individuals from the vibrant surroundings in which they are entangled. The operational closure of systems is not to be confused with rigid forms of material seclusion. Transformation in conjunction with other entities does not usually amount to the utter dissolution of individuality or the suspension of self-regulation and cognitive processes that enable survival and trigger the negotiation of one's position in systems of all kinds. Mori, Czarnecki, and Saraceno's works do not absolve participants of responsibility. Despite their immersive perceptual qualities, they do not simply elicit abandonment to sensory enchantment but trigger affective disjunction with the aim of exposing shifting levels of contingency and autonomy. In her writings on the heterogeneous factors that influence human agency, Jane Bennett argues that "a vital materialism does not reject self-interest as a motivation for ethical behavior although it does seek to cultivate a broader definition of self and of interest."[23] In the same vein, Mori, Czarnecki, and Saraceno call on individuals to establish an active role in systems while keeping in mind the inevitable limitations these roles impose on their ability to trigger transformations with predictable outcomes.

All three works ask participants to step into unfamiliar grounds without having a clear sense of how the system will respond to their presence. Relinquishing a degree of control over the experiential situation is a prerequisite for the encounter with these environments. As one puts on electrodes in *Wave UFO*, steps into a zone of virtual contamination in *Contagion*, or loses balance in the steel net of *In Orbit*, a sense of unease inevitably emerges.

However, these anxieties are counterbalanced by the sensitivity of the environments to change and the lack of a clear center from which the situation is controlled. Far from rigid territories, these are elastic spaces that evolve in conjunction with the presence, movement, psychic moods, and thoughts of their participants, who repeatedly model and are modeled by dynamic relationships established between biological and social systems.

Interestingly, the works include visual elements that evoke the potential for extension and temporary containment. The neural connections established between the three participants in *Wave UFO* could potentially evolve beyond the three-minute interval in which their brain frequencies become visible. The *Connected World* animation suggests that participants may also be virtually on the same wavelength while witnessing a similar set of images. This latter possibility may elicit discontent at the thought of spectacle's controlling effect over both neural modulations and cognitive processes. Some hope can be retrieved as viewers consider the latent instability inherent in neural systems and the mere temporary alignment of their brainwave frequencies.

Czarnecki confronts participants with a more disquieting system experience. The perimeter of viral contagion has alluring visual qualities and gives the viewer agency by allowing her to influence the color of the plumes and to activate hidden video content. Yet, in the process of shaping visual projections, one is virtually challenged to assume the risk of contamination. The environment is made even more visceral by the fact that territorial demarcations would have limited effectiveness in the event of the spread of a virus. Ironically, the red circle on the floor would offer no guarantee of safety if an actual airborne virus were present.

Contagion encourages viewers to ponder the relation between singularity and holism. Singularity is signaled by color at the level of the floating plumes that correspond to human presence. Yet, these seemingly imponderable formations also connote open, multicellular systems that are perpetually in flux and can be thrown into upheaval upon coming into contact with viruses. The holism of an individual body system is thus counterposed to the holism of broader biological systems of micro- and macroorganisms in which it is engulfed. Czarnecki has long been preoccupied with the way notions of singularity and sameness are dependent on different degrees of distance from a system. Her interest in enacting information systems that prompt viewers to perform roles with which they may or may not be entirely comfortable is motivated by deeply ethical concerns. Her father was held captive in a Nazi camp in which the detained were subjected to scientific experiments. This traumatic family history, along with an interest in the dehumanizing impact of surveillance systems, has led the artist to consider under what circumstances individuals cease to grasp their shared human condition and end up perpetrating aggressive acts.

In *Contagion*, Czarnecki chose to overlap images captured from above by a motion-tracking camera with close-up mass media and scientific representations of human bodies to expose their transforming potential. By juxtaposing an ultrasound image of a fetus to an aerial view of a city grid resembling a video game setting, the artist attempts to sensitize participants to the way our relation to others transforms depending on our distance from biological and social systems. Drawing on Primo Levi's philosophy, she notes that under precarious conditions we all appear the same.[24] While this shared sense of vulnerability may encourage a more planetary mode of thinking that values equanimity and respect for a shared environment, Czarnecki feels that it may also pose problems unless one also contemplates singularity. She asks, "How far or close do you have to be to recognize difference? How close in can you get before the visual ceases to become relevant information for you? When does data become information become knowledge?"[25] *Contagion* challenges participants to oscillate between distant and proximate views on their existence in relation to a shifting web of visual information. It invites "resingularization" as one participates within a system that is responsive to acts that can have a potentially harmful effect on others.[26] In the installation, participants need to accept the limitations of their agency while simultaneously assuming responsibility for the way their individual acts can influence the balance of the system as a whole. Moreover, interaction with the environment invites involvement in acts of interpretation of blurry images that extend the sphere of associations between personal experience, sociopolitical events, and biological systems. Meaning making is as important as kinetic engagement in the space of *Contagion*. It suggests that responsibility is attained to a greater degree if one contemplates one's role across both biotic and metabiotic systems observable from shifting vantage points.

While Czarnecki metaphorically alludes to states of physical and psychic instability, Saraceno literally places participants in a vulnerable position. Whether contemplating the gravity-defying web of *In Orbit* from the ground level or tottering on its vibrating steel rods, visitors experience a degree of anxiety. His suspended environments do not merely express longing for the freedom associated with play and exhilarating sensorial experiences. They are deeply inspired by the artist's ecological concerns and the need for envisioning alternative modes of subsistence under threatening environmental circumstances. Notions of nomadism and ethical responsibility inform his discourse on the position of individuals within ecosystems. Saraceno espouses Félix Guattari's "ecosophic" views according to which survival will be possible only "through the articulation of a nascent subjectivity, a constantly mutating socius, an environment in the process of being reinvented."[27] While Guattari sometimes used the term *system* to designate a fixed structure that impedes transformation, his thinking on the interconnections between subjective projections, social relations, and the environment evokes the behavior of dynamic systems. The tensile space of Saraceno's *In Orbit* calls for an ecosophical engagement with multiple levels of experience, albeit one that does not permit too prolonged of a subjective analysis since participants need to be constantly on the lookout for emerging solidarities or tensions that impact their balance in the net. Consonant with the principle of "heterogenesis," defined by Guattari in terms of "processes of continuous resingularization" that permit individuals to "become both more united and increasingly different," the installation prompts a sensation of attentive alertness to psychic and bodily cues, as well as to unpredictable environmental modulations.[28] In Saraceno's vibrating net, one is challenged to intuit the evolution of the system while concomitantly sensing that no fixed rules of movement could guarantee equilibrium. Attempts at maintaining balance are contingent on individual attention, weight, and kinetic responsiveness, as well as on the behavior of coparticipants and the flexibility of the web underlying the open system.

In contrast to Czarnecki's and Saraceno's works, Mori's *Wave UFO* offers a much more circumspect view on processes of heterogenesis that depend on singularity. While singularity is not discounted, especially since viewers can observe visual representations of their individual neural activity, it is seen more as a hurdle to acquiring a sense of oneness. Mori's approach underscores the value of relinquishing individual control and cultivates an awareness of limited individual agency. Mori argues that "the idea of 'open mind,' and the idea of looking at the universe as though we are only a part of it, might help us to not contaminate nature and to not exploit nature and kill life unnecessarily."[29] In this sense, her approach departs from Guattari's ecosophic view, which builds on persistent conflicts within planetary systems even if their components and spaces are deeply intertwined. Espousing a more universal approach infused with Buddhist ideas, Mori remains averse to singularity and somewhat skeptical of human interventions meant to redress ecological balance. She invites a change in attitude, hoping that it would trigger significant changes at all the other levels of society. Despite these differences, her perspective shares some affinities with the ecosophic stance, especially in terms of the value it assigns to interconnections between cosmic and molecular domains. The *Connected World* animation in *Wave UFO* bespeaks the intricate relationship between transformations occurring at micro- and macrolevels. Through merging spherical patterns, it invites analogies between molecular changes, fluctuations in the neural activity of participants, and cosmic energy flux. Perceiving complexity at different scales facilitates a systemic consciousness that is pertinent both to Guattari's ecosophy and Mori's practice.

Notwithstanding subtle distinctions in terms of ecological views, all three works suggest that grasping our intrinsic interdependence facilitates a behavior that can ensure survival through more careful attunement to changes in our environment. Given that the porosity of systems and the pace at which they are changing may lie beneath the visible threshold, Mori, Czarnecki, and Saraceno are engaging participants' broader sensorium and their imagination in order to channel alternative modes of experiencing the complexity of the environment. They contribute to the consolidation of "ecologicity," a term coined by art historian Amanda Boetzkes to define a new "cultural orientation" which implies an enhanced ability to calibrate perceptual processes to environmental variables.[30] She notes that this orientation arises in response to the limited legibility of the signs of the Anthropocene and the need to move past binary divides between "a physical reality and a phenomenal one."[31] While Boetzkes mainly discusses these perceptual changes in relation to visuality, the practices of Mori, Czarnecki, and Saraceno suggest that a shift in ecological perspective would call for a reattunement of multiple senses and an increased openness to potentially invisible clues to the dynamic behavior of planetary systems.

Mori's *Wave UFO* and Saraceno's *In Orbit* portray more utopian outlooks on the world, whereas Czarnecki's *Contagion* carries more dystopian connotations given both the ambiguity of the visual images and the correlations between participants' movements and the spread of diseases. Nonetheless, none of these three installations offers a black-and-white image of the implications of increasingly interdependent systems. Understanding that one's behavior within a complex system is dependent on social and cultural factors as well as on biological processes signals the need for recalibrating one's attention to the near and distant components of a system and the space between them. In Jane Bennett's words, "the *its* outnumber the *mes*" and, in a world threatened by ecological imbalances, it is essential to recall that we are "an array of bodies, many different kinds of them in a nested set of microbiomes."[32] It is precisely such an understanding that Mori, Czarnecki, and Saraceno seek to inspire by unveiling the commingling of participants' bodies in vibrant matter that does not abide by the Cartesian divides between subjects, objects, and environments. Their works testify to the physicality of hybrid assemblages that resist individual control but do not suppress human agency. Perceiving this tension between the contingency and autonomy of their acts, participants in the three installations become more attuned to changes that occur across multiple system boundaries, within and outside their bodies.

In 1969, Jack Burnham argued that artists are "'deviation-amplifying' systems, or individuals who, because of psychological makeup, are compelled to reveal psychic truths at the expense of the existing societal homeostasis."[33] Mori, Czarnecki, and Saraceno confirm his notion that artists can act as agents of disorder by inviting participants to consider scenarios that wreak havoc with preestablished roles. Yet, with the rise of new materialist theories, it is now also clearer than ever that they do this in conjunction with other actants that enter into complex relations with the variables of their works. *Wave UFO*, *Contagion*, and *In Orbit* entail orderly patterns and allow for recurrent reconfigurations of their material components, independently of the intent of the artist or the free will of individual participants. Through a heightened sense of embodied presence, they emphasize the inseparability of the biological from the social, the individual from the collective, the living beings from complex ecosystems. By plunging participants into overly sensitive environments, Mori, Czarnecki, and Saraceno impede a detached visualization of complex systems and reveal the limits of individual control. Their works indicate that a systems approach to art does not necessarily suppress tension and difference, but actually instills an enhanced awareness of contingent relations established among multiple agents. Sensing biological, social, and cognitive instability in participatory environments channels both attunement and differentiation, collective awareness and self-questioning.

NOTES

1 Melanie Mitchell, *Complexity: A Guided Tour* (Oxford: Oxford University Press, 2009), 12–13.

2 Jack Burnham, "Systems Esthetics," *Artforum* 7, no. 1 (1968): 31.

3 Jack Burnham, *Beyond Modern Sculpture: The Effects of Science and Technology on the Sculpture of This Century* (London: Allen Lane, 1968), 369–70.

4 Bruce Clarke, *Neocybernetics and Narrative* (Minneapolis: University of Minnesota Press, 2014), 13.

5 Mariko Mori, *Wave UFO* (Köln: W. König; New York: Distributed Art Publishers, 2003), 43–49.

6   Mariko Mori, "Interview with Mariko Mori, Japan's Most Radical Fine Artist," *Art Review* 3 (September 2006): 45.

7   Czarnecki designed *Contagion* in collaboration with the epidemiologist James Fielding, public health specialists Stephen Corbett and Nick Crofts, the natural historian Keith Skene, programmers Tim Kreger and Rob Stewart, and the composer Christian Fennesz.

8   For a detailed account of the two iterations in the interface design of *Contagion* and its growing degree of complexity, see Elizabeth Muller, "The Experience of Interactive Art: A Curatorial Study" (PhD diss., University of Technology, Sydney, 2008).

9   Bruce Clarke, "The Planetary Imaginary: Gaian Ecologies from Dune to Neuromancer," in *Earth, Life, and System: Evolution and Ecology on a Gaian Planet*, ed. Bruce Clarke (New York: Fordham University Press, 2015), 153.

10 Examples of such participatory pneumatic environments include *On Air* (2004), presented in the Palazzo Ducale in Genoa, and *On Space Time Foam* (2012), displayed at the Pirelli HangarBicocca in Milan. They are part of Saraceno's ongoing investigation in the design of suspended ecosystems called *Cloud Cities*.

11 Tomás Saraceno, artist lecture, at "Seeing/Sensing/Sounding," CAST Symposium, MIT, Cambridge, MA, September 27, 2014.

12 Safety instructions were found at Kunstsammlung Nordrhein-Westfalen, accessed October 12, 2015, http://www.kunstsammlung.de/en/discover/exhibitions/tomas -saraceno/sicherheitshinweise.html (link no longer accessible).

13 Jane Bennett, *Vibrant Matter: A Political Ecology of Things* (Durham, NC: Duke University Press, 2010), 31, 36.

14 Caroline A. Jones, "Biennial Culture and the Aesthetics of Experience," in *Contemporary Art: 1989 to the Present*, ed. Suzanne Hudson and Alexander Dumbadze (Chichester, UK: Wiley-Blackwell, 2013), 198.

15 Teresa Brennan, *The Transmission of Affect* (Ithaca, NY: Cornell University Press, 2004).

16 Burnham, "Systems Esthetics," 35.

17 Brennan, *Transmission of Affect*, 17.

18 Burnham, *Beyond Modern Sculpture*, 370.

19 Mariko Mori, "Mary Jane Jacob in conversation with Mariko Mori," in *Buddha Mind in Contemporary Art*, ed. Jacquelynn Baas and Mary Jane Jacob (Berkeley: University of California Press, 2004), 263.

20 Kate Mondloch, "Wave of the Future? Reconsidering the Neuroscientific Turn in Art History," in *Perception and Agency in Shared Spaces of Contemporary Art*, ed. Cristina Albu and Dawna Schuld (New York: Routledge, 2018), 44.

21 Sean Cubitt, "Moiré Sinister," *Contagion*, exhibition brochure (Brisbane: Queensland University of Technology and Brisbane Festival, 2008), n.p.

22 Tomás Saraceno, "Conversation with Tomás Saraceno, Luca Cerizza and pinksummer" (2004), pinksummer contemporary art, accessed September 5, 2015, https://www.pinksummer.com/en/tomas-saraceno-on-air/ (link no longer accessible).

23 Bennett, *Vibrant Matter*, 13.

24 Czarnecki in Marco Mancuso, "The Art and the Epidemiological Criticism of Gina Czarnecki," *Digimag* 46 (July/August 2009), accessed March 26, 2020, http://digicult.it/digimag/issue-046/the-art-and-the-epidemiological-criticism-of -gina-czarnecki/.

25 Gina Czarnecki, "Silvers Alter," in *Humancraft: Contaminating Science with Art*, ed. Gina Czarnecki, Boo Chapple, and Sara-Jayne Parsons (Liverpool: Bluecoat, 2011), 87.

26 Félix Guattari, *The Three Ecologies*, trans. Ian Pindar and Paul Sutton (1989; repr., London: Athlone Press, 2000), 23.

27 Guattari, *Three Ecologies*, 45.

28 Guattari, *Three Ecologies*, 45.

29 Mori, *Buddha Mind in Contemporary Art*, 260.

30 Boetzkes, "Ecologicity, Vision, and the Neurological System," in *Art in the Anthropocene: Encounters among Aesthetics, Politics, Environments, and Epistemologies*, ed. Heather M. Davis and Etienne Turpin (London: Open Humanities Press, 2015), 272.

31 Boetzkes, "Ecologicity, Vision, and the Neurological System," 273.

32 Bennett, *Vibrant Matter*, 112–13.

33 Burnham, "Real Time Systems," *Artforum* 8, no. 1 (1969): 55.

The Contemporary Art World Described as a System

Abstraction, Dispersion, Deflation, and Noise

Liam Gillick's Disappointing Systems

FRANCIS HALSALL

If you try and use art as a fragmented mirror of the complexity of contemporary society you might try and develop a system of art production that is equally multi-faceted and *misleading* and that functions as a series of parallels rather than reflections of the dominant culture. . . . [And] you must also dissolve a little as an author. —Liam Gillick, "Berlin Statement"

We live in an age of systems. The condition of late capitalism is characterized by, on the one hand, the predominance of information as an organizing principle, and on the other, the distribution and dispersion of that information across complex systems of communication and control. This dispersion is experienced in the effects of a dispersed subjectivity as human subjects find themselves distributed across global systems. This chapter examines how the contemporary British artist Liam Gillick works with and through these complex information systems, and in doing so, mimics their logic of dispersion and distribution. However, rather than either celebrating these systems, or conversely, offering an antagonistic critique of them, Gillick does something else. His work is neither a spectacular nor even satisfactory aesthetic experience; one is not rewarded by spending more time with it, and it is not absorptive in the high-modernist sense of the word. But neither does it perform in the traditional avant-garde manner as an oppositional gesture directed toward bourgeois property relations and a fissure between art and life. Neither beautiful nor revolutionary, Gillick's work operates according to what, as is unpacked below, might be called strategies of "denial and deferment," where what is denied and deferred is both aesthetic satisfaction and critique. As he says: "In the current context this means that the abstract is a realm of denial and deferment—a continual reminder to various publics that varied acts of art has [*sic*] taken place and the authors were probably artists."[1]

Through a type of imitative excess, Gillick uses systems to provide what is a disappointing, deflationary, and ultimately unsatisfactory experience, either aesthetically or as a form of avant-garde opposition. This has the potential to act as a strategy of alienation whereby, through disrupting the usual function of the systems he uses, Gillick draws attention to their function. Gillick makes things that look like and fulfill the role of contemporary art. These objects and actions are, I argue, the tokens that provide access to the systems of distribution and display that support contemporary art. These are the economic and institutional systems such as galleries, biennials, art fairs, journals, websites, and so on; but the tokens Gillick provides are, ultimately, hollowed of meaning. Examining Gillick's work through the logic of systems brings some consistency to a set of practices that are otherwise too pluralistic, dispersed, and diffuse to be considered a coherent practice. It also allows me to employ some specific terms from systems theory to describe what Gillick is doing; specifically, Bateson's use of *noise* and *restraint*. In doing so, as I argue below, Gillick's work can be put to work to do what Fredric Jameson calls "cognitive mapping," that is, a means of giving discernible forms to abstracted systems of contemporary life and opening up their conditions to scrutiny, albeit in ways that are, ultimately, disappointing.

The advantage of the kind of "cognitive mapping" that Gillick's disappointing systems can produce is that, through these deflationary acts, Gillick engages in a subtle form of critique in which viewers are confronted with the dispersion of their own subjectivity. The work is unsatisfactory because, ultimately, that is the condition of subjectivity in late capitalism. This produces disappointing work as a strategy for avoiding the double risk of being complicit in the logic of neoliberal market fundamentalism either through valorizing these conditions of dispersion through empty spectacle or reducing critique to part of that spectacle.

Cognitive Mapping in the Age of the World System

Fredric Jameson argues that the contemporary ubiquity of systems—which I am arguing is Gillick's subject matter—was established in the mid-twentieth century with the emergence of the "world system of late capitalism" and is "inconceivable without the computerized media which eclipses its former spaces and faxes an unheard-of simultaneity across its branches."[2] This historical condition has also been called the "network society" by Manuel Castells and the "postmodern condition" by many others, including Jean-François Lyotard.[3]

Common to all these accounts is a challenge to the notion of an autonomous human subject and to the value of communicative rationality that is commonly identified as the outcome of the European Enlightenment. In the age of the world system, humans are repositioned within existing economic, technological, and ecological systems that are beyond their control. The influence of electronic technologies such as computing and telecommunication systems coincided with shifts in economic policies and the rise of the market fundamentalism that is often called neoliberalism. This led to both the subsequent dominance of information as the predominant metaphor for communication and organization and the reconfigurations of those social systems that were established in modernity, including economics, law, education, and forms of modern liberal democracy.

All these developments coincided with the power of nation states becoming eclipsed by global systems of communication and control in which capital has migrated into information—which has subsequently become the primary unit of capitalist exchange—and power is distributed and dispersed across systems. These effects of production and power create new experiences of subjectivity that, like information, is similarly understood to be both distributed and dispersed across different systems while being produced and mediated by them. In the age of the world system, human subjectivity is understood not to exist a priori to these processes but rather to emerge from an ecology of social, historical, and material conditions within which it is positioned, such as economic transactions, communication systems, and social media. In other words, subjectivity does not preexist processes of production and power but is instead constituted by them. For subjects that are distributed and dispersed across different systems, the alienating effects of late capitalism constitute historically specific modes of experience and, therefore, are the conditions of their subjectivity. In turn this means the ideological foundations of the world system operate on the level of perceived reality itself.[4]

That the world system operates on the level of perceived reality itself creates a problem in how it may be represented and critiqued, as subjects are too immersed in these systems to have an effective critical purchase on their effects. The problem is that if we are always *in* a social system, then a position of observation from outside of the system is impossible. As Fredric Jameson observes, such a system is too "vast" to be effectively represented, because it "cannot be encompassed by the natural and historically developed categories of perception with which human beings normally orient themselves."[5]

Jameson used the term *cognitive mapping* to describe aesthetic strategies for revealing the conditions of the present in a manner that uncouples them from their situation within late-capitalist ideology.[6] Cognitive mapping is a form of sociological description that aims to reveal the actual effects of ideology on the individual prior to acts of representation that will themselves be inflected with that ideology. To cognitively map a social system is to begin to describe how the subjective and the intersubjective are intertwined through the social spaces people occupy or are excluded from. Hence it suggests the potential, within aesthetic practices, of mimicking its effects. For instance, Jameson argues for the potential in films like conspiracy thrillers and science-fiction to offer forms of critique, as they can, through fiction, suggest existing hierarchies and power structures that are embedded in capitalism. Crucially for my argument, this critique does not depend on the authorial motivations or intentions of the filmmakers, but rather how the work might be subsequently employed in the process of cognitive mapping. And, as is unpacked below, Gillick's work provides a similar opportunity to cognitively map the systems of late capitalism through presenting some of these systems in a way that thwarts the usual expectations of them.

Gillick's Use of Systems

The diversity and abstraction of Gillick's practice exemplifies the conditions of contemporary art and, therefore, as I argue below, the conditions of contemporary subjectivity. Gillick is a prolific collaborator, working not only with curators and other artists but also with designers, architects, filmmakers, municipal entities, rock bands, and fashion lines. This has included collaborating with Pringle under the tagline "liamgillickforpringleofscotland," producing knitwear, bags, and display structures for a pop-up store at Art Basel Miami Beach (2011). He has also produced architectural interventions on the facades of buildings including the Home Office (*Home Office London* [2002–2005]) and the Lufthansa Aviation Center in Frankfurt (*Four Levels of Exchange* [2005]). For $\Sigma(N_o 12k, L_g 17M_{if})$ *New Order + Liam Gillick: So It Goes . . .* , he worked with the band New Order at the Manchester International Festival to design the set for performances in which the group deconstructed its back catalog. He regularly contributes to the online contemporary art journal *e-flux*, and he writes and edits books such as the anthology *All Books* and multiple volumes of his own collected writings.[7] In 2009, Gillick represented Germany at the 53rd Venice Biennale with *How Are You Going to Behave? A Kitchen Cat Speaks*, an installation comprising bare pine structures that recalled functional domestic architecture such as a kitchen. The installation featured an animatronic cat, an obscure text about the cat that could be heard being read out in the space, and a model of Arnold Bode's 1957 proposal for the new German Pavilion.

As Sean Keller puts it: "Here is an artist who wants to take it all on: global capitalism, corporate identity, product design, institutional critique, modernism and its aftermath, Minimalism and its aftermath, literary conventions, the linearity of time itself. . . . All of this is guided by an unresolved combination of the Marxist desire to explain everything with a single system (centered on economics) and a post-Marxist realization that no system can ever achieve this goal."[8] Yet, in spite of its diversity of medium and method, Gillick's art has a recognizable style and formal consistency. His signature pieces are modular forms made from aluminum frames, often including plexiglass, and colored with powder coated finish using a standard process of industrial production and the RAL Color chart. For instance, *Complete Bin Development* (2013, Kerlin Gallery, Dublin; figures 7.1 and 7.2) is a series of abstract, brightly colored boxes that recall the minimalist forms of Donald Judd. They are sculptural frames standing three meters high and paneled with brightly colored, transparent plexiglass. The objects stylistically allude to systemic structures insofar as, according to the descriptions for their fabrication, any number of structures can be used as long as they are separated by at least 1.5 meters. Hence the piece is a series of open frameworks, allowing for multiple iterations according to different exhibition conditions (indoors or outdoors, for example). The work also refers specifically to standard processes of mechanical engineering. In particular, Gillick draws on his extensive research into processes of automobile production, such as the Kalmar plant in Sweden, which produced cars for Volvo between 1974 and 1994 and which he proposes as a model for how social systems operate in a post-Fordist context.[9]

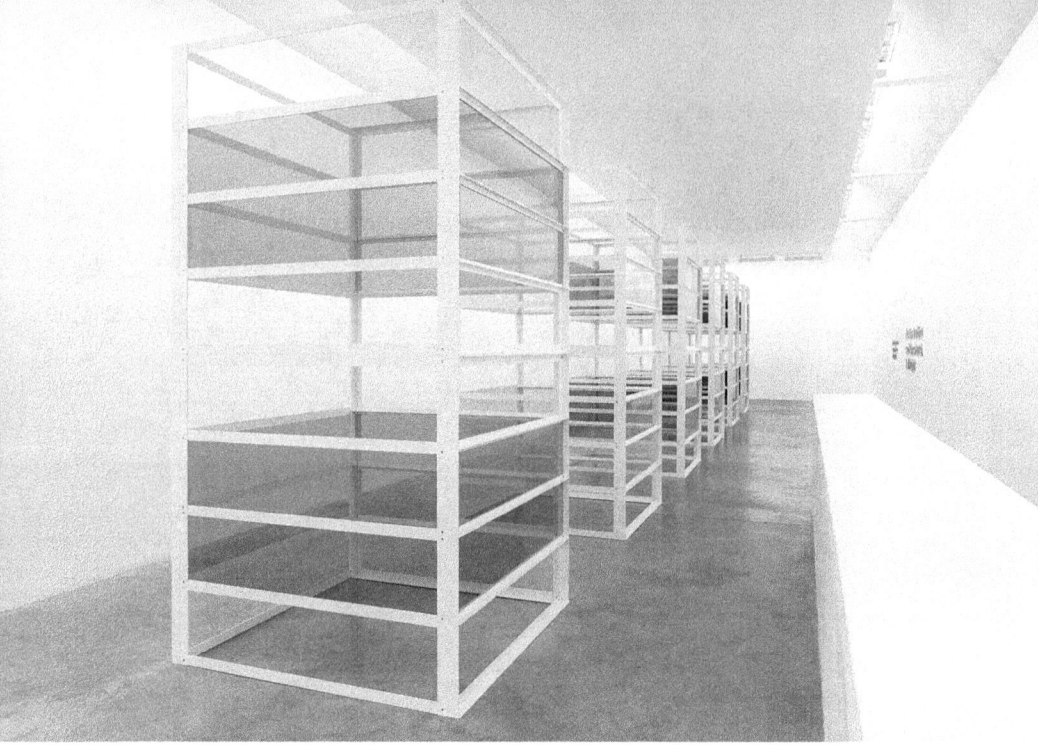

FIGURE 7.1. Liam Gillick, *Complete Bin Development*, Kerlin Gallery, Dublin, 2013. Powder coated aluminum, six plexiglass elements, each element 118.1×59.1×59.1 in. / 300×150×150 cm. Image courtesy of the artist and Kerlin Gallery, Dublin.

Complete Bin Development, as with all his work, no matter the medium, points beyond its formal structure to a complex series of reference points that involve processes of abstraction and obfuscation. What, exactly, a work like *Complete Bin Development* is actually about remains unclear. But, looking beyond its formal consistency, Gillick's broader body of work reflects a consistent engagement with systems of distribution, communication, and control. It is my argument that the concept of systems provides a meaningful way for understanding what Gillick does. His use of systems, like his work in general, is abstract and obscure; they also seem to frustrate viewers' attempts to appreciate or grasp them. While they are handsome objects, they are, ultimately, aesthetically bland and hollowed of meaning as either phenomenologically absorbing experiences or instances of politically charged polemic. Instead, if there are systems in Gillick's work, these systems are revealed to be dysfunctional, or in collapse, and will ultimately disappoint any attempt to enter a sustained or earnest engagement with them.

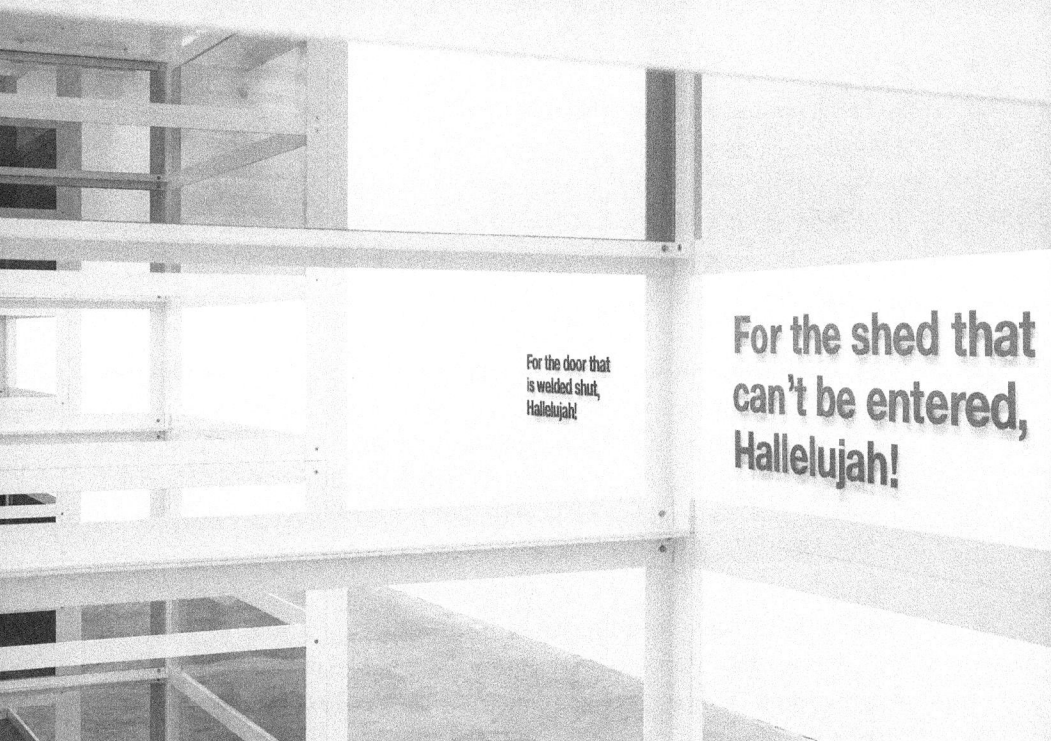

For the door that
is welded shut,
Hallelujah!

For the shed that
can't be entered,
Hallelujah!

FIGURE 7.2. Liam Gillick, *Complete Bin Development* (detail), Kerlin Gallery, Dublin, 2013. Powder coated aluminum, six plexiglass elements, each element 118.1×59.1×59.1 in. / 300×150×150 cm. Image courtesy of the artist and Kerlin Gallery, Dublin.

Art, Systems, and Subjects

Considering Gillick's work through the vocabularies of systems brings into relief how the systems approach challenges two long-standing preconceptions about the ontological status of art. First, it requires a recalibration in thinking about what works of art are, whether representations of the appearance of the world or instances of self-expression. Second, it also means we need to reconsider the forms of human subjectivity that generate and experience these works of art. Any understanding of what art is will always be underwritten by a correlated view of what a human being is. Consider the humanist model of art exemplified in the Western European Renaissance. Here, art is understood as an expression of some common values predicated on the universality of human reason, in contrast to the model of both art and subjectivity found in the expressionism, beginning in the late nineteenth century, that is often coupled with Western modernism. This perceives art not as the product of shared human values but as an index of a unique and individual expressive act.

Conversely, the systems paradigm considers phenomena in terms of information and not objects. As Gregory Bateson puts it, "After all, the subject matter of cybernetics is not events and objects, but the *information* 'carried' by events and objects. We consider the objects or events only as proposing facts, propositions, messages, percepts and the like."[10] When both art and the human subject are understood through the lens of systems, the idea that either is the expression of either a set of universal human values or an autonomous instance of individual expression needs to be jettisoned. Instead they are both objects and subjects that are radically distributed and dispersed across systems of communication and control.

Considering art under the sign of systems means not focusing on any essential or intrinsic properties but recognizing instead that its identity is organized, mediated, and thus constituted through a system of relations. Art, objects, and observers are triangulated through a complex and dynamic relationship with their context. In other words, art objects do not exist outside of the systems of communication and control that they are positioned within. Acknowledging this requires a shift, one that Jack Burnham already identified as moving away from "the cultural obsession with the art object" and toward a "systems consciousness" in which art is understood as being dispersed throughout systems of distribution and display.[11]

"Contemporary Art Does Not Account for That Which Is Taking Place"

As in the previous examples from Gillick, the techniques and media available to the contemporary artist are so diffuse that any historical specificity of established media—such as painting, sculpture, performance, and so on—have become emptied of certainty. In contemporary art, three fundamental concepts that have shaped art history are called into question: the notion of the discrete work of art as the focus of specific aesthetic attention; the concept of an artistic medium with specific constitutive elements and protocols; and finally, the role of the individual artist as one who engages in a particular type of activity (making and exhibiting art) within particular environments (art schools, studios, museums, galleries, fairs).

In an essay titled "Contemporary Art Does Not Account for That Which Is Taking Place," Gillick acknowledges this condition of uncertainty with his claim that "the flexibility of contemporary art is no longer sufficiently capable of encompassing all dynamic current art, if only because an increasing number of artists seek a radical differentiation."[12] Here Gillick reiterates established philosophical arguments about the end of art by a range of prominent critics, art historians, and aesthetic philosophers, including Hans Belting, Donald Kuspit, Arthur Danto, Thierry de Duve, and Peter Osborne, that I am claiming here, bring forth the condition of systems as a medium for art and of artworks as instances of communication dispersed across those systems.

Belting has reflected on the relationship between contemporary conditions of production and exchange in the era of postwar globalization, noting, "The commonplace concept of art can no longer cope with this [such conditions]. Everyone knows that art with an implied capital *A* has meanwhile fragmented into a spectrum of resistant phenomena that are accepted as art long before we are able to define them."[13] Here, Belting recalls earlier claims that modernism marked the end of the history of art by critics like Kuspit and Danto.[14] The general position which these arguments share is that the art historical moment of high modernism was an end point in a historical teleology of art. What followed this ending was a spirit of artistic pluralism and the dispersal of distinctions between specific media. Thierry de Duve similarly argued that this dispersal was necessitated by the figure of the readymade. Duchamp's gesture necessitated a shift in philosophical aesthetics from judgments on stylistic value to ones of ontology, in which the question, "Is this beautiful?" is replaced by, "Is this art?"[15] The condition of absolute indeterminacy that de Duve identifies is elaborated on by Peter Osborne in terms of a periodization which he dubs "post-contemporary." By this Osborne means that contemporary practices have become separated from any historical period or associated style. Instead, art is understood through a set of situational, rather than stylistic, conditions that are, crucially for my argument, distributed and dispersed over systems.[16] In contrast to other art historical categories like *Renaissance* or *baroque*, which have identifiable stylistic, historical, and geographical characteristics, postcontemporary art is "a radically distributive— that is, irreducibly relational—unity of the individual artwork across the totality of its multiple material instantiations, at any particular time."[17]

To impose some art historical order on this radically distributive character of art practices after modernism, Jack Burnham's borrowing of the term *systems* from cybernetic discourse has a renewed contemporary relevance. Writing in 1969, Burnham was prescient in identifying the effects of new technologies on how artistic media were understood and configured. Much more recently, both David Joselit and Lane Relyea have also considered the relationships between technologies and media through the vocabularies of systems and networks.[18] Joselit ascertains how the ubiquity of mobile screen technologies such as smartphones and tablets intensifies, accelerates, and expands the free circulation of images, leading to a condition in which the production of contemporary art is determined by format rather than medium. Format, Joselit argues, is "a heterogeneous and often provisional structure that channels content." Formats are opposed to objects, which are characterized by "discernible limits and relative stability [and which] lend themselves to singular meanings," while formats "regulate image currencies (image power) by modulating their force, speed, and clarity." "After art," Joselit explains, "comes the logic of networks where links can cross space, time, genre and scale in surprising and multiple ways."[19]

With a similar focus on systems of distribution, Lane Relyea argues that contemporary art is characterized by "the rise to dominance of network structures and behaviors and their enabling manifestations: the database, the platform, the project and the free agent or do-it-yourselfer."[20] A consequence of what Relyea identifies is the blurring of the lines between artist, cultural agent, and entrepreneur, with the effect that the identifiable figure of the artist becomes dispersed and distributed into other systems of communication and control.

The effect of this dispersal of art and artists into systems means that contemporary art practices increasingly tend to marshal relations in systems as both their medium and primary subject matter. In the mid-1990s, the French curator Nicolas Bourriaud dubbed this tendency "relational aesthetics" and applied it to the collective practice of a group of young artists, including Gillick, who came to prominence in Europe in the 1990s. Bourriaud identified that such practices operate within "the realm of human interactions and its social context rather than the assertion of an independent and private symbolic space."[21] In doing so, he argues, they place an "emphasis on a parallel engineering, on open forms based on the affirmation of the trans-individual."[22]

A characteristic work of relational aesthetics is *No Ghost Just a Shell* (1999–2002), initiated by the artists Pierre Huyghe and Philippe Parreno, who invited other artists, including Gillick, to contribute to the project.[23] For $400 (46,000 Japanese yen), Huyghe and Parreno acquired the copyright and likeness of generic female Manga character called Annlee. The character was a prepubescent girl, with wide eyes and blue hair but otherwise few characteristic features, who Parreno described as "a character without a biography and without qualities, very cheap, which had that melancholic look, as if it were conscious of the fact that its capacity to survive stories was very limited."[24] The somewhat anonymous and adaptable figure of AnnLee served as both the "shell" of the title for a variety of different manifestations and the medium for those manifestations, which included video works, graphic design, and animations. The whole work was presented as a series of relations between its different constituent elements within systems. As Huyghe observed of Ann-Lee: "It's a sign around which a community has established itself and which this community also established. Unlike a logo, it is a fragile sign without autonomy; it has that ability to become plural and complex. A hologram requires several beams of light to exist. Each author is the amplifier of an echo that he or she has not emitted and does not own."[25] Gillick's contribution to this project was *AnnLee You Proposes* (2001), a three-minute video in which AnnLee discusses her situation in fragmented and abstract terms. The work was exhibited as an installation at Tate Britain (2001), with accompanying sculptural elements of colored, modular forms typical of Gillick's practice.

For Bourriaud, the potential of such practices is political and lies in how they can represent contemporary conditions of subjectivity. By participating in social relations, art participates in social systems and carries the potential to transform them. Relational practices are inherently and necessarily systemic. However, as I will argue below, where Bourriaud is attempting to recoup the emancipatory social potential of art by inserting it back into systems of relations, Gillick's strategic use of systems is more obtuse and deflationary. Because of this deflationary air his work is, ultimately, unsatisfactory. It does not seem to reward sustained aesthetic attention. The result is to produce a form of alienation from those systems. We are not immersed in them; they cannot easily be engaged in. They offer no spectacle, entertainment, or solutions. They are disappointing, and in this lies their potential to be used as an apparatus for critique.

Disappointing Systems

Gillick produces with and within the systems of contemporary life, adopting them as his medium. For example, within the economic system Gillick's objects have a commodity value within the art market. But their identity is awkward because they remain unsatisfactory aesthetic experiences. The work is not reducible to the systems within which they circulate because they also declare and perform their position within other systems. In addition to the art-world system and the economic system, his work engages other, parallel social systems. For instance, as a professor at Columbia University and Bard College, he participates in the higher education system. As an actor, Gillick has performed in a feature film, where he plays a character indistinguishable from himself (an example discussed in greater depth in the conclusion). Similarly, for his contribution to the *No Ghost Just a Shell* project, his work was entangled in the legal system, since Huyghe and Parreno acquired the copyright of the AnnLee character. The project culminated in 2002 with a legal document that supposedly guaranteed (in a legal sleight of hand) ownership of all rights and copyright of AnnLee to AnnLee herself.

Gillick works with these systems to generate an aesthetic that is awkward, deflationary, and disappointing. In a discussion with Beatrix Ruf, Gillick described his work as something that might disappoint expectations: "People either functionalize the work, instrumentalize it, or use it as a metaphorical structure. The truth is that the work is none of these things alone. The object is neither just functional nor is it exactly a metaphor of the idea of place for something to happen. It has potential, it is in a constant state of 'becoming.'"[26] In addition to *Discussion Platform*, Gillick has produced several other works with the terms *discussion* or *platform* in the title, including *Discussion Island* and *Denominator Platform* (figure 7.3). As with much of Gillick's work, the materials follow the logic of corporate design with use of machined, powder coated aluminum, plexiglass, and the reiteration of modular elements. As Gillick observed: "Plexiglass and aluminum are the materials of renovation and refurbishment. They are the materials of McDonald's signs, and display cases in Prada, of airplanes and bullet-proof screens in banks, of really sexy nightclub floors and riot shields."[27]

Corporate vocabularies are also used in the publication *Discussion Island/ Big Conference Centre*,[28] which involves a story that is abstracted, fragmented, and hard to follow. As it describes itself, it is a text that "sweeps across various locations and situations in order to create a complex picture of how decisions are made at a point where there is no strong shared ideological consensus about how the future should be. . . . [it] starts in the new big conference centre of the title. A large space has gone unplanned and unnoticed in the new building to create a crisis, which will permit some degree of freedom within the planned structure."[29] Given that *Discussion Island* comprises multiple elements, it is left ambiguous as to the primacy of either text or object within the work. This was Gillick's intention for the work, and he claimed, "With this book the artworks related to it occurred both before and after the writing of the text and in many cases set the scene for a text that had few clear locations."[30] Through this strategy of the deferral of aesthetic focus *Discussion Island* is comparable to Robert Smithson's concept of the site/nonsite. It is constantly referring to itself as a complex, recursive, and yet never fully intuitable system of interconnected elements. As Bill Roberts

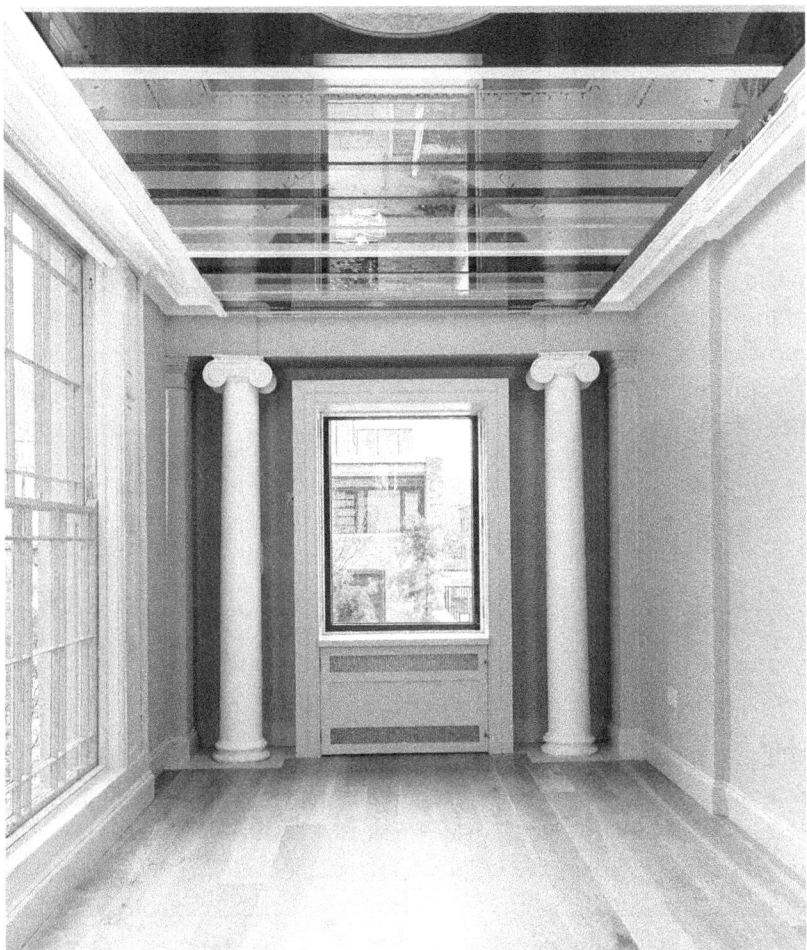

FIGURE 7.3. Liam Gillick, *Denominator Platform*, Goethe Institut, Dublin, 2018. Powder coated aluminum, plexiglass, 78.7 × 118.1 × 2 in. / 200 × 300 × 5 cm. Image courtesy of the artist and Kerlin Gallery, Dublin.

observes: "Gillick's visual and sculptural production therefore ought not to be taken to stand for his practice. It is, instead, a part of a more complex constellation of elements, which has the effect of relativizing the apparent claims of sculpture itself."[31]

Gillick's writing is prolific, but prolix and partial. It can be full of jargon and hard to follow. It frequently refers to his objects tangentially. Consider this passage, for example, which accompanied his contribution to the German Pavilion at the Venice Biennale (2009): "There will be a cat that can speak.

All the people of the town will be very proud of their speaking cat. People will come every day to hear what it has to say. It will be very cynical but never mean. It will see everything and understand it all. After a while people will only come on the weekends or drop by on the way home from work or school." The text concludes: "It will take a deep surreptitious suck of the children's breath and as they reel and swoon, glide and dream, it will begin to tell them a true story about the wisdom of a kitchen cat."[32] What exactly this might mean is unclear, and it does not help in unpacking the formal elements of the installation. And while the objects Gillick produces might be read as merely what Sven Lütticken calls: "quasi-illustrations of his discourse,"[33] any clear correspondence between text and object is obscured or frustrated. Gillick acknowledges this in his somewhat cryptic claims for one of the works:

> By leaving the first platform . . . alone in a room with nothing else and no other explanation, I was hoping to indicate that there was a revision of ideas and a visual shift about to take place. It functioned as an abstracted discussion space designating a move away from a text heavy, dinner party history play into attempts to look at the conditions around the planned middle ground. It echoed those socio-political spaces which are fought over within a neo-liberal consensus.[34]

Gillick makes objects and performs gestures that look like and perform the role of art. They are the tokens that give him access to a number of different systems of distribution and display, circulating in the economic and institutional systems that form the support structure for contemporary art, such as the market, galleries, biennials, art fairs, and so on. Gillick's objects become instances of communication that give him access to the various systems that he operates within. However, rather than being entirely complicit with such systems, the objects do not communicate any clear meaning. The works reveal their performative function and contingency through the very nature of their unsatisfactoriness. Gillick presents a discursive engagement with them, in order to "confront a socio-economic system that bases its growth and collapse upon 'projections.'"[35] Yet while doing so, they disrupt and render the communications of those systems ambiguous, abstract, and diffuse.

It is thus my argument that Gillick engages in an aesthetics of systems in a different mode than that of a formal, stylistic engagement with seriality. His work invokes systems to challenge the autonomy of both the art object and the process of authorship by demonstrating that, although inanimate, these objects circulate between different systems of communication and control and require these systems to frame and articulate their identity. These systems include the galleries, art fairs, and exhibitions where the objects are shown; economic systems in which they appear as commodities; and the discursive systems of contemporary criticism and art history where they circulate as discursive objects. Yet these objects are also, crucially, not entirely reducible to such systems. They also disrupt them through strategies of contradiction and abstraction: "The abstract draws artists towards itself as a semi-autonomous zone just out of reach. It produces the illusion of a series of havens and places that might reduce the contingent everyday to a sequence of distant inconveniences. It is the concretization of the abstract into a series of failed forms that lures the artist into repeated attempts to 'create' the abstract—fully aware that this very act produces things that are the representation of impossibilities."[36] When considered in the cybernetic vocabulary of Gregory Bateson, Gillick's processes of what he calls the "concretization of the abstract" can also be considered as the identification of *restraints* and *noise*. Such restraints, for Bateson, are the logic of the functioning of systems:

> In cybernetic language, the course of events is said to be subject to restraints, and it is assumed that, apart from such restraints, the pathways of change would be governed only by equality of probability. In fact, the "restraints" upon which cybernetic explanation depends can in all cases be regarded as factors which determine inequality of probability.... Restraints of many different kinds may combine to generate this unique determination.... From the cybernetic point of view, a work in a sentence, or a letter within the word, or the role of a species in an ecosystem, or the behavior of a member within a family—these are all to be (negatively) explained by an analysis of restraints.[37]

In systems theory, noise is that which accompanies communication but which is not communication. This has its origin in Claude Shannon and Warren Weaver's information theory, in which the information transmitted by noise is useless to the communication and introduces indeterminacy: "Uncertainty which arises because of errors or because of the influence of noise is undesirable uncertainty. It is thus clear where the joker is in saying that the received signal has more information. Some of this information is spurious and undesirable and has been introduced via the noise. To get the useful information in the received signal we must subtract out this spurious portion."[38] By contrast, Bateson emphasizes the usefulness of noise, due to its capacity to introduce novelty and a creative dimension into systems: "All that is not information, not redundancy, not form and not restraints—is noise, the only possible source of *new* patterns."[39] Following Bateson, Gillick acknowledges the noise and restraints of the systems he engages, but, rather than blatantly celebrate or critique them, he offers up a disappointing mirror image of their logics and effects.

Conclusion

In the feature film *Exhibition* (Joanna Hogg, UK, 2014), Gillick plays, in what is plausibly a disappointing mirror image of himself, the role of a conceptual artist living with his partner in a modernist house in North London. Neither Gillick nor his costar, the musician Viv Albertine, are professional actors, and his performance is naturalistic. His filmic presence is deadpan, down-beat, and somewhat inscrutable; it is disrupting and deflationary. In the film Gillick appears to be acting in much the same way that his objects perform in other exhibitionary contexts; that is, through a certain difficult-to-read obstinacy. His body, like his objects, present some disruption to a system of communication. Gillick admitted that he gave Hogg "a hard time. Not giving someone their line. Having my back to the camera. Just playing." He describes the process thus:

> Although we had no time between her request and the start of the shoot, she did suggest that I look at Bresson's *Notes on Cinema* before the shoot-ing started. He writes about the actor as mannequin. I decided to take this route. I often cleared my mind completely before scenes and just played them as a body in space. Sometimes I didn't even listen to the other actors around me—just sensed myself in space. I didn't think my character would be a good listener so I played him as someone aware of his body who doesn't hear everything first time—who is hearing every-thing for the first time—and mishearing some of it.[40]

Here Gillick is describing his approach to acting as being a body that doesn't communicate well and which interacts only awkwardly with its environment and other actors. My argument is that this is an apt description for how all his work responds to the environments and systems within which it is posi-tioned. Using modular and iterative processes, Gillick generates new systems within his own oeuvre. Inasmuch as they give the superficial appearance of being operational and communicative, his systems are incomplete, imper-fect, dysfunctional, and disappointing. His art does not offer a satisfactory aesthetic experience, but rather frustrates attempts to understand, enjoy, or like it. Through this disappointment, Gillick alienates us from the systems he deploys. Our attention is drawn away from the art objects toward the systems they sit within and, consequently, to our position within and reliance on the systems of communication and control of late capitalism. In doing so, Gillick's systems also present an aesthetic analogue for the contingent and dispersed conditions of subjectivity in the age of the world system. Through strategies of abstraction and deflation, Gillick's work is doubly disappointing: it frustrates any expectations of immersive spectacle in the face of the industries of entertainment and culture, while it also frustrates the supposedly radical antagonistic gestures of those avant-garde practices that were historically opposed to such spectacle. Gillick neither valorizes nor attacks systems but rather presents something more deflationary and, thus, provides an opportunity to engage in a critique of two systems—the system of capital and the system of art—by illuminating their mutual complicity in the production of contemporary subjectivity.

NOTES

Epigraph from Liam Gillick, "Berlin Statement," February 12, 2009, Hamburger Bahnhof, Berlin, published in Liam Gillick, *Wie würden Sie sich verhalten? Eine küchenkatze spricht/How are You Going to Behave? A Kitchen Cat Speaks*, ed. Nicolaus Schafhausen (Berlin: Sternberg, 2009). I am enormously grateful to Judith Wilkinson, Tate, for her help on this chapter.

1   Liam Gillick, "Abstract" (2011), originally commissioned by the Museo Tamayo in Mexico City for the exhibition catalog *Microhistorias y macromundos*, vol. 3, as part of the exhibition *Abstracción possible/Abstract Possible*. Available online at Liam Gillick, "Abstract," On-Curating, accessed February 26, 2019, http://www.on-curating.org/issue-20-reader/abstract.html#.XHgWeMD7Row.

2   Fredric Jameson, *The Geopolitical Aesthetic: Cinema and Space in the World System* (Bloomington: Indiana University Press, 1992), 10.

3   Manuel Castells, *The Rise of the Network Society* (Oxford: Blackwell, 2000); Jean-François Lyotard, *The Postmodern Condition: A Report on Knowledge*, trans. Geoff Bennington and Brian Massumi (Manchester: Manchester University Press, 1984).

4   Mark Fisher named this condition "capitalist realism" and argued with Jameson that in this condition it is easier to imagine the end of the world than the end of capitalism. Mark Fisher, *Capitalist Realism: Is There No Alternative?* (Winchester, UK: Zero Books, 2009).

5   Jameson, *The Geopolitical Aesthetic*, 2.

6   The term *cognitive mapping* is taken from the geographer Kevin Lynch's *The Image of the City*, where it is used to describe how people understand their environments by looking at relationships between physical and psychological space in urban contexts. This recognizes how the subjective and the intersubjective are intertwined through the social spaces people occupy or are excluded from.

Further, because it is related to the experience of space, it applies to bodily (aesthetic) practices rather than conceptual ones. Kevin Lynch, *The Image of the City* (Cambridge, MA: MIT Press, 1960).

7   See Liam Gillick, *Proxemics: Selected Writings (1988–2006)* (Zurich: JRP-Ringier, 2007); Liam Gillick, *All Books* (London: Book Works, 2009); and Liam Gillick, *Industry and Intelligence: Contemporary Art since 1820* (New York: Columbia University Press, 2016).

8   Sean Keller, "Liam Gillick, Museum of Contemporary Art, Chicago." *Artforum* 48, no. 8 (2010): 188–89.

9   Liam Gillick, "Maybe It Would Be Better If We Worked in Groups of Three?," *e-flux Journal*, no. 2 (January 2009), http://www.e-flux.com/journal/maybe-it-would-be-better-if-we-worked-in-groups-of-three-part-1-of-2-the-discursive/.

10 Gregory Bateson, "Cybernetic Explanation," reprinted in Gregory Bateson, *Steps to an Ecology of Mind* (Chicago: University of Chicago Press, 2000), 410.

11 Jack Burnham, *Beyond Modern Sculpture: The Effects of Science and Technology on the Sculpture of This Century* (London: Allen Lane, 1968), 369.

12 Gillick, *Industry and Intelligence*, 1.

13 Hans Belting, *Art History after Modernism*, trans. Caroline Saltzwedel, Kenneth J. Northcott, and Mitch Cohen (Chicago: University of Chicago Press, 2003), 4.

14 Hans Belting, *The End of the History of Art*, trans. Christopher Wood (Chicago: University of Chicago Press, 1987); see also Donald Kuspit, *The End of Art* (Cambridge: Cambridge University Press, 2005); and Arthur Danto, *After the End of Art* (Princeton, NJ: Princeton University Press, 2014).

15 Thierry de Duve, *Kant after Duchamp* (Cambridge, MA: MIT Press, 1997), 73.

16 Peter Osborne, *Anywhere or Not at All: Philosophy of Contemporary Art* (London: Verso, 2013), 51.

17 Osborne, *Anywhere*, 48.

18 In this chapter I take the terms *network* and *system* as being synonymous while recognizing that the relationships between the terms is complex and can be troubled.

19 David Joselit, *After Art* (Princeton, NJ: Princeton University Press, 2012).

20 Lane Relyea, *Your Everyday Art World* (Cambridge, MA: MIT Press, 2017), x.

21 Nicolas Bourriaud, *Relational Aesthetics*, trans. Simon Pleasance and Fronza Woods (Dijon, France: Les presses du réel, 1998), 113.

22 Nicolas Bourriaud, "Berlin Letter about Relational Aesthetics," in *Contemporary Art: From Studio to Situation*, ed. Claire Docherty (London: Black Dog, 2004), 48–49.

23 Huyghe and Parreno commissioned other artists to produce animations, paintings, posters, books, neon works, and sculpture which were shown at the Kunsthalle Zürich (2002) and the San Francisco MOMA (2003). The shows included Rirkrit Tiravanija's *Untitled (Even Electric Sheep Can Dream)* (2002), an eight-hour digital animation in which the character AnnLee reads the entire text of Philip K. Dick's *Do Androids Dream of Electric Sheep?*, and silkscreen posters by the artist collective M/M (2002).

24 Pierre Huyghe and Philippe Parreno, eds., *No Ghost Just a Shell* (Cologne: Walther König, 2002), 15.

25 Huyghe and Parreno, *No Ghost*, 17.

26 John Baldessari, Liam Gillick, Lawrence Weiner, and Beatrix Ruf, *Again the Metaphor Problem and Other Engaged Critical Discourses about Art* (New York: Springer, 2007), 24.

27 Sean O'Hagan, "This Is Not an Art Gallery," *Guardian*, May 5, 2002, https://www.theguardian.com/education/2002/may/05/arts.highereducation/.

28 Liam Gillick, *Discussion Island/Big Conference Centre* (Ludwigsburg, Germany: Kunstverein Ludwigsburg; and Derry, UK: Orchard Gallery, 1997), reprinted in Gillick, *All Books*, 141–98.

29 Gillick, *All Books*, 140.

30 Gillick, *All Books*, 140.

31 Bill Roberts, "Burnout: Liam Gillick's Post-Fordist Aesthetics," *Art History* 36, no. 1 (2013): 201.

32 Liam Gillick, "A Kitchen Cat Speaks," Helicotrema, accessed March 9, 2021, http://helicotrema.blauerhase.com/liam-gillick/.

33 Sven Lütticken, "(Stop) Making Sense," in *Meaning Liam Gillick*, ed. Monika Szewczyk (Cambridge, MA: MIT Press, 2009), 40.

34 Liam Gillick and Anthony Spira, "Speculation and Planning," in Liam Gillick, *The Wood Way* (London: Whitechapel Art Gallery, 2002), 15.

35 Gillick, "Berlin Statement."

36 Gillick, "Abstract."

37 Bateson, "Cybernetic Explanation," 405–6.

38 Claude E. Shannon and Warren Weaver, *The Mathematical Theory of Communication* (Champaign: University of Illinois Press, 1963), 29.

39 Bateson, "Cybernetic Explanation," 417.

40 "Exhibition: An Interview with Liam Gillick," ICA, April 30, 2014, https://archive.ica.art/bulletin/exhibition-interview-liam-gillick/.

Aesthetic Action as Planetary Praxis

Mel Chin's *The Arctic Is . . .*

AMANDA BOETZKES

It is a mild November morning in Paris. Yellowed autumn leaves drift to the ground in the parks. As people awaken and begin their daily routines, the streets begin to hum. The city is preparing to host the 2015 United Nations Climate Change Conference (COP 21). Jens Danielsen, an Inuit subsistence hunter from Qaanaaq, Greenland, drives his handmade wooden sledge and a team of seven French poodles down the boulevard. Covered in exquisite seal-fur coat, pants, and boots, he poses to have his picture taken with his harpoon in front of Notre-Dame, the Arc de Triomphe, and the River Seine. A delegate from the Inuit Circumpolar Council, he has come to Paris with his fellow hunter, Mamarut Kristiansen, to deliver a message about the rapid environmental changes in the northern Arctic that have dramatically affected their livelihood. These uncanny scenes of Inuit hunters in Paris were filmed and photographed as part of an artwork titled *The Arctic Is . . .* , orchestrated by the conceptual artist Mel Chin (figure 8.1).

Unexpectedly, on November 16 of that same year, the terrorist group ISIL executed a series of distributed attacks on the city of Paris, involving suicide bombers and gunmen with assault rifles who killed 131 people. France went into a three-month state of emergency. As soon as it was possible to leave the city, Jens Danielsen returned to Greenland baffled and appalled by this sudden explosion of global political conflict during the artwork's production. He

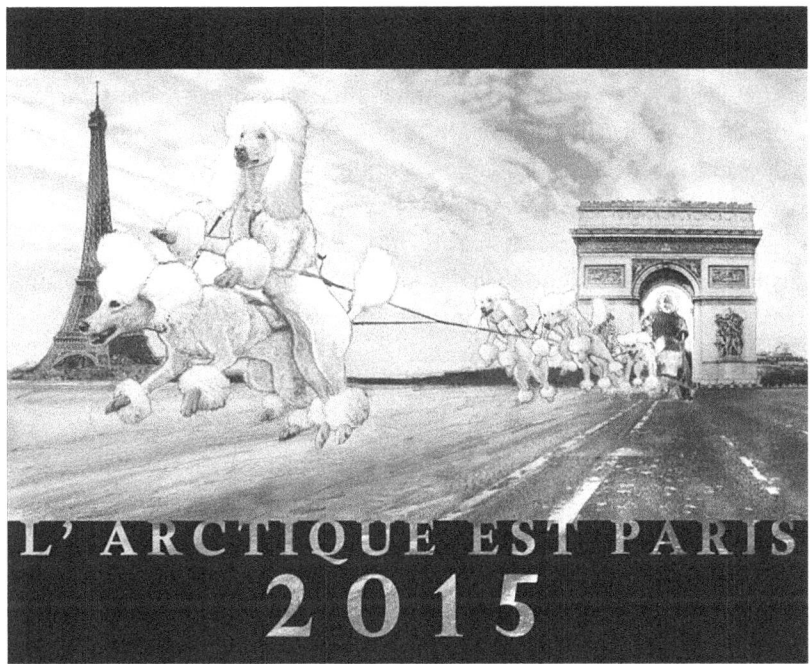

FIGURE 8.1. Mel Chin, *The Arctic Is* . . . (2015), hand-drawn poster. Image courtesy of the artist.

vowed never to return. Nevertheless, he delivered a message by way of Mel Chin's film for *The Arctic Is* . . . :

> The world has a mortal fever. I am a witness to this sickness. I see our way of life, thousands of years old, facing storms we can no longer read. . . . We do not ask for help, and we are not afraid. We have always adapted, and we will survive. We see the Gulf Stream warming; your Spring filled with floods, your Summer of unforgiving heat, your Fall of furious storms, your Winter of unbreakable days of ice. The Arctic is Paris, the Arctic is Kiribati, Beirut, Jakarta, New York, Rio, Santiago, Dallas, Dakar, Mumbai, Miami, Haiti, Helsinki. . . . The Arctic has always been part of the climate you know. Now that Arctic is no more.

Mel Chin was one of over a hundred artists and architects invited to spearhead a campaign of public engagement with the COP 21 conference. *The Arctic Is* . . . summarizes an ecological predicament: while climate change appears as a localized problem for the Arctic, its effects are planet-wide and appear in systemic feedback loops, whether social, political, or environmental.

The planetary condition perturbs all domains of human activity. But the unfolding of the artwork in tandem with the terrorist attack is also revealing. Global conflicts are not merely peripheral to climate change but rather are enmeshed with it. The scenes of Inuit hunters appearing and posing in the streets of Paris are an assertion of how Indigenous knowledge, lifestyle, and culture have an unprecedented contemporary relevance and urgency on the world stage. The work anticipates how major art centers of the West are changing their orientation to create an ecological perspective of the planet. Further, it demonstrates how climate crisis has transformed all natural and cultural landscapes and has fundamentally altered the terms *nature* and *culture*. Mel Chin's staging of a visitor from Greenland who had come to speak about a planetary problem was, however, accompanied by other visitors who came to this hub of Western culture in a violent expression and extension of the global perturbations between oil nations (ISIL claimed that the attacks were retaliation against France for its air strikes over Syria and Iraq). The work was therefore also the site at which a complex knot of relations and realities appears.

The Arctic Is . . . can be located at the conjunction of three interlocking systems: globalization, planetarity, and art. Taken together, we might see these systems as integral to an emergent paradigm of political ecology, as Bruno Latour defines it. To take these three domains as systems per se is to suggest that they are not merely areas of disciplinary knowledge—knowledge of economy, climate change, or aesthetics, respectively. Rather, it is to suggest that they are self-organizing entities that define the spatiotemporal coordinates of environmental reality. In turn, they orient and shape human perception and sensibility.

Importantly, though, the artwork gathers these three systems together with a supplementary circuit that mutually catalyzes all of them, making each visible in and through one another. The three systems are *energized* in and through the artwork: it reveals the dynamics in operation among them. In other words, art is an integral system of meaning chained to globalization and planetarity, but the particular work of art introduces a fourth term in its activity of knotting the three systems together in such a way as to alter the movement of energy among them. Systems aesthetics therefore demands an account of the dimension of energy that animates this exchange among systems. It requires understanding art as a form of *energy metabolism*. Mel Chin's *The Arctic Is* . . . is not merely a representation of systems but is rather a representational praxis that transects otherwise disparate systems and, like an energy circuit, sets vital forces in motion in an attempt to redistribute the points of connection between those systems.

In what follows, I will suggest that political ecology has become central to contemporary art's engagement with systems aesthetics. I will consider how Mel Chin's aesthetic actions transform the terms of systems aesthetics by engaging with planetary energies. Chin locates his work in a critical zone between globalization and planetarity; in a domain of invisible alterity and visual possibility where it mediates a reciprocal exchange of energies between systems. His aesthetic actions mobilize globalization, planetarity, and art in a circuit of reciprocal vital energies. Further, I argue that Mel Chin's praxis achieves this reciprocity by *anticipating* planetary activity and expressing its vitality in and through the existing field of globalization. It therefore operationalizes planetary energy against the grain of globalization's entropy.

Three Ecologies, Two Knots, and the Work of Art:
Reordering the Order of Globalization

In the late 1980s and early 1990s, the discourse of globalization instigated a reframing of ecology as both an environmental system and a politicized form of thinking. The concept of "political ecology" emerged out of a set of quandaries over how to order knowledge of the world in ways that would account for a certain gap between a scientific understanding of planetary systems and a political understanding of global environmental crises. It was at this time that a number of theorists began to consider what Isabelle Stengers describes as "the intrusion of Gaia" into their understanding of globalization. However, the theorization of politics at stake in political ecology is not to be mistaken for any existing ideological struggle (a bad politics) but rather should be understood as a resetting of the terms of collective articulation and negotiation, as well as an acknowledgment of planetary forces as an integral part of that collective.

This account of globalization as a reordering of knowledge of the planet appears in Bruno Latour's introduction to his 1991 *We Have Never Been Modern*.[1] He opens with a description of newspaper headlines: statements about the depletion of the ozone layer, Monsanto's use of chlorofluorocarbons, drought in Third World countries, public debate about aerosols and inert gases. The headlines signal hybrid forms of knowledge across science and politics, but they also alert us to conditions of crisis. While the media seeks ever more information from "experts" (particularly scientists), it offers no consensus as to how to categorize the imbroglios of science, politics, economy, law, religion, technology, and fiction that characterize the effects of globalization.

Latour suggests that the recourse to scientific expertise is a fundamental cut to the Gordian knot that binds knowledge, interest, justice, and power.[2] This severing of an existing nexus of thought consequently polarizes knowledge of things on one side and human politics on the other. Latour's opening question is therefore, How might we retie the Gordian knot by crisscrossing the divide that separates exact knowledge from the exercise of power, nature, and culture? Invoking the image of the Gordian knot again in his 2004 *Politics of Nature*, Latour maps out a preliminary model of such a redistribution of knowledge, which he designates "political ecology."[3] Not only does political ecology replace the false binary of human politics and "nature" as the object of scientific study, it designates the philosophy of ecology itself as a systemic operation. To overcome the paradigm of globalization in modern philosophy, Latour proposes political ecology as its own auto-activation of thinking. Thus, as an alternative to "modernizing," we might instead "ecologize."[4]

Globalization's hybrid forms well up in the epistemological gap between science and politics. Latour's political ecology is an exercise in retying the Gordian knot in such a way as to account for these new forms. He insistently works the figure of the knot into a series of diagrams that bring coherence to the hybrid forms signaling an end of science and politics as discrete entities. This endeavor is crucial to understanding the specific ecology of Mel Chin's practice; I will return to this point. But before doing so it is worth considering that Latour's imperative to retie the Gordian knot of political ecology—in and as an operation of bringing this very political ecology about—has a theoretical kinship to Félix Guattari's figuration of ecology as an entangled tripartite form in his 1989 *The Three Ecologies*. Political ecology can be understood as a new development from Guattari's formulation of the three ecologies, and the latter's debt to Gregory Bateson's understanding of ecology as a cybernetic system imbricated with consciousness. Political ecology therefore has a history rooted in second-order cybernetics through Guattari's exegesis. But as I will suggest, political ecology charts a new path in systems thinking in its capacity to account for aesthetic actions as vital components of intertwining ecologies. Latour opens the way for thinking aesthetic meaning and planetary expression together as a common ontological form.

Guattari opens *The Three Ecologies* with an epigraph from Bateson: "There is an ecology of ideas, just as there is an ecology of weeds."[5] The confrontation between globalization and planetarity that informs political ecology can be traced to this genealogy of ecological thinking by which concepts are taken together with and against their chaotic alterities. Guattari maps out three intersecting systems—the environment, the social, and the subjective—in response to global-scale perturbations and environmental disequilibria that interfere with human modes of life: "The Earth is undergoing a period of intense techno-scientific transformation. . . . Domestic life is being poisoned by the gangrene of mass-media consumption. . . . Otherness [*l'altérité*] tends to lose all its asperity. . . . Despite having recently initiated a partial realization of the most obvious dangers that threaten the natural environment of our societies, they are generally content to simply tackle industrial pollution and then from a purely technocratic perspective. . . . Henceforth it is the ways of living on this planet that are in question."[6]

Guattari approaches this enigmatic crossing of the planetary condition with a technoscientific perspective of the globe by calling for an "ecosophy": a philosophy that would orient thinking toward the relationship between the three registers that constitute ecosystemic thinking. Guattari's ecosophy is not merely a reordering of thought but the operationalization of thinking ecologically across the disjoined scales and registers of the three ecologies. Ecological thinking is therefore a systemic process that interweaves the environment, society, and the subject through recursions between them. While these domains had historically been theorized in isolation, and through specialized disciplines, Guattari makes a case for thinking about their development in synchrony: the three ecologies are *fractal*, signaling to and co-shaping one another though they are autopoietic organizations.

Guattari's conceptualization of the three ecologies also drew from Jacques Lacan's diagram of the Borromean knot. Though the two theorists are often thought to have divergent trajectories, in their late careers they were both challenging their respective distributions of consciousness by considering the interplay between threefold systems. While Guattari theorized the three ecologies, Lacan embarked on his famous "topological turn," by which he employed the figure of the Borromean knot to visualize the intertwined (but untouching) spheres of the real, the symbolic, and the imaginary. In taking a topological turn, Lacan's theory of the subject invigorated studies on the ecology of mind, and ecopsychoanalysis, particularly in times of ecological crisis.[7] Lacan's Borromean knot figures the way in which the respective domains of the subject behave as interwoven rings of meaning that bind and separate spheres of the unthought. The rings of the knot overlap or undergird the continuity of meaning; they never meet but nevertheless produce effects such as anxiety, symptoms, and inhibition in one another. To cut one

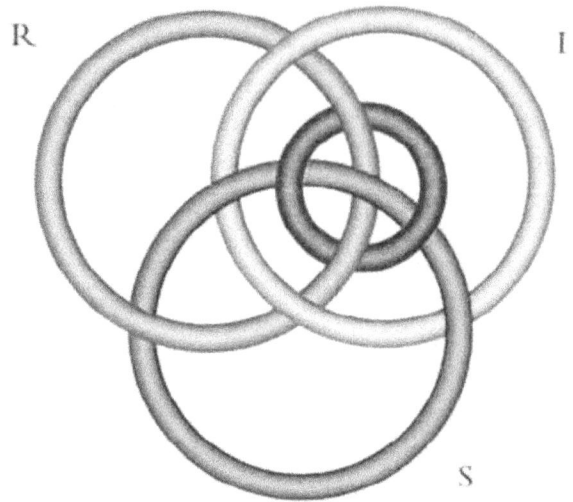

FIGURE 8.2. Jacques Lacan, "The Borromean Knot for Joyce with the Sinthome as That Which Restores the Knot" (1975). Reproduced in Jacques Lacan, *The Sinthome: The Seminar of Jacques Lacan Book XXIII*, ed. Jacques-Alain Miller, trans. A. R. Price (Cambridge: Polity, 2016), 131.

ring would be to sever the chain of meaning of the entire system. It thus exemplifies the fundamental enchainment of the subject to the real in such a way that the subject always proceeds "on the basis of the One."[8] Analysis would therefore be a task of untying and retying the Borromean knot to reconfigure the subject position.

In his Seminar 23, however, Lacan introduces the concept of the *sinthome*, a fourth component to the knot that is irreducible to the other three orders but that yields the capacity to rebind the Borromean knot and instigate a new chain of meaning (figure 8.2).[9] The *sinthome* is a prosthetic invention of the subject; it is singular and particular to the individual and an essential component for transforming the Borromean knot in such a way as to articulate and produce jouissance. In his analysis of James Joyce, Lacan submits that writing literature was Joyce's sinthome—a creative, though spontaneous, innovation of the subject that mediates an exit from the unconscious search for the phallus that marks the Oedipal subject and instead charts a course toward a desire beyond neurosis.[10] As Scott Wilson suggests, Lacan's deployment of the sinthome as a "beyond-Oedipus" may have been a mutual inspiration between Lacan and Deleuze and Guattari as they formulated their anti-Oedipus theory of jouissance.[11]

Lacan repositions the subject as a knotted topology, essentially, as an ecology of the mind. The creative flourish of the sinthome becomes a material agent that binds the topology together. It is also an opening by which to reconsider Guattari's siting of the mind as a planetary place (a topos) that can drive and be transformed by an ethico-aesthetic paradigm. For Guattari's three ecologies do not merely suggest a fractal homology between the environment, society, and the subject. Rather, each is activated and reformed through the energies of its intersection and co-constitution. In this respect, Guattari situates aesthetics as a planetary mode of existence, a primary force to activate systemic interplay between the three ecologies. Lacan's development of the sinthome within the topology of the subject is therefore also a valuable lens through which to consider the Latourian imperative for a political ecology through the knotting of global politics and planetary consciousness.

The alternative modality of creative expression—what Lacan calls the sinthome and what Guattari terms a "line of flight"—signals the departure of consciousness from the discursive framing of a technocratic global regime. The creative flourish is a metabolic *process*, as distinct from the machinic operations of systems in the service of what Guattari calls "integrated world capitalism."[12] It is in this respect that *The Three Ecologies* contributes an "ethico-aesthetic" component to a Latourian political ecology. The surplus activity that permits a recasting of the system—a retying of knots across epistemology and ontology—is a creative activity born of a different logic. We might therefore consider how works of art break out of the totalizing frame of any given system, and instead work to capture existence in the very weave that spans systems by introjecting alternative expressions across and between them.

It is in this context that we can return to Mel Chin's conceptual art practice and to the orchestration of systems at stake in his ongoing intervention. With *The Arctic Is . . .* Chin reknots epistemological zones by setting up the artwork as a synthetic representational form that integrates itself into planetary intrusions and then feeds those intrusions back into other systems as a meaningful form. An early example of this intrasystemic activity is his *Revival Field* project (1991–present; figure 8.3), for which Chin earned recognition as an eco-artist early in his career. For this work, Chin created a hybrid entity: a sculpture built into the Pig's Eye Landfill in St. Paul, Minnesota. The work doubled as a scientific laboratory to test hyperaccumulator plants and prove the hypothesis that they could absorb lead and heavy metals. The sculpture was defined in accordance with the parameters of a replicable scientific experiment. The area was separated from the rest of the landfill by a circular chain-link fence, surrounded by a square chain-link fence. The center of the test site was subdivided into two crossing paths to form an *x*, completing the shape of a pinpoint target, a reference to the focalized parameters of the work's remediation activity. The four equal sections of the circle were

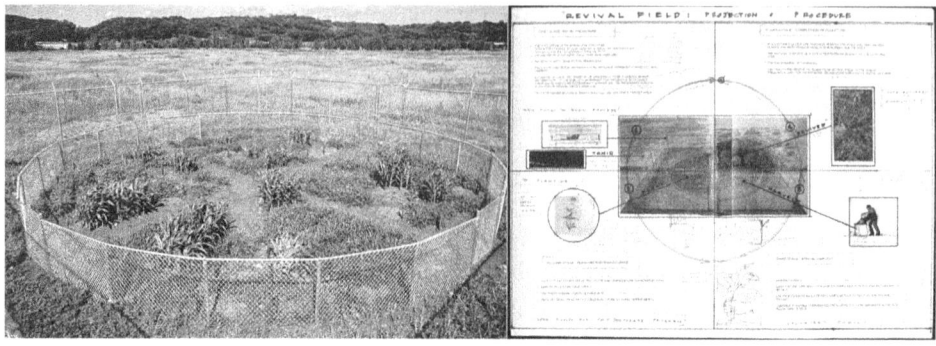

FIGURE 8.3. Mel Chin, *Revival Field* (1991–ongoing). Pig's Eye Landfill, St. Paul, Minnesota. 60 × 60 × 9 ft. Image courtesy of the artist.

planted with six species of hyperaccumulators, each arranged in its own separate domain so the plants could be harvested and compared over the course of the experiment, ideally with the proceeds from the plants generating revenue to replant the work. The final step in the process would be to remove the fence and return the site to the community as a growing, proliferating, and decaying ecosystem.

But while *Revival Field* acts as a laboratory experiment, Chin conceived of the biochemical remediation of the subsurface soil as an invisible sculptural process since the plants transform the soil at a molecular level as they extract the heavy metals. The process of biochemically purifying the soil is akin to the act of sculpting, which extracts form from raw materials such as marble, bronze, or stone. Chin therefore resituates the scientific disciplines of biochemistry and agriculture as sculpting tools that shape remediated soil, the resulting artwork. Otherwise put, he employs the tools and knowledge of science as an artistic operation.

An essential component of the artwork was therefore its artistic mediation of scientific research and its use of scientific research as an aesthetic form of environmental mediation. But in invoking science as a medium, the work also activated a political ecology. *Revival Field* was produced in collaboration with the geochemist Rufus Chaney, a scientist who had been forced to shelve his research on hyperaccumulators before being able to test them, due to cuts to his research funding during the years of the George W. Bush administration.[13] Mel Chin's arts grant was a salutary opportunity for Chaney to test hyperaccumulators, though this test would take place only adjacent to the scientific apparatus where this might normally take place. Chin and Chaney proved the phenomenon of phytoextraction and published their results in the peer-reviewed science journal *Applied and Environmental Microbiology.*[14] But more than being a resource for environmental research, Chin imagined the artwork itself as economically generous. He designed the work to "give back" to the community through the harvesting of ore from the plants, provided it with the tools to remediate the soil, and developed a model of site restoration that the community could sustainably uphold.

Revival Field was threaded across domains of knowledge and against the grain of the industrial resource economy that led to toxic dumping in an open landfill. Instead, its aesthetic form drew together a political ecology. The work's reconstitution of soil as sculpture also doubled as the production of a "proven fact" of science (a fact that was later published in a peer-reviewed scientific study), and tripled as a sustainable resource for the community, enacting a retying of the Gordian knot of the modern episteme that separates science and politics in Latour's terms. Furthermore, it did so in its deployment of a processual ecology that energized the pathways of knowledge, politics, and environment in and through the aesthetic form of the artwork, namely, its link to vital planetary activity. We might therefore also think of *Revival Field* as the prosthetic figure of Lacan's sinthome, a fourth term that precipitates a new logic of intertwinement. The aesthetic procedure of the work invoked a reciprocity of vital energies between its original social, environmental, and economic systems.

From this perspective, *Revival Field* can be understood as a vitalist cosmogram. It is both a diagram of a knotted cosmopolitics and a living processual system that works itself into and against the toxic space in the landfill through its own generative energies. Chin's diagram of the work from 1991 charts a counterclockwise circular movement across its four quadrants, from the administrative preparation of the site, to the planting of the hyperaccumulators, to their harvest, and finally to the return of the site to the community. Where Latour identifies a blind spot amid the condition of globalization, *Revival Field* enacts a remediation in this forgotten zone. Not only is the artwork located exactly where industrial waste has accumulated, it generates new symbolic meanings from this undesignated space. It is activated by and activates the site through the reciprocity between ecologies. Thus, the form begins with the more insidious implications of a target; land that is marked for toxic dumping, as though held in the crosshairs of a rifle. But these formal partitions are repurposed for producing a scientific proof of the (invisible) phenomenon of phytoextraction. The terms of visibility change as the remediation takes place. Ultimately, the artwork generates a flourishing of plants to be harvested, which reconstitutes the target as a zone of ecological abundance. Finally, then, the demarcated area comes to fruition through the redistribution of its systemic coordinates. The aesthetic paradigm configures scientific knowledge, political concern, and planetary agency to enact one another in concert.

Aesthetic Action as Planetary Expression

Chin's transection of science and art as the constitution of a political ecology must also be understood as a movement in systems aesthetics toward a planetary praxis. However, it is important to specify that what designates "the planetary" as such remains a zone of alterity. The vital energies that the artwork sets forth are not symbolic representations but rather real forces that are channeled into configurations of aesthetic expression. In other words, planetarity in and of itself cannot be reduced to political ecology. Rather, planetarity is the intrusion of forces and energies that occasions new ecologies of sense, knowledge, and practice. Planetarity is the ur-form of the spectral Other; an original alterity that, like Lacan's real, appears eventfully, sometimes even catastrophically. It expresses itself with particular urgency in its destabilization of the material conditions produced by globalization.

In her initial formulation of the concept of planetarity, Gayatri Spivak presents it as an undecidable figure of alterity.[15] It makes an uncanny appearance that is not derived from identifications with globalization. To think ourselves as planetary, rather than as global or worldly, she argues, is to radicalize alterity itself (one's own and others) in ways that are not derived from the global imaginary that is still rooted in a colonizing framework. Nor can it appear within the "gridlines of electronic capital," those virtual delineations that constitute geographic information systems. "The globe is in our computers," she summarizes.[16]

Despite the command of globalization to schematize the imagination, Spivak argues, humans always tend toward an alterity, a transcendental figure, whether nature, mother, or god, that is attributed an original, animating force. Yet, this original force is prefigured by the imaginary structure of globalization. Planetarity is therefore a continuously receding domain, never bound to the strictures of the figure. It is both a radical figure of alterity in contrast to "nature," but also an insistent operation of disfiguration by which the planet, and planet-thought, preserves its zone of irreducibility within the dominance of globalization. Such a procedure is not merely a matter of representation, then; it is a matter of cultivating a response-ability within the rhythm of figuration and disfiguration of the planet's alterity.

In this way, Spivak defines planetarity as both a force and a philosophical disposition. Planetarity entails an embrace of an "inexhaustible taxonomy of names" for this force that can overwrite the globe and sensitize us to new forms of nomination and designation.[17] It is in following this impulse that Isabelle Stengers, Bruno Latour, and Donna Haraway, among others, introduce a panoply of mythological, classical, or fictional figures into their philosophies of planetary modes of existence. All three invoke the name and concept of Gaia, following from the climate scientist James Lovelock's Gaia hypothesis, which theorized the planet as an autopoietic, self-regulating entity. But despite, or perhaps because of, the vitalist assumption at the heart of planetarity, it is precisely its uncanny quality—the eventful perturbation of planetarity—that inflects the hermeneutics of Gaia.

In her description of the contemporary era as one of catastrophe and immanent barbarism, for example, Stengers describes Gaia's expressivity as an indifferent, but nevertheless intractable, *intrusion* into the confusion of globalization.[18] This notion of intrusion endows the appearance of planetarity with an ontological force. Further, Stengers's elucidation of Gaia invokes a theoretical praxis, an entire mode and language that is attuned to planetary forces. To name Gaia's expressivity as an intrusion is not to designate what is true (with scientific authority) but rather to execute a maneuver that confers the power to experience and think the planet in consonance with its indifference. Gaia is, after all, "blind to the damage she causes," a characteristic fundamental to the nature of intrusion.[19] The intrusion reveals the asymmetry of the ontological relation—or rather, the *arelationality* of the relation—between planetarity as primordial *physis* and globalization as a human-oriented (and capital-oriented) system. Intrusion is both the rupture of planetarity and the figure of that rupture.

The language of Gaia redirects the pathways of agential force: it is not merely symbolic but also pragmatic. The nomination of Gaia is not merely a naming but an action of ushering in an alternative regime of intention and causality. For Stengers this amounts to a reflection on the mode of address, not simply to Gaia but to those with the authority to govern and who will be forced to take responsibility for Gaia's intrusion. Stengers calls these people "the guardians," with a view to redesignating the domain of responsibility of those with public authority (scholars, economists, scientists) from the guardianship of rationality and disciplinary knowledge to the creation of a legibility and responsiveness to the planetary assemblage in the midst of catastrophe.[20] Such a designation must be undertaken in the mode of compassion, she suggests, with the proviso that such compassion is neither sympathy nor engagement with the deep ignorance of the global paradigm. Rather, compassion is a simultaneous refusal of the epistemologies of globalization and a recognition of the futility of heated confrontation in the public discourse, when such conflicts are deliberating over an uprooted and obsolete episteme.

Language itself is therefore a carrier and purveyor of planetarity. This efficacy, however, must be likened to practices of visualization, as Timothy Morton suggests with his concept of *phantasia*.[21] Morton argues that language has the sublime effect of producing a sense of object-like alterity in its very articulation. This effect—phantasia—is the way in which words provoke sensation in the imagination. The word *spice* in a poem, for example, presents an imagined olfactory sense that will produce a stoppage in the narrative flow. This sensual visualization is an ontological passage to the irreducible planet. As he puts it, "Visualization should be slightly scary: you are summoning a real deity after all: you are asking to be overwhelmed, touched, moved, stirred."[22] More schematically, however, he suggests that phantasia is the capacity of an object to imagine another object through their sensual contact.

The relay of the planetary through its sensual appearance makes it possible to consider aesthetic actions in terms of planetary praxis. Drawing from Sylvia Wynter's notion of *being human as praxis*, a means by which to address and overturn the racialization of entangled human and planetary differences, Jennifer Gabrys suggests how visual media constitute a *planetary praxis*.[23] By overcoming the human being (being human as difference from the planet), and instead becoming collective as a response to planetary thinking, Gabrys responds to Spivak's call to overwrite the globe through planetarity. She suggests that through its very procedure of image making, technological media become integrated into the environment. From the cartographic survey to satellite imaging or other virtualizations, media reconstellate collective responsibility through practices of partitioning and reimagining environments. A planetary ethic might therefore emerge from within the technicity of global media imaging, such that the practice of imaging becomes the medium for becoming planetary.

Planetary praxis is not without its complications, however. As Donna Haraway points out, the question of how to usher in planetary thinking is not a matter of technical ability but of consciousness in particular.[24] To specify her focus, Haraway draws from Hannah Arendt's analysis of the trial of the Nazi Adolf Eichmann, which raised the fundamental issue of the evil of thoughtlessness—Eichmann 's incapacity to think. Haraway argues for a distinction between the inconsequential thinking without mattering from disciplines that focus on evaluating information (especially the sciences, but not exclusively), and a thinking that is open and attends to the presence of planetary alterity. A core issue, then, is how to contend with the aggressive refusal of a thought toward what is not the self, amid the spaces that are filled with assessing information. Haraway answers this challenge with a bi-directional formulation of a planetary imperative: "Think we must: we must think!"[25] Importantly, this thinking is not just the occasion of a thought but rather the operation of thought mattering and opening to matter's processes as integral to systems of thinking. She therefore recapitulates the bidirectionality of thought and matter as a living system. Her statement, "It matters what thoughts think thoughts," insists on the implicit thoughtfulness of matter in the operation of it being thought.[26] In this vein, Haraway takes up Stengers's concept of Gaia's intrusion by suggesting that Gaia is an intrusive event that undoes thinking as usual and demands redistributions of thought in order to be thought at all.

Planetary praxis is precisely this operation of mattering a planetary system of thought. It is much more than an attentiveness to everyday practice or a diligence to materiality. Rather, it stems from the actionability that arises in the convergence of planetary matter, expression (language, affect, or other forms of communication), and thinking itself. Planetary praxis mediates the planet's alterity by attending to its intrusions. It registers within the human symbolic but also resists identification within it. As Haraway points out, "Gaia is not reducible to the sum of its parts but achieves finite systemic coherence in the face of perturbations within parameters that are themselves responsive to dynamic systemic processes. Gaia does not and could not care about human or other biological beings' intentions or desires or needs, but Gaia puts into question our very existence."[27]

Mel Chin's artwork seizes planetary intrusion as a condition of actionability—planetarity thus becomes an imperative and a domain of possibility for thinking. It is in this vein that we can return to *The Arctic Is . . .* and reflect on its aesthetic *modus operandi* as political ecology. It is perhaps precisely because planetarity raises the question of actionability that Mel Chin's work is impossible to categorize in terms of its medium. Even the categories of conceptual art or eco-art fall short, since his practice is defined neither merely by the dematerialized idea, nor by the ecosystem that determines the form of the work, but rather by the affordance that arises between these domains: its capacity to "ecologize," in Latour's terms. Chin describes his approach to art as a responsiveness to what is demanded of the situation: "I'm a conceptual artist, which means everything rises from an idea or a concept, but the way I do it is . . . if the concept needs to be a film, I do a film, if it needs to be a sculpture it'll be a sculpture, if it needs to be a painting it'll be a painting, if it needs to be a piece of clay, it'll be a piece of clay. It's a very diverse way of operating."[28] In other words, the aesthetic action emerges out of the concept, and the concept demands an aesthetic action: Chin cinches together a praxis from their codetermination.

I am suggesting that what constitutes Mel Chin's aesthetic actions as a planetary praxis is precisely the way in which they operationalize planetary expression. That is to say, they anticipate a planetary presence by both addressing this domain of alterity and opening the work to the possibility that it can and will express itself, though this expression emerges from an invisible domain and will surely perturb. Rather than enacting the human system of worlding in a hermeneutic cycling that Heidegger summarizes in his phrasing "the world worlds," Chin mediates the intrusion of Gaia: "the intrusion intrudes." In *The Arctic Is . . .* planetarity makes its appearance by way of the artwork's mediation, and specifically through the uncanny presence of a climate change messenger, Jens Danielsen. The image of an Inuit subsistence hunter in Paris, tugging his sledge against the concrete sidewalks in the middle of Paris, calls forth the full political ecology of climate change. This scene is not just an issue of global justice for the Arctic Inuit whose livelihood is jeopardized by the climate effects caused by southern paradigms of environmental exploitation and negligence. More than this, Jens Danielsen's appearance *intrudes*: he struggles conspicuously with the lack of snow and ice, attracts the confusion of bystanders with his Inuit clothing, sits obtrusively on his sledge in the middle of the sidewalk. These scripted actions are all part and parcel of the planet's expression through climate change effects. Moreover, the culmination of the work is the delivery of the message. Danielsen is clear: this is not a communiqué from the Inuit, nor is it for their benefit. He specifies, "We have always adapted. We will survive." The message is the environmental intrusion of the planet into the coherence of a globalized city, with all the systemic reactions it implies, from the political disruption of seeing a displaced Inuit in Paris to the implied physical struggle with a warming climate, to the colonial reactivity precipitated by the unexpected sight of an Indigenous person in full winter hunting garb.

The staged intrusion is a mediation of planetary force with a view to provoking a movement of consciousness. Through its intervention on the global framing of climate change with a planetary intruder, the work introduces a surplus component that originates neither from science nor from politics but rather gathers the respective domains into a new domain of interaction. Like Lacan's sinthome, *The Arctic Is . . .* invokes an alien operation, an aesthetic action that knots together formerly dissociated zones (the domains of the real, the symbolic, and the imaginary for Lacan; the three ecologies for Guattari; and, in political ecology, the global and the planetary by way of art).

Redirecting Energy Systems: From Global Entropy to Planetary Negentropy

While *The Arctic Is . . .* initiates a planetary praxis, the fact remains that it also coincided with another form of intrusion: a terrorist attack on the city. The event of COP 21 was therefore subject to at least two kinds of uncanny intervention at its margins, the aesthetic action of subsistence hunters from Greenland orchestrated by Mel Chin, and the violent takeover of the city and a set of mass murders executed by ISIL insurgents. In a sense, we might view these two intrusions as a planetary sinthome, on the one hand, and an intensified symptom of globalization on the other. Another way to address them, in line with Stengers, is to distinguish the Inuit messengers of planetary catastrophe from ISIL's "harbingers of globalization's barbarism." But if both are forms of intrusion on the prevailing regime of globalization, and both signal its collapse, how might we further distinguish the role of political ecology in systems aesthetics? In other words, if we are to usher in a new system of planetary knowledge, how can we interpret the presence and coincidence of these two intruders in such a way as to distinguish political ecology from globalization's barbarism?

The answer lies in foregrounding the energic distinction between the sinthome as a form that generates vitality and the symptoms of globalization that serve to further entrench its regime of energy depletion. Recall that Guattari identifies ecosophy as thinking in and through process, rather than in and through a mere system. What lies at the heart of this distinction is the vitalism of process as distinct from the machinic repetition of the system. Ecosophy does not refute the system, but rather catalyzes systemic activity in unanticipated directions. Guattari cites Francisco Varela's concept of autopoiesis, or the living machine, to insist on the distinction between the machinic system *tout court* and its vital corollary, the "living autopoietic machine."[29] He gives two examples of this dissimilarity, one at the individual scale and the other at the collective. First, he writes, there is a distinction between a piano pupil's imitation of his teacher and the transference of a style likely to bifurcate in a singular direction. In other words, the living system could be likened to a stylistic flourish. Second, he makes a distinction between the way a crowd aggregates and "collective assemblages of enunciation, which conjoin pre-personal traits with social systems or their machinic components."[30]

What makes ecosophy, as an ethico-aesthetic paradigm, a thinking system integral to a living system is precisely the enunciatory capability released by the vital energies of art. My return to Guattari's formulation of the three ecologies (and its proximity to Lacan's sinthome) opens the possibility to reconsider systems aesthetics, the intrusion of planetarity into the machinery of globalization, and Mel Chin's conceptual practice—all in terms of their *energic* circuitry. What is crucial to the development of political ecology out of the late twentieth-century philosophies of ecology, then, is a theorization of the creative flourishes that galvanize planetarity within the register of globalization in terms of their capacity to energize.

The philosopher Bernard Stiegler argues for the primacy of energy in his characterization of the era of the Anthropocene as a regime of entropy. Indeed, he redubs the concept the Entropocene (the age of entropy).[31] Stiegler suggests that globalization is fueled by the energies of labor and life, and these energies are incorporated into a thermodynamic system of perpetually diminishing returns. The technocratic era of combustion, with the steam engine as its iconic technology, initiated a broader form of systemic entropy causing ecological disequilibria. If the Anthropocene's distinguishing drive is combustion—the entropic loss of energy and life—it becomes necessary to countervail it with processes of *negentropy*. Negentropy would intervene on the seeming inevitability of the Anthropocene's hold on life through energy depletion. Such a logic requires its own form of inquiry, which Stiegler terms a *neganthropology*, an anthropology of the technological seizure and expenditure of the energy of fire.

For Stiegler, the protension of thought—the carrying forward of systemic thinking from memory into the future—is the site at which globalization's entropic tendency becomes apparent as both a technological and an environmental condition. Because of the speed of technical thinking, the depletion of energy occurs in and through the production of knowledge of the environment, particularly in predictive statements about the futurity of the world. Thoughts and environments are mediated within the same entropic system, so that the transformation of the environment through its depletion appears to be a foregone conclusion, even before it is carried through its technological seizure. In other words, while human thinking of the environment is processual, unless we become conscious of its tendency to extract energy, our thinking inadvertently forecloses the capacity to transform the future.[32] Entropy appears to be inevitable. Stiegler even characterizes this depletion of the future's vitality as a giant digital Leviathan that exerts its power over the entire Earth by penetrating the reticulation of thought (the ways in which we conceive of processes that have already transpired). The ways we assess the depletion of energy that has already taken place thereby preface the ways we attempt to think forward into the future.[33] In other words, the hallmark of the Anthropocene is not just the entropic depletion of energy in and of itself, but an entropic mentality by which humans carry forward foreclosures of the possibilities of the future into that future. Negentropy would, however, anticipate the heterogeneity of the world to come against the grain of entropy.

By distinguishing their respective energy movement—whether entropy or catalysis, we can consider the two intrusions that converged on Paris during COP 21. Whereas the terrorist attack intensifies the entropy of globalization, the uncanny appearance of Jens Danielsen recasts the perspective of that entropic system by delivering a message from an alternative knowledge base, value system, and awareness of unstoppable planetary forces. The content of that message stems from an Inuit perspective, but it also exerts force that is planetary in nature. The message describes in vivid and poetic detail the effects of climate change in the Arctic. The intrusion is shot through with an Inuit understanding of that planetary activity as an ontological force. The effect of the artwork is thus to assume and welcome an unknown knowledge, belief, and lived experience of the planet. It does not merely attempt a different production of knowledge as an epistemological endeavor ("here is a different cultural way of knowing") but rather effects an alternative way of knowing the planet through the messenger, Jens Danielsen ("my reality is your reality").

The messenger is a bidirectional circuit: Jens Danielsen transmits the planetary intrusion of climate change with an address to the logic of globalization: "The Arctic is . . . [every global city, including yours]." His message also speaks to the introjection of the planetary condition of the Arctic into the visual field of globalization. The message *expresses* and *is* the end of the Arctic at the hands of global warming, but also *expresses* and *is* the extension of the Arctic to every other global place. The planetary *is* the global; "the Arctic is Paris."

More than this, the message is implanted as an a priori reticulation of the planetary within the global and a simultaneous refusal of its absorption into the regime of the global: "The Arctic has always been a part of the climate you know. Now, that Arctic is no more." The message is manifest—it extends across the globe while nevertheless effacing its traces from that globe. It remains a withdrawn zone of alterity while it nevertheless sparks an emergent planetary perspective: a world that has absorbed the Arctic and in which climate change has fundamentally changed the way we map the world's geography. At the same time, the message deploys the demise of the Arctic as its catalytic material, as the very way in which we can see the future differently, though it is a way that embraces the reality of a world without the Arctic, defined as it has been through a history of resource extraction, colonial projection, the displacement of Inuit people, and military occupation. It therefore exemplifies a reversal of entropy to give articulation to a planetary future in which climate change is a reality, perturbing as this may be. The messenger/message enacts a neganthropology, a planetary thinking that thinks the planetary as knotted to the global, as an imminent future. *The Arctic Is . . .* ecologizes.

Conclusion

I opened this chapter by suggesting that Mel Chin's work instigates an energic reciprocity among the three respective systems of globalization, planetarity, and art. While Chin's work is "art" in the sense that it is part of an imaginary order that is knotted to the symbolic world of globalization and the planetary real, what distinguishes his practice is its introduction of a supplementary term, a mode of aesthetic action that deploys a catalytic planetary energy. This supplement is not just the added vitality of a literal energy (combustion) within the entropic logic of globalization. Rather, it introduces a planetary agent that stimulates a redistribution of vital force, orientation, and thinking among systems of knowledge. In *Revival Field*, this is immediately apparent insofar as the work transformed toxic soil into remediated land by reknotting scientific knowledge and political concern. An even more radical departure from a conventional global command of knowledge of nature, however, appears in *The Arctic Is . . .* in its capacity to harness climate change as a medium and force for altering future thinking about planetary existence. Its message enacted a reordering of the globe: there is no more Arctic, and the Arctic is everywhere. It anticipates a time and space in which climate change is indisputably present.

It is not surprising that the intrusion of the Inuit hunters was mirrored but also contrasted by their entropic global counterparts. The two sets of intruders coincided in Paris within the same zone that the artwork opened and made visible. But precisely because of the work's sensibility to intrusions, and of the eventful visibility of planetarity within globalization, the artwork's mediation of their mutual knotting activates the three systems of planetarity, globalization, and art through one another. In November 2015, during COP 21, the city of Paris was changed forever. It remains to be seen what will emerge from the reknotting of Paris with the Arctic, its planetary and global intruders, and the commingling of their interventions.

NOTES

1   Bruno Latour, *We Have Never Been Modern*, trans. Catherine Porter (Cambridge, MA: Harvard University Press, 1993).
2   Latour, *We Have Never*, 1–3.
3   Bruno Latour, *Politics of Nature: How to Bring the Sciences into Democracy*, trans. Catherine Porter (Cambridge, MA: Harvard University Press, 2004), 6.
4   Latour, *Politics of Nature*, 247.
5   Gregory Bateson, *Steps to an Ecology of Mind,* cited in Félix Guattari, *The Three Ecologies*, trans. Ian Pindar and Paul Sutton (1989; repr., London: Athlone Press, 2000), 27.
6   Guattari, *Three Ecologies*, 27.
7   See, for example, Joseph Dodds, *Psychoanalysis and Ecology at the Edge of Chaos: Complexity Theory, Deleuze/Guattari and Psychoanalysis for a Climate in Crisis* (London: Routledge, 2011).
8   Jacques Lacan, *The Seminar of Jacques Lacan, Book XX: On Feminine Sexuality, the Limits of Love and Knowledge*, ed. Jacques-Alain Miller, trans. Bruce Fink (Paris: Éditions de Seuil, 1999), 128.
9   Jacques Lacan, *The Seminar of Jacques Lacan, Book XXIII: The Sinthome*, ed. Jacques-Alain Miller, trans. A. R. Price (Cambridge: Polity, 2018).
10 Levi R. Bryant, "Notes on the Borromean Clinic," *Larval Subjects*, December 4, 2008, https://larvalsubjects.wordpress.com/2008/12/04/notes-on-the-borromean-clinic/.
11 Scott Wilson, *The Order of Joy: Beyond the Cultural Politics of Enjoyment* (Albany, NY: SUNY Press, 2008), 4.
12 Guattari, *Three Ecologies*, 47.
13 For a developed analysis of this work in relation to later works of the economy of soil remediation, see Amanda Boetzkes, *Plastic Capitalism: Contemporary Art and the Drive to Waste* (Cambridge, MA: MIT Press, 2019), 84–93.
14 Teresa E. Pawlowska, Rufus L. Chaney, and Mel Chin, "Effects of Metal Phytoextraction Practices on the Indigenous Community of Arbuscular Mycorrhizal Fungi at a Metal-Contaminated Landfill," *Applied and Environmental Microbiology* 66, no. 6 (2000): 2526–30.

15 Gayatri Spivak, "Planetarity," in *Death of a Discipline* (New York: Columbia University Press, 2003), 71–102.

16 Spivak, "Planetarity," 71.

17 Spivak, "Planetarity," 72.

18 Isabelle Stengers, *In Catastrophic Times: Resisting the Coming Barbarism* (London: Open Humanities Press, 2015), 43.

19 Stengers, *In Catastrophic Times.*

20 Stengers, *In Catastrophic Times*, 35.

21 Timothy Morton, "Sublime Objects," *Speculations* 2 (2011): 224.

22 Morton, "Sublime Objects," 224.

23 Jennifer Gabrys, "Becoming Planetary," *e-flux Architecture* (October 2018), https://www.e-flux.com/architecture/accumulation/217051/becoming-planetary/.

24 Donna J. Haraway, *Staying with the Trouble: Making Kin in the Chthulucene* (Durham, NC: Duke University Press, 2016).

25 Haraway, *Staying with the Trouble*, 57.

26 Haraway, *Staying with the Trouble*, 35.

27 Haraway, *Staying with the Trouble*, 44.

28 Mel Chin, interview, MacArthur Foundation, September 25, 2019, https://www.macfound.org/fellows/1031/.

29 Guattari, *Three Ecologies*, 102.

30 Guattari, *Three Ecologies*, 61.

31 Bernard Stiegler, *The Neganthropocene*, trans. Daniel Ross (London: Open Humanities Press, 2018), 38–39.

32 Stiegler, *Neganthropocene*, 43.

33 Stiegler, *Neganthropocene*, 47.

Mapping, *SEA STATE*, and State Violence on the Shores of Singapore

BRIANNE COHEN

In 2015, Charles Lim Yi Yong represented Singapore at the Venice Biennale with his multicomponent installation SEA STATE (2005–present). Ostensibly, it was the culmination of a ten-year art project and hailed Singapore's golden jubilee, or its fiftieth anniversary as an independent, postcolonial nation-state.[1] Yet SEA STATE also acted as a harbinger of dire planetary conditions in the form of rising sea levels and topsy-turvy land-water relations for many vulnerable coastal cities such as Singapore and Venice. As defined by the World Meteorological Organization, the sea state code describes the surface characteristics of a large body of water. Numbered from zero to nine and ranging from "calm" to "phenomenal," the statistics-based categorization specifies the height, period, and power of waves in each moment and location. Lim's SEA STATE draws metaphorically from this classification system to chart the changing socio-environmental shores of Singapore, both a powerful nation-state and a defensive city-state with a fragile coastline. The expansive artwork is composed of ten subparts (numbered 0–9), including elements of video and film, sculpture, photography, a garden, and an archival website of local stories, all exhibited in different configurations and various spaces over the last fifteen years (figure 9.1).[2] It touches on issues ranging from Singapore's postcolonial statehood and celebrated neoliberal development to

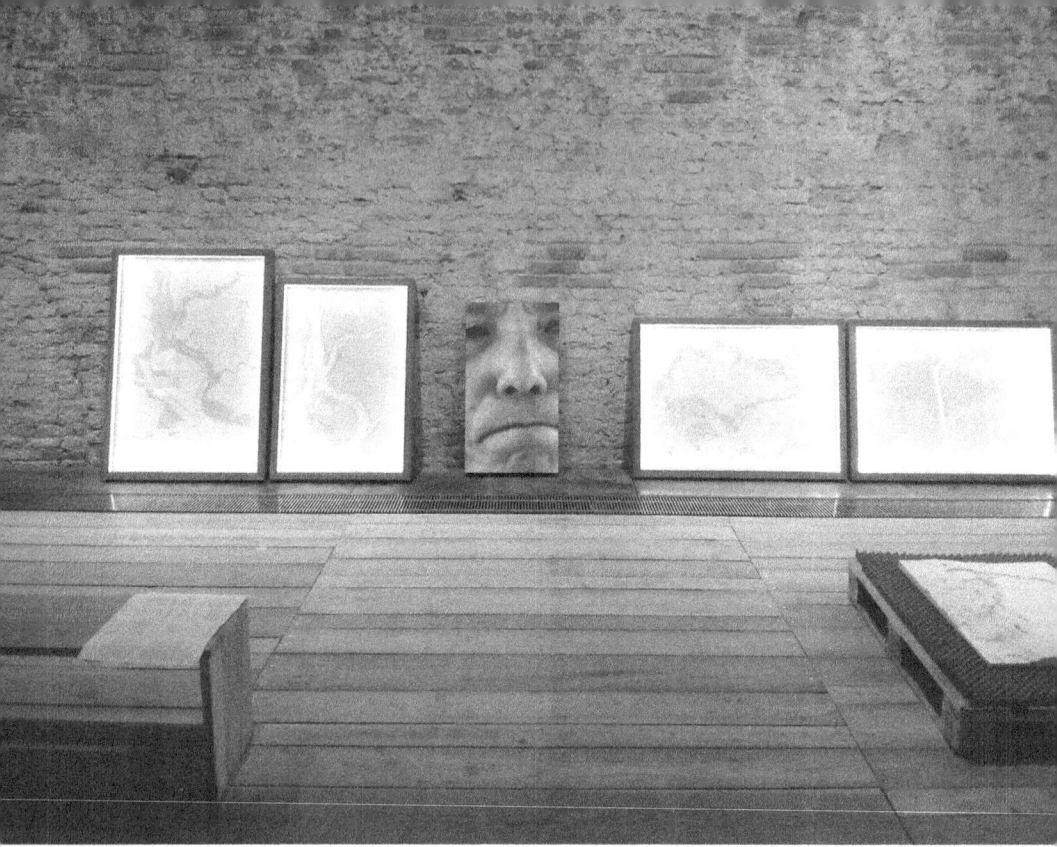

FIGURE 9.1. Charles Lim, *SEA STATE*, partial view of Venice Biennale installation (2015). Photo taken by the author.

rising sea levels and the country's violent extraction of sand throughout the region.

SEA STATE 0: all the lines flow out (2011), for instance, focuses on the porousness of Singapore's composition, documenting the city's extensive system of drains, canals, and rivers for water catchment.[3] All of these "lines" in the short film—the beating arteries of the city—eventually flow out to the ocean, and with their flow, human figures increasingly lose control over the water and their elaborate management of it. In the beginning, spectators view a lone man walking away from the camera in one such *longkang* (or drain, in Malay). He easily steps through its calm, still water, stopping at one point to devise a simple fish trap made from a plastic water bottle. Following this, a group of individuals wearing full-body, transparent white rain gear slowly walk and converge on the same low-filled drainage canal. The anonymous, spectral assemblage look as if they are speculating about a problem in the longkang, yet viewers are left with no information, only an ominous feeling created by the gray scene and monotonous noise of falling rain. The camera, however, then zooms in again on the handmade fish trap, now filled with about a half dozen small, glistening fish, suggesting that the ghostly figures still maintain some control over the waterways. Subsequently, the film transports spectators through many other longkangs and higher-filled canals of the city, offering both picturesque views of urban high-rises as well as trash-filled riverscapes. The soundtrack transitions from footfalls in the streams to paddles pushing a boat and eventually to a man treading neck-deep in one of the polluted waterways.[4]

Toward the end of the film, SEA STATE 0: all the lines flow out suddenly interjects with the voiceover of a woman, who worries about the precarity of her abandoned home on the seacoast, its frame visualized on screen. She notes the reassurances that her husband has given her regarding their house's security, with its stable, human-crafted pillars—a metaphor for Singapore. Yet the film then portrays a man bobbing up and down in the sea, the camera jerkily swaying in sync with its forceful waves. The last scene depicts this man straggling back up the coast, clearly enervated from the experience and almost walking on all four limbs. Not only do "all the lines flow out" of water-dependent Singapore back to the ocean, but any illusion of human control over this body of water becomes more and more dispelled throughout the film. In the end, SEA STATE 0: all the lines flow out presents a compressed version of the larger SEA STATE project and conceit. It displays a systematic increase in the agency and power of water as it gathers mass, concurrently with the loss of human mastery over it. "All the lines" in SEA STATE point to the hubris of humans—from attempting to capture fish as decorative pets to terraforming the entire nation into a massive, infrastructural water catchment system.

The components of Lim's installation all interlink to address the historical and contemporary violence wrought by Singapore's hegemonic attitude toward the sea, its authoritarian governance, and its neoliberal capitalist policies. Since its independence in 1965, the small yet globally ambitious nation-state has increased its landmass by almost 25 percent, often through the illegal extraction of sand from other Southeast Asian countries and the destructive dredging of the ocean bed. The SEA in SEA STATE also suggests the common acronym for Southeast Asia. To be sure, Singapore reconfigures domestic and regional territories, populations, and other-than-human life in ways that primarily seek to maximize profits and bolster a hypercentralized, technocratic systems approach ostensibly geared toward the small island's "survival." This narrative of survival—of small, vulnerable David up against global Goliaths—dominates the country's official mythology, the Singapore story. It germinated from a violent ethos of capitalist, terra nullius expansion established by British and Japanese colonialism and now continues through a top-down, technocratic approach focused on neoliberal "development" and global, financial success. In many ways, the country epitomizes what cultural theorist Macarena Gómez-Barris terms the *extractive zone*, or "the violence that capitalism does to reduce, constrain, and convert life into commodities, as well as the epistemological violence of training our academic vision to reduce life to systems."[5] In *The Extractive Zone: Social Ecologies and Decolonial Perspectives*, Gómez-Barris argues that extractive capitalism materially and affectively destroys heterogeneous, vernacular life through flattening technologies and perspectives.[6] SEA STATE registers the leveling technological apparatus and purview of Singapore—the literal destruction of its vibrant ecologies and the littoral violence of its border expansion—in order to contest and resist it.

In this essay, I contend that SEA STATE inverts and subverts official mapping systems to allow diverse, submerged perspectives—both human and nonhuman—to resurface against the tightly managed infrastructure of Singapore. In this multielement installation, reconfigured modes of perception challenge the managerial administration of the land, the sea, and its peoples, countering a tabula rasa violently crafted for governmental, military, and commercial purposes. In her book, Gómez-Barris offers examples of such "submerged perspectives" from five marginalized regions in South America and the global South, places with little power yet with central status in the global economy. These are tropical areas that both teem with life and recognize the richness of that brimming life. Ecuador's Yasuní region, for example, is registered as a UNESCO World Heritage Site yet is still quite vulnerable against national and multinational oil companies; and Indigenous, Afro-Ecuadoran, LGBT, ecofeminist, and labor union assemblages are fighting to save it from exploitation and extraction.[7] Yet what happens when such resistance seems largely foreclosed in the mainstream public's imagination? When submerged perspectives seem drowned and the tropical landscape mostly domesticated? In other words, what forms of creative resistance are available when the neocolonialism of a state like Singapore seems so rooted and accepted, even embraced, as to be impenetrable? It is important to note that this is not necessarily the case in Singapore. Yet the state can strategically dispel or absorb much resistance to its corporatist and extractivist methods. This is because the government offers a livable, acceptable status quo for many of its citizens, for example with financial security and hygienic city water, which are at a premium in other parts of the region.

SEA STATE's response is to push systematically against Singapore's entrenched, technocratic edifice—exposing in its cracked foundation a type of bottom-up and weed-like, "ecosystemic" life. On the one hand, SEA STATE denaturalizes Singapore's violent relationship with the sea inch by inch, nautical mile by nautical mile, through strategies of fragmentation, inversion, and dislocation. This deconstructive impulse manifests mostly through artistic-documentary methods of photography, film, and video, including in the subparts SEA STATE 0: all the lines flow out, SEA STATE 1: inside/outside, SEA STATE 2: as evil disappears (Pulau Sajahat), SEA STATE 3: inversion (sculptural documentation, not lens-based), SEA STATE 4: line in the chart, SEA STATE 5: drift (two versions), SEA STATE 6: phase 1 and SEA STATE 6: capsize, SEA STATE 7: the inarticulate sandman, and SEA STATE 9: proclamation. These documentary pieces challenge the charting and surveying reach of the state's totalizing view, which attempts to control and manage the island through an artificially imposed, materially and visually bound ordering apparatus. On the other hand, the artwork also generates and continually reprises a more organic "ecosystemic" landscape and seascape through other diverse and interrelated components. I employ the term ecosystem in a poetic sense in order to suggest an ecosocial foundation based on interdependency, heterogeneity, and what I refer to as "undergrowth," or a less visible type of grassroots agency and life that emphasizes the background (environment) rather than the foreground (humans). SEA STATE 9: proclamation garden (2015), SEA STATE 2: as evil disappears (Sajahat Buoy) (2014), and SEA STATE 8: seabook, for example, all revivify Singapore's historically razed environment with more plural and submerged viewpoints. Ultimately, Lim employs an ecosystemic approach in SEA STATE not only in order to challenge the state's technocratic, neoliberal system of extraction, bit by bit, but also to dwell in tension with it, slowly resedimenting its cracked foundation with a more ecosocially holistic ground cover. Let me now begin with the official story: Singapore's position as a humble speck on the map.

The Singapore Story

In the twenty-first century, Singapore has come to acquire the affectionate moniker, Little Red Dot. The government branding for the country's golden jubilee anniversary, for example, employs an image of a red dot filled in with the logo "SG50" (i.e., Singapore's fifty years of independence). The nickname originates from a supposedly offhand remark made in 1998 by the former president of Indonesia, B. J. (Bacharuddin Jusuf) Habibie. As first reported in the *Asian Wall Street Journal*, Habibie criticized Singapore for a less-than-friendly attitude toward Indonesia and himself (comments he later denied). Habibie apparently pointed to a map of the region, stating, "It's OK with me, there are 211 million people [in Indonesia]. Look at that map. All the green [area] is Indonesia. And that red dot is Singapore. Look at that."[8] The comment gained traction in popular media and soon became a rallying cry for Singaporean politicians and citizens, as a term and image of pride. In a 2003 speech, "Learning and Living the Singapore Story," for example, Lee Hsien Loong, the former deputy prime minister and now prime minister, expressed gratitude for Habibie's "vivid and valuable reminder that we are indeed very small and very vulnerable."[9] The former Indonesian president's injunction to "look at that"—the little red dot on the map—actually played perfectly well into Singapore's own projection of itself on the larger world screen.

To be sure, the Singapore story referenced in Prime Minister Lee's speech title is a long-established, state-constructed narrative of nationhood. Put another way, it is the country's standardized mythology. Since the introduction of the National Education Programme in 1997, the island's schools and junior colleges have all taught this official history, and it also dominates the universities and media.[10] Essentially, it communicates that Singapore's triumphant progress can be traced primarily to its histories of British colonialism (namely, with the putative founder Sir Stamford Raffles's introduction of free trade) and Chinese immigration, deeming precolonial histories as irrelevant to the island's modern success.[11] As historian Michael D. Barr describes it: "The explicit premise of the national narrative is that before Raffles arrived in 1819 there was, basically, nothing on the island and nothing in the region that need be considered when accounting for Singapore's success; and without the leadership of Lee Kuan Yew and the followership of industrious, clever and frugal Chinese citizens, Singapore would still be in the Third World."[12] The Cambridge-trained lawyer Lee Kuan Yew was the first prime minister of Singapore, serving in that capacity from 1965 until 1990, and his son, Lee Hsien Loong, has served as prime minister since 2004.

Crucially, the Singapore story also emphasizes Singapore's smallness, vulnerability, and struggle for survival and development against a backdrop of numerous domestic and international threats since its "expulsion" from a brief, two-year union with Malaysia and its necessary declaration of independence in 1965.[13] The citizens of postcolonial Singapore in the 1960s and 1970s experienced and knew these threats firsthand (i.e., Chinese communism, domestic interreligious conflict, Malaysia, the United States and "Western liberalism," and so on), but as a younger generation came of age in the 1980s, the government suddenly took a greater interest in teaching them the "tale of great men" who had founded and built such an "exceptional" nation-state.[14] The regime's paternalistic, technocratic approach to development and industrialization helped the small island survive and prosper on a global stage, and to an exceptional degree, but it has also codified an ethos of colonial expansion (i.e., "nothing existed before Raffles's establishment of a free port on the island").[15]

It is therefore not surprising that Singapore also espouses a more literal system of terra nullius, in the form of neocolonial land expansion. SEA STATE 9: proclamation (2015), highlights the fact that any "reclaimed," or physically created, land within Singapore's borders automatically becomes property of the state, despite any former historical uses as sea bed or extracted land material from other countries. The artwork reprints and displays Singapore's Foreshore Act, including chapter 5, "Declaration Regarding Reclaimed Lands," which decrees the state's territorial authority. A video counterpart to the textual declaration, SEA STATE 9: proclamation: DRAG DROP POUR poetically documents the government's top-down "reclamation" of land. The aerial-view, three-screen installation displays the dragging of sand by barge, the dropping of sand via large excavator into the sea, and the pouring of it to fill in new landmass. In other words, the official Singapore story—of the peaceful struggle, survival, and entrepreneurship of this "little red dot"—masks an administratively and technically intricate, large-scale operation to colonize and dominate vast new stretches of land "reclaimed" not out of thin air, but rather from previously existing, fragile ecosystems and specific, sociohistorically situated places.

Such territorialized land, moreover, is not barren. Sometimes the land fill must first settle and stabilize, and as it awaits state "development," rogue ecologies find a way of taking root in the terrain. SEA STATE 9: proclamation garden (2019) consists of a rooftop garden on the National Gallery Singapore, arranged with planter boxes of thirty lesser-known plants that typically populate extended land areas around Singapore.[16] These plants are often ignored and neglected—not the ornamental landscaping that usually adorns the national museum's rooftop. However, here they are granted special status, placed in a pedestaled, overviewing position within the city center. Ultimately, they are constrained within an institutional master plan, yet they serve as reminders of the disposable-yet-not-quite-controllable ecologies that manage to circumvent such planned environments, as hardy "weeds." In the end, the full *SEA STATE 9: proclamation* challenges the top-down mythology of the Singapore story, which discursively legitimates the staking and colonization of so-called new land on the map.

It should be stressed, however, that the state has also been strategic at adapting its master narrative in light of recent counterstories and a nascent chorus of oppositional voices in Singaporean society. As the political scientist Kenneth Paul Tan elaborates, there has been a growing body of literary, theatrical, artistic, and academic work—particularly leading up to the golden jubilee year—which has challenged the discursive hegemony of the Singapore story.[17] The state has allowed much of this to circulate. According to Tan, Singapore has attempted to craft itself as a "creative global city" since the beginning of the twenty-first century, and this has in large part required more leniency toward alternative views in the arts sector.

Simultaneous to Singapore's "creative global city" branding, however, in 2011 the People's Action Party (PAP) suffered its worst electoral results ever, and it has worked to retrench its official version of the national imagined community for the larger electorate.[18] Thus, for instance, it staged the year-long, nationwide platform, Our Singapore Conversation, in 2012. Including 47,000 participants, it was a "kind of state-organised public ritual, designed to bring Singaporeans together to perform their national identity," weaving personal stories "into a national tapestry to dress up The Singapore Story in more vibrant and complex colours."[19] Relatedly, the historian Ramakrishna Kumar calls for a tactical pluralizing of the state's official history into a Singapore Story 2.0, which would include more marginalized voices and a longer historical view of Singapore beyond its colonization by the British in 1819.[20] In the end, through state-inspired, calculated adaptations, including those meant to "diversify" Singapore's centralizing mythology, the state's hegemonic, neoliberal narrative prevails in the mainstream public sphere. Above all, its "survival story" seeks to justify and scaffold the nation-state's tightly controlled material armature—its infrastructure, economy, and geography—to which I will now turn in more detail.

A Systems Approach to Statehood

What Singapore may lack in size or population, it makes up for in location. Namely, Singapore sits along the shortest, shallowest, and most placid water route between the Pacific and Indian Oceans, which helps position it at the nexus of important shipping and exchange networks.[21] Less visible, more-over, is the fact that this waterway holds a global node of submarine fiber-optic cables, or a communication network that now carries 95 percent of intercontinental data traffic.[22] As part of the art collective tsunamii.net, Charles Lim highlighted Singapore's strategic position as a global informa-tion nerve center in his earlier work.[23] At *Documenta 11* in 2002, the col-lective performed a piece in which they walked away from the exhibition site in Kassel toward the location of the exhibition's internet server in Kiel. For this walk, they followed a GPS signal and moved several hundred kilo-meters north.[24] The long, slow trek worked to highlight the more invisible, instantaneous transmission of massive amounts of information via such electronic data cables. In drawing attention to our reliance on these frag-ile, materially bound networks, tsunamii.net utilized a "systems approach" themselves, tethering their art piece to specific protocols for the walk and ultimately tying it more closely to the physical "undergrowth" beneath their feet. Their contribution to *Documenta 11* both echoed Allan Sekula's sys-tematized, photographic artwork in the show—*Fish Story* (1989–95), which exposes the material framework of a globalized, "postindustrial" shipping industry—and recalled numerous other documentary, walking/mapping performances by figures such as Richard Long, Gianni Motti, Iain Sinclair, and François Maspero and Anaïk Frantz.[25] Even the art collective's name, tsunamii.net, playfully signals their attention to mapping more invisible networks within an otherwise overwhelming flood of information and big-picture movement.

Their piece stands in contrast to the Singaporean state's employment of a top-down "systems approach," a term and concept explicated by the urban theorists P. C. Lui and T. S. Tan. According to them, the government tightly manages every possible infrastructural system, from land, sea, and air transport to public housing, information and communication services, and petrochemical industries.[26] The state addressed all of these areas right from the beginning: due to the country's small size and anxieties about survival, a systems approach necessitated master planning and a centralized, "multi-dimensional integration" of different infrastructures, the best technologies available, and quick and decisive implementation by an empowered elite.[27] In the 1980s, Lee Kuan Yew facilitated this systems approach by nurturing a new top tier of civil servants, or "uber-technocrats," and this enabled the PAP to monopolize control over the government. The press and trade unions, and the political Left in general, were dismantled.[28] Multinational corporations supplanted local businesses and banks, and a new type of entity arose: the government-linked company "through which the government could inter-polate itself directly into the heart of local capitalism."[29]

Today the small island has also acquired the nickname of Singapore Inc.[30] In its neoliberal developmental model, the state and international capital work together. The government is enabled by two monolithic sovereign wealth funds, estimated to hold just under $1 trillion and managed by trusted friends of Lee Kuan Yew's family.[31] Furthermore, Singapore follows a Japanese rather than an Anglo-American model, with a tripartite relationship among a strong state, strong bureaucracy, and big business that still maintains a paternalistic (authoritarian) attention to the welfare of its domestic constituencies.[32] Some experts regard it as the "most efficient form of state capitalism in the world."[33] Less acknowledged and touted in terms of its economic development, however, is the country's tremendous reliance on low-paid and vulnerable foreign labor.[34]

When the art collective tsunamii.net dissolved and SEA STATE began to germinate in 2005, Lim continued to work with roving documentary methods to expose the shifting boundaries and infrastructure of Singapore. The installation SEA STATE 1: inside/outside (2005), for instance, includes 168 photographs marking the port limit of the city-state, as well as a chattering marine VHF radio and an altered map of those limits. The photographs mostly depict buoys (but also some other territorial markers) around the island, which Lim circled three times in order to document the structures from vantage points both inside and outside the state's port limits.[35] As the curator Pauline J. Yao notes, the buoy photographs recall the typological grids of Bernd and Hilla Becher.[36] Yet here the buoys are meant to signify borders and, moreover, borders that are anything but static or stable. Lim's documentation, looking both out from and in toward the island of Singapore, reveals the fluidity of the buoys' environment. The oppositional lighting conditions from each point, as circumnavigated around the whole island, imbues the "makeshift wallpaper" of topographical, grid-like photographs with a type of dynamic difference-through-repetition. Furthermore, the installation's live VHF radio, a communication system typically found on seafaring vessels, also disrupts the fixedness of the programmatic photographs. In other words, SEA STATE 1: inside/outside exposes an underlying porosity, ephemerality, and malleability characterizing one of Singapore's most firmly managed systems of border infrastructure.[37] This idea, moreover, resonates with the photographic work of SEA STATE 4: line in the chart (2008), which portrays a rigid sheet-metal fence out in the middle of the ocean. Situated along Singapore's northeastern sea border, the wall warns, "No Entry Restricted Zone," in English, Chinese, and Malay; it is an area designated for future development by the Housing and Development Board of Singapore.[38] The wall is surrounded by flowing sea on both sides, however, and the thought that a person might trespass against this wall seems absurd. Ultimately, both SEA STATE 1: *inside/outside* and SEA STATE 4: *line in the chart* emphasize the fluidity of Singapore's surveyed sea limits, highlighting the porosity and unfixedness of its border infrastructure.

Similarly, the moving-image works SEA STATE 5: *drift (rope sketch)* (2012) and SEA STATE 5: *drift (stay still now to move)* (2012) counter any sense of dominion over, or possible containment of, the ocean. They depict, respectively, a straight rope lying in the Straits of Johor, which yields to the currents and twists into a snaking jumble despite resting on one of the most placid, calm waterways in the region; and an orange-life-vested man floating in the ocean who becomes an abstract and then invisible fleck in the current as the camera assumes more distant angles. Both the passive, isolated man and the cut of sailor's rope—the latter a symbol of jurisdiction and enclosure—lose any sense of anchorage in the vastness of the animated sea, which continually churns and pushes its surface riders in haphazard directions.

In the end, Singapore may attempt to shore up its borders against the tides of its surroundings, but the ocean—and now even more so with rising sea levels—will continue to threaten its tightly controlled borders, material armature, and changing geography. Its metamorphosis from "survival" to "success" on a globalized stage is a hyperdefensive claim backed up by a totalizing, technocratic, and technologized infrastructure that can never truly find solid ground against the unpredictability and power of the sea. As addressed below, Singapore's infrastructure and economy are now destructively bound to a practice and ethos of extractive capitalism.

On and off the Grid: The Extractive Zone

Critical to the state's economic success has been its ability to facilitate fast, cheap transportation of bulk goods by sea.[39] Singapore has maintained its leading position as a shipping hub, for example, by being among the first countries to join the mid-twentieth-century containerization revolution and the first in Southeast Asia to do so.[40] SEA STATE 7: *sandwich* (2015) visually evokes such containerization (figure 9.2). It is composed of dozens of screens compressed, rotated 90 degrees from a normal viewing angle, and "sandwiched" together in a long, horizontal wall of moving imagery. Each individual screen displays a landscape surrounding Singapore: for example, people

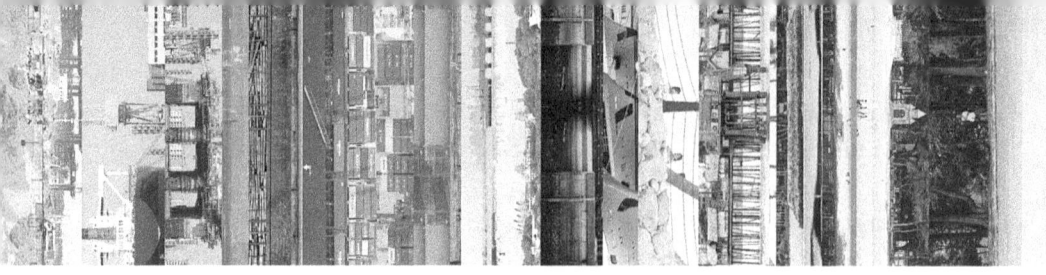

FIGURE 9.2. Charles Lim, SEA STATE 7: *Sandwich* (2015), video still. Image courtesy of the artist.

on the beach, an outlying island, a container port, petrochemical towers, a sand barge on the sea, and many more scenes along the horizon, now flipped to a vertical position and incongruously flattened together. The visual chaos of the extended "seawall" recalls the jumbled yet efficiently organized, continually moving stacks of containers on Singapore's shores. Instead of being oriented around a traditional horizon line, the landscape now appears more akin to a commodifying, machinic barcode.

Of course, mapping and signification are key to Singapore's shipping efficiency. Sea navigation is enhanced by the Grid, for instance, a system developed in 1972 by the former chief hydrographer of the Port of Singapore Authority (now Maritime and Port Authority of Singapore), Captain Wilson Chua.[41] Based on one of Singapore's official nautical charts, the GSP1 hydrographic chart, the Grid segments the sea into one-square-mile units, and these are further divided into quadrants A, B, C, and D.[42] Whereas longitude and latitude can be hard to plot, the Grid employs simple numbers and letters, making it easy to identify where vessels are located.[43]

In the 1970s, the Grid led to a massive cleanup operation of the seabed, because submerged objects could pose a threat to a ship's anchorage. This included hundreds of unexploded bombs dumped by the British military during its withdrawal from the island when the Japanese invaded.[44] In SEA STATE 7: *the inarticulate sandman* (2015), an experienced seaman and sand mover, or "sandman," Foo Say Juan, explains that his crew would often suction up pieces of ordnance, which would then damage the sand-dredging gear.[45] Lim's video interview of Foo offers a form of oral testimony of this commercialized practice, depicted through an extreme close-up of Foo's face and mouth as he narrates his past experiences as a "sandman." The single shot tightly frames Foo's words and mostly monologue, excluding Lim's physical presence in the interview and effectively filtering out any other visual or aural distractions from Foo's often disjointed account. What viewers learn is that Foo was probably an accomplice to illegal sand extraction. At one point, for example, he was forced to remain in Indonesia for a month because he and his crew did not have a permit to take sand from that country. In different mythologies, the figure of the sandman is said to bring either happy dreams or nightmares—symbolic of the contested status of Singapore's shores. At the very least, the sandman is said to induce sleep, and Singapore has surely benefited from its "sleepy" attention to how it receives all of the necessary sand for its landfill ambitions.

Since its independence in 1965, Singapore has increased its land mass by almost 25 percent, and it aims to increase this to 30 percent by 2030.[46] The country has a long history of land extension projects, which are typically referred to and euphemized as acts of land reclamation. Singapore's most basic efforts began in the 1960s, when infill came from local, hill-cut material, but since 1980, infill has arrived in the form of sand imported from around the region.[47] In 2003, for example, an island on the Singapore-Indonesia border, Nipah Island, was wiped off the map, and an additional twenty-four islands are reported to have vanished between 2005 and 2010.[48]

SEA STATE 2: *as evil disappears (Pulau Sajahat)* (2012) highlights such disappearances through the juxtaposition of two altered GSP1 charts that display Grid 0124, quadrant C, published in 2000 and 2010 by the Maritime and Port Authority of Singapore.[49] The two discrepant maps register and expose in a measured fashion the erasure of the one-hectare Pulau Sajahat, or "Evil Island," off the northeast coast of Singapore.[50] The island vanished along with its smaller neighbor Pulau Sajahat Kechil, both subsumed within the larger island of Pulau Tekong, which used to be covered with rubber estates and now functions as a military training base.[51] *Jahat* means "evil" in Malay but can also mean "naughty" colloquially.[52] In 2002, the island fell off the Grid—along with its marking buoy—and was "cleansed" of that negative connotation, as part of a state directive and for state military purposes. SEA STATE 2: *as evil disappears (Sajahat Buoy)* (2014) is a five-meter-tall buoy meant to replicate and evoke the original buoy from the island of Sajahat.[53] Buoys are created to accommodate specific tidal conditions, and Lim contacted the company that initially produced the Sahajat buoy in order to commission its doppelgänger. The artist then submerged this near Pulau Sajahat for four weeks, and it quickly grew a skin of barnacles due to the tropical climate.

The buoy sculpture reveals the bountiful ocean life that official Singaporean charts "disappear" or officially mark as absent. According to a team of geographers and marine ecologists, Singapore's mangrove forests, coral reefs, and sand and mudflats largely disappeared between the 1920s and 1990s, and the amount of coastline in its natural state decreased to 40 percent of its former area. The team predicts that all will shrink further in fifteen- and fifty-year projections according to Singapore's 2008 Master Plan and longer-term 2011 Concept Plan.⁵⁴ To give a more vivid picture: for instance, Singapore's mudflats harbor 77 fish species, 62 snail species, 37 crab species, and many types of seagrass meadow.⁵⁵ All this life is absent from the extensively charted seabed and the few remaining sand flats on the Grid. A three-dimensional sand print of the seabed in *SEA STATE 3: inversion* (2014) shows the state's championed cable lines running across the ocean floor but cannot display any of the ocean's diverse, nonhuman residents. Instead, *SEA STATE 2: as evil disappears (Sajahat Buoy)* evidences this, exposing the vibrant yet disposable, other-than-human life that does not register on the state's grid and extractive optic, wiped off the slate of "new," empty land construction. The buoy is an exhumed, spectral figure brought back to life in order to haunt the unnatural inversion enforced between land and sea in Singapore's master plans.

In other words, the barnacled buoy marks a submerged, revivified perspective against the violence of the extractive zone. Typically, a buoy acts as an anchored float to signal hazards such as wrecks, to aid navigation, or to serve as a mooring device. In *SEA STATE*, it embodies all three modes in order to warn, steer, and support viewers in resisting an operation and ethos of extractive capitalism. According to Macarena Gómez-Barris, extractive capitalism is an economic system based on "thefts, borrowings, and forced removals, violently reorganizing social life as well as the land," in which "the extractive view sees territories as commodities, rendering land as for the taking, while also devalorizing the hidden worlds that form the nexus of human and nonhuman multiplicity."⁵⁶ Furthermore, she connects such extractivism to longer histories of colonial capitalism and the pursuit of conquest and control. Challenging a universalizing rhetoric and discourse concerning the age of the Anthropocene, she considers colonial capitalism to be the primary cataclysmic event of planetary inhabitation. Put simply, not all humans are equally responsible for global warming, and many suffer far worse effects than others. Whereas colonial capitalism historically erased difference and life through enslavement, dispossession, and environmental destruction, it now remanifests in a neocolonial and neoliberal ethos of "corporate bio-territorialization."⁵⁷ Gómez-Barris aims both to document the flattening violence of this neocolonial extraction and to analyze alternative, vibrant viewpoints of and from an ecosystem that refute such a "monocultural imperative."⁵⁸ Submerged or emergent perspectives challenge how we conceive of progress and insist that we revalue entangled human and other-than-human life in all its thick relationality and heterogeneity.[59] As understood in Lim's artwork, this is the ecosystemic *ground* that may exist just as vibrantly as its dominating, human *figures*. Such a revisioning or reperceiving requires an "epistemological unmooring."[60]

Lim's exhumed and "reappeared" buoy resonates with this call, as a marker of renewed life-giving that is simultaneously mooring and unmooring. This re-barnacled doppelgänger is not the same as the one that used to mark Singapore's borders as part of the island's infrastructure of containment in *SEA STATE 1: inside/outside*. Instead, it has reemerged to bear witness to the thriving, unbridled life found beneath the ocean's surface against the deadened opacity of the state's technocratic and gridded purview. It reflects the heterogeneous and interdependent undergrowth of a more organic type of ecosystem.

Submerged Stories

The Singaporean government realizes that it can only extend its land so far. At some point it becomes technically impractical and commercially unprofitable to fill in coastal areas whose sea beds plunge more deeply and steeply away from sea level.[61] Thus the island has become creative in not only building higher into the sky but also tunneling farther into the ground for storage capacity. The Jurong Rock Caverns, for instance, are a series of 130-meter-deep, 61-hectare (about the size of 84 football fields) rock caves underneath Jurong Island, as of 2017 being used to cache 126 million gallons of liquid carbons (oil, gas, naphtha) for companies such as Chevron Phillips, ExxonMobil, and Shell.[62] Remarkably, the facility constitutes the first time a country has terraformed storage space *underneath* the seabed.[63] Further, Jurong Island itself, Singapore's largest outlying island, was created through the amalgamation of eight smaller islands in order to serve the nation-state's petrochemical industries.[64] The cavern facility opened in 2014, and it helps Singapore maintain its status as the third-largest oil exporter in the world.[65]

The short film *SEA STATE 6: phase 1* (2014) explores the submerged space and story of Jurong Island's artificial caverns. It opens with a ghostly figure of a lone sailboat sinking to the depths of the ocean. The film then transports viewers down the length of one of Jurong Rock Cavern's main shafts, while loud sounds inundate the space: heavy machinery, noise from the surrounding water, and a female-voiced cover of the popular 1962 song, "There's a Reason," by the Cascades, whose sound is like that of the Beach Boys. The sentimental, harmonically pleasant love song's lyrics explain that "there's a reason" for all of nature's elements—like snowfall, cloudy skies, glowing moons, sunbeams—but the singer does not "know why I should cry just because you said goodbye." Its upbeat melody contrasts starkly with the machinic, subterranean descent. Once the elevator reaches the bottom of the long shaft, viewers then encounter an inert man lying on the watery cave floor. It might be a corpse (or one of the sandman's soporific workers), but he soon rises and begins to lead viewers farther into the depths of the hellish caverns, its tunnels reminiscent of the longkangs in SEA STATE 0: *all the lines flow out*. Discordant images and sounds follow, including an alarm, a suggested explosion, a sand barge on the sea's surface, and isolated workers in the murky tunnels. The most unusual image is that of a group of workers, again walking away from the camera and carrying a sailboat above their heads through the tunnel (figure 9.3). The sailboat easily fits within the spacious cavern, well below the ocean's surface. Yet the image is jarring, barely fathomable. Finally, the film ends with a slow shot aimed up and out of the shaft as the elevator brings viewers to the "light at the end of the tunnel." The eerie, machinic shaft reminds one of an uncanny science-fiction scenario, in which one attempts to escape a Death Star–like space station.

With this film, Lim takes spectators into the belly of the beast. SEA STATE 6: *phase 1* excavates Singapore's topsy-turvy relationship with the land and the sea through inverted, bizarre, and denaturalized sounds and images in the human-made caves. Particularly the image of the sailboat strikes one as unintelligible. Lifted like a special dais, it rather seems kidnapped, an empty shell in the gloomy space, deprived of the wind and sea that would "give it a reason" for existing. Instead, its movement signals not only a disjunctive departure—a sad farewell as the incongruously upbeat pop song intimates—but also an officially sanctioned and state-enforced one. Lim laments the fact that small boats no longer populate the shores of Singapore; instead, containerization facilities and petrochemical plants dominate its littoral zones. Singaporeans no longer imagine the sea as a space of leisure or pleasure, like Lim did growing up in his grandmother's *kampong* (village) near Changi, before the city transformed the stockpiles of sand around his neighborhood into land for its international airport.[66] According to Lim, there used to be frequent *kolek* races around the island, and they brought many people together for events such as the festive New Year Regatta. Koleks are personal boats native to the shores of Singapore, Johor, and surrounding islands that are used for both racing and small-scale fishing, but today these are a rare sight.[67] Lim himself trained as a sailor when young, representing Singapore in the Olympics for sailing. SEA STATE 6: *capsize* (2015) draws on these skills, portraying Lim in a

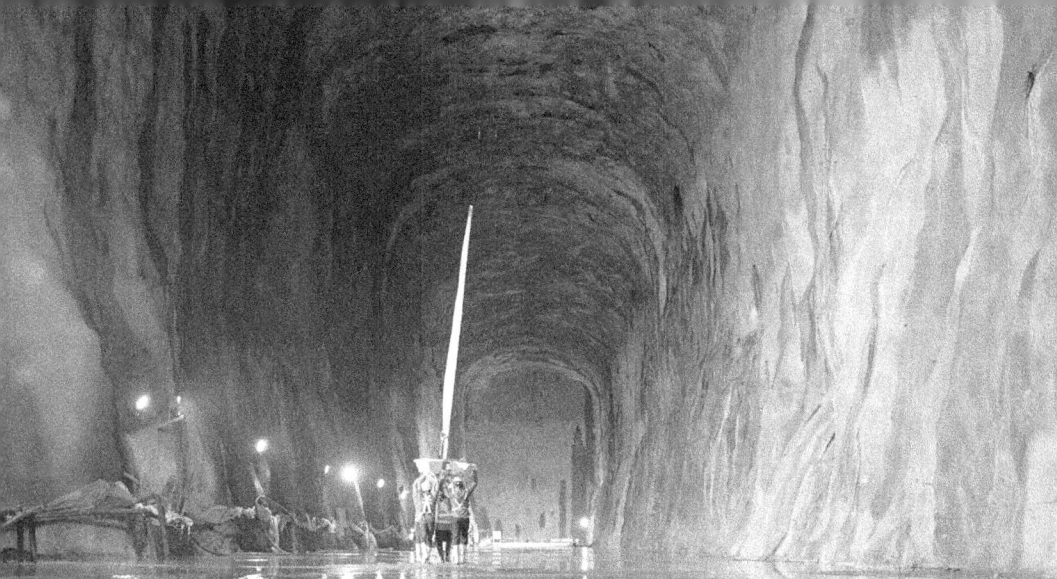

FIGURE 9.3. Charles Lim, *SEA STATE 6: Phase 1* (2014), video still. Image courtesy of the artist.

sailboat as it repeatedly capsizes in the ocean. The process is exhausting even to watch, as if he is constantly on the verge of drowning yet somehow always manages to resurface to flip the boat back upright. Round and round the sailboat goes for eight minutes, often in split-screen mode to heighten a sense of splitting and inversion. In the end, the short film complements *SEA STATE 6: phase 1*, by drawing attention, for instance, to the submerged perspective of local coastal experiences that have become subsumed by much larger state-corporate actors and agendas. As the art historian Kevin Chua notes about the Singaporean citizens' now-transformed relationship with the sea, "The country has an existential denial of its surrounding waters."[68] Extractive capitalism has already remodeled the coast to an unrecognizable degree, burying a palimpsest of rich, vernacular stories.

Not Fully Subsumed, Not Quite Concluded

Today only one kampong still exists on mainland Singapore, home to about thirty families.[69] Its fate is uncertain, but Singapore's "reclaimed" horizon seems set. Innumerable communities and villages have been forcibly relocated since Singapore's independence to make way for a more "secure" future, to transfigure a story of precarious, local survival into solid, global success. The nation-state has reconfigured, mythologized, and officially instituted that narrative—the Singapore story—through an infrastructure of neocolonial development, an ethos of neoliberal technocracy, and a project of extractive capitalism. Yet alternative stories are emerging and resurfacing against the top-down proclamations and imposed land fill of such state violence, in resistant spaces such as SEA STATE. SEA STATE 8: seabook attempts to explicitly exhume and collect such heterogeneous tales of "undergrowth." It is an unfinished, yet-to-be-published website, www.seabook.sg, which documents archival sources as well as personal anecdotes and memories. In a preview clip, for instance, Eric Ronald Alfred (a marine zoologist and the director of the Raffles Museum) describes the vast, historical resettlement of village populations to pave the way for Singapore's grand vision.[70]

Singapore has been unyielding in its manifest destiny–like quest for control over the sea and land. Many laud its developments and point to its technological feats, such as the NEWater program, which desalinates and makes fresh water from the ocean. Not surprisingly, Singapore's dependence on Malaysia for fresh water was once a source of insecurity: the NEWater program was developed to address and mitigate this fear.[71] Yet Singapore's hyperdefensive attitude has also justified and nurtured a neocolonial, extractive policy toward the environment. To "survive," the Little Red Dot has upended and reorganized whole landscapes, peoples, and human-nonhuman ecologies, simultaneously monetizing and devaluing them in the name of capitalist "progress," technological innovation, and social order. Against the top-down, state-constructed Singapore story, SEA STATE attempts to offer grassroots, seagrassed, and barnacled voices that are submerged yet not quite drowned out by that hegemonic narrative. The long-term artwork charts off-the-grid coordinates and perspectives in order to resist the violent abstraction of official maps that "disappear" these marginalized bodies and normalize the state's extractive territorialization of the sea. Ostensibly, SEA STATE culminated after ten years at and for the 2015 Venice Biennale, where Lim represented the nation-state and heralded Singapore's celebratory jubilee year, yet it in fact remains unfinished and still unsettling. SEA STATE 8: seabook will continue to archive alternative emerging stories of Singapore's relationship with the sea that disturb the island's official narrative and subsuming vision. Crucially, when the mainstream public sphere accepts and even espouses this status quo, a more interrelational, organic, and diverse "ecosystemic" approach can help challenge the system from the ground up. Lim's ecosystemic creation of SEA STATE counters but cannot dispel the technocratic, top-down systems approach centralized by the government. Instead, it offers a more holistic vision that may exist in tandem and in tension with the state's armature, giving space and "voice" to a less visible though no less vibrant undergrowth of ecosocial life.

As ecocultural theorists such as Gómez-Barris and Donna Haraway insist, we must pay heed to stories of the "muck" or "mud" as "muddle"—and more, we must dwell in them.[72] Imagine the biomatter on the underwater pillar of jetties, the primordial stuff that clings for life and proliferates despite and in tandem with ordered human architecture. The undergrowth is often there but overlooked, a disposable nuisance that humans attempt to cleanse of their surroundings. In Lim's companion piece to *SEA STATE 0: all the lines flow out*—the film *SEA STATE 0: it's not that i forgot, but rather i chose not to mention* (2008)—a lone swimmer attempts to rid the former Singapore Airlines Country Club pool in Changi of all this earthy slime, the algae and leaves that always manage to collect at the bottom of the pool.[73] For the entirety of its forty-four minutes, the film displays only one static framing of the pool from above. In the beginning, it is swamped in green and brown sludge, but by the end, the swimmer has managed to brush away the majority with his bare hands, amphibiously and arduously breathing underwater for his Sisyphean task. His efforts do yield some "success," exposing the gridded, white-tile floor as well as its demarcated pool lanes, to which the swimmer largely adheres in his slow-going movement. In the process, however, he also loosens much of the confined muck from the background, letting it float to the surface of what was once a strictly maintained and artificially cleansed pool. In another life, the biomatter would exist in a more hospitable environment, thriving in a tropical climate and lively body of water. Yet here it is trapped on the pool's grid, and it is only the swimmer's methodical, though somewhat veering approach, that turns our sustained attention to the neglected underbelly of the water. In the end, as throughout the larger project of *SEA STATE*, the artwork calls on us to also jump in and dwell in this messy muddle.

NOTES

I would like to thank Johanna Gosse and Tim Stott for their excellent editorial suggestions. My deep gratitude also extends to Roger Nelson for reading an earlier draft of this essay.

1   Shabbir Hussain Mustafa, ed., *SEA STATE: Charles Lim Yi Yong* (Singapore: National Arts Council, 2015), 5.

2   This includes, most notably, solo exhibitions at NTU CCA Singapore (2016) and the National Gallery Singapore (2019).

3   Akshita Nanda, "Singapore Signs 20-Year Lease in Venice," *Straits Times*, May 8, 2015.

4   Unless otherwise specified, much of my analysis is based on materials available on the artist's website or from an interview conducted in Singapore on May 24, 2018; see http://www.charleslimyiyong.com. As of publication the site has gone inactive, and may reappear edited or at a new location.

5   Macarena Gómez-Barris, *The Extractive Zone: Social Ecologies and Decolonial Perspectives* (Durham, NC: Duke University Press, 2017), xix.

6   Gómez-Barris, *Extractive Zone*, xviii.

7   Gómez-Barris, *Extractive Zone*, 19.

8   Richard Borsuk and Reginald Chua, "Singapore Strains Relations with Indonesia's President," *Wall Street Journal*, August 4, 1998, https://www.wsj.com/articles /SB902170180588248000.

9   Lee Hsien Loong, "Learning and Living the Singapore Story: Keynote Address by Deputy Prime Minister, Mr. Lee Hsien Loong at the Network Conference 2003, Government of Singapore," May 3, 2003, https://www.nas.gov.sg/archivesonline /data/pdfdoc/2003050301.htm.

10 Michael D. Barr, *Singapore: A Modern History* (London: I. B. Tauris, 2018), 3.

11 Barr, *Singapore*, 4.

12 Barr, *Singapore*.

13 Barr, *Singapore*, 120.

14 Barr, *Singapore*, 23–25, xii.

15 Barr, *Singapore*, 3–4. It should be noted that the Singapore Story has also emphasized the state's establishment of social order through the quelling of various culturally, religiously, and politically inflected riots and demonstrations throughout the 1950s and on through the 1980s. Barr, *Singapore*, 20–24.

16 Adele Tan, ed., *Ng Teng Fong Roof Garden Commission: Charles Lim Yi Yong*, exhibition catalog (Singapore: National Gallery Singapore, 2019).

17 Kenneth Paul Tan, "Choosing What to Remember in Neoliberal Singapore: The Singapore Story, State Censorship and State-Sponsored Nostalgia," *Asian Studies Review* 40, no. 2 (2016): 231–49. Also see Lee Weng Choy, "The Assumption of Love: Friendship and the Search for Discursive Density," in *Modern and Contemporary Southeast Asian Art: An Anthology*, ed. Nora A. Taylor and Boreth Ly (Ithaca, NY: Cornell Southeast Asia Program Publications, 2012), 189–209.

18 Tan, "Choosing," 233–35. I also refer here to Benedict Anderson's seminal book, *Imagined Communities: Reflections on the Origin and Spread of Nationalism* (1983; repr., London: Verso, 2006).

19 Tan, "Choosing," 237.

20 Ramakirshna Kumar, *"Original Sin"? Revising the Revisionist Critique of the 1963 Operation Coldstone in Singapore* (Singapore: Institute of Southeast Asian Studies, 2015), 126–28. According to Pi-Chun Chang, Lee's successor Goh Chok Tong championed the "Singapore Story Version 2.0." Pi-Chun Chang, "Going Global and Staying Local: Nation-Building Discourses in Singapore's Cultural Policies," *Identities: Global Studies in Culture and Power* 19, no. 6 (November 2012): 695.

21 Barr, *Singapore*, 35.

22 Barr, *Singapore*, 33.

23 This group existed approximately from 2001 to 2005 and was composed of Charles Lim, Woon Tien Wei, and Melvin Phua. Mustafa, SEA STATE, 113.

24 Mustafa, SEA STATE, 30.

25 For more information concerning such documentary walking projects, see Karen O'Rourke, "A Map, No Directions," in *Walking and Mapping: Artists as Cartographers* (Cambridge, MA: MIT Press, 2013), 47–72.

26 P. C. Lui and Thiam-Soon Tan, "Building Integrated Large-Scale Urban Infrastructures: Singapore's Experience," *Journal of Urban Technology* 8, no. 1 (August 4, 2010): 49–68.

27 Lui and Tan, "Building," 53.

28 Barr, *Singapore*, 129, 161.

29 Barr, *Singapore*, 129.

30 Barr, *Singapore*, 159.

31 Barr, *Singapore*, 159, 155. Samanth Subramanian, "How Singapore Is Creating More Land for Itself," *New York Times*, April 20, 2017, https://www.nytimes .com/2017/04/20/magazine/how-singapore-is-creating-more-land-for-itself .html.

32 Barr, *Singapore*, 125.

33 Barr, *Singapore*, 159.

34 Barr, *Singapore*, 161–62.

35 Lucy Rees, "Expanding the Horizon: Future Perfect and the Singapore Scene," *Art Monthly Australia* 279 (May 2015): 30.

36 Pauline J. Yao, "Floating World: Pauline J. Yao on Charles Lim's 'Sea State,' 2005–," *Artforum International* 53, no. 8 (2015): 236–39.

37 Chua Beng Huat, "The Sahajat Buoy: Notes on a Disappearance," in Mustafa, SEA STATE, 61, 65n33.

38 Mustafa, SEA STATE, 25.

39 Barr, *Singapore*, 157.

40 Barr, *Singapore*, 157–58.

41 Barr, *Singapore*, 122.

42 Mustafa, "'Mr.' Anthrobalanus," in Mustafa, SEA STATE, 22–23.

43 Chua, Lim, and Mustafa, "THE GRID," in Mustafa, SEA STATE, 118.

44 Chua, Lim, and Mustafa, "THE GRID," 119–121.

45 Foo Say Juan, in conversation with Charles Lim, "Sand Man," in Mustafa, SEA STATE, 105.

46 Subramanian, "How Singapore Is Creating."

47 Barr, *Singapore*, 165; Lui and Tan, "Building," 54.

48 Chris Milton, "The Sand Smugglers," *Foreign Policy*, August 4, 2010, http://www .foreignpolicy.com/articles/2010/08/04/the_sand_smugglers. Khvay Samnang's art practice provides an important complement to SEA STATE in exploring the ramifications of sand extraction from Cambodia. See my essay, "Breathing, Carrying, Pouring: Khvay Samnang's Eco-Aesthetic Gestures of Non-violence,"

in *Khvay Samnang: The Land Beneath My Feet*, exhibition catalog, ed. Nicola Müllerschön and Christoph Tanner (Berlin: Künstlerhaus Bethanien, 2015), 8–23.

49 Mustafa, *SEA STATE*, 52.

50 Mustafa, "'Mr.' Anthrobalanus," 26; Yao, "Floating World."

51 Mustafa, *SEA STATE*, 130.

52 Mustafa, "'Mr.' Anthrobalanus," 26.

53 Charles Lim, "Charles Lim: *SEA STATE*," interview at the Pavilion of Singapore, Arsenale—Sale d'Armi, Venice Biennale 2015, https://vimeo.com/134812753.

54 Samantha Lai, Lynette H. L. Loke, Michael J. Hilton, Tjeerd J. Bouma, and Peter A. Todd, "The Effects of Urbanisation on Coastal Habitats and the Potential for Ecological Engineering: A Singapore Case Study," *Ocean and Coastal Management*, November 2014, 79.

55 Lai et al., "The Effects of Urbanisation," 81.

56 Gómez-Barris, *Extractive Zone*, xvii, 5.

57 Gómez-Barris, *Extractive Zone*, 4.

58 Gómez-Barris, *Extractive Zone*, xvi.

59 Gómez-Barris, *Extractive Zone*, 137.

60 Gómez-Barris, *Extractive Zone*, xix.

61 Subramanian, "How Singapore Is Creating."

62 "Five Things to Know about the Jurong Rock Caverns," *Straits Times*, September 2, 2014, https://www.straitstimes.com/singapore/five-things-to-know-about -the-jurong-rock-caverns; Subramanian, "How Singapore is Creating."

63 Lui Pao Chuen, in conversation with Shabbir Hussain Mustafa, "The Department of Dreaming," in Mustafa, *SEA STATE*, 90.

64 Chua Beng Huat, "Singapore as Model: Planning Innovations, Knowledge Experts," in *Worlding Cities: Asian Experiments and the Art of Being Global*, ed. Ananya Roy and Aihwa Ong (Hoboken, NJ: Blackwell, 2011), 38.

65 Singapore's oil and shipping industries have long developed hand in hand; see Barr, *Singapore*, 151–52.

66 Ahmad Mashadi, "Drifting Conversations," in Mustafa, *SEA STATE*, 117n3.

67 Chua, Lim, and Mustafa, "THE GRID," 126.

68 Chua, "The Sahajat Buoy," 57.

69 There are numerous tourist blogs and websites that sentimentalize Kampong Lorong Buangkok, such as https://thehoneycombers.com/singapore/kampong -lorong-buangkok-singapore-secrets/.

70 Charles Lim artist website, "*SEA STATE* 8," accessed September 26, 2019, http:// www.charleslimyiyong.com/8.

71 Barr, *Singapore*, 25.

72 Gómez-Barris, *The Extractive Zone*, xiii, 134. See especially Donna J. Haraway, "Tentacular Thinking: Anthropocene, Capitalocene, Chthulucene," in *Staying with the Trouble: Making Kin in the Chthulucene* (Durham, NC: Duke University Press), 30–57.

73 Prasenjit Duara, "Island Territoriality: Charles Lim Yi Yong's Water-Bounded Singapore," in Mustafa, *SEA STATE*, 44.

Toward Infrastructure Art
Containerization, Black Box Logistics, and New Distribution Complexes

JAIMEY HAMILTON FARIS

Globally, every theory of systems became a graph of either a simplex or a complex, all things being first of all situated in the depths of a black box. We despise contents, we administer flow charts. —Michel Serres, *Genesis*

When Jack Burnham wrote his now-famous 1968 essay "Systems Esthetics," he described the new role of art as bringing visibility to "the way things are done."[1] What did he mean exactly by this phrase? Most obviously, he meant systems. His essay now stands as an important and clear identification of artistic practices that shifted from a sole focus on the art object or "thing" to the ways, methods, processes, relations, and connections *between* things. Burnham discussed in particular minimalists' and postminimalists' attention to the logic of component parts and contextual relationships—likening Donald Judd's instructional style of writing to a computer programmer's list structure, noting how Dan Flavin's fluorescent lights articulated "illumination systems for given spaces," and recognizing that Robert Morris's *Steam*, which captured hot vapor from the water pipes underneath the streets of Philadelphia for the *Air Art* exhibition, was an intervention in the city's civil engineering.[2]

Much of Burnham's discussion of art made around 1968 was imbued with an understanding of artists as systems analysts—who "have an ever-expanding grasp of human needs and limitations."[3] One of the most prominent strains of art to arise out of this new interest in systems was institutional critique and its varied performative methods of visualizing the motivated connections among players, parts, and sites in any named institution, including art museums, governments, and businesses.[4] Burnham's argument has informed a history of contemporary art dominated by institutional critique in which embedded artists trace, mimic, exaggerate, and expose the heretofore hidden power relations that circulate within organizations.

Yet, there are many clues in Burnham's text that what he might have meant by likening artists to systems analysts was leading to something even more mundane than what we now call institutional critique. The artists he admired used pipes, lights, and software routines, all pointing beyond institutions as systems and toward more diffuse material and informational networks that support and connect institutions. At the beginning of the essay, Burnham underscores the importance of systems art as a means to seriously contend with problems of an "emergent 'superscientific culture' . . . precipitating vast crises in human ecology."[5] Citing John Kenneth Galbraith's *The New Industrial State* (1967), he describes the key issues of this "superscientific culture" in terms of the Cold War military-industrial complex: "Already in California think-tanks and in the central committees of each soviet, futurologists are concentrating on the role of the technocracy, that is, its decision-making autonomy, how it handles the central storage of information, and the techniques used for smoothly implementing social change. In the automated state power resides less in the control of the traditional symbols of wealth than in information."[6] In 1968 it was radical to point to the rise of technocracy—to make note of automated information *as power*—and moreover as a "technique of implementing social change," of inducing massive behavioral shifts across nations and even the world.

Looking back at the statement, after the advent of the internet and big data, we can now see that Burnham's focus on "ways," systems, and complex interactions was part of a larger growing interest in the methods through which power was accumulated and instrumentalized in everyday structures. Information systems were linked into networks of schools, prisons, hospitals, governments, businesses, and houses, which in turn were increasingly interconnected and managed by mass manufacturing, energy grids, water systems, roadways, and ports. Technocratic algorithms and databases were making key visionary decisions about how life would be lived—about lifestyles, certainly, but also about how bare life itself would be supported.

Systems within and across systems have grown exponentially since Burnham's statement. Information and technology operate in fundamentally different ways than Burnham could have imagined in 1968. They now define our present world-spanning networks of water management, agriculture, mining, high-speed fiber-optic cables, global shipping ports, airports, computerized logistics and management, cookies linking browser data to ads, financial algorithms, and more. Now more than ever, we need to look deeper into Burnham's call for art to attend to the "way things are done."

With new recognition for the postwar histories of global informational and material development and distribution, how can we think about Judd's algorithmic boxes, Flavin's lights, and Morris's rerouting of pipes as laying a "groundwork" for the importance of contemporary art in a global neoliberal landscape? To begin, take the evolving project *Puerto Rican Light* by the Puerto Rico–based artists Jennifer Allora and Guillermo Calzadilla. Since 2003 they have been recontextualizing Dan Flavin's 1965 piece *Puerto Rican Light (to Jeanie Blake)* by reinstalling it in various locations around New York with solar-powered batteries renewed by vast solar arrays in Puerto Rico. A 2015 iteration in which the Flavin sculpture was installed in a remote cave in Puerto Rico and linked to the nearby arrays extends the discussion of the politics of energy.[7] The piece relates the disparate military and energy histories of New York and Puerto Rico and questions the United States' extractive relationship with the islands. In this work Allora and Calzadilla consciously cue viewers to the geopolitics of the energy grid beyond the white cube. Art practices such as these signal that perhaps we need an art historical framework for this shift that moves from "systems art" (and veers slightly away from the dominance of institutional critique) and toward "infrastructure art."

First, it would be helpful to briefly identify the relationship between systems and infrastructure as well as the rise of infrastructure studies in the early 2000s that parallels art practices such as Allora and Calzadilla's.[8] The sociologist Susan Leigh Star's foundational article "The Ethnography of Infrastructure" (1999) gives an overview of the issues and potentials of the new field. She points out that the sociological or anthropological study of information systems struggles with how infrastructure is built into the very fabric of technical work.[9] In studying computing power, one also has to look at the standardization of computing and telecommunications machines, conventions of practice, and so on. Seeing infrastructure, she argues, is a difficult interpretive tactic: one that involves identifying which systems subtend or motivate other systems and then separating a system to analyze it, even though it may be simultaneously integrated with others and also operating on multiple levels. She sees infrastructure not just in terms of material networks but as the "embodiments of standards." Since Star's writing the field has expanded into multiple domains looking at histories of civil engineering, transportation, migration, waste, communication, and more. The media anthropologist Brian Larkin has refined many of Star's key points not only by reiterating a clear definition of infrastructure—as the materials or technologies that create the grounds on which other materials or technologies run—but in looking at the larger historical (especially the colonial and postcolonial) implications of infrastructure.[10]

There have been many other efforts to detail the histories of modern infrastructures as they have intensively developed in the name of Cold War defense and out of the reconfigured geographies of postcolonialism.[11] As David Harvey, Keller Easterling, and others point out, the infrastructural processes of neoliberalization—built in pieces, in fits and starts (and always with gaps or lacunae in its uneven development)—have become increasingly maintained, managed, and expanded not by the state but by private enterprise often operating as de facto monopolies (think here of the electric utilities in the United States).[12] With the exception of highways, much of our global commerce infrastructure is now self-regulated through NGOs like the World Trade Organization, the International Organization for Standardization, and the International Chamber of Commerce.[13] These infrastructure systems operate through what the architect and urbanist Keller Easterling calls "extrastatecraft," "undisclosed activities beyond, in addition to, and sometimes even in partnerships with statecraft."[14]

In *Extrastatecraft: The Power of Infrastructure Space*, Easterling pushes beyond Burnham's concern for the "centralized" power of the Cold War state to describe new distributions of power among a global economic elite. The "infrastructure space" to which the subtitle of her book alludes is energy grids, linked oil extraction projects, transoceanic cables, free-trade zones, special economic zones, and more.[15] As other scholars have looked into environmental infrastructures—or, better, environment *as* infrastructure—a broader infrastructural analysis of contemporary technocracies now also includes interconnected human relations to material, energy, and ecology.[16] This critical infrastructure cohort is looking at the way systems within systems tend to bury the violent extraction of human and earth externalities alike.

If one were to pinpoint a moment of awareness in the art world toward the power of globally connected information-material infrastructure, it would be when global trade and finance became automated and more widely distributed in the 1990s via extrastatecraft processes.[17] Since then, artists have been developing more explicit projects about the integrated physical, economic, and data infrastructures of our world. In retrospect, we can begin to identify the emergence of art in the late twentieth century based in systems aesthetics and related to the social structures of relational art practices but pointedly more attentive to global sociality's imbrication in material, informational, and distributive complexes. Indeed, investigating the systemic means of circulation and distribution of capital (whether as information or as goods) is a key component of infrastructure art.

Toward Infrastructure Art

One of the most interesting threads in the development of infrastructure art from the 1990s to the present is artistic concern over the rise of containerization—an absolutely essential infrastructure for global trade and markets.[18] In the interest of sketching out some key issues of infrastructure art, I'd like to focus the rest of this essay on three historical moments in the representation of containerization, beginning with the late photographer and filmmaker Allan Sekula, whose photo essay *Fish Story* (1989–95) documented all the newly constructed automated superports around the world. I will then look at two artists who signal a new intensity in the geopolitics of containerization by the early 2000s: the Chinese artist Ni Haifeng, whose *Return of the Shreds* (2007) and *Para-Production* (2008) highlight the obfuscations of factory outsourcing through containerization, and the Swiss artist Christoph Büchel, whose *Training Ground for Training Ground for Democracy* (2007) connects commercial, political, art-world, and military infrastructures. I will end with a look at the digital media artist Hito Steyerl's art installation *Duty Free Art* (2015) and book (2017), which focus on the interrelated functions of containers, free ports, and art markets to launder money for a global elite. The trajectory running from Sekula, at the advent of trade liberalization, to Haifeng and Büchel's extensive material articulations of the global trade infrastructure at full steam, lead us finally to Steyerl's most recent projects that clearly expose the operations of data capitalism as it depends on the real material infrastructure of containers. The arc traces infrastructural concerns as the artists have gained more access and more insight into the operations of containerization over the decades. It also traces, through the material shifts and strategies of the art practices, the containerization of the art-world infrastructure itself.

These projects focus on the two major units of container infrastructure: the metal shipping box and the cybernetic black box of logistics software. The world-spanning automated intermodal global distribution system is composed of modular boxes (typically 20 by 40 feet) moving through integrated and standardized transportation networks from factory to port to warehouse to store. With ports, ships, containers, roadways, railways, and trucks built, modified, remodified, and expanded over decades and across continents, the system now moves 90 percent of the world's consumer goods.[19]

The physical system is supported by networked logistical "just-in-time" supply chain software. In 1968, software was built by each company to keep track of manufacturing costs and inventory, as supply chains began to intensively expanded outside national boundaries. Now pre-packaged networked just-in-time supply chain software is available at many levels and connects to five million data centers and transfer stations, which in turn use GPS tracking information cross-referenced with port and trucking logs. This system is integrated with standardized enterprise software that calculates the daily costs of materials and oil prices, makes labor market comparisons, and tracks inventory.[20]

Containerization, then, is both a material and an informational complex of black box routines, flowcharts, and massive amounts of material and energy. The interconnected trade system appears at first sight to be the most efficient, apolitical, necessarily algorithmic, and automated of all contemporary infrastructures. It is just "the way things are done" (à la Burnham's original statement). Yet, as the basis of much of the world's everyday material life, it has ramifications for everything from workers' wages to health care coverage, to rural and suburban development, to the politics of migration, nationalism, borders, and even climate change.

In tracing the developing visibility of containerization in a few art practices over the last three decades, I hope to indicate the ways in which contemporary infrastructure art is part of the larger history of systems art. But I also want to indicate that it is an increasingly important and distinctive approach to visualizing the ways our informational and material-intensive infrastructures impact social and environmental justice around the world. Infrastructure art practices are concerned generally, like all systems-based art, with the interdependence of relationships and how to represent their value-defining boundaries. But infrastructure art's ethico-aesthetic mode is different from typical "institutional critique." Infrastructure artists are often searching for ways to make visible deep subtending operations between and beyond corporate, commercial, and state institutions. Infrastructure artists are interested in the relations between institutions, the pervasive practices and processes that link them and that would, by implication, survive even if

the institutions are transformed. Infrastructure artists' forms of critique usually are focused not on systems "within institutions" but on the systems that
link across the spaces between and below institutions. In short, infrastructure art provides a language for talking about systems aesthetics as extra- or
intra-institutional critique.

What makes infrastructure art, particularly art about containerization, distinctive within a pervasive systems approach to art making in the contemporary
era is its attention to how certain kinds of information and material substruc-
ture have buried themselves deep down below political and social oversight.
Technocratic and informational infrastructures insinuate themselves into the
material, factual basis of the present *and* the immediate future. It is hard now
to imagine a world without containerization. Yet its historical development
since the 1950s is rife with stories of million-dollar container ships and ports
made almost immediately defunct by the development of newer technology,
methods, and standards.[21] Containerization's development appears, from the
contemporary consumer's vantage point, to have arisen "smoothly" and quietly,
never as a specific political choice or concern. Infrastructures such as these,
so ubiquitous as to become invisible, appear as fixtures of the world. Many
Euro-Americans (and increasingly "middle-income" earners from around the

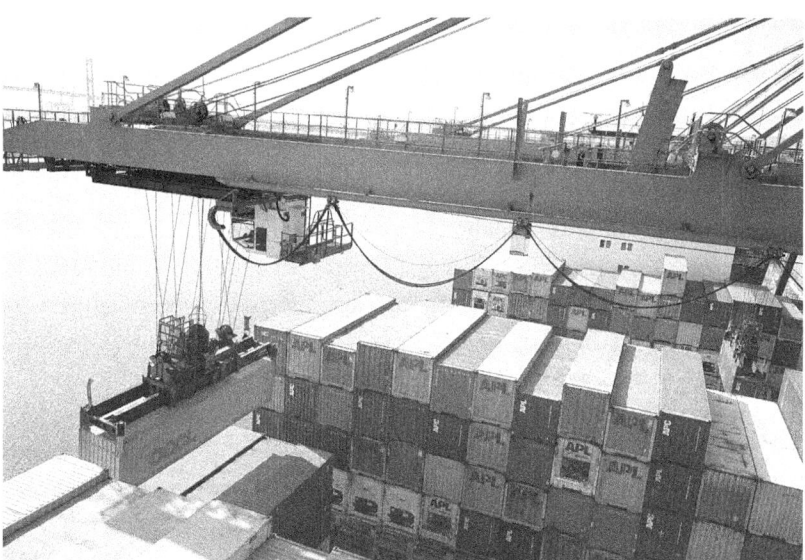

FIGURE 10.1. Allan Sekula, *Hammerhead crane unloading forty-foot containers from
Asian ports. American President Lines terminal. Los Angeles harbor, San Pedro, California.*
From the series *Fish Story*, 1992. Photograph courtesy of the Allan Sekula Studio.

world) take these substructures and logics for granted because they are implemented on a routine basis, adding convenience and a sense of security and modernization to everyday life.[22] These infrastructures are also now a key basis of global power as an ever-evolving, decentralized network. Thus, there is all the more reason to examine our various assumptions about and attachments to them, as well as the ways in which they have subtended many of the darkest aspects of contemporary neoliberal political institutions. The following art historical sketch offers some views into these infrastructural concerns and the ways they have evolved.

The Container Principle

In 1989, Allan Sekula began working on *Fish Story*, a long-term research project documenting the impact of containerization on maritime trade. Based on his interest in the US labor movement since the 1980s, he started following a growing number of dockworker strikes organized against the automation of the port system.[23] Sekula's documentation developed into a series of photographs about working and living at port and on board the new massive container ships then coming into operation. The photos were collected into a book and also exhibited in museums and galleries as a combination of photographs, texts, and slideshows. Sekula focused on the lives and dwellings of laid-off dockworkers (often dwarfed by the new loading machines) as well as the seamen on the new ships (often working in small spaces and at awkward angles to scrape rust, paint, and maintain machines and pipes on the massive ships).

In the book, the images were punctuated by the artist's essays, which clearly detailed the advent of transnational capital rising from a "fluctuating web of connections, lines of exploitation that run from London to Hong Kong, to Shenzhen to Taipei. . . . Drawing ravenously on the rock-bottom labor costs of the new factory in the border city of Shenzhen."[24] The reasoning behind this infrastructure, as Sekula saw it, was a new politics of neoliberal trade agreements and a new economics of profit maximization based on cheap ocean transit.[25] Value is added to material goods simply in the way their circulation is managed through the supply chain. The cheaper the factory labor, the cheaper the shipper, the lower the costs at ports and at customs, the sooner it can get to its destination, and the more profit is earned. Trade liberalization also enabled shippers to register in countries with the least regulatory oversight (so-called flags of convenience)—basically building the global port and container system on sweatshop conditions, not just in factories but also at port and sea.[26]

Sekula positioned the development of containerization as the key element in this new system with dramatic effects on labor. In a long section of *Fish Story* called "Dismal Science: Part II," he relates this to a history of packaging by juxtaposing an image of Andy Warhol's *Brillo Box* with diagrams of the first intermodal containers of the 1970s that ushered in the mechanization of ports. Sekula argues that, with containerization, dockworkers were no longer considered necessary for onloading and offloading individual boxes. The container's "superficial clarity of straight lines" linked the factory immediately to the store, erasing everything in between, including the radical deregulation of dock and ship labor, the deregulation of tariffs and taxes between countries protected by special economic zones, and the sea itself.[27] In the end, Sekula declares, "The container has become the very emblem of capitalist disavowal."[28]

Sekula attempted to overcome the container's classic structure of disavowal ("I know but nevertheless") with his "critical realist" photographs highlighting the work of the laborers in relation to the gigantic scale of super-ports and super-ships and giving viewers a specific image of the human cost in maintaining such an infrastructure.[29] His tracing of the systemic effects on global labor throughout interconnected port systems was a hallmark shift in contemporary art toward explicit attention to the processes of globalization as it affected lives in every country around the world. *Fish Story*, with its flexible exhibition format and clear Marxist methodology, became a foundational piece for the art world's revival of materialist critique.[30] The first chapters were shown in the 1993 Whitney Biennial, but its acclaim was sealed when it was included in the 2002 *Documenta 11* among other more recent documentaries also critiquing processes of globalization, many of which referenced or paid homage to Sekula.

There are now many projects indebted to Sekula that focus on how containerization and globalization impact the precarity of global labor—and not just in photographic or video documentary modes, as with Ursula Biemann's *Contained Mobility* (2004), a video installation about a man who found illegal passage in a container. There are also social practice–based projects like the Center for Urban Pedagogy's "Cargo Chain" booklet poster (2007), in which the collective worked in collaboration with the Longshore Workers Coalition to make an organizing tool in which the workers could visualize how the shippers pit the unions at different ports against each other to drive down costs. Martha Atienza's *Gilubong ang Akon Pusod sa Dagat (My Navel Is Buried at Sea)* (2011) combined critical realist documentary with social practice by asking her neighbors on Bantayan Island in the Philippines to help her film and discuss the co-constitutive demise of fishermen and the rise of a migrant seaman class traveling around the world on container ships. The film not only looked at containerization's impact on the Filipino economy but also examined its connection to the destruction of fishing ecologies, unraveling family dynamics, and perceptions of wealth in the community.

Since Sekula, political scientists, theorists, and artists have taken on the task of digging deeper into the visual epistemology of the container to understand why it works so elegantly to "disavow" the darker realities of global trade and labor. Alexander Klose's *The Container Principle: How a Box Changes the Way We Think* (2009) argues that the container's pervasive visibility makes our questions about its existence superfluous.[31] It becomes a visotype, or empty signifier, of globalization that stands in for the space between locales and naturalizes the connection between cities. The world becomes a picture composed as a flowchart of easily movable boxes.

In diagrams of containerization, the key to flow is the "container principle." Essentially, as Klose argues, it the same principle as the black box in computing—an object that can be viewed in terms of its inputs and outputs (or transfer characteristics), without any knowledge of its contents and the operations subtending them. All the information locked inside is trumped by the priority of the all-important networked information encoded in the number on the container. Indeed, one of the most important aspects of global trade is the container's unbroken seal, which makes it faster to move contents through each transfer point.

Klose uses Michel Serres's metaphor of the "parasite" to explain the intermodal system.[32] The container climbs on the backs of trucks, trains, and ships, using the energy of these hosts to move, but always in relation to them (*para-*)—beside, not a part of, in contradiction to—and therefore able to detach easily. Shippers are no longer even required to carry manifests of their cargo; the space of circulation does not have to depend at all on knowledge about the goods in the container—in what conditions they are made or sold. As Klose puts it: "Millions of tons of metal appear weightless and frictionless, moved as if by magic. . . . It evokes the image of a neutral medium, a pure movement of units of information, production, and consumption on the circuits of a system."[33] This black box logic also insulates its movement through the potentially dangerous and vulnerable realities of shipping. It can move seamlessly through port cities run by authoritarian and exploitative regimes, is insured against inclement weather, and so on.

To understand the full import of Klose's argument about how container-ization is a *parasitical* infrastructure, it is worth backtracking for just a moment. The title of his book, *The Container Principle*, was a phrase coined much earlier (this is never mentioned by Klose) by avant-garde artist Asger Jorn, a founding member of the Situationist International, formed in 1957. Jorn's essay "The End of the Economy and the Realization of Art" (1960) is included in the Situationist International's fourth publication.[34] In a section called "The Container Principle and the Concept of Form," he writes, "We have always perceived form as constancy and stability." Yet, as Jorn continues, this is an illusion: "A container's form is a form that exists *only as a direct opposite to the content*, its function being to prevent the content entering into a process except under controlled and severely limited conditions. . . . Gen-erally the container hides the content's own form that thus possesses a third form, the sensual form or the apparent form." He concludes, "The content is neutralized by the container's function as a unit. . . . This . . . is the basis for the whole of the modern tin-can philosophy."[35]

With disaffected tone, Jorn essentially critiques formalism in art and de-sign for helping to give rise to the new logic of capitalism's abstraction of value, "neutralizing" labor, energy, and time by packaging or containing it in regularized sizes. Jorn's argument actually runs parallel to and elucidates the political tenor of Burnham's own subtle argument in "System's Esthetics," made a few years later, in which the latter similarly lambastes the "syndrome of formalist invention in art."[36] It is picked up again by Sekula in his critique of the "serial discipline of the box."[37] This network of citations provides a loop back to reinforce an understanding that systems art was not merely a postfor-malist aesthetic but a critique of formalism's own infrastructural past (hence minimalists' attention to boxes as algorithmic structures).[38]

While it is unclear whether Klose was riffing off of Jorn's text in describing his own version of the container principle, he does cite Sekula's argument about seriality. There is a connecting thread in Klose's use of Serres, who is generally known to be indebted to the Situationist International's critique of capitalism. Serres's understanding of the black box logic of capitalism as parasitical, laid out in both *The Parasite* (1980) and *Genesis* (1982), is consis-tent with Jorn's statement that the container functions in direct opposition to its contents—an abstraction of the real conditions of labor production and Sekula's structure of disavowal. Serres's *Genesis* is part of Sekula's own library of Marxist literature now archived at the Clark Art Institute.[39] The strategic deferment of both content and site operating in the container principle has naturally made artists not only want to mimic the black box function of the closed container (as minimalists did) and then trace the parasitical exploitative movement of the container through ports in relation to labor (as Sekula and the other artists just mentioned above did), but also to open the box and see what is inside.

Paraproduction and Paraconsumption

The container as parasite acts *para-* to its surroundings, feeding on *and* interrupting relations, all with a certain political and social immunity to itself. The container situation is parasitical not just to the port and transportation systems, as Klose argues, but also to labor, resources, and other relations in the lengthening supply chains of the early 2000s.[40] Essentially, containerization was initially grafted onto existing mining and factory structures (and national road and railway structures) but was then also leveraged by emerging big-box stores like Walmart to encourage an expanded system in keeping with its appetites. This led artists to take an interest in containerization as an infrastructure that orchestrated the transnational phenomenon of outsourced factory production related to frenzied consumption. In 2006 the Chinese artist Liu Jianhua tried to materialize this in *Yiwa Survey*, arranging a plastic spill out of a container onto the floor of the gallery of the Sixth Shanghai Biennale. In 2007, compatriot Ni Haifeng took that logic further with *Return of the Shreds*.

Ni, part of the first generation of internationally recognized Chinese installation artists, has lived in Amsterdam since the early 1990s. In 2007, at the height of his career, he was commissioned to do an art installation for the Museum De Lakenhal, located in a defunct textile factory in Leiden. He reanimated the space with the "ghosts" of past and present trade relations between China and the Netherlands. He shipped boxes of porcelain to the gallery to evoke the historical beginnings of this relation. He also requested ten days' worth of remnants of high-fashion garments collected from ten Chinese factories, which he piled on the museum floor up to the ceiling. The size of the pile quickly overwhelmed the space, making it seem like a small stockroom in comparison to the half-mile-long metal sheds now used in China for apparel manufacture. Loose threads tangled in viewers' feet were pulled slightly apart from the body of the fabric pile.

The symbolic remnants of contemporary labor half a world away were returned to the nineteenth-century factory floor as a way of invoking the material memory of the textile workers and the historical displacement of their labor across the globe. This relation was overlaid by the idea that the waste or "shreds" made by the Chinese workers were there to haunt the Europeans who consumed the related swaths of fabric fashioned into shirts and coats that populated shops across Europe.

The adjoining room was filled with the paperwork that Ni had to fill out to ship the remnants to Amsterdam. Ni discovered that, because it was not normally desired by another country, postproduction waste did not have a harmonized system (HS) code. These are the codes used by Comtrade to classify and track transnational trade and calculate the value of the global economy.[41] This gap in the container principle made it extremely difficult for Ni to ship the fabric. It exposed other systems of bureaucracy through the letters he wrote explaining to officials why he wanted such quantities of trash from across the ocean.

Ni became fascinated by the details of the HS code as well as its fundamental importance as a standardized information infrastructure to the trade system. In his next installation, *Para-production* (2008), mounted this time in an old factory in Beijing, he filled one room with a pile of cloth remnants and then added an additional room in which he pasted vinyl text of the HS codes directly on the walls from floor to ceiling. Resonant with Serres's parasite, this installation references the invisible labor a few miles away in new textile factories. Ni also provided a few old-fashioned Singer sewing machines that could be used by visitors to help create a single patchwork fabric—a "para"-production at a "para"-site that existed next to, but apart from, the real ones nearby. This also made the installation hauntingly relational, as visitors became symbolic laborers—linked to but not part of the global force of garment workers. The room with HS codes gave the impression of a juggernaut as large as the mass of fabric in the other room.

Both of Ni's installations put visitors in a space to understand how container infrastructures, connected to factory infrastructures, connected through a "harmonized system" of logistics software, are parasitical extrastatecraft structures of biopower, making invisible and abstracting the actual labor conditions in the factories popping up all over China. The connections made by Ni in 2007–8 were possible not only because of the mounting number of exposés of factory production in China but also because of the new online accessibility of Comtrade software.[42] As artists and galleries scaled up in the transnationally configured art world, which demanded large, sophisticated, and immersive installations like Ni's, they now had need of this logistics software. Despite the political and ethical limitations of the highly circumscribed representational space that the luxury Chinese art world offered, Ni saw an opportunity to point out how the implicit violence and inequity of production contained by the black box logic of parasitical standardization and regulation systems occlude the activities happening in the open economic zones just outside of Beijing.

Since then, Deborah Cowen has dug deeper into this "network space of circulation" in her 2014 book *The Deadly Life of Logistics: Mapping Violence in Global Trade*, arguing that the current system, historically related to the military supply chain, relies heavily on externalizing costs to national governments, which not only protect the right of open oceans for shipping companies but also wage wars that keep oil prices low and reinforce the devaluation of labor by upholding national borders.[43] In this sense, the container rationalizes and erases both the political spaces of the port and the ocean and the political spaces of the mine, the factory, the suburb, the highway, and big-box store. Cowen sums up the logic of the container as essentially "conceal[ing] histories of organized violence."[44]

As a complement to Ni's focus on paraproduction in China, another rising star of the global art world, the Swiss artist Christoph Büchel focused on the American citizen-consumer end of the container infrastructure. His installation *Training Ground for Training Ground for Democracy* featured a container plopped in the middle of Hauser and Wirth's booth at Art Basel Miami Beach in 2007. A sandwich board out front invited art patrons to "Vote Here." Entering the container, visitors were suddenly immersed in a typical American public school classroom set up as a temporary polling place. Accoutrements of elementary education were everywhere—chairs, chalkboard, Play-Doh, Legos, and paper cutouts. Voting booths, complete with ballots, lined one wall; and pictures of US soldiers in Iraq and Afghanistan decorated the room. There was also a television set on low volume and broadcasting *Tomorrow's Pioneers*, a Mickey Mouse–like show in Arabic with English subtitles. If visitors weren't paying attention, they would miss the subtle anomaly of the programming. Again outside, visitors were then invited to climb the ladder propped up against the container. On the roof they were engulfed in another surreal scene of an abandoned party in which every imaginable snack food was left on the tables, half-eaten. Surveillance cameras decorated in white lights were set at the perimeter. A decommissioned missile hanging above the table festooned the whole scene like a gigantic militarized piñata.

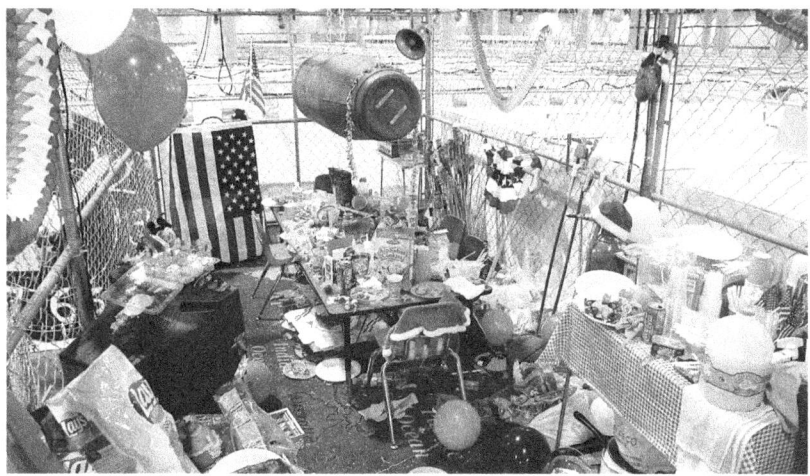

FIGURE 10.2. Christoph Büchel, *Training Ground for Training Ground for Democracy*, 2007. Installation, dimensions variable. Installation view on top of the container, Art Basel Miami Beach. © Christoph Büchel. Courtesy of the artist, Hauser and Wirth, and Nationalgalerie, Staatliche Museen zu Berlin, gift of the Friedrich Christian Flick Collection/DE. Photo by Christoph Büchel.

If the title of the installation suggested a "training ground for democracy," then commodity objects, television and surveillance cameras, and the voting booths, were displayed as training tools. The absurd implication was that Büchel's training ground was the container itself—reproducible and mobile. It could be sent anywhere and used to teach others an American lifestyle in which democracy, militarism, education, and consumerism were four sides of the same coin. The Arabic Mickey Mouse show, cameras, and the missile were there as reminders of the strange mirror worlds that container circulation instantiates.[45] In effect, his work materialized the situation that Cowen articulates in the *Deadly Life of Logistics*: "The entire network of infrastructures, technologies, spaces, workers, and violence that makes the circulation of stuff possible remains tucked out of sight for those who engage with logistics only as consumers. Yet, alongside billions of commodities, the management of global supply chains imports elaborate transactions into the socius—transactions that are political, financial, legal, and often martial."[46] Büchel's conception of these weirdly collapsed sectors created an atmosphere in which commercial and military logistics were seen to be intimately entangled. The whole Miami installation was presented as a feedback loop of supply chain security in response to President George W. Bush's advocacy of consumption as a way to show enemies that nothing could disrupt the American way of life. Only two weeks after 9/11, the president had urged the public to "get down to Disney World in Florida. Take your families and enjoy life, the way we want it to be enjoyed."[47] The logic of the statement is ultimately tautological: the manufacture of cheap goods and cartoon characters perpetuates resource wars (conducted in large part by private logistics operators) and fear of the other, leading to heightened anxiety that can then be assuaged only by more consumption and the expansion of that lifestyle of consumption beyond borders, supported by more capital, more military penetration, and more training. Büchel's subtle inclusion of such details as *Tomorrow's Pioneers* begins to unravel this logic.[48]

For the Art Basel Miami Beach installation made a few years after 9/11, there was an additional layer of critique leveled against the art world. Büchel has long been known for pushing institutional buttons with the extravagance of his installations. The Art Basel installation was actually part of a larger project (titled *Training Ground for Democracy*) that was abandoned by MASS MoCA for this reason.[49] Doubling the title in reference to that abandoned project, Büchel wanted to see how far he could coopt the budget of his gallery, Hauser and Wirth, for materials, labor, shipping, and art fair space to create this "training ground" that, ostensibly, no art investor in their right mind would purchase. (Of course, one did—the piece is now in Berlin's National-galerie collection, gifted by Friedrich Christian Flick.[50]) Büchel's tactic, if not really disruptive of the art-world system, was to invite viewers on top of the container to stand amidst the abandoned party scene and look out over the top of the art fair cubicles. At this moment the whole fair became part of Büchel's installation, a big-box commercial structure, easily dismantled, containerized, and reinstalled in yet another city for the art-world elite. A paraconsumption experience.

Ni and Büchel's use of containers in art projects parallels the rise of their use in the art world in general: as ticket booths, food courts, and even galleries within old schools and factories that were converted into contemporary art project spaces. In the 1990s and early 2000s, containers seemed to signal a rehabbed, DIY world of cultural revitalization. Beyond the surface appeal of the mobile and modular box, the presence of containers in art-world spaces was actually an early marker of the historical transformation of the entire art world's distribution and circulation infrastructure. Art fairs and biennials, as well as multinational galleries with locations around the globe, could not exist without the cost-effective shipping, delivering, and storing mechanisms invented with containerization.

One can easily dismiss the paralogic of Ni's multinational material poetics or Büchel's cynical tableau as part of the rise of the spectacle-experience-oriented art world, but there is also something undeniably effective about the hyperreality of infrastructure space at the core of their installation aesthetics.[51] Both focus on what Brian Larkin calls the "ambient experience of infrastructure: our sense of temperature, speed, florescence, and the ideas we have associated with these conditions."[52] Büchel's accumulation of detail, for example, inspires the desire to open the ballot boxes and taste the food to see how real they are, which then evolves into a desire to touch the screws holding the art fair's cubicles together. There is a sudden realization that the art fair is also part of the elaborate theatrical set, a temporarily composed infrastructural environment acting partially as a training ground for art consumers. In essence, these para-sites, by grafting onto the parasitical logic of containerization, begin to expose its logic. To understand this strange loop, Carrie Lambert-Beatty's notion of artistic parafictional strategies is appropriate here.[53] Both Ni and Büchel create fictional para-site spaces that intersect with the real structures of containerization. But they do not create a critique through fictionality alone; rather, they cultivate a lack of clarity about where their spaces end and the real world begins, thereby creating a certain amount of skepticism about the reality beyond. Both installations heighten the viewer's awareness of infrastructure as a sort of omnipresent mise-en-scène cultivating our producing and consuming performances even as we walk outside the gallery.

Duty Free Art

Just a few years after, in *Duty Free Art* (2015), a video installation for Artists Space in New York, Hito Steyerl was able to map the containerization of the art world with far more precision and specificity than Büchel or Ni. A conceptual filmmaker and writer, Steyerl is known for her interest in data capitalism, the processes by which information is not only collected but also circulated, redistributed, and monetized. In earlier essays published in *e-flux*, such as "Too Much World, Is the Internet Dead?," she explored the ways in which this condition has impacted the artist's job—not only to make art but also to market, launch, and "accelerate" it so that worth accrues through its promotion.[54] *Duty Free Art* explores aspects of data capitalism on the buyer's end, particularly the motivations of the elite financial sector to buy art at art fairs (especially in low-tax or tax-free countries like Switzerland or Hong Kong) and then literally to keep their purchases in sealed containers stored in

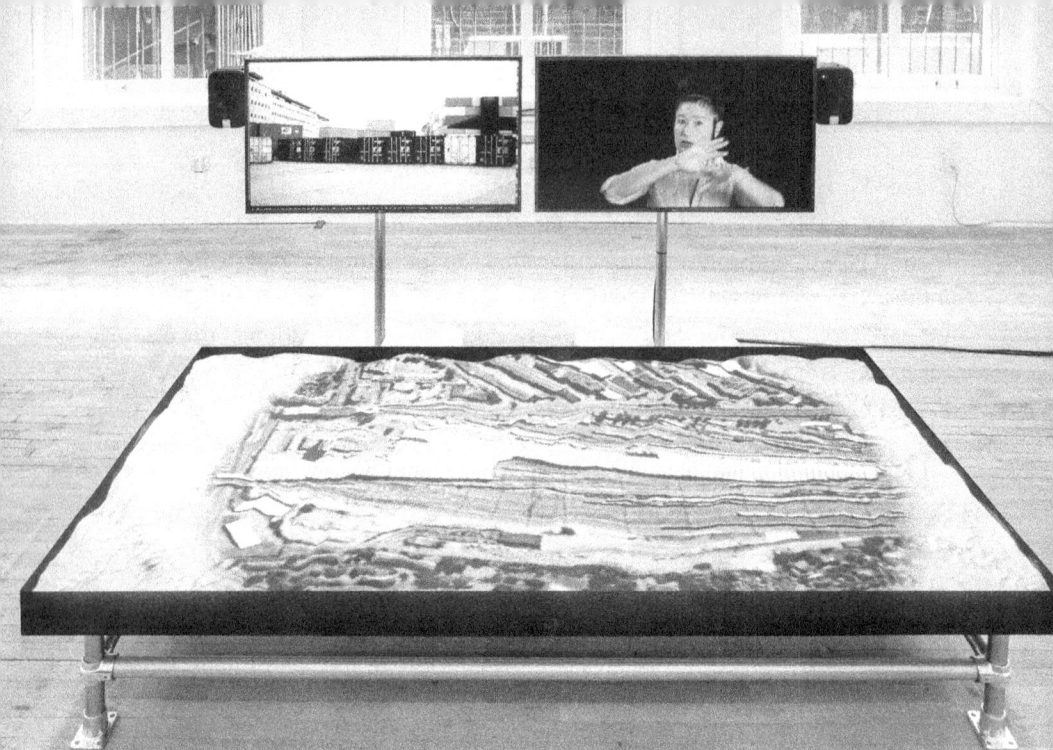

FIGURE 10.3. Hito Steyerl, *Duty Free Art*, 2015. Three-channel HD video with sound, 38 minutes, 21 seconds. Installation view from Artists Space, New York. Image courtesy of the artist, Andrew Kreps Gallery, New York, and Esther Schipper, Berlin. Photo by Matthew Septimus.

nearby special economic zones (SEZS) in order to avoid taxes. The containers can then be moved around the world at a moment's notice to pay for nefarious other economic and political activities, and to launder money. She essentially charts data capitalism's increased reliance on a containerized system of art-world distribution as a method of not only accruing power and wealth, but also deferring responsibility to the public by always keeping art en route.[55]

In the performance lecture that is part of the installation (also published as an essay in *e-flux*), Steyerl spins a characteristically convoluted and elliptical story through a few data points. The style of the lecture and essay correlates to the feeling of surfing hyperlinks on the web. She begins with an email dated February 11, 2011, between Syria's Assad regime and the architect Rem Koolhaas, that had been exposed by Wikileaks.[56] The email outlines the family's attempt to build nationalist sentiment by inviting the globally recognized Koolhaas to build a museum. At the time of the correspondence, a civil war broke out, one that continues and has provoked a chaotic exodus of

Syrian refugees. In her essay, Steyerl includes a photograph found on the internet of Syrian refugees who took shelter in a Turkish municipal art gallery in August 2014. This veneer of humanitarianism that accompanies the infrastructure of the art world—building and launching museums to promote national unity, and sheltering refugees of war within a gallery's walls—are superficially altruistic and ultimately inadequate responses to real world problems, ones that Steyerl claims are merely a "proxy for the global commons."[57]

Steyerl then brings the discussion around to containers and freeports as the ideal infrastructure for hiding the elite art economy. She focuses particular attention on the Geneva freeport, owned by art handler Yves Bouvier (indicted in September 2015 for fraud, and still under investigation for tax evasion as of 2021), describing it as a model facility located amid shipping containers at the airport in an old freight station. Despite its location and cloistered collection of artworks, the Geneva freeport nevertheless presents itself as analogous in scale and opulence to a contemporary art museum, with climate control, security measures, and a well-designed, well-lit, and decorated lobby area. Amid the world's catastrophic wars and displaced populations, Steyerl argues, there has been a shift: from the expression of wealth through art on public display in a national museum to its utter occlusion in freeport storage facilities around the world that serve as repositories for billions of dollars' worth of art.

These structures offer an array of tax advantages because goods in freeports (as part of SEZs) are technically considered "in transit," even if in reality the ports are used more and more as permanent homes for accumulated wealth.[58] The strategic en route status of duty-free art is known and understood widely by investors as part of the larger financialization of the global economy.[59] Just as the shipping and manufacturing world depends on the value gaps of labor forces and raw materials available between nations and the quickness of containerization to exploit those gaps; and just as high-frequency stock market investors make profit on the miniscule discrepancies of value that can be culled from millisecond gaps between the computer systems that share proprietary stock information; so too the art market exploits gaps and loopholes within the unregulated gallery and auction systems as a convenient way to move capital around the world without having to pay taxes.[60]

Looking at Steyerl's *Duty Free Art*, especially in combination with Büchel's Art Basel Miami Beach intervention, also exposes the role that art fairs and art biennials play in substantiating art's luxury and investment value by constantly packing, containerizing, unpacking, and staging its importance. This opens onto a consideration of how the logic of containerization undergirds art and culture's middle market and grassroots networked artistic communities as well. Virtual art gallery sites like Artsy promote themselves as revolutionizing the market by expanding it to bring distant buyers and artists together, thereby becoming, as Artsy's CEO claims, the "Amazon of the art world."[61] These structures are changing the model of production and distribution at every level of the art market.

The ethical problems that arise within the financialized art economy is aptly summarized by Steyerl: "If art is produced more and more for a high-finance tax shelter system, and only shown strategically, it becomes duty-free art—no duty to perform, to represent, to teach, to embody value. . . . It's only duty is to be an asset."[62] While Steyerl may be painting too stark a picture (one would hope that works of contemporary art embody value in ways that cannot be quantified economically), her point stands. More attention needs to be paid to how multiple layers of the contemporary art world now factor into the parasitic container principle. Steyerl's focus on big data and new massive luxury port systems has tied together the motivations and calculations of big capital in ways that affect all modes of distribution and representation.

The Art of Disassembly

The narrative I have threaded through these art practices only schematically represents a much larger field of representations that deal with the material and informational power of global infrastructure. There are many other networks to trace (oil pipelines, roads, fiberoptic cables, and other less concrete "data" infrastructures like the financial market) and many other artists who have built visibility toward them. As they begin to be put in conversation with one another, they can even more powerfully remediate our lack of knowledge about the interconnected basis of everyday life.

In terms of representing containerization as infrastructure, I've chosen artists who offer a diversity of realisms: Sekula's heavily narrated, Marxist-toned mode of "critical realism," Ni's and Büchel's parafictional factories and picnics, and Steyerl's conspiratorial narratives of the uber-wealthy, composed of evidence found on the dark web. These realisms have lots in common. They reveal the instabilities in the networked systems. To quote Deborah Cowen, they "highlight the 'perverse installed within.'"[63] Indeed, looking at their work together helps one see the perversity of infrastructure—pretending that it has always been there, not up to anything in particular, despite the fact that it is a very recent, highly contingent, volatile, and often darkly motivated series of systems. They also demonstrate that there is a deep resistance to oversight or behavioral change within these systems. With each decade, they have represented how the stakes of containerization get higher and more complex. Obversely, their practices also might appear perverse to the average citizen-consumer—obstinate or self-righteously obnoxious in their commitment to expose a reality that most don't really want exposed.

I offer this notion of perverse realism as a way to deepen our discussions of the representational modes of infrastructure art beyond contemporary art discourses of appropriation and hacking. For instance, at the end of *Extrastatecraft* Keller Easterling compiles a list of what she sees as useful creative resistance tactics against extrastatecraft culled from such discourses. They include rumor and exaggerated compliance, doubling, comedy, irrationality, and more.[64] It is true that these terms could be applied to the art under discussion. Steyerl masterfully disseminates secret documents with various levels of credibility in her work in order to trace information's digital amplification and manipulation, and Ni's exhibition of customs paperwork operates as a mode of exaggerated compliance. That said, Easterling's discussion is provisional. The tactics she identifies are more convincingly encompassed by a notion such as perverse realism. Rumor and exaggerated compliance are forms of realism in that they are different ways to mimetically represent, extend, and expose the logic of algorithmic efficiency as the basis of our contemporary reality, one which so far has failed to take into account critical human and ecological values that outweigh economic efficiencies: a livable wage, safe working conditions, a sense of community, clean air and water, and so on. As Geoff Mann argues in *Disassembly Required*, we need less analysis of the way capitalism works, in terms of black box relays, and more analysis of "how it *actually* works" if one were to attempt to look inside its occluded routines, read between the lines of its flowcharts, and open the seals on containers.[65] This is precisely what infrastructure artists try to demonstrate: how workers are *actually* laboring on the ships, what *actually* gets produced and what *actually* gets trashed, who *actually* benefits from the global system of perpetual circulation—and going back to Burnham's phrase, the way things are *actually* done.

Finally, through the refractive lens of Hito Steyerl's obsessive charting of the world's distributive complexes of sequestered and contained wealth, we can reconsider the historical importance of systems aesthetics's own engagement in the politicization of the everyday. As our infrastructures begin to crack and collapse under the pressures of economic, political, and environmental transitions (and pandemics), so infrastructure art will become more prominent and vital, not just in creating visibility for the mundanity (and often, perversity) of the world's automated systems, but also in reimagining and reconfiguring what systems and infrastructures are, can be, and—most important—for whom they operate. Pointing out the power, as well as the contingency, of global infrastructural givens can become a platform for imagining global frameworks for new socialities beyond economic circulationism and distribution.

NOTES

1   Jack Burnham, "Systems Esthetics," *Artforum* 7, no. 1 (September 1968), 31.

2   Burnham, "Systems Esthetics," 35.

3   Burnham, "Systems Esthetics," 31.

4   Benjamin Buchloh, "Conceptual Art 1962–1969: From the Aesthetics of Administration to the Critique of Institutions," *October*, no. 55 (1999): 105–43; Alexander Alberro and Black Stimson, eds., *Institutional Critique: An Anthology of Artist's Writings* (Cambridge, MA: MIT Press, 2009); and John C. Welchman, ed., *Institutional Critique and After* (Zurich: JRP-Ringier, 2006).

5   Burnham, "Systems Esthetics," 31.

6   Burnham, "Systems Esthetics," 31.

7   See Irene Small, "Close Up: Allora and Calzadilla's *Puerto Rican Light (Cueva Vientos)*, 2015," *Artforum* 55, no. 9 (2017): 286.

8   For a good bibliography that defines the scope of critical infrastructure studies, see "CI Studies Bibliography," accessed February 1, 2021, https://cistudies.org/critical-infrastructures-bibliography/.

9   Susan Leigh Star, "The Ethnography of Infrastructure," *American Behavioral Scientist* 43, no. 3 (1999): 377–91.

10 Brian Larkin, "The Politics and Poetics of Infrastructure," *Annual Review of Anthropology* 42 (2013): 330. That same year *Orion* magazine published a special issue called "Reimagining Infrastructure." See also Brian Larkin, *Signal and Noise: Media, Infrastructure, and Urban Culture in Nigeria* (Durham, NC: Duke University Press, 2008).

11 Deborah Cowen, *Infrastructures of Empire and Resistance* (New York: Verso, 2017).

12 David Harvey, *Spaces of Global Capitalism: Towards a Theory of Uneven Development* (New York: Verso, 2006); Keller Easterling, *Extrastatecraft: The Power of Infrastructure Space* (New York: Verso, 2014); Stephen Collier, James Mizes, and Anita von Schnitzler, "Preface: Public Infrastructures/Infrastructural Publics," *Limn*, no. 7 (July 2016): 2–7.

13 Larkin, "Politics and Poetics of Infrastructure," 335.

14 Easterling, *Extrastatecraft*, 15.

15 Lisa Parks and Nicole Starosielski, eds., *Signal Traffic: Critical Studies of Media Infrastructures* (Urbana: University of Illinois Press, 2015).

16 Kregg Hetherington, ed., *Infrastructure, Environment, and Life in the Anthropocene* (Durham, NC: Duke University Press, 2019); Nicole Starosielski and Janet Walker, eds., *Sustainable Media: Critical Approaches to Media and Environment* (New York: Routledge, 2016); Imre Szeman and Dominic Boyer, eds., *Energy Humanities: An Anthology* (Baltimore, MD: Johns Hopkins University Press, 2017).

17 Jaimey Hamilton Faris, *Uncommon Goods: Global Dimensions of the Readymade* (London: Intellect, 2013). See also Pamela M. Lee, *Forgetting the Art World* (Cambridge, MA: MIT Press, 2012); and Nato Thompson and Independent Curators International, *Experimental Geography: Radical Approaches to Landscape, Cartography, and Urbanism* (New York: Melville House, 2015), the formative exhibition and catalog curated by Nato Thompson in 2009. Reaching further back, Hein van Bohemen, "Infrastructure, Ecology and Art," *Landscape and Urban Planning* 59, no. 4 (2002): 187–201.

18 In terms of art about containerization, beyond the works discussed in this essay, see also Andreas Gursky's *Salerno* (1990) project, discussed in Pamela M. Lee's *Forgetting the Art World*; Edward Butynsky's *Container Port* photographs from the early 2000s; Peter Hutton, *At Sea* (2007); and António Ole's *The Entire World/ Transitory Geometry* (2010), installed at the Hamburger Bahnhof.

19 Marc Levinson, *The Box: How the Shipping Container Made the World Smaller and the World Economy Bigger* (Princeton, NJ: Princeton University Press, 2008); Rose George, *Ninety Percent of Everything: Inside Shipping, the Invisible Industry That Puts Clothes on Your Back, Gas in Your Car, and Food on Your Plate* (New York: Metropolitan Books, 2013).

20 Alexander Klose, *The Container Principle: How a Box Changes the Way We Think* (Cambridge, MA: MIT Press, 2015).

21 As Levinson, George, Easterling, and Klose all attest, the material development and standardization of containerization was massively *uncoordinated* and hugely political.

22 Rachel Heiman, Carla Freeman, and Mark Liechty, eds., *The Global Middle Class: Theorizing through Ethnography* (Santa Fe, NM: School for Advanced Research, 2012).

23 Two chapters of *Fish Story* were included in the 1993 Whitney Biennial and were shown again in *Trade Routes* at the New Museum in 1993. Chapters were also exhibited at the major port cities of Rotterdam, Stockholm, Glasgow, Calais, and Seattle in the late 1990s. The entire project was exhibited at *Documenta 11* in 2002, which cemented the project's reputation.

24 Allan Sekula, *Fish Story* (Düsseldorf: Richter Verlag, 1995), 48. *Fish Story* propelled related projects for Sekula, including two films, *Lottery at Sea* (2006) and *Forgotten Space* (2010), codirected with Noël Burch, both of which focus on the even newer, even more massive automated ports at Rotterdam, San Pedro, and Hong Kong.

25 David Harvey, *A Brief History of Neoliberalism* (Oxford: Oxford University, 2007).

26 Charmaine Chua, "Logistics, Capitalist Circulation, Chokepoints," The Disorder of Things, September 9, 2014, https://thedisorderofthings.com/2014/09/09 /logistics-capitalist-circulation-chokepoints/.

27 Sekula, *Fish Story*, 50.

28 Sekula, *Fish Story*, 248.

29 While Sekula focuses on labor conditions of neoliberal trade, he does not link these systems back to colonial slave trade and thus erases stories of black dispossession. For a critique of Sekula's oversight in this regard, see Christina Sharpe, *In the Wake: On Blackness and Being* (Durham, NC: Duke University Press, 2016), 25–34.

30 Bill Roberts, "Production in View: Allan Sekula's *Fish Story* and the Thawing of Postmodernism," *Tate Papers* no. 18 (August 2012), https://www.tate.org.uk /research/publications/tate-papers/18/production-in-view-allan-sekulas-fish -story-and-the-thawing-of-postmodernism/.

31 Klose, *Container Principle*, 74.

32 Klose, *Container Principle*, 46; citing Michael Serres, *The Parasite*, trans. Lawrence R. Schehr (Minneapolis: University of Minnesota, 2007).

33 Klose, *Container Principle*, 74.

34 Asger Jorn, "End of the Economy and the Realization of Art," trans. Reuben Keehan, in *Internationale Situationniste* 4 (June 1960): n.p. Anthologized in Asger Jorn, *The Natural Order and Other Texts* (New York: Ashgate, 2002), 133–35.

35 Jorn, "End of the Economy," in *Natural Order*, 135, emphasis added.

36 Burnham, "Systems Esthetics," 31–32.

37 Sekula, *Fish Story*, 55.

38 It is worth charting these connections in more detail at another time (especially with regard to the history of the Bauhaus, which, in moving to Chicago, was initially supported by the Container Corporation of America). Suffice it to say that artistic interest in the container principle could be traced back through an expanded history of systems aesthetics that looks at Judd's boxes, as well as Warhol's, through the lens of infrastructure.

39 Reading room call number NE2698 S4637L 02394, Allan Sekula Library, Clark Art Institute, Williamstown, MA.

40 Klose, *Container Principle*, 81.

41 The strange name refers to its origins in 1988 when the World Trade Organization coordinated multiple databases between various trading partners into one centralized, and hence "harmonized," system. The Comtrade database has 200,000 general commodity classifications for the over ten billion goods and services. See more at the International Trade Administration's website: https://www.trade.gov /harmonized-system-hs-codes

42 Hamilton Faris, *Uncommon Goods*, 77.

43 Deborah Cowen, *The Deadly Life of Logistics: Mapping Violence in Global Trade* (Minneapolis: University of Minnesota Press, 2014), 10.

44 Cowen, *Deadly Life of Logistics*, 18.

45 This is a controversial live-action children's program broadcast between 2007–2009 on the Hamas-affiliated Palestinian television station Al-Aqsa TV.

46 Cowen, *Deadly Life of Logistics*, 1.

47 Büchel's installation begs the question that Brian Holmes asks: "Do containers dream of electric people?" Riffing off of Philip K. Dick's famous title *Do Androids*

Dream of Electric Sheep?, Holmes asks how container systems imagine and shape their hosts. Brian Holmes, "Do Containers Dream of Electric People?," *Open* 21 (2011), http://massivelyinvisibleobjects.org/wpcontent/uploads/2015/04/Holmes_Do-Containers-dream.pdf.

48 Though it seems on the surface to be an instance of global American market penetration, the show actually advocated anti-Israeli, anti-American sentiment. Büchel, well aware of these kinds of cultural appropriations, loves to embed them as paradoxes into his displays in order to distort and disrupt his otherwise "accurate," over-the-top scenes of democratic consumption. The installation's voting booths reference the hanging chad incident of the 2000 presidential election that eventually led to war and to Bush's speech.

49 MASS MoCA commissioned the artist to build one of his signature environments with a $160,000 budget. The artist composed a long list of items to acquire for the project that included houses, a tavern, a movie theater, trailers, mobile homes, nine full-size shipping containers, and more. As the list and the budget grew to more than double the original figure, the museum and Büchel became entangled in a fight over authorship rights. MASS MoCA left the incomplete installation in place and lackadaisically threw up some tarps, so that it was "closed" but still easily viewable. This led to a brilliant retaliation in which Büchel exhibited the documents accumulated during the resulting lawsuits as a finished artwork unto itself. He then also exhibited a small fraction of some of the objects acquired for the MASS MoCA installation as a purchasable installation at Art Basel.

50 Friedrich Christian Flick, a German now living in Switzerland, is known for using his collection to whitewash the origins of his family fortune made in arms manufacturing during Third Reich. See Isabelle Graw and Rosalyn Deutsche, "(De)Facing the Flick Collection: Should Art Replace Political Reparations for Nazi War Crimes?," *Texte zur Kunst*, no. 58 (June 2005): 143–45.

51 As a side note, Büchel's recent projects also highlight politically charged material infrastructures, but they lack the same framing of mundane bureaucracy that lent his earlier projects such as *Training Ground* their uncanny potency. In 2018, he tried to preserve the installed prototypes of President Trump's United States–Mexico border wall as a national monument. In another controversial move at the Venice Biennale in 2019, he displayed the recovered wreck of a barge that had sunk off the coast of Italy, taking the lives of 1,100 African migrants. Displayed on a dock without the typical art infrastructure that usually lends his work a heightened eeriness, the object failed to rupture the logic of art-world spectacle and bring productive discussion to border politics in Europe.

52 Larkin, "Poetics of Infrastructure," 336.

53 Carrie Lambert-Beatty, "Make-Believe: Parafiction and Plausibility," *October*, no. 129 (2009): 51–84.

54 Hito Steyerl, "Too Much World, Is the Internet Dead?," *e-flux* 49 (November 2013), https://www.e-flux.com/journal/49/60004/too-much-world-is-the-internet-dead/.

55 Hito Steyerl, "Duty Free Art," *e-flux* 63 (March 2015), https://www.e-flux.com
    /journal/63/60894/duty-free-art/.

56 Steyerl, "Duty Free Art," 1.

57 Steyerl, "Duty Free Art," 4.

58 Steyerl, "Duty Free Art," 14.

59 Financialization refers to financial markets and financial institutions, especially in
    postindustrial nations, gaining greater influence over economic policy and opera-
    tions. There is an increased importance in the role of the shareholder, cultivation
    of outsourcing, and corporate disaggregation, while increasing compensation at
    the top. Gerald Davis and Suntae Kim, "Financialization of the Economy," *Annual
    Review of Sociology* 41 (August 2015): 203–21. See also Luc Boltanski and Eve
    Chiapello, *The New Spirit of Capitalism*, trans. Gregory Elliot (New York: Verso,
    2005); and "Freeports: Uber Warehouses for the Ultra-Rich," *Economist*, Novem-
    ber 23, 2013.

60 The auction system is key to raising the value of collections through "chandelier
    bidding," and the container system also raises value by occluding key pieces in an
    artist's oeuvre in containers. Georgina Adam, *Big Bucks: The Explosion of the Art
    Market in the 21st Century* (New York: Ashgate, 2014).

61 Carter Cleveland, quoted in Natalie Robehmed, "Why Artsy Is Succeeding at
    Putting the Art World Online," *Forbes*, September 6, 2013, https://www.forbes
    .com/sites/natalierobehmed/2013/09/06/why-artsy-is-succeeding-in-putting-the
    -art-world-online/?sh=a400eec18945.

62 Steyerl, "Duty Free Art," 18.

63 Cowen, *Deadly Life of Logistics*, 5. She cites Jasbir K. Puar, "Queer Times, Queer
    Assemblages," *Social Text* 23, nos. 3–4 (2005): 121–39.

64 Easterling, *Extrastatecraft*, 415–61.

65 Geoff Mann, *Disassembly Required: A Field Guide to Actually Existing Capitalism*
    (Chico, CA: AK Press, 2013), 10.

Selected Bibliography

Adam, Georgina. *Big Bucks: The Explosion of the Art Market in the 21st Century.* Farnham, UK: Ashgate, 2014.

Alberro, Alexander. *Conceptual Art and the Politics of Publicity.* Cambridge, MA: MIT Press, 2003.

Alberro, Alexander, ed. *Working Conditions: The Writings of Hans Haacke.* Cambridge, MA: MIT Press, 2016.

Alberro, Alexander, and Blake Stimson, eds. *Institutional Critique: An Anthology of Artists' Writings.* Cambridge, MA: MIT Press, 2011.

Alexander, Christopher. "Systems Generating Systems." In *Systemat.* Berkeley, CA: Inland Steel Products Company, 1967.

Alloway, Lawrence. *Systemic Painting.* New York: Solomon R. Guggenheim Foundation, 1966.

American Artist. "Black Gooey Universe." *Unbag,* no. 2 (January 5, 2018). http://unbag .net/issue-2-end/black-gooey-universe/.

Amor, Mónica. *Theories of the Nonobject: Argentina, Brazil, Venezuela, 1944–1969.* Oakland: University of California Press, 2016.

Anderson, Benedict. *Imagined Communities: Reflections on the Origin and Spread of Nationalism.* 1983. Reprint, London: Verso, 2006.

Apter, Michael J. "Cybernetics and Art." *Leonardo* 2, no. 3 (1969): 257–65.

Armstrong, Helen. *Digital Design Theory: Readings from the Field.* New York: Princeton Architectural Press, 2016.

Ascott, Roy. "Behaviourist Art and the Cybernetic Vision." In *Telematic Embrace: Visionary Theories of Art, Technology, and Consciousness,* edited by Edward Shanken, 109–56. Berkeley: University of California Press, 2003.

Asher, Michael. *Writings, 1973–1983, on Works, 1969–1979.* Edited by Benjamin Buchloh. Nova Scotia: Press of the Nova Scotia School of Art and Design; and Los Angeles: Museum of Contemporary Art, 1983.

Ashton, Dore. "Marketing Techniques in the Promotion of Art." *Studio International* 172, no. 884 (1966): 270–73.

Avanessian, Armen, and Luke Skrebowski, eds. *Aesthetics and Contemporary Art.* Berlin: Sternberg, 2011.

Baldessari, John, Liam Gillick, Lawrence Weiner, and Beatrix Ruf. *Again the Metaphor Problem and Other Engaged Critical Discourses about Art.* New York: Springer, 2007.

Bardini, Thierry. *Bootstrapping: Douglas Engelbart, Coevolution, and the Origins of Personal Computing.* Stanford, CA: Stanford University Press, 2000.

Bateson, Gregory. *Steps to an Ecology of Mind.* New ed. Chicago: University of Chicago Press, 2000.

Battcock, Gregory, ed. *New Ideas in Art Education: A Critical Anthology*. New York: Dutton, 1974.

Bearden, Romare, Sam Gilliam Jr., Richard Hunt, Jacob Lawrence, Tom Lloyd, William Williams, and Hale Woodruff. "The Black Artist in America: A Symposium." *Metropolitan Museum of Art Bulletin* 27, no. 5 (1969): 245–61.

Bednarz, John. "Complexity and Intersubjectivity: Towards the Theory of Niklas Luhmann." *Human Studies* 7 (1984): 55–69.

Belting, Hans. *Art History after Modernism*. Translated by Caroline Saltzwedel, Kenneth J. Northcott, and Mitch Cohen. Chicago: University of Chicago Press, 2003.

Belting, Hans. *The End of the History of Art*. Translated by Christopher Wood. Chicago: University of Chicago Press, 1987.

Berger, Maurice. *Labyrinths: Robert Morris, Minimalism, and the 1960s*. New York: Icon, 1990.

Best, Stephen. *None Like Us: Blackness, Belonging, Aesthetic Life*. Durham, NC: Duke University Press, 2018.

Bianconi, Giampaolo. "Agnes Denes in the 1970s: Toward the Hologram." In *Agnes Denes: Absolutes and Intermediates*, edited by Emma Enderby, 165–68. New York: The Shed, 2020.

Bijvoet, Marga. *Art as Inquiry: Toward New Collaborations between Art, Science, and Technology*. Bern: Peter Lang, 1999.

Bird, Jon. "Minding the Body: Robert Morris's 1971 Tate Gallery Retrospective." In *Rewriting Conceptual Art*, edited by Michael Newman and Jon Bird, 88–106. London: Reaktion, 1999.

Bishop, Claire. "Antagonism and Relational Aesthetics." *October*, no. 110 (2004): 51–79.

Bishop, Claire. *Artificial Hells: Participatory Art and the Politics of Spectatorship*. London: Verso, 2012.

Boetzkes, Amanda. *Plastic Capitalism: Contemporary Art and the Drive to Waste*. Cambridge, MA: MIT Press, 2019.

Bois, Yve-Alain. "What If . . ." In Mel Bochner, *Solar Systems and Restrooms: Writings and Interviews 1965–2007*, edited by Roger Conover, xi–xvi. Cambridge, MA: MIT Press, 2008.

Boltanski, Luc, and Eve Chiapello. *The New Spirit of Capitalism*. Translated by Gregory Elliott. London: Verso, 2005.

Bourriaud, Nicolas. "Modelised Politics." *Flash Art* 26, no. 171 (1993): 142–43.

Bourriaud, Nicolas. *Relational Aesthetics*. Translated by Simon Pleasance and Fronza Woods, with Mathieu Copeland. Dijon, France: Les presses du réel, 1998.

Brodsky, Estrellita. "Latin American Artists in Postwar Paris: Jesús Rafael Soto and Julio Le Parc, 1950–1970." PhD diss., New York University, 2009.

Brown, Tony. "Artist as Corporate Critic: An Interview with Hans Haacke by Tony Brown." In *Hans Haacke*, vol. 2, *Works, 1978–1983*. London: Tate Gallery; Eindhoven: Van Abbemuseum, 1984.

Brown, Wendy. *Undoing the Demos: Neoliberalism's Stealth Revolution*. Cambridge, MA: MIT Press, 2015.

Bryan-Wilson, Julia. *Art Workers: Radical Practice in the Vietnam War Era*. Berkeley: University of California Press, 2009.

Buchloh, Benjamin H. D. "Cold War Constructivism." In *Formalism and Historicity: Models and Methods in Twentieth-Century Art*. Cambridge, MA: MIT Press, 2015, 375–408.

Buchloh, Benjamin H. D. "Conceptual Art 1962–69: From the Aesthetic of Administration to the Critique of Institutions." *October*, no. 55 (1990): 105–43.

Buchloh, Benjamin H. D. "Hans Haacke: Memory and Instrumental Reason." In *Neo-Avantgarde and Culture Industry: Essays on European and American Art from 1955 to 1975*, 203–41. Cambridge, MA: MIT Press, 2000.

Buchloh, Benjamin H. D. "Hans Haacke: The Entwinement of Myth and Enlightenment." In *Hans Haacke: "Obra Social,"* edited by Walter Grasskamp, 45–60. Barcelona: Fundació Antoni Tàpies, 1995.

Burnham, Jack. "Art and Technology: The Panacea That Failed." In *The Myths of Information: Technology and Postindustrial Culture*, edited by Kathleen Woodward, 200–215. Madison, WI: Coda, 1980.

Burnham, Jack. *Art in the Marcusean Analysis*. University Park: Pennsylvania State University Press, 1969.

Burnham, Jack. *Beyond Modern Sculpture: The Effects of Science and Technology on the Sculpture of This Century*. London: Allen Lane, 1968.

Burnham, Jack. *Dissolve into Comprehension: Writings and Interviews, 1964–2004*. Edited by Melissa Ragain. Cambridge, MA: MIT Press, 2016.

Burnham, Jack. *Great Western Salt Works: Essays on the Meaning of Post-formalist Art*. New York: George Braziller, 1974.

Burnham, Jack. "Hans Haacke's Cancelled Show at the Guggenheim." *Artforum* 9, no. 10 (1971): 67–71.

Burnham, Jack. "Jack Burnham, Terry Fenton: An Exchange." *Artforum* 7, no. 8 (1969): 60–61.

Burnham, Jack. "Notes on Art and Information Processing." In *Software: Information Technology; Its New Meaning for Art*, 10–14. New York: Jewish Museum, 1970.

Burnham, Jack. "Real Time Systems." *Artforum* 8, no. 1 (1969): 49–55.

Burnham, Jack. "Steps in the Formulation of Real-Time Political Art." In *Hans Haacke: Framing and Being Framed; 7 Works, 1970–75*, edited by Kasper Koenig, 127–43. Halifax: Press of the Nova Scotia College of Art and Design; New York: New York University Press, 1975.

Burnham, Jack. *The Structure of Art*. New York: George Braziller, 1971.

Burnham, Jack. "Systems and Art." *Arts in Society* 6, no. 2 (1969): 194–203.

Burnham, Jack. "Systems Esthetics." *Artforum* 7, no. 1 (1968): 30–35.

Busbea, Larry. "Kineticism—Spectacle—Environment." *October*, no. 144 (2013): 92–144.

Butterfield, Jan. *The Art of Light and Space*. New York: Abbeville, 1993.

Camnitzer, Luis. *Conceptualism in Latin American Art: Didactics of Liberation*. Austin: University of Texas Press, 2007.

Caplan, Lindsay A. "Open Works between the Programmed and the Free: Art in Italy 1962–1972." PhD diss, City University of New York, 2017. https://academicworks.cuny.edu/gc_etds/1776.

Carnevale, Graciela, Marcelo Exposito, Andre Mesquita, and Jaime Vindel. *Desinventario: Esquirlas de Tucumán Arde en el Archivo de Graciela Carnevale*. Santiago,

Chile: Ocho Libros, con la colaboracion del Museo Nacional Centro de Arte Reina Sofia, 2015.

Castells, Manuel. *The Rise of the Network Society*. Oxford: Blackwell, 2000.

Chakrabarty, Dipesh. "The Climate of History: Four Theses." *Critical Inquiry* 35, no. 4 (2009): 197–222.

Chang, Pi-Chun. "Going Global and Staying Local: Nation-Building Discourses in Singapore's Cultural Policies." *Identities: Global Studies in Culture and Power* 19, no. 6 (2012): 691–707.

Choy, Lee Weng. "The Assumption of Love: Friendship and the Search for Discursive Density." In *Modern and Contemporary Southeast Asian Art: An Anthology*, edited by Nora A. Taylor and Boreth Ly, 189–209. Ithaca, NY: Cornell Southeast Asia Program Publications, 2012.

Clapp, James A. *The City: A Dictionary of Quotable Thoughts on Cities and Urban Life*. Piscataway, NJ: Rutgers University Press, 1984.

Clark, Robin, and Hugh Davies, eds. *Phenomenal: Light, Space, and Surface*. Berkeley: University of California Press, 2011.

Clarke, Bruce. "From Information to Cognition: The Systems Counterculture, Heinz von Foerster's Pedagogy, and Second-Order Cybernetics." *Constructivist Foundations* 7, no. 3 (2012): 196–207.

Clarke, Bruce, and Mark B. N. Hansen, eds. *Emergence and Embodiment: New Essays on Second-Order Systems Theory*. Durham, NC: Duke University Press, 2009.

Cohen, Brianne. "Breathing, Carrying, Pouring: Khvay Samnang's Eco-Aesthetic Gestures of Non-violence." In *Khvay Samnang: The Land beneath My Feet*, edited by Nicola Müllerschön and Christoph Tannert, 8–23. Berlin: Künstlerhaus Bethanien, 2015.

Cohen, Kris. "Abstraction, the Irreconcilable: An Interview with American Artist." *Open Set*, January 16, 2019. http://www.open-set.com/krcohen/essay-clusters /abstraction-the-irreconcilable-an-interview-with-american-artist/.

Collier, Stephen, James Mizes, and Anita von Schnitzler. "Public Infrastructures/Infra-structural Publics." *Limn*, no. 7 (July 2016).

Compton, Michael. *Larry Bell, Robert Irwin, Doug Wheeler*. London: Tate Gallery, 1970.

Compton, Michael. "UK Commentary." *Studio International* 179, no. 923 (June 1970): 269–70.

Corris, Michael, ed. *Conceptual Art: Theory, Myth, Practice*. Cambridge: Cambridge University Press, 2004.

Coughlan, Gráinne. "An Organisational Analysis of Participatory Art in Art Institu-tions." PhD diss., Dublin School of Creative Arts, Technological University Dublin, 2021.

Cowen, Deborah. *The Deadly Life of Logistics: Mapping Violence in Global Trade*. Min-neapolis: University of Minnesota Press, 2014.

Cowen, Deborah. *Infrastructures of Empire and Resistance*. New York: Verso, 2017.

Crawford, Margo Natalie. *Black Post-blackness: The Black Arts Movement and Twenty-First-Century Aesthetics*. Urbana: University of Illinois Press, 2017.

Danto, Arthur. *After the End of Art*. Rev. ed. Princeton, NJ: Princeton University Press, 2014.

Davis, Gerald F., and Suntae Kim. "Financialization of the Economy." *Annual Review of Sociology* 41 (2015): 203–21.

de Duve, Thierry. *Kant after Duchamp*. Cambridge, MA: MIT Press, 1997.

Demos, T. J. *Decolonizing Nature: Contemporary Art and the Politics of Ecology*. Berlin: Sternberg, 2016.

Denes, Agnes. "The Dream." *Critical Inquiry* 16, no. 4 (1990): 919–39.

Docherty, Claire. *Contemporary Art: From Studio to Situation*. London: Black Dog, 2004.

Dodds, Joseph. *Psychoanalysis and Ecology at the Edge of Chaos: Complexity Theory, Deleuze/Guattari and Psychoanalysis for a Climate in Crisis*. London: Routledge, 2011.

Dubberly, Hugh, and Paul Pangaro. "How Cybernetics Connects Computing, Counterculture, and Design." In *Hippie Modernism: The Struggle for Utopia*, edited by Andrew Blauvelt, 126–41. Minneapolis, MN: Walker Art Center, 2015.

Duggan, Lisa. *The Twilight of Equality? Neoliberalism, Cultural Politics, and the Attack on Democracy*. Boston: Beacon, 2003.

Easterling, Keller. *Extrastatecraft: The Power of Infrastructure Space*. New York: Verso, 2014.

Eco, Umberto. *Opera aperta*: *Forma e indeterminazione nelle poetiche contemporanee*. Milan: Bompiani, 1962.

Edwards, Paul. *A Vast Machine: Computer Models, Climate Data, and the Politics of Global Warming*. Cambridge, MA: MIT Press, 2013.

Eglash, Ron, "Cybernetics in American Youth Subculture." *Cultural Studies* 12, no. 3 (1998): 382–409.

Elkins, James, and Harper Montgomery, eds. *Beyond the Aesthetic and the Anti-aesthetic*. University Park: Pennsylvania State University Press, 2013.

Ellul, Jacques. *The Technological Society*. Translated by John Wilkinson. New York: Knopf, 1964.

Engelbart, Douglas C. "Special Considerations of the Individual as a User, Generator, and Retriever of Information." *American Documentation* 12 (1961): 121–25.

Engelbart, Douglas C. "Toward High-Performance Knowledge Workers." *OAC '82 Digest: Proceedings of the AFIPS Office Automation Conference* (April 1982): 279–90.

English, Darby. *How to See a Work of Art in Total Darkness*. Cambridge, MA: MIT Press, 2007.

English, Darby. *1971: A Year in the Life of Color*. Chicago: University of Chicago Press, 2016.

Fantoni, Guillermo. *Arte, vanguardia y política en los años '60: Conversaciones con Juan Pablo Renzi*. Buenos Aires: El Cielo por Asalto, 1998.

Faris, Jaimey Hamilton. *Uncommon Goods: Global Dimensions of the Readymade*. London: Intellect, 2013.

Farver, Jane, ed. *Global Conceptualism: Points of Origin, 1950s–1980s*. New York: Queens Museum, 1999.

Fernández, María. "Detached from HiStory: Jasia Reichardt and *Cybernetic Serendipity.*" *Art Journal* 67, no. 3 (2008): 6–23.

Filippone, Christine. *Science, Technology, and Utopias: Women Artists and Cold War America*. New York: Routledge, 2017.

Fisher, Mark. *Capitalist Realism: Is There No Alternative?* Winchester, UK: Zero Books, 2009.

Foster, Hal, ed. *The Anti-aesthetic: Essays on Postmodern Culture*. New York: New Press, 1998.

Foucault, Michel. *The Birth of Biopolitics: Lectures at the Collège de France, 1978–1979*. Translated by Graham Burchell. New York: Picador, 2008.

Foucault, Michel. *Madness and Civilization: A History of Insanity in the Age of Reason*. Translated by Richard Howard. London: Routledge, 2001.

François, Charles. "Systemics and Cybernetics in a Historical Perspective." *Systems Research and Behavioral Science* 16, no. 3 (1999): 203–19.

Franklin, Seb. *Control: Digitality as Cultural Logic*. Cambridge, MA: MIT Press, 2015.

Fraser, Andrea. "What's Intangible, Transitory, Mediating, Participatory, and Rendered in the Public Sphere, Part II." In *Museum Highlights: The Writings of Andrea Fraser*, edited by Alexander Alberro, 55–80. Cambridge, MA: MIT Press, 2005.

Gaboury, Jacob. "The Random-Access Image: Memory and the History of the Computer Screen." *Grey Room*, no. 70 (2018): 24–53.

Gabrys, Jennifer. "Becoming Planetary." *e-flux Architecture*, no. (October 2018). https://www.e-flux.com/architecture/accumulation/217051/becoming-planetary/.

Gaines, Charles. "Reconsidering Metaphor/Metonymy: Art and the Suppression of Thought." *Art Lies: A Contemporary Art Journal*, no. 64 (Winter 2009): 48–57.

Galison, Peter. "The Ontology of the Enemy: Norbert Wiener and the Cybernetic Vision." *Critical Inquiry* 21, no. 1 (1994): 228–66.

Galloway, Alexander R. *The Interface Effect*. Cambridge: Polity, 2012.

George, Rose. *Ninety Percent of Everything: Inside Shipping, the Invisible Industry That Puts Clothes on Your Back, Gas in Your Car, and Food on Your Plate*. New York: Metropolitan, 2013.

Gillick, Liam. *All Books*. London: Book Works, 2009.

Gillick, Liam. *Discussion Island/Big Conference Centre*. Ludwigsburg, Germany: Kunstverein Ludwigsburg; and Derry, UK: Orchard Gallery, 1997.

Gillick, Liam. *Industry and Intelligence: Contemporary Art since 1820*. New York: Columbia University Press, 2016.

Gillick, Liam. *Proxemics: Selected Writings (1988–2006)*. Zurich: JRP-Ringier, 2007.

Gillick, Liam, and Anthony Spira. "Speculation and Planning." In *Liam Gillick, The Wood Way*, 14–18. London: Whitechapel Art Gallery, 2002.

Giunta, Andrea. *Avant-Garde, Internationalism, and Politics: Argentine Art in the Sixties*. Durham, NC: Duke University Press, 2007.

Glusberg, Jorge. *El Grupo de los trece en arte de sistemas*. Buenos Aires: Centro de Arte y Comunicación, 1971.

Gómez-Barris, Macarena. *The Extractive Zone: Social Ecologies and Decolonial Perspectives*. Durham, NC: Duke University Press, 2017.

Goodyear, Anne Collins. "From Technophilia to Technophobia: The Impact of the Vietnam War on the Reception of 'Art and Technology.'" *Leonardo* 41 (2008): 169–74.

Grant, Simon. "Grant Simon Interviews Robert Morris." *Tate Etc*, September 1, 2008. http://www.tate.org.uk/context-comment/articles/simon-grant-interviews-robert -morris.

Graw, Isabelle, and Rosalyn Deutsche. "(De)Facing the Flick Collection: Should Art Replace Political Reparations for Nazi War Crimes?" *Texte zur Kunst*, no. 58 (2005): 143–45.

Greenberg, Clement. "The Case for Abstract Art." In *Clement Greenberg: The Collected Essays and Criticism*, vol. 4: *Modernism with a Vengeance, 1957–1969*, edited by John O'Brian, 75–82. Chicago: University of Chicago Press, 1993.

Guattari, Félix. *The Three Ecologies*. Translated by Ian Pindar and Paul Sutton. 1989. Reprint, London: Athlone Press, 2000.

Haacke, Hans. *Hans Haacke: Framing and Being Framed; 7 Works, 1970–75*. Edited by Kasper Koenig. Halifax: Press of the Nova Scotia College of Art and Design; New York: New York University Press, 1975.

Halsall, Francis. *Systems of Art: Art, History and Systems Theory*. Oxford: Peter Lang, 2008.

Halsall, Francis, Julia Jansen, and Tony O'Connor, eds. *Rediscovering Aesthetics: Trans-disciplinary Voices from Art History, Philosophy, and Art Practice*. Stanford, CA: Stanford University Press, 2009.

Hanegraaf, Wouter. *Esotericism and the Academy: Rejected Knowledge in Western Culture*. Cambridge: Cambridge University Press, 2014.

Haraway, Donna J. *Staying with the Trouble: Making Kin in the Chthulucene*. Durham, NC: Duke University Press, 2016.

Harrison, Charles. *Conceptual Art and Painting: Further Essays on Art & Language*. Cambridge, MA: MIT Press, 2001.

Hartman, Saidiya V. *Scenes of Subjection: Terror, Slavery, and Self-Making in Nineteenth-Century America*. Oxford: Oxford University Press, 1997.

Harvey, David. *A Brief History of Neoliberalism*. Oxford: Oxford University Press, 2007.

Harvey, David. *Spaces of Global Capitalism: Towards a Theory of Uneven Development*. London: Verso, 2006.

Hayles, N. Katherine. *How We Became Posthuman: Virtual Bodies in Cybernetics, Literature, and Informatics*. Chicago: University of Chicago Press, 1999.

Hayles, N. Katherine. "Narrating Consciousness: Language, Media, and Embodiment." *History of Human Sciences* 23 (2013): 131–48.

Heidegger, Martin. "The Question concerning Technology." In *Martin Heidegger: Basic Writings*, translated by D. F. Krell, 283–317. San Francisco: HarperCollins, 1977.

Heiman, Rachel, Carla Freeman, and Mark Liechty, eds. *The Global Middle Classes: Theorizing through Ethnography*. Santa Fe, NM: School for Advanced Research, 2012.

Heims, Steve. *Constructing a Social Science for Postwar America: The Cybernetics Group, 1946–1953*. Cambridge, MA: MIT Press, 1991.

Hetherington, Kregg, ed. *Infrastructure, Environment, and Life in the Anthropocene.* Durham, NC: Duke University Press, 2019.

Holmes, Brian. "Do Containers Dream of Electric People?" *Open* 21 (2011). http://massivelyinvisibleobjects.org/wpcontent/uploads/2015/04/Holmes_Do-Containers-dream.pdf.

Huyghe, Pierre, and Philippe Parreno, eds. *No Ghost Just a Shell.* Cologne: Walther König, 2002.

Ilfield, Etan J. "Contemporary Art and Cybernetics: Waves of Cybernetic Discourse within Conceptual, Video, and New Media Art." *Leonardo* 45 (2012): 57–63.

Irwin, Robert. *Being and Circumstance: Notes toward a Conditional Art.* Culver City, CA: Lapis, 1985.

Irwin, Robert. "Statement on Reproductions." *Artforum* 3, no. 9 (1965): 23.

Jameson, Fredric. *The Geopolitical Aesthetic: Cinema and Space in the World System.* Bloomington: Indiana University Press, 1992.

Jezer, Marty. *Abbie Hoffman: American Rebel.* New Brunswick, NJ: Rutgers University Press, 1992.

Jones, Caroline A. *Eyesight Alone: Clement Greenberg's Modernism and the Bureaucratization of the Senses.* Chicago: University of Chicago Press, 2005.

Jones, Caroline A. *Hans Haacke 1967.* Cambridge, MA: MIT Press, 2011.

Jorn, Asger. *The Natural Order and Other Texts.* New York: Ashgate, 2002.

Joselit, David. *After Art.* Princeton, NJ: Princeton University Press, 2012.

Joseph, Branden W. *Beyond the Dream Syndicate: Tony Conrad and the Arts after Cage; A "Minor" History.* New York: Zone, 2008.

Katzenstein, Ines, ed. *Listen Here Now! Argentine Art of the 1960s; Writings of the Avant-Garde.* New York: Museum of Modern Art, 2004.

Keith, Naima J., ed. *Charles Gaines: Gridwork 1974–1989.* New York: Studio Museum in Harlem, 2014.

Keller, Sean. "Liam Gillick, Museum of Contemporary Art, Chicago." *Artforum* 48, no. 8 (2010): 188–89.

Kline, Ronald. *The Cybernetics Moment: Or Why We Call Our Age the Information Age.* Baltimore, MD: John Hopkins University Press, 2015.

Klose, Alexander. *The Container Principle: How a Box Changes the Way We Think.* Cambridge, MA: MIT Press, 2015.

Kotz, Liz. *Words to Be Looked At: Language in 1960s Art.* Cambridge, MA: MIT Press, 2007.

Kozloff, Max. "The Multimillion Dollar Boondoggle." *Artforum* 10, no. 2 (1971): 72–76.

Krauss, Rosalind E. *Passages in Modern Sculpture.* Cambridge, MA: MIT Press, 1981.

Kumar, Ramakrishna. *"Original Sin"? Revising the Revisionist Critique of the 1963 Operation Coldstone in Singapore.* Singapore: Institute of Southeast Asian Studies, 2015.

Kuspit, Donald. *The End of Art.* Cambridge: Cambridge University Press, 2005.

Lacan, Jacques. *The Seminar of Jacques Lacan, Book XX: On Feminine Sexuality, the Limits of Love and Knowledge.* Edited by Jacques-Alain Miller. Translated by Bruce Fink. Paris: Éditions de Seuil, 1999.

Lacan, Jacques. *The Seminar of Jacques Lacan, Book XXIII: The Sinthome.* Edited by Jacques-Alain Miller. Translated by A. R. Price. Cambridge: Polity, 2018.

Lai, Samantha, Lynette H. L. Loke, Michael J. Hilton, Tjeerd J. Bouma, and Peter A. Todd. "The Effects of Urbanisation on Coastal Habitats and the Potential for Ecological Engineering: A Singapore Case Study." *Ocean and Coastal Management* 103 (2015): 78–85.

Lambert, Nick. "The Cybernetic Moment: Roy Ascott and the British Cybernetic Pioneers, 1955–1965." *Interdisciplinary Science Reviews* 42 (2017): 42–53.

Lambert-Beatty, Carrie. "Make-Believe: Parafiction and Plausibility." *October*, no. 129 (2009): 51–84.

Lambert-Beatty, Carrie. "Moving Still: Mediating Yvonne Rainer's *Trio A*." *October*, no. 89 (1999): 87–112.

Larkin, Brian. "The Politics and Poetics of Infrastructure." *Annual Review of Anthropology* 42 (2013): 327–43.

Larkin, Brian. *Signal and Noise: Media, Infrastructure, and Urban Culture in Nigeria*. Durham, NC: Duke University Press, 2008.

Latour, Bruno. *Politics of Nature: How to Bring the Sciences into Democracy*. Translated by Catherine Porter. Cambridge, MA: Harvard University Press, 2004.

Latour, Bruno. *We Have Never Been Modern*. Translated by Catherine Porter. Cambridge, MA: Harvard University Press, 1993.

Laurel, Brenda, and S. Joy Mountford. *The Art of Human-Computer Interface Design*. Reading, MA: Addison-Wesley, 1990.

Lee, Pamela M. "Art as a Social System: Nancy Holt and the Second-Order Observer." In *Nancy Holt: Sightlines*, edited by Alena J. Williams, 39–58. Berkeley: University of California Press, 2011.

Lee, Pamela M. *Chronophobia: On Time in the Art of the 1960s*. Cambridge, MA: MIT Press, 2004.

Lee, Pamela M. *Forgetting the Art World*. Cambridge, MA: MIT Press, 2012.

Leslie, Stuart W. *The Cold War and American Science: The Military-Industrial-Academic Complex at MIT and Stanford*. New York: Columbia University Press, 1993.

Levinson, Marc. *The Box: How the Shipping Container Made the World Smaller and the World Economy Bigger*. Princeton, NJ: Princeton University Press, 2008.

Licht, Jennifer, ed. *Spaces*. New York: Museum of Modern Art, 1969.

Lippard, Lucy R. *Six Years: The Dematerialization of the Art Object from 1966 to 1972*. New York: Praeger, 1973.

Liu, Alan. *The Laws of Cool: Knowledge Work and the Culture of Information*. Chicago: University of Chicago Press, 2004.

Longoni, Ana. *Vanguardia y revolución: Arte e izquierdas en la Argentina de los sesenta-setenta*. Buenos Aires: Editorial Paidós SAIF, 2014.

Longoni, Ana, and Mariano Mestman. *Del Di Tella a "Tucumán Arde": Vanguardia artística y política en el 68 Argentino*. Buenos Aires: EUDEBA, 2010.

Lui, P. C., and T. S. Tan. "Building Integrated Large-Scale Urban Infrastructures: Singapore's Experience." *Journal of Urban Technology* 8, no. 1 (2010): 49–68.

Lynch, Kevin. *The Image of the City*. Cambridge, MA: MIT Press, 1960.

Lyotard, Jean-François. *The Postmodern Condition: A Report on Knowledge*. Translated by Geoff Bennington and Brian Massumi. Manchester: Manchester University Press, 1984.

Macón, Cecilia. *Sexual Violence in the Argentinean Crimes against Humanity Trials: Rethinking Victimhood*. Lanham, MD: Lexington Books, 2017.

Mann, Geoff. *Disassembly Required: A Field Guide to Actually Existing Capitalism*. Chico, CA: AK Press, 2013.

Marcuse, Herbert. "Art as a Form of Reality." In *On the Future of Art*, edited by Edward Fry, 123–34. New York: Viking, 1970.

Marcuse, Herbert. *An Essay on Liberation*. Boston: Beacon, 1969.

Marcuse, Herbert. *One-Dimensional Man: Studies in the Ideology of Advanced Industrial Society*. Boston: Beacon, 1964.

Masotta, Oscar. *Conciencia y estructura*. Buenos Aires: Eterna Cadencia Editora, 2010.

McKittrick, Katherine. "Mathematics Black Life." *Black Scholar* 44, no. 2 (2014): 16–28.

McLuhan, Marshall. *Understanding Media: The Extensions of Man*. New York: McGraw Hill, 1964.

McQuillan, Dan. "The Countercultural Potential of Citizen Science." *Media/Culture Journal* 17, no. 6 (2014). https://doi.org/10.5204/mcj.919/.

Meireles, Cildo. *Cildo Meireles*. Valencia, Spain: IVAM Centre del Carme, 1995.

Meltzer, Eve. *Systems We Have Loved: Conceptual Art, Affect, and the Antihumanist Turn*. Chicago: University of Chicago Press, 2013.

Merleau-Ponty, Maurice. *The Visible and the Invisible*. Translated by Alphonso Lingis. Evanston, IL: Northwestern University Press, 1968.

Milton, Chris. "The Sand Smugglers." *Foreign Policy*, August 4, 2010. http://www.foreignpolicy.com/articles/2010/08/04/the_sand_smugglers.

Morton, Timothy. "Sublime Objects." *Speculations* 2 (2011): 207–27.

Moten, Fred. *Stolen Life*. Durham, NC: Duke University Press, 2018.

Mumford, Lewis. *The Myth of the Machine*. New York: Harcourt, 1967.

Murray, Derek Conrad. *Queering Post-Black Art: Artists Transforming African-American Identity after Civil Rights*. London: I. B. Tauris, 2016.

Mustafa, Shabbir Hussain, ed. SEA STATE: *Charles Lim Yi Yong*. Singapore: National Arts Council, 2015.

Nelson, Georges. *Problems of Design*. New York: Whitney, 1957.

Nieland, Justus. "Happy Furniture: On the Media Environments of the Eames Chair." *Places Journal* (January 2020). https://placesjournal.org/article/happy-furniture/.

Nisbet, James. *Ecologies, Environments, and Energy Systems in Art of the 1960s and 1970s*. Cambridge, MA: MIT Press, 2014.

Norvell, Patricia. "Interview with Robert Smithson, June 20, 1969." In *Recording Conceptual Art: Early Interviews with Barry, Huebler, Kaltenbach, LeWitt, Morris, Oppenheim, Sigelaub, Smithson, and Weiner by Patricia Norvell*, edited by Alexander Alberro and Patricia Norvell, 124–34. Berkeley: University of California Press, 2001.

Nusberg, Lev. "Cybertheatre." *Leonardo* 2 (1969): 61–62.

Ong, Aihwa. *Neoliberalism as Exception: Mutations in Citizenship and Sovereignty*. Durham, NC: Duke University Press, 2006.

O'Rourke, Karen. "A Map, No Directions." In *Walking and Mapping: Artists as Cartographers*, 47–72. Cambridge, MA: MIT Press, 2013.

Osborne, Peter. "Aesthetic Autonomy and the Crisis of Theory: Greenberg, Adorno, and the Problem of Postmodernism in the Visual Arts." *New Formations* 9 (Winter 1989): 31–50.

Osborne, Peter. *Anywhere or Not At All: Philosophy of Contemporary Art*. London: Verso, 2013.

Owens, Craig. "From Work to Frame: or, Is There Life after 'The Death of the Author'?" In *Beyond Recognition: Representation, Power, and Culture*, edited by Scott Bryson, Barbara Kruger, Lynne Tillman, and Jane Weinstock, 122–39. Berkeley: University of California Press, 1992.

Parks, Lisa, and Nicole Starosielski, eds. *Signal Traffic: Critical Studies of Media Infrastructures*. Urbana: University of Illinois Press, 2015.

Patterson, Orlando. *Slavery and Social Death: A Comparative Study*. Cambridge, MA: Harvard University Press, 1982.

Pawlowska, Teresa E., Rufus L. Chaney, and Mel Chin. "Effects of Metal Phytoextraction Practices on the Indigenous Community of Arbuscular Mycorrhizal Fungi at a Metal-Contaminated Landfill." *Applied and Environmental Microbiology* 66, no. 6 (2000): 2526–30.

Peltomäki, Kirsi. *Situation Aesthetics: The Work of Michael Asher*. Cambridge, MA: MIT Press, 2010.

Pickering, Andrew. *The Cybernetic Brain: Sketches of Another Future*. Chicago: University of Chicago Press, 2010.

Popper, Frank. *Art Action Participation*. London: Cassel and Collier Macmillan, 1975.

Puar, Jasbir. "Queer Times, Queer Assemblages." *Social Text* 23, nos. 3–4 (2005): 121–39.

Quinz, Emanuel. "From Programme to Behaviour: The Experience of Arte Programmata in Italy 1958–1968." In *Practicable: From Participation to Interaction in Contemporary Art*, edited by Samuel Bianchini and Erik Verhagen, 91–111. Cambridge, MA: MIT Press, 2016.

Ramirez, J. Jesse. "Marcuse among the Technocrats: America, Automation, and Postcapitalist Utopias, 1900–1941." *Amerikastudien/American Studies* 57 (2012): 31–50.

Rampley, Matthew. "Systems Aesthetics: Burnham and Others." *Vector* 12 (January 2005). http://www.virose.pt/vector/b_12/rampley.html.

Randerson, Janine. *Weather as Medium: Toward a Meteorological Art*. Cambridge, MA: MIT Press, 2018.

Rees, Lucy. "Expanding the Horizon: Future Perfect and the Singapore Scene." *Art Monthly Australia* 279 (May 2015): 30.

Reiss, Julie. *From Margin to Center: The Spaces of Installation Art*. Cambridge, MA: MIT Press, 1999.

Relyea, Lane. *Your Everyday Art World*. Cambridge, MA: MIT Press, 2017.

Ricco, John Paul. "The Commerce of Anonymity." *Qui Parle: Critical Humanities and Social Sciences* 26, no. 1 (2017): 101–42.

Roach, Tom. "Becoming Fungible: Queer Intimacies in Social Media." *Qui Parle: Critical Humanities and Social Sciences* 23, no. 2 (2015): 55–87.

Robbins, David, ed. *The Independent Group: Postwar Britain and the Aesthetics of Plenty*. London: Institute of Contemporary Arts, 1990.

Roberts, Bill. "Burnout: Liam Gillick's Post-Fordist Aesthetics." *Art History* 36, no. 1 (2013): 180–205.

Roberts, Bill. "Production in View: Allan Sekula's *Fish Story* and the Thawing of Post-modernism." *Tate Papers*, no. 18 (August 2012). https://www.tate.org.uk/research /publications/tate-papers/18/production-in-view-allan-sekulas-fish-story-and-the -thawing-of-postmodernism.

Robinson, Cedric J. *Black Marxism: The Making of the Black Radical Tradition*. Chapel Hill: University of North Carolina Press, 2000.

Rodenbeck, Judith. "Poeisis in Bali: Notes on Feedback." *Media-N: Journal of the New Media Caucus* 10, no. 3 (2014). http://median.newmediacaucus.org/art -infrastructures-information/poeisis-in-bali-notes-on-feedback/.

Rosler, Martha. *Decoys and Disruptions: Selected Writings, 1975–2001*. Cambridge, MA: MIT Press, 2004.

Ross, Andrew. *No-Collar: The Humane Workplace and Its Hidden Costs*. New York: Basic, 2003.

Rothenstein, Sir John. *A Brief History of the Tate Gallery*. London: Pitkin Pictorials, 1963.

Roy, Ananya, and Aihwa Ong, eds, *Worlding Cities: Asian Experiments and the Art of Being Global*. Hoboken, NJ: Blackwell, 2011.

Sagen Gil, Guillermo. *La CGT de los argentinos en Rosario, 1968–69*. Rosario, Argentina: Universidad Nacional de Rosario, 2005.

Sartre, Jean-Paul. *No Exit*. Translated by Stuart Gilbert. New York: Vintage International, 1946.

Schneemann, Carolee. "II. Recent Work." In *Carolee Schneemann: Early and Recent Work*. New Paltz, NY: Max Hutchinson Gallery–Documentext, 1983.

Schuld, Dawna. "Beyond Method and without Object." In *Hybrid Practices: Art in Collaboration with Science and Technology in the Long 1960s*, edited by David Cateforis, Steven Duval, and Shepherd Steiner, 79–90. Berkeley: University of California Press, 2018.

Schuld, Dawna. *Minimal Conditions*. Berkeley: University of California Press, 2018.

Sekula, Allan. *Fish Story*. Dusseldorf: Richter Verlag, 1995.

Selz, Peter, and Kristine Stiles, eds. *Theories and Documents of Contemporary Art: A Sourcebook of Artist's Writings*. Berkeley: University of California Press, 1996.

Serres, Michael. *The Parasite*. Translated by Lawrence R. Schehr. Minneapolis: University of Minnesota, 1980.

Shaked, Nizan. *The Synthetic Proposition: Conceptualism and the Political Referent in Contemporary Art*. Manchester: Manchester University Press, 2017.

Shanken, Edward. *Art and Electronic Media*. London: Phaidon Press, 2009.

Shanken, Edward. "The House That Jack Built: Jack Burnham's Concept of 'Software' as a Metaphor for Art." *Leonardo Electronic Almanac* 6, no. 10 (1998).

Shanken, Edward. "Reprogramming Systems Aesthetics: A Strategic Historiography." *UC Irvine: Digital Arts and Culture 2009*. http://escholarship.org/uc/item/6bv363d4/.

Shanken, Edward, ed. *Systems*. Cambridge, MA: MIT Press; London: Whitechapel, 2015.

Shannon, Claude E, and Warren Weaver. *The Mathematical Theory of Communication*. Champaign: University of Illinois Press, 1963.

Sharp, Willoughby. *Cinetismo: Systems Sculpture in Environmental Situations*. Mexico City: UNAM Press, 1968.

Sharp, Willoughby. "Luminism and Kineticism." In *Minimal Art: A Critical Anthology*, edited by Gregory Battcock, 317–58. New York: E. P. Dutton, 1968.

Sharp, Willoughby. "Place and Process." *Artforum* 8, no. 3 (1969): 46–49.

Sharpe, Christina. *In the Wake: On Blackness and Being*. Durham, NC: Duke University Press, 2016.

Shiff, Richard. "Photographic Soul." In *Where Is the Photograph?*, edited by David Green, 95–112. London: Gardners, 2003.

Siegel, Jeanne. *Artworks: Discourse on the '60s and '70s*. Ann Arbor, MI: Da Capo Press, 1985.

Skrebowski, Luke. "All Systems Go: Recovering Hans Haacke's Systems Art." *Grey Room*, no. 30 (2008): 54–83.

Skrebowski, Luke. "The Artist as Homo Arbiter Formae: Art and Interaction in Jack Burnham's Systems Essays." In *Practicable: From Participation to Interaction in Contemporary Art*, edited by Samuel Bianchini and Erik Verhagen, 39–54. Cambridge, MA: MIT Press, 2016.

Skrebowski, Luke. "Jack Burnham Redux: The Obsolete in Reverse?" *Grey Room*, no. 65 (2016): 88–113.

Skrebowski, Luke. "Systems, Contexts, Relations: An Alternative Genealogy of Conceptual Art." PhD diss., Middlesex University, 2009.

Small, Irene V. "Close Up: Allora and Calzadilla's *Puerto Rican Light (Cueva Vientos)*, 2015." *Artforum* 55, no. 9 (2017): 286–95.

Spivak, Gayatri Chakravorty. "Planetarity." In *Death of a Discipline*, 71–102. New York: Columbia University Press, 2003.

Spreiregen, Paul D. *Urban Design: The Architecture of Towns and Cities*. New York: McGraw-Hill, 1965.

Star, Susan Leigh. "The Ethnography of Infrastructure." *American Behavioral Scientist* 43, no. 3 (1999): 377–91.

Starosielski, Nicole, and Janet Walker, eds. *Sustainable Media: Critical Approaches to Media and Environment*. New York: Routledge, 2016.

Steiner, Shep. "It Must Be the Weather: Today's Forecast—Again, Mainly Capitalism." *Afterall* 2 (2000): 74–81.

Stengers, Isabelle. *In Catastrophic Times: Resisting the Coming Barbarism*. London: Open Humanities Press, 2015.

Stephenson, Neal. *In the Beginning . . . Was the Command Line*. New York: Avon, 1999.

Steyerl, Hito. "Duty Free Art." *e-flux*, no. 63 (March 2015). https://www.e-flux.com/journal/63/60894/duty-free-art/.

Steyerl, Hito. "Too Much World, Is the Internet Dead?" *e-flux*, no. 49 (November 2013). https://www.e-flux.com/journal/49/60004/too-much-world-is-the-internet-dead/.

Stiegler, Bernard. *The Neganthropocene*. Translated by Daniel Ross. London: Open Humanities Press, 2018.

Stiegler, Bernard. *Technics and Time 1: The Fault of Epimetheus*. Translated by Richard Beardsworth and George Collins. Stanford, CA: Stanford University Press, 1998.

Stiegler, Bernard. *Technics and Time 2: Disorientation.* Translated by Stephen Barker. Stanford, CA: Stanford University Press, 2008.

Stott, Timothy. *Play and Participation in Contemporary Arts Practices.* New York: Routledge, 2015.

Stott, Timothy. "When Attitudes Became Toys: Jasia Reichardt's *Play Orbit.*" *Art History* 41, no. 2 (2018): 344–69.

Szeman, Imre, and Dominic Boyer, eds. *Energy Humanities: An Anthology.* Baltimore, MD: Johns Hopkins University Press, 2017.

Szewczyk, Monika, ed. *Meaning Liam Gillick.* Cambridge, MA: MIT Press, 2009.

Tan, Kenneth Paul. "Choosing What to Remember in Neoliberal Singapore: The Singapore Story, State Censorship and State-Sponsored Nostalgia." *Asian Studies Review* 40, no. 2 (2016): 231–49.

Tani, Ellen Yoshi. "Black Conceptualism and the Atmospheric Turn, 1968–2008." PhD diss., Stanford University, 2015.

Taussig, Michael. *The Nervous System.* New York: Routledge, 1992.

Tickner, Lisa. *Hornsey 1968: The Art School Revolution.* London: Frances Lincoln, 2008.

Tillberg, Margareta. "You Are Now Leaving the American Sector: The Russian Group *Dvizhenie, 1962–1978.*" In *Place Studies in Art, Media, Science and Technology: Historical Investigations on the Sites and the Migration of Knowledge,* edited by Andreas Broeckmann and Gunalan Nadarajan, 147–65. Weimar: VDG, 2008.

Tuchman, Maurice. *Art and Technology: A Report on the Art and Technology Program of the Los Angeles County Museum of Art 1967–1971.* Los Angeles: Los Angeles County Museum of Art, 1971.

Turner, Fred. *The Democratic Surround: Multimedia and American Liberalism from World War II to the Psychedelic Sixties.* Chicago: University of Chicago Press, 2013.

Turner, Fred. *From Counterculture to Cyberculture: Stewart Brand, the Whole Earth Network, and the Rise of Digital Utopianism.* Chicago: University of Chicago Press, 2006.

Tyson, John A. "The Context as Host: Hans Haacke's Art of Textual Exhibition." *Word and Image* 31, no. 3 (2015): 213–32.

Umpleby, Stuart. "A History of the Cybernetics Movement in the United States." *Journal of the Washington Academy of Sciences* 91, no. 2 (2005): 54–66.

van Bohemen, Hein. "Infrastructure, Ecology and Art." *Landscape and Urban Planning* 59, no. 4 (2002): 187–201.

Van der Ryn, Sim. "Advertisements for a Counter Culture." *Progressive Architecture* 51, no. 6 (1970): 71–93.

Verón, Eliseo. *Conducta, estructura y comunicacion.* Buenos Aires: Editorial Jorge Álvarez, 1968.

von Bertalanffy, Ludwig. *General System Theory: Foundations, Development, Applications.* London: Allen Lane, 1971.

von Bertalanffy, Ludwig. *Lebenswissenschaft und Bildung.* Erfurt, Germany: Stenger, 1930.

von Bertalanffy, Ludwig. "An Outline of General System Theory." *British Journal for the Philosophy of Science* 1, no. 2 (1950): 134–65.

von Bertalanffy, Ludwig. "Untersuchungen über die Gesetzlichkeit des Wachstums, I. Teil: Allgemeine Grundlagen der Theorie; Mathematische und physiologische Gesetzlichkeiten des Wachstums bei Wassertieren," *Wilhelm Roux Archiv für Entwicklungsmechanik der Organismen: Organ für d. gesamte kausal Morphologie* 131, no. 4 (1934): 613–52.

Warren, Calvin L. *Ontological Terror: Blackness, Nihilism, and Emancipation*. Durham, NC: Duke University Press, 2018.

Weheliye, Alexander G. "Engendering Phonographies: Sonic Technologies of Blackness." *Small Axe* 18, no. 2 (2014): 180–90.

Welchman, John C., ed. *Institutional Critique and After*. Zurich: JRP-Ringier, 2006.

Weschler, Lawrence. *Seeing Is Forgetting the Name of the Thing One Sees*. Berkeley: University of California Press, 2008.

Whitelaw, Mitchell. "1968/1998: Rethinking a Systems Aesthetic." *ANAT Newsletter*, no. 33 (May 1998): n.p.

Whyte, William H. *The Organization Man*. New York: Simon and Schuster, 1956.

Wiener, Norbert. *Cybernetics: Or Control and Communication in the Animal and the Machine*. Cambridge, MA: MIT Press, 1948.

Wiener, Norbert. *The Human Use of Human Beings: Cybernetics and Society*. New York: Avon Books, 1967.

Wilderson, Frank B., III. *Red, White and Black: Cinema and the Structure of U.S. Antagonisms*. Durham, NC: Duke University Press, 2010.

Wilson, Scott. *The Order of Joy: Beyond the Cultural Politics of Enjoyment*. Albany, NY: SUNY Press, 2008.

Winnubst, Shannon. "The Queer Thing about Neoliberal Pleasure: A Foucauldian Warning." *Foucault Studies* 14 (2012): 79–97.

Woodruff, Lily. "The Groupe de Recherche d'Art Visuel against the Technocrats." *Art Journal* 73, no. 3 (2014): 18–37.

Wortz, Ed, ed. *First National Symposium on Habitability*. 4 vols. Venice, CA: Garrett AiResearch, 1970.

Yao, Pauline J. "Floating World: Pauline J. Yao on Charles Lim's 'SEA STATE,' 2005–." *Artforum International* 53, no. 8 (2015): 236–39.

Contributors

CRISTINA ALBU is associate professor of contemporary art history at the University of Missouri–Kansas City. Her research focuses on the intersections between contemporary art, cognitive sciences, and technology. She is the author of *Mirror Affect: Seeing Self, Observing Others in Contemporary Art* (2016) and the coeditor of *Perception and Agency in Shared Spaces of Contemporary Art* (2018). Her writings have appeared in numerous scholarly anthologies and journals (*Afterimage*, *Artnodes*, and *Camera Obscura*). She is currently working on a book project that explores the affective and social implications of biofeedback art.

AMANDA BOETZKES is professor of contemporary art history and theory at the University of Guelph. Her writing examines the politics, aesthetics, and ecologies of contemporary art through the lens of human waste, energy consumption and expenditure, and most recently, climate crisis and glacier melt in the circumpolar north. She is the author of *Plastic Capitalism: Contemporary Art and the Drive to Waste* (2019), *The Ethics of Earth Art* (2010), and the editor of *Heidegger and the Work of Art History* (2014). She has published in the journals *South Atlantic Quarterly*, *e-flux*, *Postmodern Culture*, and *Afterimage*, among others. Recent book chapters appear in *Climate Realism*; *The Routledge Handbook of Waste Studies*; *The Edinburgh Companion for Animal Studies*; and *Art in the Anthropocene: Encounters among Politics, Aesthetics, Environments, and Epistemologies*.

BRIANNE COHEN is assistant professor in the Department of Art and Art History at the University of Colorado Boulder, where she teaches contemporary art history and visual culture. From participatory art to lens-based activism, she explores artistic practices concerned with public sphere formation, decolonization, political violence, and ecology and environmentalism. Her current book project, "Preventive Publics: Contemporary Art and Nonviolence in Twenty-First-Century Europe," examines contemporary art that grapples with cross-cultural affiliation and the active imagining of nonviolence in twenty-first-century Europe. She is the coeditor of *The Photofilmic: Entangled Images in Contemporary Art and Visual Culture* (2016) and has published in journals such as *Representations*, *Afterimage*, *Journal of European Studies*, *Third Text*, and *Image [&] Narrative*. Her new research addresses questions of ecological devastation and the formation of critical publics in Southeast Asia, particularly in Vietnam, Cambodia, and Singapore.

KRIS COHEN is associate professor of art and humanities at Reed College. He works on the relationship between art, economy, and media technologies, focusing especially on the aesthetics of collective life. His first book, *Never Alone, Except for Now* (2017), addresses these concerns in the context of electronic networks. He is working on a new manuscript that accounts for how a group of Black artists working from the 1960s to the present were addressing, in ways both belied and surprisingly revealed by the language of abstraction and conceptualism, nascent configurations of the computer screen and the forms of labor and personhood associated with those configurations.

JAIMEY HAMILTON FARIS is associate professor of art history and critical theory at the University of Hawaiʻi at Mānoa. Her research focuses on global infrastructure and ecologies. She has contributed articles and essays to *Art Journal*, *October*, *Art Margins*, *The Contemporary Pacific*, *Art Journal Open*, *Shima*, and more. Her book *Uncommon Goods: The Global Dimensions of the Readymade* (2013) examines artistic practices of the 1990s and 2000s concerned with neoliberal trade. She is the editor of a special issue of *Art Margins* on capitalist realism (2015) and a volume of experimental ecocriticism, *The Almanac for the Beyond* (2019). Her current focus is on water infrastructures, ecologies, and creativities. She curated *Inundation: Art and Climate Change in the Pacific* in spring 2020 in Hawaiʻi and is working on a water art book project tentatively titled "Liquid Archives Liquid Futures."

CHRISTINE FILIPPONE is associate professor of art history at Millersville University of Pennsylvania. Recipient of the 2017 SECAC Award for Excellence in Scholarly Research and Publication, her book *Science, Technology, and Utopias: Women Artists and Cold War America* (2017) examines feminist aesthetic approaches to science and technology. Her research has been supported by a Mellon Postdoctoral Fellowship, an American Fellowship from the American Association of University Women, and a Guggenheim Fellowship from the National Air and Space Museum of the Smithsonian Institution. She has served as executive director of the Print Center in Philadelphia and in curatorial departments at the Philadelphia Museum of Art, Brooklyn Museum of Art, International Center of Photography, and the Nasher Museum of Art. Currently, she is researching the intersection of systems theory and political utopias in Latin American conceptual art of the 1960s and 1970s.

JOHANNA GOSSE is assistant professor of art history and visual culture at the University of Idaho and the executive editor of *Media-N: Journal of the New Media Caucus*. A historian of postwar art specializing in experimental film and media, she researches the intersection of art history, film and media studies, and visual studies. Gosse has published in journals such as *Journal of Cinema and Media Studies*, *Camera Obscura*, *Millennium Film Journal*, *Art Journal*, and *Radical History Review*, as well as in numerous edited collections and exhibition catalogs. Gosse was a Mellon Postdoctoral Fellow in the Department of Art History and Archaeology at Columbia University and received an Arts Writers Grant from the Andy Warhol Foundation for her forthcoming book on the mail artist Ray Johnson.

FRANCIS HALSALL is codirector of the Art in the Contemporary World MA/MFA program at the National College of Art and Design, Dublin, and a research fellow in the Department of Art History and Image Studies, University of the Free State, South Africa. Halsall's forthcoming publications include the books *The Dispersed Subjects of Contemporary Art* and *Systems Aesthetics*.

JUDITH RODENBECK is a cultural historian and writer whose work focuses on the movement lexicons of intermedia. She is associate professor and chair of the Department of Media and Cultural Studies at the University of California, Riverside.

DAWNA SCHULD is assistant professor of modern and contemporary art history in the Department of Visualization at Texas A&M University. Her research concentrates on points of intersection between art, technology, and biology, with an emphasis on how the perceptual phenomena of human experience are implemented in art. She is the author of *Minimal Conditions: Light, Space, and Subjectivity* (2018) and the coeditor (with Cristina Albu) of *Perception and Agency in Shared Spaces of Contemporary Art* (2018). Schuld has been awarded a Dana and David Dornsife Research Fellowship at the Huntington Library in Pasadena, California, and a Senior Research Fellowship at the Henry Moore Institute in Leeds.

LUKE SKREBOWSKI is lecturer in contemporary art at the University of Manchester. He is the coauthor of *Trevor Paglen: Sites Unseen* (2018) and the coeditor of *Aesthetics and Contemporary Art* (2011). His articles have appeared in journals including *Amodern*, *Art History*, *Art Margins*, *Grey Room*, *Manifesta Journal*, *Tate Papers*, and *Third Text*, and he has written catalog essays for the Tate's *Conceptual Art in Britain: 1964–79* (2016) and the Generali Foundation's twenty-fifth anniversary show *Amazing! Clever! Linguistic! An Adventure in Conceptual Art* (2013). He cocurated the exhibitions *Plastic Words* (2014–15) at Raven Row and *Counter-Production* (2012) at the Generali Foundation. His current research explores two areas: the exhaustion of institutional critique and the ecological turn by contemporary artists; and the relationship between postconceptual art and the novel.

TIMOTHY STOTT is associate professor in modern and contemporary art history at Trinity College Dublin, the University of Dublin. His research focuses on ecocritical art and design history, the visual culture of science, and the contribution of art/design history to the environmental humanities. His recent book projects include the monograph *Buckminster Fuller's World Game and Its Legacy* (2021), which studies the design strategies of the World Game, a series of projects beginning in the late 1960s to redistribute planetary resources, and he is now working on a visual history of earth systems science. He is chair of the Environmental Humanities Working Group for the Irish Humanities Alliance at the Royal Irish Academy and a member of the Trinity Centre for Environmental Humanities.

JOHN TYSON is assistant professor of art history at the University of Massachusetts Boston and served as Andrew W. Mellon Postdoctoral Curatorial Fellow at the National Gallery of Art (Washington, DC) from 2015 to 2017. Tyson's scholarship focuses on art and technology since the 1960s, as well as on early twentieth-century American art. In 2019, he curated (with Sam Toabe) *From Theory to Practice: Artistic Legacies of the Whitney Independent Study Program*. He is presently developing a book on Hans Haacke's works from the 1960s and 1970s. His recent publications include "Politics of the Press: Newspapers and the Representation of Art by African Americans in the Nation's Capital," in *American Art* (2019); "Beyond Systems Aesthetics: Politics, Performance, and Para-Sites," in the catalog for the New Museum's *Hans Haacke: All Connected* (2019); and "Nineteen Notes for Elena del Rivero's Nineteen Flags," an online project created for Rivers Institute for Contemporary Art and Thought.

Index

An italic *f* following a page number refers to a figure.

abstraction: blackness and, 103; Gillick and concretization of the abstract, 187; graphical user interface and, 103–4

Adorno, Theodor, 42, 50

affect: complex participatory art and, 158; cybernetics and, 15; "nervous systems" and, 7; Rosario Group's Tucumán Arde and, 92; *The Transmission of Affect* (Brennan), 159–60

Afrofuturism, 9–10

Akomfrah, John: *The Last Angel of History*, 9–10; *Vertigo Sea*, 10

Albers, Josef, 38–39

Alexander, Christopher, 13

Alfred, Eric Ronald, 230

Allora, Jennifer: *Puerto Rican Light* (with Calzadilla), 237

Alloway, Lawrence, 10–11, 14, 19–20

Angry Arts, 1, 3, 70, 76n68

Anthropocene, 208–9, 226

Apple Computer, 110–11

Apter, Michael, 13

Arendt, Hannah, 204–5

Argentina: Noche de los Bastones Largos (Night of the Big Sticks) (July 29,1966), 85–86; "Operation Tucumán" and disinformation in, 79, 88–89; political history, 78–79. *See also* Tucumán Arde

Art and Technology exhibition (LACMA, 1971), 125–28

Arte programmata, 16–17

Arte programmata exhibition (GRAV, 1962), 83

Artsy, 254

Artway of Thinking, 28n70

Art Workers' Coalition (AWC), 22n3, 67–69, 134

Ascott, Roy, 15

Asher, Michael, 138

Atienza, Martha: *Gilubong ang Akon Pusod sa Dagat (My Navel Is Buried at Sea)*, 244

avant-garde: "becoming classical," 145n21; Burnham and, 38; ecology and, 64; First National Meeting on Avant-Garde Art (Rosario, Argentina, 1968), 85; Gillick and, 174, 189; open systems and, 87–88; Torcuato di Tella Institute and, 78

Baas, Jacquelynn, 14

Baer, Jo, 10

Banham, Reyner, 141

Barr, Michael D., 218

Barry, Robert, 31

Barthes, Roland, 48–49

Bateson, Gregory: cybernetics, planetary ecology, and, 5; Gillick and, 187; Guattari and, 196; on noise and restraint, 174; on objects vs. events, 180; on open systems, 13; Rosario Group and, 82

Battcock, Gregory, 67–68

Bauhaus, 38–42, 258n38

Becher, Bernd and Hilla, 222

Beer, Stafford, 5

Bell, Larry: habitability symposium (Venice Beach, 1970), 133–34; phenomenal art and, 127–28; in *Primary Structures* exhibition (Jewish Museum, 1966), 138; in *Spaces* exhibition (MoMA, 1969), 133–34; *Three Artists from Los Angeles* exhibition (Tate Gallery, 1970), 130–41, 132*f*; untitled 1971 environmental glass work, 143. *See also* light and space art

Belting, Hans, 181

Benedit, Luis Fernando, 16

Benjamin, Walter, 50, 58

Bennett, Jane, 158

Berger, Maurice, 141

Bianconi, Giampaolo, 18

Biemann, Ursula: *Contained Mobility*, 243; *Egyptian Chemistry*, 19

biopolitics, 162

Bishop, Claire, 17, 137

black box logic, 239–40, 244–46

Bochner, Mel: *Domain of the Great Bear* (with Smithson), 76n65

Boetzkes, Amanda, 167

Borromean knot, 197–99, 198*f*

Bourdieu, Pierre, 141

Bourriaud, Nicolas, 17–18, 43, 182–83

Bouvier, Yves, 253

Bread and Puppet Theater, 65

Brennan, Teresa, 159–60

Broodthaers, Marcel, 82

Brown, Trisha, 115–17

Büchel, Christoph, 254, 259n51; *Training Ground for Training Ground for Democracy*, 239, 248–51, 249*f*

Buchloh, Benjamin H. D., 32, 38, 72n4

Buchmann, Sabeth, 32

Burch, Noël, 257n24

Buren, Daniel, 47, 60, 82

Burn, Ian, 60

Burnham, Jack, 40*f*; "The Aesthetics of Intelligent Systems", 40; on *Art and Technology* exhibition, 126; "Art and Technology: The Panacea That Failed", 48–49; *Art in the Marcusean Analysis*, 44, 46*f*; the art object vs. systems consciousness and, 180; *Atom*, 41; *Beyond Modern Sculpture*, 14, 31, 36, 41, 49; career, 33–38; on conceptual art, 142; on deviation-amplifying systems, 168; *Dissolve into Comprehension*, 32; exhibitions curated by, 18; *Great Western Salt Works*, 35, 35*f*, 37; Haacke and, 1–3, 2*f*, 48–50, 57, 150; "nervous breakdown" and, 50; ocular bias, critique of, 149–50; postcontemporary art and, 181; professional formation and revolt against New Bauhaus, 38–42; Shanken on, 7; "sociotechnical," 6; *Software: Information Technology; Its New Meaning for Art*, curation of, 36, 45–47, 143n5; "Steps in the Formulation of Real-Time Political Art," 4; *The Structure of Art*, 36, 47–48; systems aesthetics uncoupled from, 10; "Systems and Art," 43; systems counterculture and,

5; "Systems Esthetics," 4–5, 11, 14, 36, 42–43, 49, 60, 149–50, 160–61, 235–37, 245; theory of systems aesthetics, 31–32, 42–49

Butterfield, Jan, 137–38

Cage, John, 50

Calder, Alexander, 48

Calzadilla, Guillermo: *Puerto Rican Light* (with Allora), 237

capitalism: capitalist realism, 189n4; data capitalism and financialized art economy, 251–54; extractive, 216, 223–27, 229; "how it *actually* works," 255; late, 175

Caplan, Lindsay, 16

Carnevale, Graciela: Le Parc and, 97n23; *Lock Up Action*, 85–86; Tucumán Arde and, 83, 92

Castells, Manuel, 175

Center for Advanced Visual Studies (CAVS), MIT, 39–41

Centro de arte y comunicación, 16

Chandler, Dorothy, 125

Chaney, Rufus, 200–201

Chin, Mel: *The Arctic Is . . .* , 192–95, 193*f*, 199, 205–11; energy metabolism and, 194–95; globalization and, 194–95, 201–4, 208–11; negentropy and, 207–10; planetarity and, 194–99, 202–5, 209–11; planetary praxis and, 202–7; political ecology and, 194–202, 205, 207; *Revival Field*, 199–202, 200*f*, 210

Chomsky, Noam, 66

Chua, Kevin, 229

Chua, Wilson, 224

Clarke, Bruce, 5, 151, 156

Clay, Jean, 75n45

Clinton, George, 9

closed systems: Alloway's concept of, 11, 19–20; entropy and, 12, 93; open systems vs., 5, 12, 82–83, 87–88, 95; Rosario Group's Tucumán Arde and, 79–80; second-order awareness of, 128; Wiener on, 82

cognitive mapping, 174–76, 189n6

complex participatory art systems: about complex systems, 148; Burnham's systems aesthetics and, 149–50, 160–61; distributed agency and, 158; embodied complexity and making the invisible perceptible, 158–63; inward and outward complex systems, 151–58; sensing system instability, 163–68

Compton, Michael, 128, 130–32, 135–42

conceptualism: Burnham on, 42, 142; Gaines and, 103, 119–20; Rosario Group's Tucumán Arde and, 81; Shaked on, 108–9

constructivism, 38–39, 45

Contagion (Czarnecki), 155*f*; inward and outward complex systems, 153–54, 158; making the invisible perceptible, 158–63; overview, 149; sensing system instability, 163–68

containerization: art of disassembly, 254–56; black box logic, 239–40, 244–46; Büchel's *Training Ground for Training Ground for Democracy*, 239, 248–51, 249*f*; Burnham's systems aesthetics and, 235–37, 245; Cowen's *The Deadly Life of Logistics*, 248–49; data capitalism and financialized art economy, 251–54; Easterling's extrastatecraft and, 238–39, 247, 255; historical development of, 241–42; as infrastructure art, 237, 239–42; Klose's *The Container Principle*, 244–45; Ni's *Para-production*, 239, 247; Ni's *Return of the Shreds*, 239, 246–47; paraproduction and paraconsumption, 246–51; parasitical logic of, 244–48, 251; Sekula's *Fish Story*, 241*f*, 242–43; Singapore and, 223–24, 228; Steyerl's *Duty Free Art*, 239, 251–53

contemporary art: Burnham and, 11, 33, 36, 38, 42, 50, 236; concepts called into question by, 180; containers and, 250; Eco on, 82, 88; financialization and, 254; Gillick and, 174–77, 180–81, 186; Joselit on format vs. medium, 182; Lippard on, 3; nervousness and, 7; new media art, relationship with, 7, 33; ontology of, 33, 38, 50; political ecology and, 195; postcontemporary art, 181; relational aesthetics and, 17–18; Relyea on network structures and, 182; Sekula, globalization, and, 243; social turn in, 17; systems ecology and, 18–19; Tate Gallery and, 130; turn outward and, 9. *See also specific artists*

Corbett, John, 9

Corris, Michael, 32

Costa, Eduardo, 82

Cowen, Deborah, 248–49, 254

Cubitt, Sean, 162

cybernetics: Bateson on, 180; first-order, 12; genealogy of, 11–16; Le Parc on, 83; second-order, 5–6, 12

Cybernetic Serendipity (ICA, 1968), 15

Czarnecki, Gina: biotechnology and cultural beliefs, 149; Burnham's systems aesthetics and, 149–50; Levi and, 165; participatory environments and, 148–49; traumatic family history, 164–65. *See also Contagion*

Dada, 52n21, 74n37

Danielsen, Jens, 192, 206, 209

Danto, Arthur, 181

Darger, Henry, 5

de Duve, Thierry, 32, 181

Dee, Elizabeth, 77n71

Deleuze, Gilles, 198

dematerialization, 1–3, 64, 87

Demos, T. J., 18–19

Denes, Agnes, 15, 18, 22; *Matrix of Knowledge*, 18; *Trigonal Ballet*, 18

Dion, Mark, 59

distributed agency, 158

Documenta 11, 221, 243

Duchamp, Marcel, 34–37, 47, 61, 181

Dvizhenie, 16

Dylan, Bob, 4, 57, 69

Easterling, Keller, 238, 255

Eco, Umberto, 82–83, 88–94

ecoartists, 18–19

ecological perspective on systems, 4–5, 167

ecological turn in art, 59–61

ecologicity, 167

ecosophy, 166–67, 197, 207–8

ecosystemic approach, 217, 227, 230–31

eco-systems aesthetics, 18

Eichmann, Adolf, 205

Eisenhower, Dwight, 78

embodiment. *See* complex participatory art systems; light and space art

Engelbart, Douglas, 109–11

Entropocene, 208

environmental humanities, 19

Escandell, Noemí, 83

Escari, Raúl, 82

Eshun, Kodwo, 9

Exhibition (Hogg), 188

Experiments in Art and Technology, 60

expressionism, 179–80

extractive zone, 216, 223–27

extrastatecraft, 238–39, 247, 255

Favario, Eduardo, 82–83, 86

Fenton, Terry, 45

Ferrari, León, 83, 94; *La civilización occidental y cristiana*, 83–85, 84*f*

Filippone, Christine, 15, 18

financialized art economy, 253–54

First National Symposium on Habitability of Environments (Venice Beach, CA, 1970), 133–34

Fisher, Mark, 189n4

Flavin, Dan, 235; "luminous sculpture," 48; *Puerto Rican Light (to Jeanie Blake)*, 237

Flick, Friedrich Christian, 250, 259n50

Foo Say Juan, 224–25

Ford, Phil, 144n11

Foster, Hal, 50, 54n63

Foucault, Michel, 8, 37, 108

Frantz, Anaïk, 221

Fraser, Andrea, 142

Fried, Michael, 4

Frondizi, Arturo, 78

Fry, Edward, 61

fungibility, 115–21, 124n44

Gabo, Naum, 34, 38–39

Gaboury, Jacob, 110, 122n14

Gabrys, Jennifer, 204

Gaia, 195, 203–6

Gaines, Charles: abstraction and, 103–4; *Faces*, 105*f*, 106–9, 112, 115; *Faces 1: Identity Politics*, 112; *Falling Leaves*, 112–15, 113*f*, 114*f*; on freedom, 110–11, 119–20; GUI, history of personhood, and labor in the graphical field, 109–12; individuality, fungibility, and contiguity, 112–21; metonymy/metaphor distinction, 124n50; *Motion: Trisha Brown Dance*, 112, 115–17; rasterworks, 105–9

Galbraith, John Kenneth, 236

Galison, Peter, 13

Galton, Francis, 58

Ganzfeld effects, 126–27, 135. *See also* light and space art

general systems theory, 12–13

George, Edward, 9

Gere, Charlie, 32

Gillick, Liam: on acting process, 188; *AnnLee You Propose*, 183–84; art, systems, and subjects, 179–80; on art and contemporary society, 173; cognitive mapping and, 174–76; as collaborator, 176–77; *Complete Bin Development*, 177–78, 178*f*, 179*f*; "Contemporary Art Does Not Account for That Which Is Taking Place," 180–81; *Denominator Platform*, 184, 185*f*; disappointment, systems of, 183–89; *Discussion Island*, 184–85; *Discussion Island/Big Conference Centre*, 184; *Discussion Platform*, 184; distribution systems and, 181–82; in Hogg's *Exhibition* (film), 188; *How Are You Going to Behave? A Kitchen Cat Speaks*, 177; on noise, 187–88; postcontemporary art and, 181–82; relational aesthetics and, 182–83; strategies of denial and deferment, 174; systems, use of, 176–79

globalization, 194–95, 201–4, 208–11. *See also* containerization

Glueck, Grace, 65, 133, 138

Glusberg, Jorge, 16

Gómez-Barris, Macarena, 216, 226, 231

Goodyear, Anne Collins, 144n9

Graham, Dan, 63

Gramuglio, María Teresa, 83

graphical user interface (GUI), 103–4, 109–12

Greenberg, Clement, 10, 39, 50–51, 54n63

Groupe de Recherche d'Art Visuel (GRAV), 82–83, 94

Grupo de artistas de vanguardia de Rosario. *See* Tucumán Arde

Guattari, Félix: ecosophy, 166–67, 197, 207–8; *The Three Ecologies*, 196–99

Guevara, Ernesto "Che," 79, 95n3

Haacke, Hans: art as unpolitical, 1–3; background history of weather, art, and systems, 58–61; BONUS-Storm, 70–71; Burnham and, 1–3, 2*f*, 48–50, 57, 150; *Condensation Cube*, 55–56, 64, 72n4; *Condensation Floor*, 56; *Condensation Wall*, 56; *Fog, Swamp, Erosion*, 57; *Ice Stick*, 56; institutional critique and, 3, 56, 63, 81–82; meteorological thinking and, 57; MIT *Sky Line*, 66–68; MOMA *Poll*, 68; *Precipitation Minus Evaporation*, 63; *Rain Tower*, 56; *Recording of Climate in Art Exhibition*, 57, 63–64, 70, 71*f*; *Shapolsky et al., Manhattan Real Estate Holdings, a*

Real-Time Social System, as of May 1, 1971, 60; *Sky Line,* 57, 64–69, 65f, 75n45; *Sphere in Oblique Air Jet,* 57; *Spray of Ithaca Falls: Freezing and Melting on Rope, Feb 7, 8, 9, 1969,* 68; on systems thinking, 13; *Weather, or Not,* 57, 70–72; *Wind in Water: Snow, December 15, 1968,* 56–57, 61–63, 62f, 72; *Wind Room,* 57, 71

Habibie, B. J. (Bacharuddin Jusuf), 218

Halsall, Francis, 27n68, 32

Hampton, James, 5

Haraway, Donna, 9, 203–5, 231

harmonized system (HS) codes, 247

Hartman, Saidiya, 117–19, 124n44

Harvey, David, 238

Hayden, Tom, 59

Heckscher, August, 75n45

Heidegger, Martin, 48, 206

Hogg, Joanna, 188

Holmes, Brian, 258n47

Hopps, Walter, 130, 144n15

Hornsey College of Art, 4–5

Hulten, Pontus, 60

Huyghe, Pierre: *No Ghost Just a Shell* (with Parreno), 182–85

Independent Group (IG), 14

infrastructure art, 237, 239–42, 255–56. *See also* containerization

In Orbit (Saraceno), 157f; inward and outward complex systems, 156–58; making the invisible perceptible, 158–63; overview, 149; sensing system instability, 163–68

institutional critique: Asher and, 138; Burnham and, 236; freedom through control, 141–42; Haacke and, 3, 56, 63, 81–82; infrastructure art and, 240–41; Rosario Group's Tucumán Arde and, 80–82. *See also* light and space art

Irwin, Robert: *Art and Technology* exhibition, 126–27; on art objects, 134–35; conditional art, 135; *Fractured Light—Partial Scrim Ceiling—Eye Level Wire,* 135; habitability symposium (Venice Beach, 1970), 133–34; phenomenal art and, 127–28; *Three Artists from Los Angeles* exhibition (Tate Gallery, 1970), 130–41, 132f. *See also* light and space art

ISIL attacks in Paris (2015), 192–94, 207

Jacoby, Roberto: on aesthetic shaping, 93–94; *Closed Information Circuits,* 87; *Happening for a Dead Boar,* 86–87; Masotta reading group and, 82; Tucumán Arde and, 83

Jameson, Fredric, 174–76

Johnson, Ray, 5

Jones, Caroline, 32, 39, 50, 66, 159

Jorn, Asger, 245

Joselit, David, 181–82

Joyce, James, 198

Judd, Donald, 177, 235, 237, 258n38

just-in-time supply chain software, 240

Kant, Immanuel, 50

Kaprow, Allan, 59

Karshan, Donald, 60

Keller, Sean, 177

Kepes, György, 38–41, 45

Kinetic Environment exhibition (Central Park, NYC, 1967), 64–65

King, Martin Luther, Jr., 1, 57, 70

Klose, Alexander, 244–45

Klüver, Billy, 48

Koolhaas, Rem, 252

Kosuth, Joseph, 60, 109

Kozloff, Max, 144n13

Krauss, Rosalind, 32

Kristiansen, Mamarut, 192

Kumar, Ramakrishna, 220

Kusama, Yayoi, 6

Kuspit, Donald, 181

Lacan, Jacques, 197–201, 207

Lambert-Beatty, Carrie, 251

Larkin, Brian, 238, 251

Last Angel of History, The (Akomfrah), 9–10

Latour, Bruno, 194–96, 201, 203, 206

Lee, Pamela M., 4, 19–20, 32

Lee Hsien Loong, 218

Lee Kuan Yew, 218, 221–22

Leider, Philip, 42

Le Parc, Julio, 82–83, 97n23

Levi, Primo, 165

Levine, Les, 150

Lévi-Strauss, Claude, 36

LeWitt, Carol, 105

LeWitt, Sol, 31, 68, 105

Licht, Jennifer, 135

light and space art (phenomenal art): about, 127–28; *Art and Technology* exhibition (LACMA, 1971), 125–28; habitability symposium (Venice Beach, 1970), 133–34; Morris's *bodyspacemotionthings*, 139–43, 140*f*; orders of systems consciousness and, 128, 137; safety issues, freedom, and control, 136, 141–43; social body consciousness and, 137–43; *Spaces* exhibition (MoMA, 1969) and, 133–34, 138; *Three Artists from Los Angeles* (Tate Gallery, 1970), 130–41, 132*f*

Lilly, John, 5

Lim, Charles: ecosystemic approach and, 217, 227, 230–31; submerged perspectives and, 216–17; tsunamii.net art collective and, 221–22. See also SEA STATE

Lippard, Lucy: *577,087*, 60, 63; on Haacke, 60; *Six Years: The Dematerialization of the Art Object from 1966–1972*, 1–3

Liu Jianhua: *Yiwa Survey*, 246

Livingston, Jane, 126

Long, Richard, 221

Longoni, Ana, 79–81

Lovelock, James, 203

Lui, P. C., 221

Lütticken, Sven, 186

Lynch, Kevin, 189n6

Lyotard, Jean-François, 175

Macy conferences, 11

Mann, Geoff, 255

Mantovani, Stefania, 28n70

Marcuse, Herbert, 34, 42–45, 50, 63, 86

Martin, Agnes, 10

Marx, Karl, 45, 108

Marxism and post-Marxism, 177

Masotta, Oscar, 82, 87

Maspero, François, 221

Matilsky, Barbara, 19

McHale, John, 14–15; *Transistor*, 14

McLuhan, Marshall, 82, 86, 88

McShine, Kynaston, 68

Mead, Margaret, 5

Meireles, Cildo, 14

Meyer, E. W., 14

minimalism: *Art and Technology* exhibition and, 128; Burnham and, 43, 235; Fried's "Art and Objecthood" critique, 3; Gillick and,

177; phenomenological turn in California minimalism, 127; Saraceno and, 149

M/M, 190n23

modernism: Bauhaus and New Bauhaus, 38–42, 258n38; Burnham and, 5, 39; Gillick and, 179–81; Greenberg and, 39, 50, 54n63; Haacke on, 1–2, 7; high modernism as endpoint, 181; "nervous breakdown" of, 7, 50; Torcuato di Tella Institute and, 95n2

Moholy-Nagy, László, 38–39

Mondloch, Kate, 161–62

Mondrian, Piet, 1

Mori, Mariko: Burnham's systems aesthetics and, 149–50; *Connected World* animation, 153, 164, 167; participatory environments and, 148–49; transcendence of selfhood and, 149. See also *Wave UFO*

Morris, Robert, 31, 237; *bodyspacemotionthings*, 131, 139–43, 140*f*; *Steam*, 235

Morton, Timothy, 204

Motti, Gianni, 221

Munari, Bruno, 16

negentropy, 93, 207–10

Nelson, George, 6–7

neoliberalism, 175, 242–43

"nervous breakdown," 7, 50

nervous systems, extended, 6–7

Ni Haifeng, 246–51, 254; *Para-Production*, 239, 247; *Return of the Shreds*, 239, 246–47

Nisbet, James, 4

noise, 187–88

Noland, Kenneth, 10

Norvell, Patricia "Patsy," 31

Nusberg, Lev, 16

October group, 54n63

Olmsted, Frederick Law, 67

Onganía, Juan Carlos, 78–79, 85–86, 88

open systems: affective turn and, 92; closed systems vs., 5, 12, 82–83, 87–88, 95; defined, 81; feminist artists and, 15–16, 18; institutional critique and, 81–82; negentropy and, 93; Rosario Group's Tucumán Arde and, 80–83, 87–88; von Bertalanffy's concept of, 12–13

Oppenheim, Dennis, 31

organizational turn, 28n70

Osborne, Peter, 50, 181

Parreno, Philippe: *No Ghost Just a Shell* (with Huyghe), 182–85
participatory art. *See* complex participatory art systems; light and space art
Peltomäki, Kirsi, 138
Perón, Isabel, 86
Perry, Lee "Scratch," 9
phantasia, 204
phenomenal art. *See* light and space art
phenomenological turn, 127
Phua, Melvin, 233n23
Piene, Otto, 68
Piper, Adrian, 104, 109
planetarity, 194–99, 202–5, 209–11
planetary praxis, 202–7
political ecology, 194–202, 205, 207
postcontemporary art, 181
postmodernism: Burnham and, 50–51; "the contemporary" vs., 33; Foster on, 54n63; "postmodern condition," 175; systems and, 13
Potter, Paul, 69
Primary Structures exhibition (Jewish Museum, New York, 1966), 138
Púzzolo, Norberto, 83, 92

Raffles, Stamford, 218–19
Ragain, Melissa, 32–33, 37–38, 42
Ramsden, Mel, 7
Ratcliff, Carter, 134
Rauschenberg, Robert, 48
Reichardt, Jasia, 15, 48
Reid, Norman, 141
relational aesthetics, 7–18, 182–83
Relyea, Lane, 181–82
Renzi, Juan Pablo, 83, 95n3
Rickey, George, 48
Roberts, Bill, 184–85
Rodenbeck, Judith, 7–8
Rodia, Simon, 5
Rosa, Nicolás, 83
Rosario Group. *See* Tucumán Arde
Rosler, Martha, 15, 81
Rudd, Mark, 59
Ruf, Beatrix, 184
Ruscha, Ed, 60

Samnang, Khvay, 233n48
Saraceno, Tomás: *On Air*, 169n10; Burnham's systems aesthetics and, 149–50; *Cloud Cities*, 169n10; Guattari's ecosophy and, 166–67; habitability and, 149; participatory environments and, 148–49; *On Space Time Foam*, 169n10. See also *In Orbit*
Schiller, Friedrich, 38, 42, 44, 50
Schneemann, Carolee, 15; *Snows*, 70; *Viet-Flakes*, 70
SEA STATE (Lim), 214f; ecosystemic approach and, 217, 227, 230–31; extractive capitalism, extractive zone, and, 216, 223–27, 229; neocolonial land expansion and, 219–20, 225–27; *SEA STATE 0: all the lines flow out*, 214–15, 228; *SEA STATE 0: it's not that i forgot, but rather i chose not to mention*, 231; *SEA STATE 1: inside/outside*, 222–23; *SEA STATE 2: as evil disappears (Pulau Sajahat)*, 225; *SEA STATE 2: as evil disappears (Sajahat Buoy)*, 225–26; *SEA STATE 3: inversion*, 226; *SEA STATE 4: line in the chart*, 222–23; *SEA STATE 5: drift (rope sketch)*, 223; *SEA STATE 5: drift (stay still now to move)*, 223; *SEA STATE 6: capsize*, 228–29; *SEA STATE 6: phase 1*, 227–29, 229f; *SEA STATE 7: sandwich*, 223–24, 224f; *SEA STATE 7: the inarticulate sandman*, 224–25; *SEA STATE 8: seabook*, 217, 230; *SEA STATE 9: proclamation*, 219–20; *SEA STATE 9: proclamation: drag drop pour*, 219; *SEA STATE 9: proclamation garden*, 217, 219; sea state code and, 213; the Singapore Story and, 217–20; submerged perspectives and, 216–17; submerged space and, 227–29; systems approach and, 220–23; undergrowth and, 217
Sekula, Allan, 242–46, 254; *Fish Story*, 221, 239, 241f, 242–43, 257nn23–24; *Forgotten Space* (with Burch), 257n24; *Lottery at Sea* (with Burch), 257n24
Serres, Michel, 235, 244–47
Shaked, Nizan, 108–9, 123n33
Shames, Stephen, 57
Shanken, Edward, 7, 32
Shannon, Claude, 14, 187
Sharp, Willoughby: on art of the future, 60; *Earth Art*, 68; on Haacke's *Sky Line*, 75n45; *Kinetic Environment* exhibition, 64–65; "Place and Process," 63
Siegelaub, Seth, 68
Sinclair, Iain, 221

Singapore: the Grid and extractive zone, 223–27; Jurong Rock Caverns, 227–28; land expansion, neocolonial, 219–20, 225–27; NEWater program, 230; Our Singapore Conversation, 220; the Singapore Story, 217–20, 229–31; submerged space, 227–29; survival narrative, 215–16; systems approach to statehood, 220–23. See also *SEA STATE* (Lim)

sinthome, 198–201, 198*f*, 207

Situationist International, 245

Skrebowski, Luke, 56

Smith, Jack, 5

Smithson, Robert, 31–32, 49, 184; *Domain of the Great Bear* (with Bochner), 76n65

social turn, 17

Software: Information Technology; Its New Meaning for Art (Jewish Museum, New York, 1970), 18, 45–47, 143n5

Solanas, Valerie, 22n1

Spaces exhibition (MoMA, 1969), 133–34, 138

Spivak, Gayatri, 202–4

Spreiregen, Paul D., 67

Star, Susan Leigh, 237–38

Stella, Frank, 10

Stengers, Isabelle, 195, 203–7

Steyerl, Hito, 251–55; *Duty Free Art*, 239, 251–53, 252*f*

Stiegler, Bernard, 208–9

structuralism, 36–37, 47, 82

Students for a Democratic Society (SDS), 59, 66, 69

Sun Ra and the Arkestra, 9–10

Sutton, Gloria, 6

Systemic Painting (Guggenheim New York, 1966), 10–11

systems: bridging the postwar and the contemporary, 8; closed, 12, 19–20; deviation-amplifying, in Burnham, 168; dynamic, in Guattari, 166; exponential growth in, 237; information vs. objects and, 180; noise in, 187–88; "the system" vs. "systems," 4–5; von Bertalanffy's general systems theory, 12–13; weird, 5

systems aesthetics: art historical scope of, 7–8; Burnham's theory of, 31–32, 42–49; disembodied information and, 142; eco-, 18; energy metabolism and, 194–95; expanded genealogy of, 10–20; "nervous breakdown"

of, 7, 50; nervous systems and, 6; planetary praxis and, 202–7

systems analysts, artists as, 235–36

systems consciousness: the art object vs., 180; embodied, 142–43; orders of, 128, 137

systems ecology, 18–19

Takis, Vassilakis, 48

Tan, Kenneth Paul, 220

Tan, T. S., 221

Taussig, Michael, 23n16

technocracy: bias, technocratic, 6; broad infrastructural analysis of, 238; Burnham and, 39, 42, 45, 49; Gaines and, 119–20; Guattari on, 197, 199; infrastructure art and, 241; Marcuse on, 33; open systems and, 13; as power, 236; Singapore and, 215–23, 229–30; Stiegler's Entropocene and, 208

technologies of experience, 126–27, 144n11. *See also* light and space art

TekArt, 45

Thiene, Federica, 28n70

Thomson, Garry, 60–61

Three Artists from Los Angeles exhibition (Tate Gallery, London, 1970), 130–41, 132*f*

Tillberg, Margareta, 16

Tinguely, Jean, 48

Tiravanija, Rirkrit: *Untitled (Even Electric Sheep Can Dream)*, 190n23

Torcuato di Tella Institute, 78, 83, 95n2

tsunamii.net art collective, 221–22

Tuchman, Maurice, 45, 125–28, 143n1

Tucumán Arde (Rosario Group): about, 79–80; archive and publication (phase four), 92; background, 78–79; Carnevale's *Lock Up Action*, 85–86; as collective work of art, 94–95; *desalinear* (disordering) and, 79, 92–95; exhibition-condemnations (phase three), 80*f*, 90–92; First National Meeting on Avant-Garde Art, 85; Happenings, 85–89; institutional critique and, 80–82; manifesto, 88, 94; open systems and, 80–83, 87–88; research trips to Tucumán (phase two), 89–90, 91*f*

Turner, Fred, 111, 116–18

Turner, J. M. W., 47

"turn outward," 9, 19, 22

Turrell, James: *Art and Technology* exhibition, 126–27; lawsuit against, 147n77; phenomenal art and, 127–28; projection pieces, 130, 144n16; *Three Artists from Los Angeles* and, 130

United Nations Climate Change Conference (COP 21), 192, 207, 209

van der Marck, Jan, 60
Van der Ryn, Sim, 13
Varela, Francisco, 207
Verón, Eliseo, 82, 88
Vietnam War, 3, 60, 65–70
von Bertalanffy, Ludwig, 12–13, 43, 81, 93
von Foerster, Heinz, 5, 25n32
von Neumann, John, 59
von Neumann, Klára Dán, 59

Warhol, Andy, 22n1, 258n38; *Brillo Box*, 243
Wave UFO (Mori), 152f; *Connected World* animation, 153, 164, 167; inward and outward complex systems, 151–53, 158; making the invisible perceptible, 158–63; overview, 149; sensing system instability, 163–68
weather, art, and systems, history of, 58–61. *See also* Haacke, Hans
Weathermen (later Weather Underground Organization), 59, 69

Weaver, Warren, 187
weird systems, 5
Wheeler, Doug: phenomenal art and, 127–28; *Three Artists from Los Angeles* exhibition (Tate Gallery, 1970), 130–41, 132f. *See also* light and space art
Whitelaw, Mitchell, 9, 19
Whitman, Robert, 144n13
Whyte, William H., 4
Wiener, Norbert: *Cybernetics*, 11–12, 59; *Human Use of Human Beings*, 82; information theory, 93; on meteorology, 59
Wilderson, Frank B., III, 118
Willats, Stephen, 15
Wilson, Scott, 198
Women Artists in Revolution (WAR), 22n3
Woodruff, Lily, 83
Woon Tien Wei, 233n23
Wortz, Ed: *Art and Technology* exhibition, 126–27
Wynter, Sylvia, 204

Xerox, 111

Yao, Pauline J., 222

ZERO, 59, 66

www.ingramcontent.com/pod-product-compliance
Lightning Source LLC
Chambersburg PA
CBHW051210170526
45166CB00005B/1827